WILEY

PATHWAYS

E-BUSINESS

WILEY

PATHWAYS

E-BUSINESS

GREG HOLDEN
Stylus Media

SHANNON BELEW
Bizoffice.com

JOEL ELAD

JASON R. RICH

with
DON GULBRANDSEN

John Wiley & Sons, Inc.
New York • Chichester • Weinheim • Brisbane • Toronto • Singapore

PUBLISHER	Anne Smith
PROJECT EDITOR	Beth Tripmacher
SENIOR EDITORIAL ASSISTANT	Tiara Kelly
PRODUCTION MANAGER	Micheline Frederick
PRODUCTION EDITOR	Kerry Weinstein
COPYEDITOR	Camelot Editorial Services
CREATIVE DIRECTOR	Harry Nolan
ART DIRECTOR	Jeof Vita
COVER PHOTO	© Tetra Images/Getty Images

This book was set in Times New Roman PS 10.5/13 pt by Aptara Inc., and printed and bound by R. R. Donnelley. The cover was printed by R. R. Donnelley.

To order books or for customer service, please call 1-800-CALL WILEY (225-5945).

ISBN 978-0-470-19857-5

Printed in the United States of America

10 9 8 7 6 5 4 3 2 1

PREFACE

Today's students have different goals, different life experiences, and different academic backgrounds, but they are all on the same path to success in the real world. This diversity, coupled with the reality that these learners often have jobs, families, and other commitments, requires a flexibility that our nation's higher education system is addressing. Distance learning, shorter course terms, new disciplines, evening courses, and certification programs are some of the approaches that colleges employ to reach as many students as possible and help them clarify and achieve their goals.

The *Wiley Pathways* program, a suite of services and content created especially for career colleges, community colleges, and continuing education institutions, is designed to help you address this diversity and the need for flexibility. *Wiley Pathways* content puts a focus on the fundamentals to help students grasp the subject, bringing them all to the same basic understanding. Content from the *Wiley Pathways* program has an emphasis on teaching job-related skills and practical applications of concepts with clear and professional language. The core competencies and skills help students succeed in the classroom and beyond, whether in another course or in a professional setting. A variety of built-in learning resources allow the students to practice what they need to perform and help instructors and students gauge students' understanding of the content. These resources enable students to think critically about their new knowledge and apply their skills in any situation.

Our goal with *Wiley Pathways* is to celebrate the many students in your courses, respect their needs, and help you guide them on their way.

LEARNING SYSTEM

To meet the needs of working college students, *Wiley Pathways* uses a learning system based on Bloom's Taxonomy. Key topics in *Wiley Pathways E-Business* are presented in easy-to-follow chapters. The text then prompts analysis, evaluation, and creation with a variety of learning aids and assessment tools. Students move efficiently from reviewing what they have learned, to acquiring new information and skills, to applying their new knowledge and skills to real-life scenarios.

Using this learning system, students not only achieve academic mastery of e-business *topics,* but they master real-world *skills* related to that content. The learning system also helps students become independent learners, giving them a distinct advantage in the field, whether they are just starting out or seeking to advance in their careers.

ORGANIZATION, DEPTH, AND BREADTH OF THE TEXT

Modular Format

Research on college students shows that they access information from textbooks in a non-linear way. Instructors also often wish to reorder textbook content to suit the needs of a particular class. Therefore, although *Wiley Pathways* proceeds logically from the basics to increasingly more challenging material, chapters are further organized into sections that are self-contained for maximum teaching and learning flexibility.

Numeric System of Headings

Wiley Pathways uses a numeric system for headings (e.g., 2.3.4 identifies the fourth subsection of Section 3 of Chapter 2). With this system, students and teachers can quickly and easily pinpoint topics in the table of contents and the text, keeping class time and study sessions focused.

Core Content

PART I: Getting Started in Business

Chapter 1, An Introduction to E-Business, demonstrates the importance of an online presence for new businesses, especially small entrepreneurial ventures. The chapter includes a brief history of the Internet and how it currently serves e-businesses. The chapter also examines the types of products that can be sold online as well as three common e-business models.

Chapter 2, The Law, Ethics, and Customer Policies, explains the legal implications of starting and running a business. Applicable licenses and laws are outlined, and the often confusing topics of trademark and copyright are covered. A business must create a code of conduct for itself as well as create and adhere to policies that serve its customers; this chapter discusses the value of policies that address privacy, shipping, and returns.

Chapter 3, Planning an E-Business, outlines the steps involved in taking an e-business from an idea to a working Web site, with tips for factoring existing competition into the development of a business. Entrepreneurs can evaluate a business idea using three methods detailed in the chapter; once an idea is approved, the chapter details how a target market can be identified.

Finally, the chapter explores the importance of the business plan and includes a helpful section-by-section review of a typical plan.

Chapter 4, Financing and Launching an E-Business, introduces readers to the concepts of business funding, with an initial focus on the idea of bootstrapping, or starting with limited funds. A wide range of funding sources are examined—including angel investors and venture capitalists—each with their respective advantages and disadvantages. The chapter concludes with a discussion of the benefits and pitfalls associated with buying an existing Web site as a way to start up a business.

Chapter 5, Accounting and Taxes, offers critical guidance on many accounting- and tax-related decisions associated with starting an e-business. Topics such as federal tax obligations, tax withholdings, and sales taxes are covered in detail, with information on the tax requirements of self-employed individuals. The chapter discusses the value of utilizing tax and accounting professionals such as CPAs and bookkeepers.

Part II: Operating an E-Business

Chapter 6, Online Payments and Shopping Carts, examines the methods of accepting customer payments for goods and services. Although credit cards are generally the most common and preferred method, the chapter profiles alternatives such as PayPal and offline payments. Shopping cart features have improved the online shopping experience for customers; this chapter introduces three types of shopping cart solutions as well as the advantages and disadvantages of each.

Chapter 7, Products, Inventory, and Fulfillment, outlines the stages of selling a product through a Web site: produce and price a product for profit, store a product, and pack and ship a product to customers. Types of inventory strategies are reviewed, as are methods of product fulfillment. The chapter highlights the importance of shipping for customers, offering guidance on working with shipping companies and handling international deliveries.

Chapter 8, Marketing an E-Business, provides an overview of how to build an effective marketing strategy for an e-business and highlights the concept of brand development. Types of online advertising are introduced, with real-world example and strategies for getting the best results. Creative promotional strategies such as e-newsletters, blogs, and podcasts are also reviewed.

Chapter 9, Effectively Using Search Engines, explains how search engines work and how e-businesses can use tools—keywords and <META> tags—to get search engines to notice their Web pages. The chapter offers an in-depth review of visible search tags, with instructions for creating search tags, placing search tags, and organizing Web pages for the greatest impact on search results. Search-engine rankings are a major concern for anyone with a Web site; this chapter explores the benefits of monitoring and managing rankings, as well as of evaluating competitors' rankings.

Chapter 10, E-Business Customer Service, focuses on ways that e-businesses can offer superior customer service for online shoppers, offering insight into the differences between online and traditional customers. Email is an important tool for delivering information to customers; this chapter explains how e-businesses can use email to serve customers' needs. Additional online customer service strategies are explored, including newsgroups and automated customer service features.

Part III: Creating and Operating a Web Site

Chapter 11, Equipment, Software, and Web Hosting, is devoted to the office equipment—computer and otherwise—required to keep a business running effectively. Software is a critical piece of the puzzle, and this chapter explores the major types of programs an e-business should consider purchasing. The topic of Internet service providers is also examined, with coverage of Web-hosting services and alternative host server options.

Chapter 12, Successful Web Site Design, emphasizes the value of site design to an e-business's success, explaining why site functionality is more important than aesthetics. Because an online business's success is largely hinged on its domain name, tips are included for choosing and registering the best possible name for a business. The chapter offers advice for working with designers to create a winning site—from initial design concepts to compatibility testing and launching.

Chapter 13, Tracking and Analyzing Customer Data, explains how tracking customer traffic—following a customer's online path to departments and products—can reveal what is working in a Web site and what is not. Using specialized software and customer logs generated by Web servers, e-business owners can analyze customer data and determine whether site changes are required. The chapter concludes with a discussion of how to use data gathered from cookies and sign-in forms to further improve a site.

Chapter 14, E-Business Security, reviews the online security risks faced by e-businesses, in particular stolen customer data, offering advice for creating safe online business practices. Internet thieves utilize sophisticated techniques for stealing data, and this chapter offers guidelines for how an e-business can secure customer data, avoid domain theft, and prevent hackers, viruses, and malware. The chapter concludes with strategies for protecting and backing up customer data.

PRE-READING LEARNING AIDS

Each chapter of *Wiley Pathways* features a number of learning and study aids, described in the following sections, to activate students' prior knowledge of the topics and orient them to the material.

Do You Already Know?

This bulleted list focuses on *subject matter* that will be taught. It tells students what they will be learning in this chapter and why it is significant for their careers. It also helps students understand why the chapter is important and how it relates to other chapters in the text.

The online assessment tool in multiple-choice format not only introduces chapter material, but it also helps students anticipate the chapter's learning outcomes. By focusing students' attention on what they do not know, the self-test provides students with a benchmark against which they can measure their own progress. The Pre Test is available online at www.wiley.com/college/holden.

What You Will Find Out and *What You Will Be Able To Do*

This bulleted list emphasizes *capabilities and skills* students will learn as a result of reading the chapter and notes the sections in which they will be found. It prepares students to synthesize and evaluate the chapter material and relate it to the real world.

WITHIN-TEXT LEARNING AIDS

The following learning aids are designed to encourage analysis and synthesis of the material, support the learning process, and ensure success during the evaluation phase.

Introduction

This section orients the student by introducing the chapter and explaining its practical value and relevance to the book as a whole. Short summaries of chapter sections preview the topics to follow.

In the Real World

These boxes tie section content to real-world organizations, scenarios, and applications. Engaging stories of professionals and institutions—challenges they faced, successes they had, and their ultimate outcome.

E-Business in Action

These margin boxes point out places in the text where professional applications of a concept are demonstrated. An arrow in the box points to the section of the text and a description of the application is given in the box.

For Example

These margin boxes highlight documents and Web sites from real companies that further help students understand a key concept. The boxes can reference a figure or the Toolkit found at the end of each chapter.

Career Connection

Case studies of people in the field depicting the skills that helped them succeed in the professional world. Each profile ends with a list of "Tips from the Professional" that provide relevant advice and helpful tools.

Pathway to . . .

This boxed section provides students with how-to or step-by-step lists helping them to perform specific tasks.

Summary

Each chapter concludes with a summary paragraph that reviews the major concepts in the chapter and links back to the "Do You Already Know" list.

Key Terms and Glossary

To help students develop a professional vocabulary, key terms are bolded when they first appear in the chapter and are also shown in the margin of page with their definitions. A complete list of key terms with brief definitions appears at the end of each chapter and again in a glossary at the end of the book. Knowledge of key terms is assessed by all assessment tools (see below).

Toolkit

An end-of-chapter appendix that contains relevant documents and examples from real companies.

EVALUATION AND ASSESSMENT TOOLS

The evaluation phase of the *Wiley Pathways* learning system consists of a variety of within-chapter and end-of-chapter assessment tools that test how well students have learned the material and their ability to apply it in the real world. These tools also encourage students to extend their learning into different scenarios and higher levels of understanding and thinking. The following assessment tools appear in every chapter of *Wiley Pathways*.

Self-Check

Related to the "Do You Already Know" bullets and found at the end of each section, this battery of short-answer questions emphasizes student understanding of concepts and mastery of section content. Though the questions may be either discussed in class or studied by students outside of class, students should not go on before they can answer all questions correctly.

Understand: What Have You Learned?

This online Post Test should be taken after students have completed the chapter. It includes all of the questions in the Pre Test so that students can see how their learning has progressed and improved. The Post Test is available online at www.wiley.com/college/holden.

Apply: What Would You Do?

These questions drive home key ideas by asking students to synthesize and apply chapter concepts to new, real-life situations and scenarios.

Be an E-Business Entrepreneur

Found at the end of each chapter, "Be a . . ." questions are designed to extend students' thinking and are thus ideal for discussion or writing assignments. Using an open-ended format and sometimes based on Web sources, they encourage students to draw conclusions using chapter material applied to real-world situations, which fosters both mastery and independent learning.

INSTRUCTOR AND STUDENT PACKAGE

Wiley Pathways is available with the following teaching and learning supplements. All supplements are available online at the text's Book Companion Web site, located at www.wiley.com/college/holden.

Instructor's Resource Guide

The Instructor's Resource Guide provides the following aids and supplements for teaching an e-business course:

- **Text summary aids:** For each chapter, these include a chapter summary, learning objectives, definitions of key terms, and answers to in-text question sets.
- **Teaching suggestions:** For each chapter, these include at least three suggestions for learning activities (such as ideas for speakers to invite, videos to show, and other projects), and suggestions for additional resources.

PowerPoints

Key information is summarized in ten to fifteen PowerPoints per chapter. Instructors may use these in class or choose to share them with students for class presentations or to provide additional study support.

Test Bank

The test bank features one test per chapter, as well as a mid-term and two finals—one cumulative and one non-cumulative. Each includes true/false, multiple-choice, and open-ended questions. Answers and page references are provided for the true/false and multiple-choice questions, and page references are given for the open-ended questions. Tests are available in Microsoft Word and computerized formats.

ACKNOWLEDGMENTS

Taken together, the content, pedagogy, and assessment elements of *Wiley Pathways E-Business* offer the career-oriented student the most important aspects of the electronic business field as well as ways to develop the skills and capabilities that current and future employers seek in the individuals they hire and promote. Instructors will appreciate its practical focus, conciseness, and real-world emphasis.

Special thanks are extended to Nan Nelson of Phillips Community College of the University of Arkansas for acting as an academic advisor to the text. Her careful review of the manuscript, significant contributions to the content, and assurance that the book reflects the most recent trends in e-business, were invaluable assets in our development of the manuscript.

We would like to thank the reviewers for their feedback and suggestions during the textís development. Their advice on how to shape *Wiley Pathways E-Business* into a solid learning tool that meets both their needs and those of their students is deeply appreciated.

Toni Clough, Umpqua Community College
Michael Fenick, Broward Community College
Warren Imada, Leeward Community College
Mary G. Logan, Delgado Community College
Diane Riegal, Sullivan County Community College
Martin Shapiro, Berkeley College
Terri L. Weston, Harford Community College
Diana Withrow, Cape Fear Community College

BRIEF CONTENTS

PART 1 Getting Started in E-Business

PART 2 Operating an E-Business

PART 3 Creating and Operating a Web Site

CONTENTS

PART 3 Creating and Operating a Web Site

CHAPTER 13. TRACKING AND ANALYZING CUSTOMER DATA 371

CHAPTER 14. E-BUSINESS SECURITY 401

CHAPTER 1

AN INTRODUCTION TO E-BUSINESS

Understanding the Power and Appeal of Operating an Online Venture

Do You Already Know?

- How the Internet and World Wide Web got started
- The advantages of selling on the Internet
- What kinds of products you can sell online
- The primary e-business models

For additional questions to assess your current knowledge of the Internet and e-business opportunities, go to **www.wiley.com/college/holden.**

What You Will Find Out	What You Will Be Able To Do
1.1 The history of the Internet and World Wide Web and what their developers hoped to accomplish	• Use the Internet and World Wide Web as a public space that mirrors the real world
1.2 The several advantages of operating an e-business compared to the physical business world	• Recognize and use the advantages of starting and operating an online business
1.3 That almost any product can be sold online—consumer goods, information, professional services, and much more	• Select an appropriate product or service for selling online
1.4 That there are three commonly used e-business models	• Choose an appropriate model for creating an e-business

INTRODUCTION

Many of us take the Internet for granted; it has become an integral part of our lives—so much so that many people cannot imagine living their lives without spending at least part of their time online. Furthermore, the Internet represents the great new frontier for the business world. Very few new businesses start without at least a minimal online presence, and more and more companies are relying exclusively on the Internet for interacting with their customers. And for small businesses, the Internet probably represents the best bet for entrepreneurial success.

What makes all this so amazing is that the Internet is such a relatively recent phenomena. This introductory chapter begins with a section on the brief history of the Internet and its graphical interface, the World Wide Web; the invention of the latter in the 1990s spawned the growth of e-business. The second section considers some of the advantages of operating an online business, including low startup costs and an ever-growing stream of new customers. The third section considers what types of products can be sold online—in short, almost anything—including consumer goods, information, and even professional services. The fourth section reviews the three most commonly employed e-business models: the online storefront, online auctions, and advertising-based businesses.

1.1 THE HISTORY OF THE INTERNET AND E-BUSINESSES

Once upon a time, startup businesses that operated over the Internet were considered risky ventures with uncertain futures, but that is no longer the case. Consider how many different ways there are to interact with businesses via the Internet every day. On a given day, the average person uses the Internet to buy gifts for friends and family members, look up health-related information, make vacation travel arrangements, and even get driving directions. Each of these interactions also represents a business through which people earn a living on the Internet.

In fact, U.S. consumers are expected to spend $139 billion annually for online goods and services by 2008, according to research done by eMarketer. With more than 200 million people now using the Internet in the United States alone (according to Internet World Stats), many potential customers are willing to be Internet consumers. Though Internet business—what this book calls "electronic business" or "e-business"—represents only a fraction of worldwide commerce, it remains one of the fastest-growing business sectors, and is an outstanding place for entrepreneurs to get their first taste of business ownership and management.

What makes the strength of e-business so amazing is that just a couple of decades ago, very few people had even heard of the Internet. The meteoric growth of the online world represents an incredible story.

1.1.1 In the Beginning

Many historians point to a series of memos written in 1962 by J. C. R. Licklider of the Massachusetts Institute of Technology (MIT) as giving birth to the first concept of the Internet and what it could be. In these papers, Linklider talked about a "Galactic Network" of linked computers that allowed sharing information and social interaction—very much what the Internet has evolved to become. Linklider convinced an MIT colleague, Lawrence Roberts, of the value of the concept. By 1967, Roberts had developed the first workable plan for a network of linked computers, the ARPANET. (ARPA stood for Advanced Research Projects Agency.) The first test of this concept was successfully completed in California in 1969 when computers at UCLA and Stanford were linked together and a message was transferred between them. Soon, additional host computers were added to the network at the University of California–Santa Barbara and the University of Utah—and so a rudimentary Internet had been created.

By 1972, the ARPANET network and its capabilities had expanded even further. The project was unveiled to the public at the International Computer Communications Conference thanks to a demonstration organized by Bob Kahn, who became very instrumental in the future direction of the network. That same year, an important new innovation was developed: "electronic mail" or "email." For the next two decades, sending e-mails was the primary use for the ARPANET.

In 1973, Bob Kahn and Vint Cerf began to develop the rules for how the ARPANET should operate. Their resulting Transmission Control Protocol/Internet Protocol (TCP/IP) was finally adopted in 1983 and the system that we now recognize as the "Internet" was finally in place. By the mid-1980s, the Internet was well established, especially in the research and computer development communities. Nonetheless, email was still the primary use for the system; it still lacked the graphic interface that would spur its meteoric growth. That development—the World Wide Web—was still a few years away.[1]

1.1.2 The World Wide Web

Some people mistakenly consider "Internet" and "World Wide Web" as interchangeable terms, but while the **Internet** refers to a global network of computer networks, the **World Wide Web** actually refers to a worldwide collection of electronic documents—what its inventor calls an "abstract (imaginary) space of information."

Tim Berners-Lee is the man behind this phenomena. He wrote a program that he called "WorldWideWeb" in 1990. The concept was fairly simple: Every "page" on the World Wide Web would have its own address or Universal Document Identifier—later known as a **Uniform Resource Locator** or URL—which could be reached by pointing at and clicking a

Internet:
A global network of interlinked computer networks.

World Wide Web:
A worldwide collection of electronic documents.

Uniform Resource Locator (URL):
The unique "address" that identifies every World Wide Web page and other resources on the Internet.

Hypertext link: Built-in connection to another related Web page or part of a Web page, which is accessed by the user pointing at and clicking the link.

hypertext link, kind of an activated word "tag" representing the URL. In the process, Berners-Lee's efforts led to the creation of the Hypertext Markup Language (HTML) and Hypertext Transfer Protocol (HTTP), which are standard elements in creating Web pages.

Though Berners-Lee gave us the technical tools that made the Web possible, just as important was his vision for what it could be: a common information space that would mirror how people worked, played, and socialized in the physical world.[2]

Browser: A computer program that works with the World Wide Web to provide a graphical user interface for the Internet.

Further enhancing the growth of the World Wide Web was the development of **browsers,** the computer programs that work with the World Wide Web to provide a graphical user interface for the Internet. An important browser (though not the first) was Mosaic, which was developed by the National Center for Supercomputing Applications and released to the public in 1993. Mosaic was easy to install and use and it was the first program to display images imbedded in the text rather than in a separate window.

As much as any other factor, Mosaic was the tool that spurred the Internet boom of the 1990s. Mosaic was also responsible for alerting the business

IN THE REAL WORLD

The Vision of the Man Who Created the Web

Tim Berners-Lee is the man responsible for writing the program that created the World Wide Web—the graphical interface of the Internet that makes it so easy and fun to use. But more than just doing the programming, Berners-Lee also had a vision of what the Web could do for the world. Consider his responses to questions about how the Web would affect the following:

- **E-Commerce:** "I think that Web shopping, as it is, only the tip of a huge larger change which will come when I can find things and compare prices automatically, and when electronic financial instruments are commonplace."
- **Education:** "I hope that educators will pool their resources and create a huge supply of online materials. I hope much of this will be available freely to those especially in developing countries who may not have access to it any other way."
- **Business and Government:** "The Web will open up new forms of business altogether, and make us rethink the way we run existing businesses. It can turn bureaucracy over to machines, and let people get on with the creativity. . . . It can help us work together more effectively, remove misunderstanding, and bring about peace and harmony on a global scale."[3]

E-business in Action

Use the Internet and World Wide Web as a public space that mirrors the real world.

world to the potential of the Internet. Which online store was the first is unknown, but in 1993, Internet shopping began. By 1994, a number of e-business firsts were recorded: the first online shopping "malls"; the first banner ads (for AT&T and Zima); and the first opportunity to order pizza online (from Pizza Hut). From those humble beginnings not that many years ago, the Internet has become *the* place for savvy entrepreneurs to make their mark in the business world.[2]

SELF CHECK

1. For what purposes was the "Galactic Network," first described in 1962, going to be developed?
2. For what purpose were the Internet and its predecessor networks primarily used during the first years of existence?
3. What is a URL?
4. How does a hypertext link work?

Apply Your Knowledge Web browsers were once a hot topic in software, but now people tend to take them for granted. Conduct an online search and list five currently available Web browsers and one advantage of each software package.

1.2 THE POWER OF SELLING ON THE INTERNET

What is the truth about the profit potential for an online business? In today's fast-paced business world, can someone still earn a profit by launching and operating an online business? The answer is yes. While equating the Internet to the California Gold Rush might be an exaggeration, online businesses nonetheless represent some of the best moneymaking opportunities for twenty-first-century entrepreneurs. Despite thousands of new e-businesses starting up every year, there are many reasons why this area is one that deserves the serious attention of every new entrepreneur.

1.2.1 Low Startup Cost

Advancing computer technology is driving much of the growth in online business. The prices of computers continue to drop rapidly, while with each new generation of microprocessor chips, their technological capabilities improve dramatically. Thus, the equipment needed to operate an e-business can be minimal—it is far more affordable than ever before to get started. In fact, it is possible to launch an online business with little more than a basic

E-business in Action →
Use the advantages of starting and operating an online business.

personal computer (PC) connected to the Internet, a great idea, and a product or service to sell. Compare the costs for an e-business to starting up a traditional bricks-and-mortar retail store. Even if the proprietor can locate an inexpensive storefront to lease rather than buy, there still will be an investment in fixtures and inventory, and ongoing costs for rent, utilities, employees, and more. A savvy online entrepreneur can start a business out of a spare bedroom and outsource inventory management and shipping. Eventually an e-business may grow and absorb these functions, but by avoiding a big startup investment, an entrepreneur can help improve their odds for success.

1.2.2 Steady Stream of New Customers

The same technology that makes it cheap and easy to start a business is also responsible for recruiting an ever-increasing customer base searching for products online. Thanks to faster dial-up Internet connection speeds, DSL (which stands for digital subscriber line), and cable Internet connections, moving around on the Web on these inexpensive PCs is faster than ever. With cost and access less of a barrier, more and more people of all ages are becoming computer literate and exploring the Internet. People from all walks of life and from almost all income levels are finding their way into cyberspace in record numbers.

Even more exciting for entrepreneurs is the worldwide growth of computers and the spread of high-speed communication lines around the globe. In the past, a small retail store might hope to attract customers within a reasonable driving distance. Because credit cards make transactions easy despite currency differences, and because companies like UPS, FedEx, and DHL can seemingly ship packages anywhere, an online retailer can realistically sell products to buyers around the world—and the potential customer base numbers in the billions.

1.2.3 Diverse Products

Since the Internet has become popular, virtually everything—yes, everything—has been bought and sold over the Internet. (A visit to eBay and a browse through some of the auctions will reveal the vast range of products for sale.) Because the Internet is really just a vast space in which buyers and sellers can come together, it is sometimes helpful to think about it as a giant mall, or even an enormous open-air market. In effect, anything that can be sold in the physical world can be sold through a Web site: automobiles, real estate (houses, apartments, condos, timeshares, and land), yachts, jewelry, artwork, insurance, financial services, collectibles, and furniture. For better or worse, the relative anonymity of an e-business transaction also makes a

Web site an attractive alternative for making a purchase that might otherwise embarrass the buyer. E-businesses can also sell products that are not physical, including information and professional services (such as medical or legal advice). And because they exist in an electronic environment, e-businesses are quickly becoming the preferred place to buy and sell digital products, including software and music. Section 1.3 discusses common online products in more detail.

1.2.4 Diverse Sellers

Compared to the physical business world, the Internet is a very democratic space. Because of that, the e-commerce industry is more open to everyone and includes fewer barriers to entry. Because of its lower startup costs, people with limited funds or who might have trouble getting a business loan are less likely to get shut out because of their economic situation. Geography is also not a barrier. An e-business operated out of an impoverished city or town can cater to wealthy clientele around the country (or world) and earn much-needed income. And people who sometimes get shortchanged in the traditional business world—including minorities, disabled people, and women—are finding the Internet a great place to do business. E-business owners are judged by the appearance of their Web site (and the products or services sold) and not their physical appearance.

IN THE REAL WORLD

A Fashion Challenge Turns into an E-Business Opportunity

Kathryn Kerrigan is six feet tall, a fact that helped the fitness buff enjoy a successful college basketball career, but that sometimes made it difficult to dress fashionably. Shoes were a particular problem; with size 11 feet, she faced extremely limited choices when searching for stylish footwear. Kerrigan saw a business opportunity, drafted a business plan while working on her MBA, and in 2005 launched her KathrynKerrigan.com Web site selling dress shoes to women with larger feet. Kerrigan worked with a craftsman in Italy to create her footwear designs. The original e-business has now expanded to a bricks-and-mortar flagship store in Libertyville, Illinois, and her line is also available at boutiques around the country. In 2007, Kerrigan was named one of Inc.com's top 30 entrepreneurs under the age of 30.[4]

SELF-CHECK

1. What is a primary reason that startup costs for e-businesses are so low?
2. What are two factors encouraging a steady stream of new Internet users?
3. What products can be sold on the Internet?

Apply Your Knowledge Explain why an impoverished member of a minority group who dreams of running their own business might be better served by starting an e-business instead of a traditional bricks-and-mortar business.

1.3 WHAT CAN YOU SELL ONLINE?

What can you sell over the Internet? Just about anything! Many people who have trouble grasping this concept are simply focusing too much on the delivery side of a transaction—for example, you can buy a car on the Web, but you still have to find a way to get to the car so you can drive it home. The reality is that all types of transactions have built-in delivery problems, and buyers and sellers have already worked out all kinds of solutions for the issue. Possible delivery issues cannot offset the Internet's incredible advantage in delivering information about products. For example, a car buyer can sometimes make a more informed vehicle purchase over the Internet than they can standing in a dealer's lot next to the car. With countless research tools available, buyers can discover everything they want about a given make, model, and year—and in some cases they can even research the life history of a single used vehicle.

So, in the spirit of keeping an open mind about the possibilities, the following sections will explore the various categories of products that can be effectively sold on the Internet. This discussion is by no means complete, and it is likely that the next generation of e-business entrepreneurs will identify more great ideas for making a living in cyberspace.

1.3.1 Selling Consumer Products

Using a Web site to sell consumer products is the most traditional application of e-commerce—and why not? The Web is a great venue for businesses with products to sell. It allows sellers to illustrate and provide a generous amount of information to support their products. In many cases, consumers can learn much more about a product sold online than they can learn from physically picking up or viewing the same product in a traditional bricks-and-mortar store.

That noted, the Web is not the ideal place to sell all consumer items. Commonplace inexpensive products, many types of perishable goods, and large or expensive-to-ship products are all things that might be better obtained in person in a traditional store. Instead, the Internet has become the place for consumers to find unique, customized, high-quality, or hard-to-locate items. Specialized stores selling "niche" products are well suited to the Internet because of its worldwide reach. Even a very large city might not provide an adequate customer base to support a bricks-and-mortar specialty shop that would otherwise thrive online.

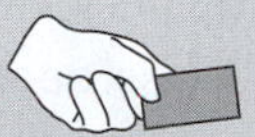

CAREER CONNECTION

By seeing what other companies were doing wrong, a young entrepreneur found a way to make his mark—and a hefty profit—with office furniture.

Office furniture is not the first thing that comes to mind when you think of ideal products for an e-business, but Sean Belnick has proven that it is just the ticket for online success. Named 2007's No. 2 entrepreneur under the age of 30 by Inc.com, the 20-year-old started his venture at the age of 14. Belnick's inspiration came while spending time at his stepfather's office at a furniture manufacturer. Furniture retailers were placing orders with Belnick's stepfather, who then shipped the furniture directly to the customers. To Belnick, it made much better business sense to provide customers with a way of ordering the furniture directly. He launched BizChair.com from his bedroom with a startup budget of just $500. In the beginning, Belnick used a Yahoo! store account to simply facilitate transport of his stepdad's furniture orders to customers. Now the company owns a 327,000-square-foot warehouse in Canton, Georgia, and counts the Pentagon and Microsoft among its customers. As an e-business, BizChair.com keeps its overhead—and thus prices—low, and as an added benefit offers free shipping for most items sold in the lower 48 states. Sean's company has built a base of satisfied customers by offering a great selection, high-quality products, a money-back guarantee, and top-notch customer service—features that consumers expect from any great retail business, online or otherwise.[4]

Tips from the Professional

- Look for business opportunities in your own life.
- Consider the benefits of direct-shipping—in particular, low startup costs.
- Maintain low overhead.
- Never overlook customer service.

1.3.2 Selling Information

The original purpose of the Internet was to share knowledge via computers; information is the commodity that has fueled the rapid growth of cyberspace. Finding valuable information and gathering a particular kind of resource in one location online is a business itself. People love to get knowledge they trust from the comfort of their own homes. For example, students and parents are eager to pay someone to help them sort through the procedures involved and the data required to apply for college (see Prince Review's Counselor-O-Matic at www.princetonreview.com/college/research/advsearch/match.asp).

Other online businesses provide gathering points or indexes to more specific areas.

Search Engines

Search engine: A Web site that provides a list of links in response to the user typing a word or phrase into a "search" box.

Some businesses succeed by connecting Web surfers with companies, organizations, and individuals that specialize in a given area. These **search engines** accomplish this by providing a list of links in response to the user typing a word or phrase into a "search" box. Google (www.google.com) and Yahoo! (www.yahoo.com) are obvious examples. Originally started by two college students, Yahoo! has become an Internet legend by gathering information in one index so that people can easily find things online.

Links Pages

These are simple Web sites that focus on a single topic and provide a comprehensive listing—and hypertext links—of Internet sites that include content related to the topic. The possible topics are endless: sports, hobbies, cities, states, music, health issues—you name it. If enough people need information on a given topic, a links page can be built around it. Links pages usually generate revenues through advertising and affiliate links as opposed to selling products.

IN THE REAL WORLD

A Web Site Linking Participants to Contests

On her Grandma Jam's Sweepstakes/Contest Guide Web site (www.grandmajam.com), Janet Marchbanks-Aulenta gathers links to current contests along with short descriptions of each one. Janet says her site receives as many as 22,000 visits per month, and generates income through advertising and affiliate links to other contest Web sites. She says she loves running her own business despite the hard work involved with keeping it updated. "The key to succeeding at this type of site is to build up a regular base of users that return each day to find new contests—the daily upkeep is very important," she says.

Personal Recommendation Sites

The personal touch sells, even on the Internet. Just look at About.com. This guide to the online world provides Web surfers with a central location where they can find virtually anything. It works because real people do the choosing and provide evaluations (albeit brief) of the sites they list.

Resource sites can transform information into money in a number of ways. In some cases, individuals pay to become members; sometimes, businesses pay to be listed on a site; other times, a site attracts so many visitors on a regular basis that other companies pay to post advertising on the site. Highly successful information sites carry a big share of ads and also strike lucrative partnerships with big companies.

1.3.3 Selling Professional Services

Selling consumer products is only the beginning. Professionals, too, have discovered the value of selling their services on the Internet. Using a Web site is an effective way to recruit new clients or patients, and it gives existing clients and patients access to busy professionals (usually using email) as well as tools for checking office hours and scheduling appointments. A variety of professionals offer their services online.

Attorneys

Many law firms consider a quality Web site an essential marketing tool. In addition, the vast reach of the Internet offers some unique opportunities to the legal profession. For example, Chicago-based immigration attorney Kevin L. Dixler uses his Web site (www.dixler.com) to reach people around the world who are interested in coming to the United States.

Physicians

Relatively few doctors are using the Internet to promote their practices, but that does not mean that the potential for online marketing of medical services is lacking. Innovative physicians have discovered the power of the Web site, especially those serving a unique niche. For example, Dr. Robert Shannon of Bear Lake, Michigan, uses his Web site (www.bearlakemichigan.com/shannon) to promote his unusual practice—which is based entirely on making house calls.

Psychotherapists

Considering how important the Internet has become as a rapid communications tool, it is not surprising that online counseling has grown in popularity.

The topic is somewhat controversial in the psychotherapy community, which promotes the value of face-to-face interaction with patients. Oregon-based Stephen Tobin, PhD, is employing new Web technology to overcome these concerns: He now offers real-time video psychotherapy through his Web site (www.doctortobin.com).

1.3.4 Technology and Computer Opportunities

What could be more natural than the Internet to sell what you need to get and stay online? The online world itself, by the very fact that it exists, has spawned all kinds of e-business opportunities for savvy entrepreneurs.

Computers

Some small discount computer houses (such as MC Electronics, www.mcelectronics.com) have become hugely successful by taking their businesses online and offering equipment for lower prices than conventional retail stores. Being on the Internet means they can save on overhead, employee compensation, and other costs, and they can pass those savings on to their customers.

Internet Service Providers

These businesses give you a dial-up or direct connection to the Internet. Smaller companies, usually catering to a geographically localized customer base, are succeeding in this area. One successful example is YourNET connection (www.ync.net) in Schaumburg, Illinois, which offers free online Web training to its customers.

Software

Big companies are not the only place for Web surfers to turn when they need software to enhance their online experience. For example, Matt Wright is well known for providing free computer scripts that add important functionality to Web sites, such as processing information that visitors submit via online forms. Matt's Script Archive site (www.scriptarchive.com) generates income from a modest number of advertisers, and also provides links to Matt's other Web sites—revenue generators in their own right.

1.3.5 Online Opportunities for Artists

Being creative no longer means starving, relying on the mercy of publishing companies or art galleries, or living in a van and driving from craft show to craft show to sell your wares. The Internet has vastly expanded opportunities for artists. Whether they are looking for more exposure or feedback on their creations, or want to sell their works, more and more artists are discovering the value of making their work available for viewing online. There are many different ways to generate very real revenue with virtual creative venues.

Host Art Galleries

Thanks to online galleries, artists whose sales were previously limited to one region can get inquiries from all over the world. Art Xpo (www.artxpo.com) reports thousands of dollars in sales through its Web site thanks to aggressive marketing. The personal Web site created by artist Marques Vickers (www.marquesv.com) has received worldwide attention—and earned him sales from customers located far from his California home.

Publish Your Writing

Blog:
Shorthand for Web log, or an online diary.

"Blogs"—shorthand for Web logs, or online diaries—have become extremely popular and have allowed thousands of people to become writers/publishers. The most successful blogs, such as "The Daily Dish" written by libertarian political commentator Andrew Sullivan (www.andrewsullivan.com), generate sizable ad revenues. To find out how to start a blog, visit www.blogger.com.

Sell Your Music

E-business in Action →
Select an appropriate product or service for selling online.

In the past, bands dreamed of getting signed by a big record company if they wanted to make it big. Now more and more bands are realizing that they can make their own success with the help of a quality Web site, selling CDs, DVDs, T-shirts, and posters online. Especially savvy bands are following the consumer trend favoring downloadable music and offering their catalog of recordings for sale direct to listeners' computers via the Internet. An example of such a site is indieTunes (www.indietunes.com), where independent artists sell downloadable music on a secure platform.

SELF-CHECK

1. What consumer products can be sold online? Are there any factors that might make the Internet less effective for selling some products?
2. List three common methods for selling information on the Internet.
3. How might a health-care professional sell their services using a Web site?

Apply Your Knowledge A photographer that you know wants some ideas for selling photos over the Internet. Brainstorm at least five unique e-business ideas for selling photographs.

1.4 POPULAR E-BUSINESS MODELS

E-business in Action →
Choose an appropriate model for creating an e-business.

Just like in the real world, there are countless ways that an individual can make money on the Internet. (And like in the real world, some of these might not necessarily be legal!) There are three commonly employed e-business models: the online storefront, online auctions, and advertising-based businesses. There are important differences among each type of business, which are detailed in the sections that follow.

It is useful at this point to make a distinction between operating an e-business and simply using a Web site to promote a traditional bricks-and-mortar firm. The e-business models that follow assume that revenues are generated directly through and because of a Web site—as opposed to using the Internet to encourage customers to physically visit a business to make their purchases. An example of the latter would be a restaurant that promotes itself online, even publishing its menu; but unless that restaurant takes food orders and payment via the Internet, it is not really an e-business.

1.4.1 The Online Storefront

Online storefront: A Web site designed to display and provide information about products or services, and then accept orders from customers for those products or services.

An **online storefront** is probably the most common type of e-commerce site. It is a Web site designed to display and provide information about products or services, and then accept orders from customers for those products or services. Most online storefronts include a shopping cart—an application built into the Web site that contains an order form and used to process orders along with payments, usually by credit card. Physical products are then shipped to the customer using mail or a courier service. Some electronic products—for example, software or music—are immediately downloaded to the customer's computer.

The most successful online storefronts are ones that emulate—or surpass—the best aspects of the bricks-and-mortar retail stores on which the model is based. This means providing quality products at a good price and placing a strong emphasis on customer service. Even though customers rarely interact directly with a human during online transactions, they still appreciate human touches during the buying process, including recommendation of related add-on products and notification of shipping and estimated arrival dates. Furthermore, most online customers fully expect to be able to talk to a real person if a problem arises, and want that person to solve that problem to their satisfaction.

1.4.2 Online Auctions

Online auction: A Web site that allows users to buy or sell items, usually through a bidding process, and pay a small fee to the site operator, who does not handle the product, but simply facilitates the transaction.

Online auction sites allow anyone to buy or sell items, usually through a bidding process, and pay a small fee to the site operator, often collected as commission on the transaction. An important aspect of auction businesses (and one that differentiates them from online storefronts) is who they do not manage the product; instead their purpose is to bring buyers and sellers together. Some would argue that auction sites represent one of the best applications of the Internet because they link people with a common interest (undertaking a transaction for a given product) who otherwise might never have an opportunity to interact. With the fast-growing popularity of these services, people have managed to supplement their incomes selling all sorts of new and used items via online auctions.

Figure 1-1

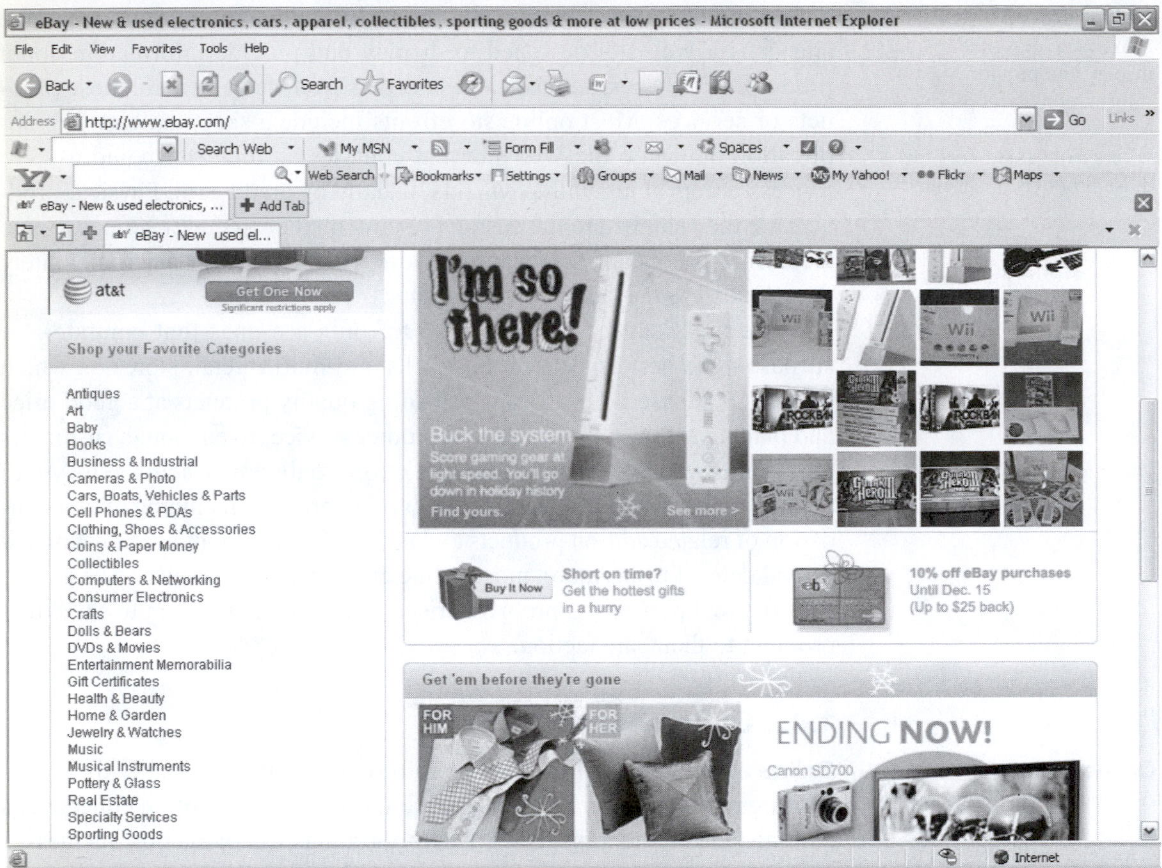

eBay's home page for a list of the product categories available.

The most successful auction site—and one of the most successful Web sites of any type—is eBay (see Figure 1-1). The online giant started in 1995 in the California living room of computer programmer Pierre Omyidar. He envisioned it operating as kind of an online garage sale. He was astonished when he sold his first item on the site—a broken laser pointer for which the buyer paid $14.93. Now eBay has more than 45 million active members in the U.S. and roughly 15 million auctions taking place at any given time.

Even though eBay is so dominant in this business, there are still opportunities for niche auction operators. For example, GunBroker.com connects buyers and sellers of firearms, a product that eBay shies away from.

IN THE REAL WORLD

Turning a Headache into an E-Business Success Story

Everybody hates dealing with the Department of Motor Vehicles and all the associated hassles of getting a driver's license or new plates for the car. And if you have just moved across state lines, the new laws can be especially confusing. Enter San Diego's Raj Lohoti and his amazing information site www.dmv.org—the "Online Unofficial Guide to the DMV." After dabbling in other Internet-related ventures, Lahoti hit it big with this domain originally developed by his brother. The site effectively gathers DMV and other auto-related information for all 50 states in one easy-to-navigate space, attracting hordes of visitors and enough advertising revenue that the e-business generated $11.6 million in 2006. For his efforts, the 25-year-old Lahoti was named one of Inc.com's top 30 entrepreneurs under the age of 30.[4]

1.4.3 Advertising-Based E-Businesses

FOR EXAMPLE

Online auction site eBay has a list of the product categories available on their home page (www.ebay.com).

A large percentage of e-commerce sites generate all or most of their revenues not by selling products or services, but by selling advertising. This is not surprising, considering how many traditional media businesses—newspapers, magazines, television, and radio—exist primarily to sell advertising. They offer news, stories, shows, and music to build a body of consumers that will attract advertisers. Because the Internet is packed with news, videos, music, and all types of content that attract visitors, it is logical that advertisers have turned their attention (and moved their dollars) to Web advertisers—much to the chagrin of companies in the traditional media.

Just about any Web site offering information and attracting a regular and measurable clientele is a candidate for selling ad space. Several popular models have developed for ad-focused sites:

Portal:
A Web site that offers a variety of Internet services from a single convenient location.

- **Portals:** One of the original Web business models, these sites provide a host of information on a specific area of interest. For example, BizOffice.com targets small-business owners and home-based businesses.
- **Search engines:** Even though Google and Yahoo! seem to have the search market cornered, some niche search engines have established themselves. For example, AllSmallBiz.com narrows their search process to topics of interest for small business owners.
- **Classifieds:** The Internet has garnered a large share of this advertising category that used to be dominated by newspapers and magazines. Personal ads are among the fast-growing categories, but sites listing jobs, housing, or businesses for sale also attract many visitors.

- **Information exchange:** This category includes blogs, user groups, and communities such as social networking sites like Facebook.com, MySpace.com, and Friendster.com.

SELF-CHECK

1. What software feature does every successful online storefront require? What functions does this feature perform?
2. What is the purpose of an auction site? How does an auction site generate revenues?
3. List four types of advertising-driven e-business sites.

Apply Your Knowledge Advertising-based businesses that cater to a narrow user group have become very popular. Brainstorm five specialized ad-driven e-business ideas. For each idea, specify the user group and briefly describe the elements that will attract ads. Who might advertise to the group?

SUMMARY

Section 1.1

- The earliest concepts outlining the Internet can be traced back to 1962, the first plans for the ARPANET were unveiled in 1967, and the first successful transmission of data over a simple predecessor of the Internet occurred in 1969.
- The World Wide Web, the graphical interface for the Internet, was developed in 1990. The first effective Web browser, Mosaic, was released in 1993 and spurred an Internet boom.

Section 1.2

- Among the many advantages of operating a business online, four reasons make it an especially attractive place for business: 1) startup costs are low; 2) there is a steady stream of new customers; 3) every product is welcome; and 4) every seller is welcome and faces fewer barriers than in the traditional business world.

Section 1.3

- Just about any product can be sold online. Some of the more popular categories for e-business products include the following:
  - consumer goods
  - information
  - professional services
  - computer/Internet products and support
  - art, writing, and other creative products

Section 1.4

- There are three commonly employed e-business models: 1) the online storefront, in which consumers browse products and make purchases using a shopping cart; 2) online auctions, in which the Web site brings buyers and sellers together (for a fee), but does not handle the product; and 3) advertising-based businesses, which attract visitors by offering information, and sell ads to other companies that want to market products or services to those visitors.

ASSESS YOUR UNDERSTANDING

UNDERSTAND: WHAT HAVE YOU LEARNED?

Go to **www.wiley.com/college/holden** to assess your knowledge of the basics of the Internet and e-business opportunities.

APPLY: WHAT WOULD YOU DO?

1. In which specific ways have the Internet and World Wide Web developed to fulfill the visions of the various people who helped create them?
2. How did the World Wide Web and browsers spur the growth of the Internet? What features of the World Wide Web make it especially well suited for online commerce?
3. You are thinking about opening a store selling Japanese-themed merchandise in a strip mall near your home, but a friend suggests that you would be better off starting up an e-business. Compare the advantages and disadvantages of each option in terms of startup costs, potential customer base, displaying products, customer service, and delivering products to consumers.
4. In theory, any product can be sold through a Web site, but some products might be inherently more difficult to market than others. For each of the following, suggest why it might be difficult to sell the product online. Then offer an idea to counteract this difficulty and make the item more saleable.
   - Fresh ocean-caught fish
   - Used single-engine airplanes
   - Custom-made evening gowns
5. Web sites for professionals are becoming increasingly popular. How might a doctor use a Web site for more than just marketing their services? What services might an attorney offer through a Web site?
6. Blogs represent just one way that a writer can make money online. Brainstorm and briefly describe three more ideas for how a writer might make money using a Web site.

7. What specific functions does a shopping cart perform in an online storefront? (Hint: Visit a popular e-commerce site and note the functions as you go through a simple transaction.)
8. Web portals remain a popular e-business model. Select an activity that interests you and locate and explore the activity via a portal. Give the name and URL of the portal. Briefly describe the content used to attract visitors and the types of ads that have been placed in the site.

BE AN E-BUSINESS ENTREPRENEUR

Purchasing Through an Online Storefront

Many traditional retail businesses now maintain a Web storefront. Visit the e-commerce site for a retailer whose physical store you have shopped. Go through a sample purchase (no purchase is required) using the shopping cart and various information-delivery features. Analyze five aspects of the transaction, comparing the online experience to a traditional in-store experience. Discuss the advantages and disadvantages for each aspect of the online purchase.

Analyzing Advertising-Based E-Businesses

Many successful Internet businesses generate all their revenues by selling advertising. The key to selling ads is to first attract a large community of regular visitors, which various Web sites do with various techniques. Search the Web and find one ad-based Web site focusing on a narrow user group for each of the following strategies:

- Search engine (other than Yahoo! or Google)
- Information exchange

For each site, describe what type of ads they sell and discuss what type of content they use to encourage repeat visits.

KEY TERMS

Blog	Shorthand for Web log, or an online diary.
Browser	A computer program that works with the World Wide Web to provide a graphical user interface for the Internet.
Hypertext link	Built-in connection to another related Web page or part of a Web page, which is accessed by the user pointing at and clicking the link.
Internet	A global network of interlinked computer networks.
Online auction	A Web site that allows users to buy or sell items, usually through a bidding process, and pay a small fee to the site operator, who does not handle the product, but simply facilitates the transaction.
Online storefront	A Web site designed to display and provide information about products or services, and then accept orders from customers for those products or services.
Portal	A Web site that offers a variety of Internet services from a single convenient location.
Search engine	A Web site that provides a list of links in response to the user typing a word or phrase into a "search" box.
Universal Resource Locator (URL)	The unique "address" that identifies every World Wide Web page and other resources on the Internet.
World Wide Web	A worldwide collection of electronic documents.

REFERENCES

1. Barry M. Leiner et al, "A Brief History of the Internet," *The Internet Society*, www.isoc.org/internet/history/brief.shtml.
2. Robert H. Zakon, "Hobbes' Internet Timeline v8.2," www.zakon.org/robert/internet/timeline.
3. Tim Berners-Lee "Frequently Asked Questions," World Wide Web Consortium, www.w3.org/People/Berners-Lee/FAQ.html.
4. Inc.com, "30 Under 30: The Coolest Young Entrepreneurs in America," finance.yahoo.com/career-work/article/103284/30-Under-30.

CHAPTER

2 THE LAW, ETHICS, AND CUSTOMER POLICIES

Creating an E-Business That Is Both Legal and Responsible

Do You Already Know?

- The four most common options for legally organizing a business
- Which licenses and identification numbers you need when starting a business
- The difference between trademark and copyright
- If running a business ethically and legally are the same thing
- How effective customer policies can help improve business

For additional questions to assess your current knowledge on business law, ethics, and customer policy, go to **www.wiley.com/college/holden.**

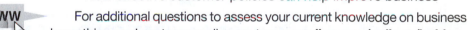

What You Will Find Out	What You Will Be Able To Do
2.1 The advantages and disadvantages of various legal options for organizing a business	• Choose whether to operate your business as a proprietorship, partnership, corporation, or LLC
2.2 How to keep your business legal with regard to licenses, zoning laws, and identification numbers	• Determine which laws apply to your e-business and ensure that you are in compliance with them
2.3 The importance of trademark and copyright protection	• How to register trademarks and file for copyrights—when it is appropriate
2.4 Why running a business ethically involves more than simply following the law	• Develop a code of conduct that outlines a business's core principles for employee behavior
2.5 That developing a strong relationship with customers requires putting policies in writing	• Write a customer pledge and online policies that explain to customers how they should expect to be treated

INTRODUCTION

Too many online entrepreneurs focus on how to create a Web site and attract customers when they begin their planning process. Yet before they attack those challenges, they need to do some very basic work to ensure that their planned enterprise will follow all the laws—federal, state, and local—regarding new businesses, that they have a plan for being responsible citizens, and that they understand the importance of establishing a trusting relationship with their future customers. This chapter covers these important topics, starting with a section that outlines the four most common options for legally organizing a business, each of which will have important effects on the owner's personal liability and taxes. The second section details the variety of licenses, identification numbers, and zoning laws that a new e-business owner should consider—long before their Web site ever goes live. Trademarks and copyrights can be confusing topics, but this chapter provides a brief overview of what each is, why they are important, and how to go about applying for them. Operating a business ethically is much more than simply obeying the law, as the third section explains. The fourth section includes information on creating a code of conduct and running a socially responsible company. The fifth section focuses on the all-important topic of making and keeping promises to customers, using such tools as a customer pledge and published policies for privacy, shipping, returns, and other issues.

2.1 LEGAL ORGANIZATION OPTIONS

Choosing the legal organization for a business demands some careful consideration. There are only four primary options—sole proprietorship, partnership, corporation, and limited liability company (LLC)—but each form has distinct advantages and disadvantages. To decide which form is right for a planned venture, a new business owner needs to examine four key issues:

- **Ownership:** How many people will have an ownership stake in the business? Who ultimately will own or control the company? Some forms of business are limited by both the number of owners and the type of owner (individual or corporation) they can have.
- **Liability:** Where should the legal responsibility for the business reside? It is important to decide whether you are comfortable accepting full liability for the actions of the company or whether you need a structure that helps protect your personal assets.

Liability: A debt or financial responsibility for which someone is responsible.

- **Taxes:** Each of the business structures is subject to varied forms of taxation. For instance, sole proprietors pay a self-employment tax based on their earnings. Corporate shareholders owe tax on the dividends paid to them by a business—and in some situations might even experience something called "double taxation." Because the tax issues can be so complex, every new business owner should first talk with a tax attorney or Certified

Public Accountant (CPA) to determine which option best fits their circumstances. Chapter 5 provides additional information on the tax liability faced by various business forms.

- **Financing:** The way in which a company is financed can play a significant role in determining its structure. If the owner is self-financing a company, any of the structures might work. However, if the owner seeks outside financing, they probably need the option of having stock available for distribution. Furthermore, if another business entity plans to own stock in the company, the choice of business structure is severely limited. Chapter 4 offers an in-depth discussion of financing options for new businesses.

The following sections provide detailed descriptions of the four most common legal forms employed by small businesses.

2.1.1 Going It Alone as a Sole Proprietor

Sole proprietorship: A business owned and controlled by one person.

If an e-business owner is interested in simplicity, they need look no further—a **sole proprietorship** is the quickest, easiest, and least expensive method of forming a business. The primary rule is that only one person can operate as a sole proprietor. The owner and the business are literally the same entity. In addition to simplicity, sole proprietorships offer owners considerable freedom and the ability to operate in secrecy, as well as the possibility of substantial financial rewards because all the profits belong exclusively to them.

The downside of being a sole proprietor is full exposure to the business's liabilities. Because the owner and the company are one, they are fully accountable for its losses and its legal matters. When the business is involved with lawsuits or problems with creditors, the proprietor is personally liable. No corporate protection is available—personal assets (such as a home) can be sold and personal bank accounts used to pay off creditors.

There are other disadvantages to sole proprietorships. Their size is usually limited in part because there is only so much work one owner can do by themselves. There is also a limit to how much money banks will loan sole proprietorships because a single person carries all the credit risk. Sole proprietorships are also limited in their life span: Because the owner and the company are one and the same, the company often dies when an owner dies. As a sole proprietor, the owner is also responsible for all taxes. See Section 5.3 for more information on taxes.

Officially becoming a sole proprietor in the e-business world can be as simple as taking a Web site live and collecting revenues (assuming any necessary business licenses have been obtained). Unless the owner chooses to operate under their exact legal name, they need to register a fictitious name with the city, county, or state. This registration is called a DBA—"doing business as"—and the name should appear on the business's checking account, licenses, and any other legal documents.

2.1.2 Operating as a Partnership

Partnerships: An association of two or more persons for the purpose of running a business for profit.

Partnerships are an association of two or more persons for the purpose of running a business for profit. In some ways, partnerships are similar to sole proprietorships. They are relatively simple and inexpensive to form, and liability and tax responsibility reside fully with the owners. With multiple owners, partnerships provide the potential for more talent and decision-making ability among the ownership. They also tend to have access to better financing, thanks in part to the willingness of banks to loan money to businesses with more than one owner to share the credit risk.

Partnerships also have some important disadvantages, not the least of which is the lack of liability protection for their owners. Those multiple owners can also be a source of conflict, leading to managerial problems. And maintaining continuity in a partnership can be just as tough as in a sole proprietorship. The departure or death of a partner can create a financial burden that the remaining partners cannot overcome.

There are actually several types of partners, though the most common is the general partner, who is active in the business and has unlimited liability. All partnerships must have at least one general partner. Other types of partners include:

- Limited partners, whose liability is limited to the amount of money they have invested
- Silent partners, who are known as partners by the public but are not active in the business
- Dormant partners, who are not known by the public and are not active in the business
- Nominal partners, who are partners in name only, such as when a celebrity lets a business use their name for promotion

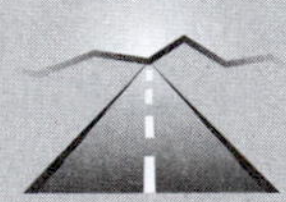

PATHWAY TO... DRAFTING A PARTNERSHIP AGREEMENT

Partnerships can be formed with a handshake, but the preferred route is to have an attorney draw up a simple partnership contract that will be signed by all the participants. This agreement should address several important topics:

- **Structure:** Show what percent of the company is owned by each partner.
- **Duties:** Define which partner is responsible for which part of the daily management of the company.

- **Profits:** Detail the division of profits and losses, and specify when profits are to be distributed to the partners.
- **Conflicts and crises:** Stipulate how disagreements between the partners will be resolved (for example, by arbitration) and how the death or departure of a partner will be managed.
- **Dissolution:** Explain how the company's assets and liabilities will be distributed if the partnership is dissolved.

Many business owners are uncomfortable contemplating crisis or failure when they are just starting a new venture, but it is essential to provide answers to tough questions in advance of forming a partnership.

IN THE REAL WORLD

Partners Need to Plan for the End—At the Beginning

Friends Dave and Mitch honed their skills brewing their own beer while sharing an apartment during college. After graduating, they decided to turn their hobby into a business and launched a Web site selling home-brewing supplies online. Dave's brother, an attorney, drew up their partnership documents. They balked when he told them the agreement needed to outline ways to dissolve the partnership—why did they want to talk about quitting before they even started? They gave in and the advice proved priceless. After two years, their e-business was doing well when Mitch announced he wanted out of the partnership: his Spanish girlfriend was returning to her home country and he was going with her. Fortunately, the partnership agreement provided a means for Dave—who loved the e-business and wanted to keep it going—to buy out Mitch over time. They parted company as friends and were able to devote their full attention to the loves of their lives.

FOR EXAMPLE

See the Toolkit at the end of this chapter for a sample partnership agreement from smallbusinessnotes.com.

Corporation: A form of business that exists independently from its owners, providing for an indefinite life and limiting the liability of its stockholders.

2.1.3 When It's Right to Incorporate

One option to consider when establishing a business is whether to incorporate. A **corporation** is a legal entity that is separate from the individuals who create or work for it. Stock in a corporation is issued to individuals or to other business entities that form the ownership of the company.

Why should a business choose to incorporate? The biggest advantage is the fact that a corporation offers protection to its owners. Individual shareholders are not personally liable as are sole proprietors or general partners. Corporations offer other advantages too. Because they are separate entities from their owners, they can exist indefinitely, even if their major stockholder dies. They also have greater growth potential than proprietorships or partnerships because they can raise money by selling stock. That stock—which in turn can be sold—also makes ownership transfers relatively simple.

Incorporating has some disadvantages too. The process of forming a corporation can be expensive, time consuming, and involve a large amount of paperwork. To file, owners must submit articles of incorporation that state (among other things) the name of the company, its location, the name of the owner(s), and the purpose of the business. In addition, the business must submit bylaws (which describe how the company is run) and a list of officers (or the people who direct the company in its daily decisions, such as a president, secretary, and treasurer).

After a corporation is approved by the state, the responsibilities don't end there. For a corporation to maintain its status, it must issue stock, hold annual board meetings (with the officers), and record minutes of those meetings. These formal requirements of a corporation can be cumbersome, especially for a new business. In addition, a corporation has to file separate tax forms, which are typically more complicated than an individual return.

Forming a corporation is not the cheapest method of starting a business either. Hiring an attorney to file the necessary paperwork with the state (a smart idea) can cost $1,000 or more in legal expenses and filing fees. There are two common types of incorporation to consider:

C corporation: A traditional corporation, with no limits on the numbers of shareholders, or who those shareholders are.

- **C corporation:** This traditional form of a corporation offers the most flexibility when seeking investors. A "C corporation" is allowed to have unlimited shareholders, usually with no restrictions on who they are. The downside is the way in which C corporations are taxed. The tax rates paid by corporations are higher than those paid by individuals, plus shareholders run the risk of something called "double taxation": The business is first taxed on its income, then its individual shareholders must also pay tax on any dividends they receive.

S corporation: A type of corporation that limits the number and type of shareholders, but avoids double taxation by allowing profits and losses to pass through to those shareholders.

- **S corporation:** Electing to form an S corporation is an option for companies with no more than 75 shareholders. The shareholders must all be individuals (they cannot be corporations or other business entities), and they must be legal U.S. residents. S corporations avoid double taxation by passing their profits and losses through to shareholders.

Limited Liability Company (LLC): A business form that combines the flexibility and tax advantages of a partnership with the formal structure and legal protection provided by a corporation.

2.1.4 The Popular Limited Liability Company

Another organizational option that has become increasingly popular is the **Limited Liability Company (LLC).** The LLC combines the flexibility and tax advantages of a partnership with the formal structure and legal protection provided by a corporation. As in a general partnership, income is passed through to the LLC members (owners), who pay taxes on their individual returns. Profits are distributed according to an organizational agreement. (Note that profit does not have to be split equally among partners.) An LLC allows an unlimited number of partners, and permits raising money for the business by taking on investors (including other corporations) as members. Additionally, members of the LLC are not personally liable for the actions. of the company.

E-business in Action

Choose whether to operate your business as a sole proprietorship, partnership, corporation, or LLC.

Choosing to form an LLC requires filing with the state, although the requirements typically are not as stringent as they are for a corporation, and the costs usually are lower.

Just because a firm selects one legal form when it is starting up does not mean that it is stuck with that structure forever. As a firm grows (or plans for growth), its needs sometimes change and it becomes apparent that the company would be better served by adopting a new structure. Changing the legal form is possible, but it should not be done without consulting with a CPA, attorney, or other trusted business advisor. In addition to the required paperwork, changing forms will sometimes require major changes in accounting practices, which demands planning and making the change at the appropriate time so as to avoid tax headaches.

SELF-CHECK

1. What are the four key issues to consider when selecting a business's legal form?
2. What are the advantages of operating as a sole proprietor? What are the disadvantages?
3. List five topics that should be addressed in every partnership agreement.
4. What are the major advantages in forming a corporation rather than a sole proprietorship or partnership?
5. How are income taxes paid by a limited liability company (LLC)?

Apply Your Knowledge Two gardening enthusiasts/entrepreneurs are planning to launch a small business selling unique flower seeds online and are unsure about what legal form to choose for their firm. They are concerned about minimizing their personal liability if the business fails, and want to make sure they can take on new investors if the business really takes off. Summarize the legal forms allowable for their situation, suggest one that best suits their needs, and briefly explain why.

2.2 IDENTIFICATION NUMBERS, LICENSES, AND ZONING

All businesses, whether online or offline, must do certain things to set themselves up and operate legally. Traditional bricks-and-mortar firms making the jump into e-business probably have a good idea of the requirements, but new online entrepreneurs may find themselves a bit overwhelmed by the world of business licenses, numbers, and laws. Like everything else in business, though, addressing the legalities of operating an online business one step at a time will make the process more manageable. The following sections provide an overview of the basic requirements that most new businesses must meet.

PATHWAY TO... GATHERING INFORMATION ON LAWS AND REGULATIONS

While the Internet is a good resource for new business owners trying to discover what licenses they need and which laws might apply to their venture, there are many organizations that can also provide assistance:

- An industry trade association
- The local chamber of commerce
- A business development center at a community college
- A city or county development association
- The Small Business Administration (www.sba.gov)

2.2.1 Federal Tax Identification Number

Employer Identification Number (EIN): A nine-digit number that is used to identify a company whenever its owner files official forms and tax returns.

Any business that has employees or is organized as a corporation, partnership, or LLC needs a federal tax identification number. Officially known as an **Employer Identification Number (EIN),** this nine-digit number is used to identify a company whenever its owner files forms and tax returns. The EIN is requested on many different types of business documents—from bank accounts to loan applications. Sole proprietors can use their Social Security number, though concerns about privacy might encourage them to get a separate number for their business.

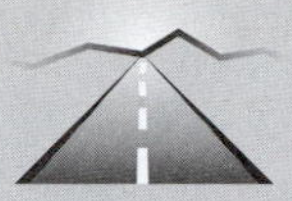

PATHWAY TO... APPLYING FOR A FEDERAL TAX ID NUMBER

Business owners can apply for a federal tax ID by calling 1-800-829-4933 or by visiting the IRS Web site: https://sa.www4.irs.gov/sa_vign/newFormSS4.do. (Or the required Form SS-4 can be downloaded, filled out, and submitted by regular U.S. mail.) Applying for an EIN on behalf of the owner is a standard task performed by attorneys hired to organize a business as a corporation or LLC.

2.2.2 Sales Taxes

The issue of sales taxes is confusing, and some people mistakenly believe that Internet sales are exempt from sales taxes. In fact, most states (all except Alaska, Delaware, Montana, New Hampshire, and Oregon as this was being written) charge sales tax and require businesses that sell products online to collect and pay tax on every sale to residents of the same state in which the firm has a physical presence. In addition, some cities and counties charge sales tax and require online sellers to comply with laws and collect tax on some or all transactions.

If an e-business is required by law to collect and pay sales tax, it must first apply for a state sales tax license. Be aware that the amount of sales tax to collect, the dates the tax is due, and the rules of collection vary by state, county, or municipality. For that reason, business owners should check the regulations for the various entities governing where their business is physically located. The good news is that many states allow—or even encourage—electronic filing and payment of sales taxes, which cuts down on the amount of paperwork involved.

2.2.3 Business Bank Account

When some owners of small online businesses start up, they simply run all their money through an existing personal bank account. This is rarely a good idea. Why do people do it? Some are just testing out a business idea and feel that opening a separate account is unnecessary. Others simply want to save some money on bank fees. Unless an e-business owner plans to maintain their Web site strictly as a hobby, however, they need to open a business bank account immediately. Otherwise, it becomes too easy to comingle personal and business expenses, which can make it difficult to distinguish legitimate business deductions. Not only can this create a headache at tax time, it can cause serious problems—including stiff penalties—in the event of an Internal Revenue Service audit.

PATHWAY TO... OPENING A BUSINESS ACCOUNT

When opening a business account, the bank needs specific information, including:

- A copy of the business license
- The federal tax ID number (or Social Security number)
- Proof of incorporation if the account is going to carry the legally incorporated business name

Owners should consider opening two bank accounts: one for daily transactions and the other for dealing with sales tax, employee withholding, and other regular tax payments. Keeping these items separate and using simple money transfers from one account to another can make it easier to manage payroll and employee finances.

IN THE REAL WORLD

Keeping Business and Personal Accounts Separate

When Joyce launched a part-time business offering online interior design advice, she convinced herself that a separate bank account was unnecessary. Over the next two years, the business grew steadily and its finances became more complicated. Joyce incurred a variety of business expenses—including travel, Web site hosting, and fabric and paint samples—all paid for with her personal credit card or checking account. Ever independent, Joyce also did her own taxes, but found herself guessing about which expenses were legitimate business deductions. When she became one of the unfortunate few to have a tax return audited by the IRS, Joyce realized she had made a big mistake. Unable to clearly distinguish business spending from personal spending in her checking and charge accounts, Joyce had some of her business deductions disallowed during the audit and ended up paying a tax penalty.

Business license: A document granting an owner the right to do business within a city, county, or state.

2.2.4 Business Licenses

Regardless of where a business is located, it will probably need a license to operate. A **business license** is a document granting the owner the right to do business within a city, county, or state. Licenses are typically valid for a one- or two-year period and are nontransferable (selling the business voids the license). Applying for a license also requires paying a fee. The amount is often based on the type of business and can range from $25 to several thousand dollars.

A firm's owner (and not a city clerk) should specify its appropriate business category when applying for a license, because a category specifically for an Internet-based, or e-commerce, business might not exist. Instead, it might be appropriate to select a broad category based on the specific activity conducted through the Web site. Some categories can require steep licensing fees and might not, in fact, apply to the business in question. Owners should carefully review the possible categories and the accompanying fees and choose one that is both appropriate and offers a low fee.

In addition to a city-issued license, counties might also require a business license. These are similar to city licenses but are often less restrictive and less expensive. Be aware that some occupations (building contractors, realtors, and other professional service providers, for example) might require obtaining a state license. Most online businesses will not require a state license, but it is important to take the time to investigate requirements, which are usually published on state government Web sites.

2.2.5 Zoning for Home-Based Businesses

A home is the ideal place to start a small online business; setup can be quick and overhead low. But before converting that spare bedroom into an office, owners need to determine whether they are legally allowed to operate from their home.

Zoning:
Ordinances that define how a particular piece of land or group of properties can be used.

The answer typically comes down to a single word: **zoning.** Most cities and towns have zoning ordinances that define how a particular piece of land or group of properties can be used. They further specify which types of activities can occur there. For example, some neighborhoods are zoned for residential use, which means that only single-family homes can be built in that area. In the area of commercial or business use, zoning gets more complicated because businesses are often separated by type of industry. An area might also be labeled mixed use, which allows both residential and some types of limited commercial activity.

E-business in Action
Determine which laws apply to your e-business and ensure that you are in compliance with them.

Some cities and counties make zoning maps, along with a detailed list of city ordinances, available online. This is the place to start an inquiry into local zoning laws. A visit to the city clerk or the city licensing or planning department will confirm whether a particular address has any restrictions that would prevent the operation of a business.

What happens if a home-based business is not allowed? Owners must ask for a variance, or an exception to the zoning ordinance. Because millions of people are working from home now, many cities have already established criteria for allowing such exceptions. To grant a variance, cities and counties typically want assurance that a home-based business does not have:

- High-volume street traffic
- Increased activity (by customers) in and out of the home
- Large trucks on-site (delivery trucks or company vehicles)
- Additional parking requirements
- Exterior signage
- The use or storage of harmful chemicals
- Warehousing of a large number of products
- The on-site sale of products to the public (such as what takes place at retail locations)
- Employees (usually more than 3 or 4) working on-site

These conditions are in place primarily to ensure that business activities do not adversely affect neighbors or residential property values. Luckily, most Internet-based endeavors don't create such nuisances or can take steps to avoid problems. For example, online businesses storing and shipping large numbers of products might want to lease an off-site storage facility or arrange to have products shipped from a distribution facility.

Increasingly, zoning is not the only concern when starting a home-based business. Many cities now require home occupational permits for businesses. The good news is that certain occupations or business types are often automatically granted permits—and computer or Internet-related businesses are almost always included. However, qualifying for a permit might be based on a long list of conditions that are similar to the criteria used in seeking a zoning variance. In addition, cities often send notices of intent to operate a home-based business to neighbors and give them an opportunity to object. Even with this caveat, obtaining a home occupational permit can be much easier (and faster) than having to get a zoning variance granted. A home occupational permit does not take the place of a business license. To operate legally, a firm must have both.

Even if a proposed home-based business clears municipal zoning ordinances and occupational permits, other obstacles can stand in the way:

- **Homeowners' associations:** Residents of subdivisions, condominiums, and some neighborhood communities often have homeowners' associations, along with restrictive covenants (or rules) that govern what can be done on each member's property. Restrictions on the operation of home-based businesses are not uncommon.

- **Landlords:** The rental agreement on a leased house or apartment might prohibit business activity on the property. Negotiating an exception to this is always a possibility, though the owner might demand an additional security deposit, higher rent, or extra insurance coverage that could prove expensive.

Choosing to ignore the legal restrictions concerning how a property can be used is a considerable risk. If illegal business activity is discovered, city officials can shut down a business, homeowners' associations can impose steep fines (and even put a lien on a house), and landlords can evict tenants, leaving an online entrepreneur without a home for his or her business or him- or herself.

SELF-CHECK

1. Are any online businesses exempt from collecting sales tax? What document do they need to obtain if they are required to collect sales tax?
2. Why is it a good idea to maintain separate business bank accounts?
3. What is a business license? What entities might require getting a business license?
4. What are an owner's options (if any) if their plans to open a home-based business are prevented by zoning laws?

Apply Your Knowledge An entrepreneur wants to launch an online business in her spare bedroom, but zoning laws forbid her from operating a business in her home. Consider the conditions created by a business that might concern neighbors, and explain why this e-business would not cause these problems and would be a good candidate for a zoning variance.

2.3 UNDERSTANDING COPYRIGHTS AND TRADEMARKS

Creating a distinctive name, symbol, or phrase for use in an online business can involve a lot of work. Professional branding companies get paid tens (or hundreds) of thousands of dollars to come up with the right name for a new product or service. The same hard work and time apply to a clever body of text used on a Web site or to an original piece of artwork. If you go to the trouble of developing something unique, it is worth protecting it as your own.

Intellectual property: Property that derives from the creative work of the mind.

To understand how to protect these valuable creative works—collectively called **intellectual property**—it is first necessary to understand some very important terms, as defined by the U.S. government:

Trademark:
A mark that legally protects the name, words, or symbols used by a firm to distinguish its products or services from those provided by another firm.

Copyright:
The exclusive legal right to reproduce, sell, or distribute a literary, artistic, or other type of creative work.

Patent:
A property right granted to an inventor excluding others from making, using, importing, or selling their invention in exchange for a public disclosure of the invention.

- **Trademark:** A device or mark that protects the words, names, symbols, sounds, or colors that distinguish goods and services offered by one firm from those sold by others. Trademarks can be renewed forever or as long as they are being used in commerce.
- **Copyright:** Intellectual property law that protects original creative works (including poetry, novels, movies, songs, computer software, and architecture) and gives the owner the exclusive right to reproduce, sell, or distribute the work. The Library of Congress registers copyrights, which last for the life of the author plus 70 years.
- **Patent:** A property right granted by the U.S. government to an inventor that excludes others from making, using, importing, or offering the invention for sale in the United States in exchange for public disclosure of the invention when the patent is granted.

Obtaining one of these legal stamps is a fairly painless process, and taking this precaution can eventually translate into dollars gained. Not having a product or logo protected makes it easier for someone to copy or steal an idea, which can be very expensive for a small business. Although having a trademark or copyright might not prevent others from infringing on a firm's intellectual property, it certainly makes it easier to go after them in court if they do.

Although the rules for these protective marks are the same whether a firm is conducting business online or off, the Internet has increased the stakes. Having information readily accessible by millions of people around the globe makes it easier for others to "borrow" what they find online. That is all the more reason for an e-business to make the effort to officially protect its intellectual property.

2.3.1 Registering Trademarks

Does a business have to register its work to be protected? No—surprisingly, a federal trademark is not a necessity. Suppose that a business designs a symbol to be used as the logo on its Web site. By placing that logo on its site and using it there and on any other business materials, the company has established rights to it. So, why bother to officially register the logo? Obtaining federal registration acts as a notice to the public that a firm owns the mark. This registration can be an important asset if a company decides to take action in a federal court to stop someone else from using its work. Also, an official U.S. registration provides the basis for registering a logo outside the United States.

Even if a business chooses not to formally register its work, it can use the trademark symbol anyway. The firm simply places a ™ (trademark) symbol next to tag lines or logos they want to protect whenever they appear on a Web page or company documents. Once a company has applied for registration and received final notification that the mark is registered, it can instead use the registered trademark ® symbol. It is important to remember that registering a trademark or correctly using the symbols will not prevent others from infringing on its use, and that it is up to the business—not a government or law enforcement agency—to enforce its own trademarks. See Figure 2-1 for examples of the correct use of trademark and registration symbols.

E-business in Action
Register a trademark.

To begin the process of applying for a trademark, go to the Web site of the U.S. Patent and Trademark office, www.uspto.gov, and follow the instructions for online filing. A $325 fee must be paid using a credit card when filing this way.

Figure 2-1

The correct use of trademark and registration symbols.

IN THE REAL WORLD

Protect That Trademark

For several years, Dan had run a successful side business tracking down and selling parts for classic Ford Mustangs. Things were going so well that he decided to quit his day job and start selling full-time through his own Web site. A friend who was both a car buff and graphic designer came up with a great new name and logo for Dan's business. The Web site was a hit and Dan decided to apply for a trademark for his company logo. It was a good idea. Within months, a new competitor also selling Mustang parts appeared online and his logo appeared to be a direct knockoff of Dan's. Dan decided to hire a lawyer and fight the competitor. The competitor claimed he had come up with his logo a couple of years earlier, but thanks to Dan's trademark application, Dan could prove prior use for business purposes. Dan won his case and was able to protect both his logo and his growing e-business.

2.3.2 Filing for Copyright

As with trademarks, a business does not have to file for copyright protection to claim a creative work as its own. Copyright protection is automatically in place at the time the work is created. However, if a firm chooses to file a lawsuit against someone that it feels is illegally using its information, the U.S. Copyright Office advises having a formal certificate of registration as proof of ownership.

The good news is that copyrighting information is not expensive. Filing fees, as this was being written, were $30 per work; a group of material typically costs a minimum of $45 (or $15 per individual work within the group). When it comes to registration, certain rules pertain specifically to Web sites and other material (such as documents offered for download) distributed online. For instance, any original information included on a Web site can be copyrighted. Table 2-1 outlines some other variables to consider.

Table 2-1 Copyright Do's and Don'ts for E-business Owners

Copyright Do's	*Copyright Don'ts*
Original computer programs can be copyrighted.	Domain names cannot be copyrighted.
Entire databases can be copyrighted.	
An electronic newsletter sent to customers each week can be protected under copyright laws—as long as the information is original.	

The rules become more complicated when discussing the period over which a work is protected, or the amount of work that can be copyrighted. For instance, the original words on Web site pages are protected. However, any updates that change the information are not protected. In other words, there is no unlimited copyright to a site's content. Any change to the information (a must to keep Web sites fresh and current) requires filing another application and paying another filing fee.

E-business in Action →
Apply for a copyright.

To file a copyright application, visit the U.S. Copyright Office Web site, www.copyright.gov, to obtain complete information on the process.

SELF-CHECK

1. What is a copyright? Which of the following can be copyrighted: a domain name; a poem; a color; a computer program?
2. If a business fails to register a trademark, will that trademark still be legally protected?
3. Who is responsible for enforcing copyrights and trademarks?

Apply Your Knowledge An online business owner wrote an interesting story that told about his life and explained how he developed the products he was selling. He applied for and received a copyright for the story. A year later, he decided to rewrite the story and added a lot of new information. Is the complete new story still copyrighted? What would the owner have to do to make sure it was all copyrighted?

2.4 THE BASICS OF BUSINESS ETHICS

Ethics:
A set of rules or moral principles that together define whether behavior is "right" or "wrong" according to society.

The word "ethics" gets mentioned often, but what does it really mean? **Ethics** are a set of moral principles that together define what is right or wrong—in effect they are the rules that tell you how to always do the right thing. Ethics are established by society, but they can be confusing because they tend to change over time and vary from one society to the next or between different segments of society.

When applied to business, behaving ethically also means doing the right thing, but deciding what is right can present significant challenges to a small-business owner. The struggle to earn a profit—or even avoid failure—sometimes pressures owners to compromise their ethical standards. Yet as high-profile, big-corporate cases of ethical lapse—Enron, for example—reveal, society as a whole suffers when businesses behave badly. The same principles that govern the Enrons of the world govern one-person online companies, and ethical failures by small e-businesses are especially troublesome at this point in history. Many new online customers are wary of shopping on their computer, and even one bad experience can undermine their confidence in the new technology.

2.4.1 Ethics and Laws

There is a lot of misunderstanding about business ethics. For example, some business owners mistakenly assume that by not breaking the law they will ensure that they are behaving ethically. Following all the laws regarding an e-business—including getting the proper licenses, paying taxes, and following legal and honest accounting practices—is an important component of behaving ethically, but sometimes that is not enough.

Though low price is important, customers often seek out firms that emphasize honesty and integrity and deliver on those promises. In today's instant-information world, it is hard to keep bad behavior a secret—consider eBay's rating system, or online service review sites like Angie's List (www.angieslist.com). Usually, the poor ratings are not received as a result of illegal acts, but rather because firms failed to deliver on promises, cut corners on packaging and shipping, or sold products that were not as advertised—in effect, they failed to conduct business in an ethical manner. While some small online sellers may feel forced into these actions by their limited resources, most will quickly learn that this is actually a formula for a quick demise.

IN THE REAL WORLD

An Ethical Test for Businesses

Consider the example offered by Rotary International, a worldwide service organization for business and professional leaders that emphasizes its members adhering to the highest possible ethical standards. The organization has adopted as its central philosophy "The Four Way Test," created in 1932 by one-time Rotary president Herbert J. Taylor when he assumed the leadership of a company threatened with bankruptcy. The test, which can be applied to any business decision, consists of four simple questions:

1. Is it the TRUTH?
2. Is it FAIR to all concerned?
3. Will it build GOODWILL and BETTER FRIENDSHIPS?
4. Will it be BENEFICIAL to all concerned?

Taylor asked his employees to follow this simple guide in all their business actions. In the end, the company survived and both employees and customers credited "The Four Way Test" as one of the reasons for the success. Regardless of the reasons behind the company's survival, what is clear from this example is that ethical behavior starts at the top—the owner or manager of a business sets the standard for ethical behavior expected in a company.

2.4.2 Codes of Conduct

Some e-business owners may find that maintaining high ethics requires more than just behaving the right way. This is especially true for small businesses that grow quickly and must add several new employees in a short time or use outside contractors that appear to be employees from the customer's viewpoint. Owners with a firm commitment to ethical behavior often find that they need to develop a formal statement about what their company believes is right or wrong. Or some owners might be so overwhelmed by rapid societal or technological change that they need to establish standards in cases where ethics are either unclear or evolving in response to change.

Code of conduct: A business's written statement of ethical practices or guidelines to which it adheres.

In such cases, small businesses often establish a **code of conduct,** a written statement of ethical guidelines that everyone in the business will follow. A code of conduct is primarily an internal document, but to be effective it should establish policies that the company would not be embarrassed to share with its customers. The range of subjects covered in a code of conduct is limitless, though establishing a core set of principles and asking employees to adhere to them usually is more effective than trying to write a giant rule book for every possible on-the-job action. Focusing on key issues such as fair employment practices, honesty in accounting and record keeping, and appropriate customer service normally yields the greatest benefits.

FOR EXAMPLE

See an excerpt from PepsiCo's corporate code of conduct (www.pepsico.com/PEP_Investors/CorporateGovernance/CodeofConduct/english/images/Conduct07-v6.pdf).

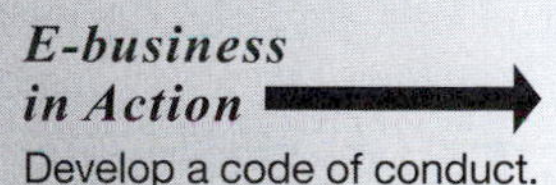

Develop a code of conduct.

Social responsibility: The obligations a business has to society.

2.4.3 Social Responsibility

In recent years, **social responsibility** has become an important issue in the business world. Closely related to ethics, the issue takes a step past simply deciding right from wrong and asks, "What obligations does a business have to society?" These obligations fall into several different areas and cover a wide variety of topics:

- **Community involvement:** Donating money, products, or time to support various public activities, including education, recreation, and the arts
- **Environment:** Employing "green" practices that minimize pollution and conserve natural resources
- **Product safety:** Refusing to sell products with known health hazards
- **Fair Business practices:** Employing and providing advancement opportunities to women, minorities, or disadvantaged individuals

In many cases, firms are not legally required to follow socially responsible practices, and, in fact, some firms choose to do only the minimum required by the law. Yet, like ethical behavior, social responsibility often demands going beyond what the law requires. Some owners find that they are more comfortable if their firm is a good citizen in the community (and that can include online communities), and others find that social responsibility can also be very good for business. The costs of supporting various community activities or embracing energy-efficient technologies are often offset by new customers attracted to the socially responsible attitudes or by savings from running a business the traditional way.

SELF-CHECK

1. Does obeying all laws ensure that a business is also behaving ethically? If not, give an example to demonstrate the difference.
2. What is a code of conduct and how would it be used by a business?
3. Give an example of a business that has demonstrated social responsibility.

Apply Your Knowledge You are the owner of an e-business that has been accused of not being a socially responsible business citizen of the community in which your business is headquartered. Suggest three ideas for improving your firm's level of social responsibility within its community.

2.5 ESTABLISHING ONLINE POLICIES

During the process of starting an e-business, it is important to think about future customers. Owners anticipate who will buy their product, research the needs of those customers, and painstakingly detail how to meet those needs in their business plan and how to turn the dollars that those customers spend into profit. Many savvy owners often realize that something is missing from the typical business plan: Where in all that research and planning is a pledge to future customers—a solemn promise of how they will be treated?

2.5.1 Creating a Customer Pledge

Customer pledge: A written guideline of what customers can expect when doing business with a firm.

What is a **customer pledge** and how is one developed? A pledge to customers is a written guideline of what they can expect when doing business with a firm. The pledge should be the basis of a company's overall customer service philosophy. A customer service pledge should first be developed internally and viewed and used only by company employees. From this

PATHWAY TO... CREATING A CUSTOMER PLEDGE

1. Answer these general questions about your attitude toward customers:
   - How do you view your customers?
   - Do you know your customers personally?
   - Do you speak with your customers on the phone?
   - Are your customers completely anonymous?
   - What are you willing to do for customers every single day?
   - What are you not willing to do for your customers?
2. Define realistic parameters of how customers will be able to communicate with you on a daily basis.
   - Can customers email your business?
   - Can customers call your e-business toll-free 24 hours a day?
3. When and how will you respond to customers?
   - Will you respond immediately or within 24 hours?
   - Will you respond to your customers only by email?
   - Will you telephone your customers?
4. Identify what, if anything, will be special about the way you treat customers.

Create a summary of your answers to questions 1 through 4; use a list of bullets or a series of short paragraphs. This is the first draft of the customer service pledge.

first internal pledge, a company can then develop an external (public) customer service pledge.

After reviewing and refining the first draft of the customer pledge, it should be finalized and distributed for internal use as a guideline and reminder of how to incorporate customers into everyday business.

E-business in Action → Write a customer pledge.

The next step is to take the internal pledge and adapt it into a version to publish on the Web site for customers to read. The pledge can be as general or specific as desired, but it should reflect the internal customer service philosophy and explain to customers how they can expect to be treated.

Creating a customer service pledge is only the beginning of an effective customer care policy. Every legitimate and successful online business must have several different policies in place. The government mandates some policies, and others are the result of common sense to minimize confusion for a firm's employees and the people with which it does business.

Policies are equally important to customers, employees, and vendors. Although not every business must create a formal printed manual filled with its policies, those policies should be written down somewhere. In most cases, it is advisable for a firm to publish policies on its Web site, to protect itself from misunderstandings and to reassure customers about how it conducts business. The following sections detail a variety of policies that the typical e-business should consider establishing and publishing on its Web site.

Privacy policy: A policy detailing how an online business collects, treats, and uses the information it receives from customers and others who visit its Web site.

Cookie: A small file placed on a user's computer when they visit a Web site. The file contains information about the user and is accessed by the Web site's server each time they visit the site.

2.5.2 Privacy Policies

A **privacy policy** details how a business collects, treats, and uses the information it receives from customers and others who visit its Web site. This policy not only covers information that customers knowingly provide, but also applies to the use of **cookies,** the information files that Web servers create to track data about people and the online sites they visit. Every privacy policy should clearly state a firm's commitment to customer privacy and data security.

PATHWAY TO... CREATING A LEGAL AND EFFECTIVE PRIVACY POLICY

A privacy policy is a requirement for online businesses based in the United States. The Federal Trade Commission (FTC) mandates this policy. The policy must be properly labeled and easily accessible on the Web site. A privacy policy should include the following elements:

- A description of how information is collected from site visitors and customers
- Details of what information is collected
- An explanation of what will be done with the collected information and how and where it will be stored
- Disclosure of those with whom the customer information might be shared
- Instructions for how visitors or customers can change their information or remove it from the records

2.5.3 User Agreements

User agreement: A document published on a Web site that specifies the terms or conditions under which visitors are allowed to use the site.

Increasingly, Web sites are implementing **user agreements.** Just like a written contract, this agreement specifies terms or conditions by which visitors or customers are allowed to use a site. One simple option is to post on a site a static (unchanging) page that lists the conditions. However, a more legally binding version of this agreement requires visitors to acknowledge that they have read the terms and agree to abide by them. Before visitors are allowed to go to certain areas of a Web site or to make a purchase, they are forced to click a button verifying that they agree to the terms.

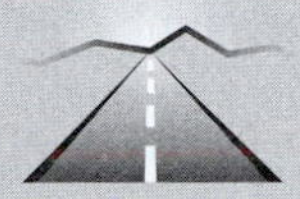

PATHWAY TO... CREATING A USER AGREEMENT

When creating a site's terms and conditions, the following information should be included:

- **How visitors or customers can or cannot use the site.** These rules are not only for customers, but for employees as well, such as posting personal information like phone numbers or physical addresses on a discussion forum.
- **Who is allowed to view the site** (whether they meet age or U.S. citizenship requirements, for example).
- **What other policies are in place,** including shipping, returns, or complaint procedures.
- **Legal and liability issues.** This includes instructions regarding responsibility of the business and third parties for providing information and taking actions, and specification of where legal disputes will be settled.

2.5.4 Shipping and Return Policies

Shipping policy: A written policy that explains how and when customer orders are to be managed and shipped.

A **shipping policy** should clearly explain the details of how and when customer orders are handled and shipped. Although a business can determine some conditions of this policy, it must also comply with the Federal Trade Commission's Mail or Telephone Order Merchandise Rule. According to the FTC, an online site must:

- Ship an order within the timeframe promised at the time of ordering or as stated in advertising or on the Web site.
- Ship a product within 30 days after the order is received, unless an earlier timeframe is specified.

- Give notice to a consumer as fast as possible whenever that person's product cannot be shipped when promised.
- Include a revised shipping date in any delay notice sent to a customer.
- Allow a customer to agree to a delay or to cancel an order. The site must provide a description of the time required for receiving a refund in the event of a cancellation.

Return policy: A written policy that details the conditions under which customers are allowed to return a product or decline a service.

A **return policy** should include the conditions under which customers are allowed to return a product or decline a service. Return policies should be specific so that customers clearly understand (and are not surprised by) the rules. A good policy should protect both the e-business and the customer. As e-commerce grows, so does the problem of customers taking advantage of online retailers. Return policies should limit the number of days returns will be accepted. Customers must have enough time to evaluate a product (three to five days is a reasonable length of time) but not use it indefinitely before demanding their money back.

An effective return policy should incorporate the following elements:

- **Time limit:** Set the maximum number of days within which a return will be accepted.
- **Conditions of use:** Maintain the right to reject a return if an item shows obvious signs of use.

IN THE REAL WORLD

Don't Forget Your Customer Policies

Shawn was a serious die-cast car collector who for several years had toyed with the idea of creating a Web site to sell rare cars. With the help of friends, Shawn launched his e-business, though he admitted he didn't know much about retail sales. His goal was to keep the venture part-time and simple, but it turned out to be a little too simple. Shawn didn't bother to write up (let alone publish) any shipping or return policies and the problems began almost immediately. First, Shawn started to get complaints that the cars were too slow in arriving. He had not bothered to tell people that because his business was a part-time, one-man show, it could take him up to a week just to get orders in the mail. Next, there were problems with returns. Shawn had no intention of accepting returned cars after 30 days, something that he had neglected to tell his customers. Soon a dispute developed with a customer who returned a car three months after purchasing it. Shawn got so frustrated that he decided to shut down his Web site, never realizing that putting a few policies in writing would have helped him develop a better relationship with his customers.

- **Restock fee:** Explain any fees that are incurred by restocking a returned item.
- **Exceptions:** Specify any items that cannot be returned.
- **Shipping responsibility:** Determine who pays for the cost of shipping when a product is returned.
- **Refunds issued as cash or credit:** Decide whether to issue store credit rather than give cash back.

2.5.5 Other Policies

Other policies that e-businesses may want to publish on their Web site include the following:

- **Message board or chat room policies:** In these areas, visitors and customers can share their opinions, ideas, and concerns. If a site offers these communication options, set up some basic guidelines for how each one is operated. The policy should specify such items as who can participate and whether someone must register (or sign on as a member) first. Also, it should explain who is monitoring these activities and in what fashion. The policy should clearly specify what type of material is inappropriate for posting, and how and when it might be removed.
- **Exporting:** If an e-commerce site sells to customers outside the United States, it might be subject to special government regulations by the U.S. Department of Commerce, the U.S. Department of Defense, or other federal departments. What is sold and to what countries might be tightly regulated. An experienced attorney should be consulted for help with developing an exporting policy.
- **Spam:** Depending on the type of business, it might be advisable to include a **spam** (unsolicited advertising emails, the online equivalent of junk mail) policy within the privacy policy. This policy states whether a site distributes marketing emails and how it responds to these emails. This type of policy has become more important since the CAN-SPAM Act of 2003 (Controlling the Assault of Non-Solicited Pornography and Marketing Act) was passed, establishing the first U.S. standards for the sending of commercial email.

Spam:
Unsolicited advertising emails, often sent in large batches; the online equivalent of junk mail.

- **Endorsing and linking to other sites' policies:** When a site sells products or services from other sites, provides links to sites owned by others, or allows other sites to link to their site, they are smart to notify customers about it. The linking policy should simply state how external links are used and whether the information found on these linked sites is endorsed. Customers should be provided with a way to provide notification of problems with external sites or violations to published linking policies.

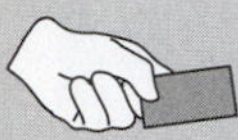

CAREER CONNECTION

While most teenagers get a job to supplement their weekly allowances, 16-year-old Jeremy Alicandri took a more high-tech approach.

With $800 in startup capital, Jeremy began purchasing and then reselling closeout consumer electronics on eBay.com. Upon discovering his business idea could become a profitable one, in 1999 he launched a stand-alone e-commerce site called SimplyCheap.com. With the goal of selling closeout consumer electronics to price-minded consumers, Jeremy saw his business grow dramatically. By 2005, SimplyCheap.com's annual revenues exceeded $2.7 million and running the business was a full-time job for Jeremy.

Asked what advice he would give someone launching a new e-commerce site, Jeremy emphasized the importance of establishing and posting clear-cut customer policies and delivering on those promises. "Providing the best possible customer service is absolutely critical," Jeremy explained. "It'll help you obtain repeat customers, increase word-of-mouth referrals, and decrease the number of credit-card chargebacks you receive. You need to be available via email and telephone.

"When you make your policies clearly known on your Web site, managing your customer-service issues is that much easier. If you have a 14-day return policy, that needs to be clearly posted.

"Also, customers hate waiting to receive their order. Make sure you can process and ship orders quickly. If there's a delay due to an item being backordered, you need to make the customer aware of this immediately. Also, never charge someone's credit card until you're ready to ship their order."

2.5.6 Delivering on Your Promises

After establishing its basic principles of operation, an e-business must deliver. Executing business policies is essential, but not always easy. These policies represent promises to customers and determine what customers come to expect from their interactions with a given e-business. Failing to meet these expectations compromises a firm's reputation and, ultimately, reduces sales.

PATHWAY TO... DEALING WITH A POLICY FAILURE

If a customer policy failure occurs, always follow these steps:

1. Notify the customer immediately.
2. Apologize for the mistake.
3. Correct the problem.
4. Offer a partial or full refund, a free gift, or a discount on future purchases.

Equally important are the consequences of failing to deliver and then incurring a legal liability. The government mandates and monitors several policies. Even a small oversight can land a company in hot water with both its customers and the Feds. Nobody is perfect, and occasional lapses might occur, but how a firm manages its failures may be more important than any other aspect of customer service.

SELF-CHECK

1. What four issues should be covered in every user agreement?
2. What are the key elements of an effective return policy?
3. What steps should a business take if it discovers it has failed to deliver on a customer policy?

Apply Your Knowledge A friend operating a small online business selling specialty hot sauces is confused about the concept of customer pledges. Create a brief customer pledge for your friend that could be published on your friend's Web site. Explain what shoppers could expect when purchasing hot sauces from your friend.

SUMMARY

Section 2.1

- In deciding which legal form a new business should take, owners should consider four important issues: The number of shareholders and who will control the company, the amount of personal liability they are comfortable in assuming, tax issues that concern them, and how the business will be financed.
- The four most common options for legal organization are sole proprietorship, partnership, corporation, and limited liability company (LLC).

Section 2.2

- All new businesses should apply for a federal employer identification number (even if they have no employees), apply for a state sales tax license, open a business bank account, obtain any necessary local business licenses, and make sure they are legal with regard to local zoning laws.

Section 2.3

- Trademarks protect the words, names, and symbols that distinguish goods and services offered by one firm from those sold by others. Copyright protects original creative works and gives the owner the exclusive right to reproduce, sell, or distribute the work. It is the responsibility of the owner to apply for, and to enforce, both trademarks and copyrights.

Section 2.4

- Ethics are a set of moral principles that together define what is right or wrong. Operating a business ethically often requires more than simply obeying laws.

Section 2.5

- Customer pledges and published online policies together constitute a promise by an e-business regarding how it will treat its customers. Delivering on these promises is essential to success.

ASSESS YOUR UNDERSTANDING

UNDERSTAND: WHAT HAVE YOU LEARNED?

Go to **www.wiley.com/college/holden** to assess your knowledge of the basics of business law, ethics, and customer policies.

APPLY: WHAT WOULD YOU DO?

1. Select the legal form that would be most appropriate for each of the following startup e-business scenarios:
   - An individual backed by a small group of investors (including a corporation) wants to provide liability protection for shareholders, but wants to avoid the complications and cost of forming a corporation.
   - Three entrepreneurs, who plan to provide all the startup funding for an e-business and are not concerned with personal exposure to liability, want to quickly and simply organize the firm.
   - A new firm supported by 30 financial backers wants to make sure it can sell stock to new investors, but is worried about those shareholders being penalized by double taxation on any dividends paid to shareholders.
2. A friend launching an e-business selling gourmet pet treats is organizing as a sole proprietorship to save time and money exploring other options. Briefly explain the disadvantages of sole proprietorship.
3. An online entrepreneur sells organic cotton T-shirts for $17.95 each. If the state in which the entrepreneur is located has a 6 percent sales tax, how much tax would the entrepreneur have to collect for each shirt sold to residents of the state in which the entrepreneur is located?
4. The owner of an online bookselling Web site would like to run a business out of a spare bedroom, but zoning laws forbid it. The firm has no other employees and uses a contract warehouse to hold and ship inventory. Make a list of reasons why the business would be a good candidate for a zoning variance.
5. Would each of the following best be protected by a trademark or a copyright, or is legal protection not possible by either means:

   (a) A database
   (b) A Web site domain name
   (c) A Web site business slogan
   (d) The original story of how a product was conceived and developed

6. An online seller of fishing equipment hired a designer to create an attractive logo for the business. After using the logo for two years, the online seller discovered a competitor using a similar design on the competitor's Web site. The online seller had never applied for a trademark. Is the logo still protected? Whose responsibility is it to police the appropriate use of trademarks?
7. An e-business owner with a dozen employees wants to create a code of conduct to give every member of the firm guidelines for ethical behavior. Suggest four different topics that should be covered by the code.
8. A friend developing a Web-based business selling designer baby bibs just discovered that a privacy policy must be published on the site. Create one for your friend that includes the information required in a privacy policy.
9. The owner of an e-commerce site is frustrated because a transaction has gone wrong several different ways and the customer is now very angry. What steps should be taken to fix this situation?

BE AN E-BUSINESS ENTREPRENEUR

Investigate the Advantages of Incorporating

Some entrepreneurs wrongly assume that it is not necessary for one-person businesses to consider organizing as a corporation. Provide at least four scenarios in which an online business owned and operated by a single person would be better served by being a corporation as opposed to being a sole proprietorship.

Establish a Code of Conduct

You have been hired to help launch the e-commerce side of an established retail store and the owner gives you the responsibility of making sure the firm and its employees follow his commitment to maintaining the highest ethical standards. To help achieve this goal, you want to create a code of conduct. Get started by selecting four topics that you think should be included in the code, and write a statement for each that defines the firm's guidelines with regard to ethical behavior.

Create a Customer Pledge

Assume you have started a simple, one-person e-business selling collectible key chains via a Web site. Following the step-by-step process outlined in Section 2.5.1, create a brief customer pledge. As you go through this process, think about how you expect to be treated when you are a customer.

KEY TERMS

Business license	A document granting an owner the right to do business within a city, county, or state.
C corporation	A traditional corporation, with no limits on the numbers of shareholders, or who those shareholders are.
Code of conduct	A business's written statement of ethical practices or guidelines to which it adheres.
Cookie	A small file placed on a user's computer when they visit a Web site. The file contains information about the user and is accessed by the Web site's server each time they visit the site.
Copyright	The exclusive legal right to reproduce, sell, or distribute a literary, artistic, or other type of creative work.
Corporation	A form of business that exists independently from its owners, providing for an indefinite life and limiting the liability of its stockholders.
Customer pledge	A written guideline of what customers can expect when doing business with a firm.
Employer Identification Number (EIN)	A nine-digit number that is used to identify a company whenever its owner files official forms and tax returns.
Ethics	A set of rules or moral principles that together define whether behavior is "right" or "wrong" according to society.
Intellectual property	Property that derives from the creative work of the mind.
Liability	A debt or financial responsibility for which someone is responsible.
Limited liability company (LLC)	A business form that combines the flexibility and tax advantages of a partnership with the formal structure and legal protection provided by a corporation.
Partnership	An association of two or more persons for the purpose of running a business for profit.
Patent	A property right granted to an inventor excluding others from making, using, importing, or selling their invention in exchange for a public disclosure of the invention.
Privacy policy	A policy detailing how an online business collects, treats, and uses the information it receives from customers and others who visit its Web site.

Return policy	A written policy that details the conditions under which customers are allowed to return a product or decline a service.
S corporation	A type of corporation that limits the number and type of shareholders, but avoids double taxation by allowing profits and losses to pass through to those shareholders.
Shipping policy	A written policy that explains how and when customer orders are to be managed and shipped.
Social responsibility	The obligations a business has to society.
Sole proprietorship	A business owned and controlled by one person.
Spam	Unsolicited advertising emails, often sent in large batches; the online equivalent of junk mail.
Trademark	A mark that legally protects the name, words, or symbols used by a firm to distinguish its products or services from those provided by another firm.
User agreement	A document published on a Web site that specifies the terms or conditions under which visitors are allowed to use the site.
Zoning	Ordinances that define how a particular piece of land or group of properties can be used.

TOOLKIT

SAMPLE PARTNERSHIP AGREEMENT

This Partnership Agreement is made on [Insert Date] between [Insert Name of Party 1] and [Insert Name of Party 2].

1. **Name and Business**
   The parties hereby form a partnership under the name of [Insert Business Name] to produce [Insert Business Product/Service]. The principal office of the business shall be [Insert Address].

2. **Term**
   The partnership shall begin on [Insert Date], and shall continue until terminated.

3. **Capital**
   The capital of the partnership shall be contributed in cash by the partners as follows:
   - A separate capital account shall be maintained for each partner.
   - Neither partner shall withdraw any part of their capital account.
   - Upon the demand of either partner, the capital accounts of the partners shall be maintained at all times in the proportions in which the partners share in the profits and losses of the partnership.

4. **Profit and Loss**
   The net profits of the partnership shall be divided equally between the partners, and the net losses shall be borne equally by them. A separate income account shall be maintained for each partner. Partnership profits and losses shall be charged or credited to the separate income account of each partner. If a partner has no credit balance in their income account, losses shall be charged to their capital account.

5. **Salaries and Withdrawals**
   Neither partner shall receive any salary for services rendered to the partnership. Each partner may, from time to time, withdraw the credit balance in their income account.

6. **Interest**
   No interest shall be paid on the initial contributions to the capital of the partnership or on any subsequent contributions of capital.

7. **Management Duties and Restrictions**
   The partners shall have equal rights in the management of the partnership business, and each partner shall devote their entire time to the conduct of the business. Without the consent of the other partner, neither partner

shall on behalf of the partnership borrow or lend money, or make, deliver, or accept any commercial paper, or execute any mortgage, security agreement, bond, or lease, or purchase or contract to purchase, or sell or contract to sell any property for or of the partnership other than the type of property bought and sold in the regular course of its business.

8. **Banking**

All funds of the partnership shall be deposited in its name in such checking account or accounts as shall be designated by the partners. All withdrawals therefrom are to be made upon checks signed by either partner.

9. **Books**

The partnership books shall be maintained at the principal office of the partnership, and each partner shall at all times have access thereto. The books shall be kept on a fiscal year basis, and shall be closed and balanced at the end of each fiscal year. An audit shall be made as of the closing date.

10. **Voluntary Termination**

The partnership may be dissolved at any time by agreement of the partners, in which event the partners shall proceed with reasonable promptness to liquidate the business of the partnership. The partnership name shall be sold with the other assets of the business. The assets of the partnership business shall be used and distributed in the following order:

(a) to pay or provide for the payment of all partnership liabilities and liquidating expenses and obligations;

(b) to equalize the income accounts of the partners;

(c) to discharge the balance of the income accounts of the partners;

(d) to equalize the capital accounts of the partners; and

(e) to discharge the balance of the capital accounts of the partners.

11. **Death**

Upon the death of either partner, the surviving partner shall have the right either to purchase the interest of the decedent in the partnership or to terminate and liquidate the partnership business. If the surviving partner elects to purchase the decedent's interest, he shall serve notice in writing of such election, within three months after the death of the decedent, upon the executor or administrator of the decedent, or, if at the time of such election no legal representative has been appointed, upon any one of the known legal heirs of the decedent at the last-known address of such heir.

(a) If the surviving partner elects to purchase the interest of the decedent in the partnership, the purchase price shall be equal to the decedent's capital account as at the date of their death plus the decedent's income account as at the end of the prior fiscal year, increased by their share of partnership profits or decreased by their share of partnership losses for the period from the beginning of the fiscal year in which their death occurred until the end of the calendar month in which their death occurred, and decreased by withdrawals charged to their income account during such period. No allowance shall be made for goodwill, trade name, patents, or other intangible assets, except as those assets have been reflected on the partnership books immediately prior to the decedent's death; but the survivor shall nevertheless be entitled to use the trade name of the partnership.

(b) Except as herein otherwise stated, the procedure as to liquidation and distribution of the assets of the partnership business shall be the same as stated in paragraph 10 with reference to voluntary termination.

12. Arbitration

Any controversy or claim arising out of or relating to this Agreement, or the breach hereof, shall be settled by arbitration in accordance with the rules, then obtaining, of the American Arbitration Association, and judgment upon the award rendered may be entered in any court having jurisdiction thereof. In witness whereof the parties have signed this Agreement.

Executed this ______________ day of ________________, [Insert Year] in [Insert City, State].

____________________ ____________________

Signature of Party 1 **Signature of Party 2**

PEPSICO CODE OF CONDUCT

WORLDWIDE CODE OF CONDUCT

Dear Employees:

PepsiCo is a large and complex organization. Our businesses reach into nearly every corner of the world. We operate in nearly every country and in every time zone, and we speak virtually every language.

There's only one way to hold together a company so big and diverse—through trust, shared values, common goals and consistent standards of conduct.

That's why we have created a Values Statement and this Code of Conduct. These documents are vitally important to PepsiCo. Together, they clarify what we stand for and the rules we live by. While they are not a substitute for individual responsibility and good judgment, they help guide us in making decisions about how we work and what we do.

Our Values Statement reflects our aspirations—the kind of company we want PepsiCo to be. Our Code of Conduct provides the operating principles that help us live up to those values. Our Values Statement and Code of Conduct apply to every PepsiCo employee throughout the world. They apply to every business transaction we make and to every business acting on our behalf. In situations not fully covered by these standards, the principles on which they are based still apply.

PepsiCo is a great company. The values we live by and our Code of Conduct help to keep it that way. Ethics and integrity are the foundation of our past success—and the keys for our future. So I ask that you please read these documents carefully and that you make a commitment to live by them—every day.

Our future depends upon it.

Indra K. Nooyi
Chief Executive Officer

PepsiCo's Mission

Our mission is to be the world's premier consumer products company focused on convenient foods and beverages. We seek to produce healthy financial rewards to investors as we provide opportunities for growth and enrichment to our employees, our business partners and the communities in which we operate. And in everything we do, we strive to act with honesty, fairness and integrity.

Respect for Our Employees/Diversity

We believe our most important strength is our employees. We seek to provide a work environment where all employees have the opportunity to reach their full potential and contribute to PepsiCo's success.

We are committed to equal opportunity in all aspects of employment for all employees and applicants; to providing a workplace free from all forms of discrimination, including sexual and other forms of harassment; and to fostering a work environment where people feel comfortable and respected, regardless of individual differences, talents or personal characteristics. Our objective is for the diversity of our employees to match the diversity of the population wherever we operate and for the performance of all employees to be judged fairly and based on their contribution to our results.

PepsiCo encourages an inclusive culture, which enables all employees to do their best. This means we:

- welcome and embrace the strengths of our differences,
- provide equal access to opportunities and information,
- treat each other with respect and dignity,
- foster an atmosphere of caring, open communications and candor.

We respect the rights of individuals to achieve professional and personal balance in their lives. We place a great deal of emphasis on personal integrity and believe long-term results are the best measure of performance.

PepsiCo respects employee privacy and dignity and will acquire and retain only that employee personal information that is required for operation of the Company or required by law.

PepsiCo follows all employment laws and regulations and respects lawful customs of the countries where we operate.

Customers, Suppliers and Competitors

We are committed to the continuation of free enterprise and the legal and regulatory frameworks that support it. Therefore, we recognize the importance of laws that prohibit restraints of trade, predatory economic activities and unfair or unethical business practices.

In all of its business dealings with suppliers, customers and competitors, PepsiCo will:

- Compete vigorously and with integrity.
- Treat all customers and suppliers honestly, fairly and objectively.
- Avoid any unfair or deceptive practice and always present our services and products in an honest and forthright manner.
- Never comment on a competitor's product without a good basis or need for such statements.
- Make clear to all suppliers that we expect them to compete fairly and vigorously for our business, and endorse the principles in our Code of Conduct. We will select our suppliers strictly on merit.
- Comply with all laws prohibiting agreements with competitors to: fix prices or other sales terms; divide or assign sales territories, customers or product lines; or coordinate bids and agreements with customers to fix their resale prices. These types of agreements are generally illegal in the United States and many other markets where we conduct business.

Outside Consultants

Where the Company (PepsiCo, its company-controlled joint ventures, and subsidiaries) hires outside consultants or agents to assist it, the consultant or agent, and its employees, will be provided with copies of this Code and informed that they will be expected to comply with its provisions with respect to their work for the Company.

Global Relations

PepsiCo firmly believes that international commerce strengthens stability and peace by fostering economic growth, opportunity and mutual understanding. As a global enterprise, we recognize our responsibility to act in concert with the legitimate interests of the countries in which we do business. We obey all laws and regulations and respect the lawful customs of host countries. Our objective is to be a good corporate citizen wherever we operate.

Health and Safety

PepsiCo is committed to providing safe and healthy work environments at its facilities for all its employees, clients, visitors, contractors and vendors. It is our policy to provide employees with a drug-free workplace. In order to create an environment free from threats, violence and intimidation, PepsiCo is committed to a policy of zero tolerance for violence.

We are dedicated to designing, constructing, maintaining and operating facilities that protect our people and physical resources. It is our policy to comply with all applicable health and safety laws and regulations, provide and require the use of adequate protective equipment and measures, and insist that all work be done in a safe and responsible manner. It is the responsibility of each employee to follow all company policies and procedures related to workplace health and safety.

Environment

PepsiCo is committed to being an environmentally responsible corporate citizen. We are committed to minimizing the impact of our businesses on the environment with methods that are socially responsible, scientifically based and economically sound. We encourage conservation, recycling and energy use programs that promote clean air and water and reduce landfill wastes.

Business Gifts and Payments

Our business decisions are made on merit. Therefore, we will never give or offer, directly or indirectly, anything of value to a government official to influence any discretionary decision by such official in his or her official capacity. Giving gifts or entertainment to governmental officials and employees is highly regulated and often prohibited Such gifts and entertainment should not be provided unless you have determined that they are permitted by law and your business unit's policies.

In circumstances where it would not create an appearance of impropriety, employees may provide existing or potential customers with reasonable entertainment or gifts. However, the gifts must be permitted by local law, the customer's own policies and your business unit's policies.

Employees may not accept a gift, favor, loan, special service, payment or special treatment of any kind from any individual or organization which conducts or seeks to conduct business with the Company, or which competes with the Company, unless:

- It would be consistent with good business practices;
- It could not be considered a business inducement;
- It is of nominal value as set forth in your Division's policy;
- Public disclosure of the transaction would not embarrass PepsiCo.

All business-related gifts, which exceed your Division's definition of nominal value, should be reported to your immediate supervisor as soon as they are received.

Political and Community Activities and Contributions

PepsiCo believes in contributing to society and encourages employees to participate in community activities.

We will continue to communicate information and opinions on issues of public concern that may affect PepsiCo. Decisions by our employees whether or not to contribute time, money or resources of their own to any political or community activity are entirely personal and voluntary.

We will obey all laws in promoting the Company's position to government authorities and in making political contributions. Contributions by the Company to political candidates may be prohibited or regulated. Any such contribution requires the approval of PepsiCo's Vice President of Government Affairs.

Conflicts of Interest

PepsiCo's conflicts of interest policy is straightforward: Don't compete with PepsiCo businesses, and never let your business dealings on behalf of any of our businesses be influenced, or appear to be influenced, by personal or family interests.

All actual or apparent conflicts of interest between personal and professional relationships must be handled honestly and ethically. Examples of conflicts that must be disclosed and resolved include:

- Having a family interest in a transaction with the Company. A family interest would include any interests of your spouse, parent, child, sibling or domestic partner.
- Having more than a nominal individual or family interest in a competitor, supplier or customer of the Company (for example, ownership of more than 1% of a supplier's equity securities).
- Having a significant individual or family interest in an organization that does, or seeks to do, business with the Company.
- Acquiring an individual or family interest in property (such as real estate, patent rights, securities or other properties) or a business where you believe the Company has, or might have, an interest.
- Having outside business interests or activities that affect job performance because of the significant amount of time and attention diverted from your responsibilities as a Company employee.

Insider Trading and Proprietary Information

PepsiCo obeys all laws designed to protect the investing public with respect to the use and disclosure of material information.

Information is considered material if a reasonable investor would consider it important to his or her decision to buy, sell or hold PepsiCo stock. Examples would be a significant upward or downward revision of earnings forecasts, a significant division restructuring, a major management change or a significant acquisition or divestiture, a significant upcoming product launch or product innovation.

Employees should not effect any transaction in the securities of PepsiCo or another company involved with PepsiCo while they have material nonpublic information about that company.

Employees should not disclose any confidential information regarding the Company to anyone outside PepsiCo, including their spouse, parents, children, siblings or domestic partner, except where disclosure is needed to enable PepsiCo to carry on its business, and there is no reason to believe—because of an agreement or otherwise—that the disclosure might cause any economic loss or substantial embarrassment to the Company or its customers, bottlers, distributors or suppliers. Examples of such confidential information include: nonpublic information about the Company's customers, suppliers, distributors and potential acquisitions; its business operations and structure; its formulas and pricing; its processing, machines and inventions; its research and know-how; its upcoming new products and other innovations, and its plans and strategies.

Within PepsiCo, employees should only discuss or disclose material nonpublic information in the ordinary course of business and when they have no reason to believe that the information will be misused or improperly disclosed by the recipient.

Accounts and Record Keeping

We will continue to observe the most stringent standards in the keeping of our financial records and accounts. Our books must reflect all components of transactions, as well as our own standard of insisting upon an honest and forthright presentation of the facts.

We will ensure that the disclosures we make in reports and documents that we submit to the Securities and Exchange Commission and in other public communications are full, fair, accurate, timely and understandable.

It is the responsibility of each employee to uphold these standards. Appropriate records must be kept of all transactions and retained based on the applicable data retention schedules. Employees are expected to cooperate fully with our internal and external auditors. Information must not be falsified or concealed under any circumstance, and an employee whose activities cause false financial reporting will be subject to disciplinary action, including discharge.

Protection and Proper Use of Company Assets

PepsiCo's technological resources, including computers, voicemail, e-mail and Internet access, are to be used for proper purposes in a manner consistent with the Code and all other Company policies, including those related to discrimination, harassment and intellectual property. As with all PepsiCo assets, these resources are to be used for business purposes.

It is generally not PepsiCo's intent to monitor Internet access or messages on the voicemail and e-mail systems. However, the Company reserves the right to do so in appropriate circumstances, consistent with applicable laws and regulations.

If you have access to PepsiCo information systems, you are responsible for taking precautions necessary to prohibit unauthorized access to the system. You should safeguard your passwords or other means of entry.

Employees must not reproduce software assets licensed to PepsiCo, use illegally obtained software, or distribute the original software media or unauthorized copies of software which the Company does not own or license.

Reporting Code of Conduct and Other Ethics Issues

PepsiCo expects its employees, contractors, subcontractors, agents and their employees to promptly report on a confidential and/or anonymous basis any conduct or situation that she/he believes conflicts with this Code or violates a local, state or federal law to their immediate supervisor, PepsiCo's General Counsel or General Auditor, or through the PepsiCo Speak Up hotline at

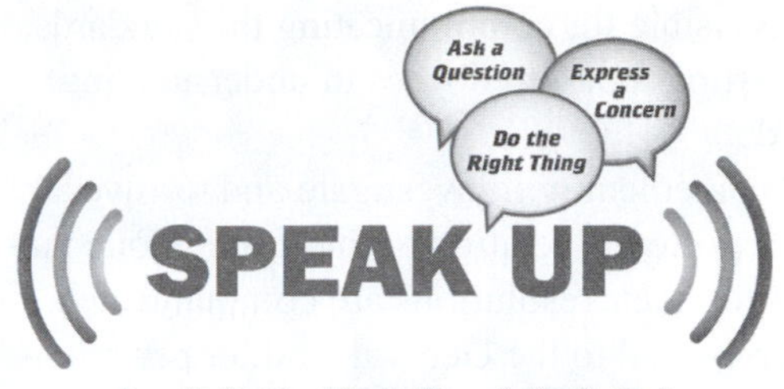

1-866-729-4888*
(from the U.S., Canada, Puerto Rico and U.S. Virgin Islands)

PepsiCo is committed to reviewing any such report in a prompt manner and taking remedial action when appropriate, and every affected employee is required to fully cooperate with any inquiry that results from any reported conduct or situation.

PepsiCo is also committed to protecting the rights of those individuals who report these issues to PepsiCo. Any PepsiCo officer or employee who is found to have engaged in retaliation against any employee who has exercised his/her rights under this Code or under applicable laws will be subject to appropriate remedial action. In addition, those individuals who violate applicable law may also be subject to civil and criminal penalties. Further, any contractor, subcontractor or agent who is found to have engaged in retaliation against any PepsiCo employee will be subject to appropriate action.

Responsibility for Compliance

All of our employees are responsible for ensuring that our standards of conduct are followed.

Each employee has a responsibility to understand and comply with this Code. Additionally, employees must seek guidance when a situation is not clear, and report all known or suspected violations of the Code to their manager, to PepsiCo's General Counsel or General Auditor, or through the Speak Up hotline.

Division management distributes this Code annually to all PepsiCo employees throughout the world, and oversees the annual certification process for its officers and key employees. Managers are responsible for communicating the standards, and assisting their employees in understanding the Code.

Management will investigate and resolve any issues reported in relation to this Code. Code violations and their resolutions are communicated and/or reported to the General Auditor per established communication and reporting guidelines.

This Code cannot provide definitive answers to all questions. For that, we must rely on each person's judgment and integrity. You are encouraged to seek guidance where a situation may not be clear. The PepsiCo Law Department and the General Auditor will respond to questions and issues of interpretation about this Code.

Waivers of this Code will be reviewed by the General Auditor and General Counsel, and in certain circumstances by the Board of Directors, and if required, will be appropriately disclosed.

*For a list of phone numbers for all other countries, go to:

http://www.pepsico.com/PEP Citizenship/CodeofConduct/SpeakUp/SpeakUpPoster.pdf

CHAPTER 3

PLANNING AN E-BUSINESS

Turning a Great Idea into an Effective Business Plan

Do You Already Know?

- What types of ideas are right for e-business
- How to analyze a business idea to see if it is viable
- What a target market is
- Why every new firm should create a business plan before it starts up
- The essential elements of every business plan

For additional questions to assess your current knowledge on planning an e-business, go to **www.wiley.com/college/holden.**

What You Will Find Out	What You Will Be Able To Do
3.1 How to identify and develop appropriate ideas for an e-business	• Identify an idea that is appropriate for e-business • Develop the idea for further analysis
3.2 The three methods for analyzing the validity of a new business idea	• Conduct a three-rings exercise, SWOT analysis, and feasibility study to evaluate the validity of a business idea
3.3 What a target market is and how to determine its makeup	• Conduct research and define the target market for a new business idea
3.4 The reasons for creating a business plan and resources to make the job easier	• Understand the value of a business plan • Find resources to help create a business plan
3.5 The eight sections of a quality business plan and what information each section should contain	• Write an effective business plan

INTRODUCTION

Coming up with a great idea is only the first step in launching an e-business. The smart e-commerce entrepreneur realizes that a lot of work needs to be done before a new Web site ever goes live and welcomes its first customer. This chapter offers a logical plan for moving from idea to launch, in the process expanding and testing and modifying the original concept so that it is fine-tuned for success. The first section talks about which ideas are appropriate for online businesses, how to begin researching and developing an idea, and how to factor competition into the development process. The second section offers three methods for evaluating business ideas: the three-rings exercise, SWOT analysis, and conducting a feasibility study. Once an idea has made it past these evaluations, it is time to clearly define a business's target market, which is detailed in the next section. Information is presented on classifying customers, conducting research, and evaluating competitors. The final two sections cover business plans, the logical product resulting from a well-conducted idea development process. Business plans are defined, the reasons for creating one are detailed, and resources for helping create one are offered. Finally, a section-by-section review of a typical plan is presented, including details on the information required to make it an effective tool for a new e-business.

3.1 DEVELOPING A BUSINESS IDEA

Every successful business begins with that first idea. Ray Kroc—the man behind the success of McDonald's—dreamed of hamburgers and milkshakes, and cosmetics queen Mary Kay visualized selling makeup door to door. One of the big myths about the business world is that most of the great concepts simply blinked on in the minds of their creator (the old light bulb cliché), the idea was unleashed on the world, and off the lucky entrepreneur went to the bank. If only it was that easy. In fact, many successful businesspeople spend years brainstorming or searching for that one great idea. And most of the good ones invest a lot of time and energy in researching and developing—and often changing—those great ideas before they ever earn their first dollar. The bottom line is that turning an idea into a successful business takes a lot of hard work.

IN THE REAL WORLD

Treat an E-Business Idea Like Any Other Business Idea

Many successful e-business entrepreneurs stress that their success was only partially a product of the Internet. Instead, many point to the effort that they put into developing their idea and treating it like any other business startup. Consider the advice of Jeff Vikari, executive director of Clickincome.com: "The biggest misconception people have is that the Internet is magic. It's the gold-rush mentality. People believe that if they invest a few thousand dollars into an online business, profits will simply start shooting out of their computer automatically. That's obviously not the case. People need to follow many of the same steps they'd take if they were to start a traditional brick-and-mortar business."

How does a budding e-business owner decide whether their idea has merit? And if the concept proves to be a good one, what is the next step? The process of moving from an idea to an actual business involves three steps. First an idea needs to be developed to its full potential. Second, an idea must be examined and carefully evaluated using a variety of methods. Finally, deserving ideas that emerge from the first two steps must be further developed into a formal business plan.

3.1.1 Appropriate Ideas for E-Business

Obviously, the strength of the original idea will have a major impact on whether the resulting online business will be successful, but it is only one ingredient. Exploring the World Wide Web reveals many successful businesses that, judging only from the product or service they offer, might seem likely to fail. In addition to the idea, many factors depend on how the idea is executed and marketed.

Unless a budding online entrepreneur has a million-dollar budget to execute the idea, it is bad business practice to attempt to compete head-on with well-established and very large online businesses (such as Amazon.com and Travelocity.com), which have spent millions changing the buying habits of online consumers. Instead, entrepreneurs planning to launch a small online business should focus on a **niche**—a small, specialized part of a market—that is not cost-effective for the larger, well-established companies to serve.

Niche:
A small specialized part of a market.

When brainstorming ideas for an online business venture, do not rule out anything initially. Early on, even if an idea seems outrageous, do not immediately dismiss it until closely examining its viability and doing some research on the potential market. Ideas that would not necessarily work as traditional retail or mail-order businesses might have potential on the Web. Make sure, however, that the ideas making the final cut are manageable and based on available resources and budget.

Fad:
An intense, widespread, and short-lived enthusiasm for a product or activity.

At any given time, one **fad**—an intense, widespread, and short-lived enthusiasm for a product or activity—or another is sweeping across

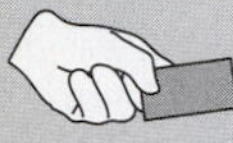

CAREER CONNECTION

A college grad follows the scent of Internet success and finds a way to sell perfume online.

Jacquelyn Tran's parents had emigrated from Vietnam in 1980 and spent the next two decades developing the family's successful retail perfume operation in Orange County, California. When Jacquelyn graduated from college in 1999, she was convinced that selling perfume on the Web was an idea whose time had come. Using a $50,000 startup loan from her parents, Jacquelyn launched Perfume Bay (www.perfumebay.com) an online fragrance and beauty products store that grew so quickly it boasted annual revenues of $9 million by 2005.

The key to Perfume Bay's success was becoming intimately familiar with both the customers and the products. Though buyers cannot smell the scents, they can clearly imagine them thanks to richly detailed descriptions. Customers have fallen in love with Perfume Bay, and Jacquelyn has achieved her goal of growing the family business so that her hard-working parents could slow down a little.

Jacquelyn, however, doesn't have any plans for slowing down. She continues to think about ways to expand Perfume Bay—she hopes to be able to open brick-and-mortar outlets—and develop other business opportunities.[1]

Tips from the Professional

- Draw on the experiences of friends and family to plan an e-business.
- Just because it hasn't been done online doesn't mean it can't be done.
- Keep opportunities for expansion in mind.

America. People will spend almost anything in order to participate in the fad and get their hands on whatever items relating to the fad are for sale. Consider Beanie Babies, Pokémon, and countless items spawned by popular movies. While it may look attractive to capitalize on a fad by launching a related online business, watch out! Just as quickly as a fad starts, it can—and will—end, causing the market for those products to quickly decline. The fast-in, fast-out approach of chasing fads goes against the rules for establishing a small online business. Small e-businesses rarely have a huge budget, meaning they must invest lots of time in planning, launching the operation, and building traffic to a Web site.

E-business in Action →
Identify an idea that is appropriate for e-business.

3.1.2 Developing an Idea: Becoming an Expert

As noted in Section 3.1.1, most online entrepreneurs will be best served by focusing on some specialty or niche market. While this strategy is smart for a small e-business, it offers special challenges. The owner must have an in-depth knowledge of their products or services and a clear idea of why their target or niche market wants, or needs, them. In other words, the owner needs to be an expert in this specialty market.

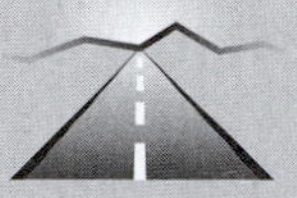

PATHWAY TO... BECOMING AN EXPERT IN AN E-BUSINESS NICHE MARKET

As a first step in developing a niche market e-business idea, the following questions should be researched and answered:

- Do the products (or services) have good market potential for sale online?
- Who is the target audience for these products?
- How does the product or service address the needs, wants, or interests of potential customers?
- What type of design and content will a Web site need in order to cater to the target audience?
- What will be the best ways to promote and advertise the Web site to reach the target audience?

If the business owner cannot adequately answer these questions, it is unlikely the potential customers will respond to the advertisements and purchase the goods or services.

Consider that once a Web site is online, traffic must be generated to the site. Once visitors arrive at the site, the information must motivate the potential customers to make a purchase. Before an e-business can attract and sell products to theoretical customers, an e-business must first figure out *who* these people are. Section 3.3 discusses target markets in greater detail, especially with regard to business planning, but it is never too early to focus on customers. Investing time researching potential customers can help determine whether an e-business idea is worth pursuing before too much time and money is invested in the concept.

E-business in Action →
Develop an e-business idea for future analysis.

3.1.3 Considering the Competition

Thousands of new Web sites pop up every day. Although not all of these sites are designed to sell products or services, the number of individuals and businesses trying to exploit the Internet is growing rapidly. Because virtually anyone can launch a successful business in cyberspace, people from all walks of life, as well as companies of all sizes, are now marking their turf on the Information Superhighway. Almost every Fortune 500 company has some type of Web presence. Likewise, many large retail-store chains are as well established online as they are they are at the local mall. These traditional retail-store chains have branched out into cyberspace because they see it as a fast-growing trend in how consumers shop.

Because of the relative ease and speed of entry, every type of business launched on the Web will ultimately face competition. That means that an online entrepreneur needs to figure out how to do things better, faster, cheaper, or more aggressively than other businesses in cyberspace, or to find innovative ways to differentiate their products. Furthermore, every truly innovative and successful e-business idea will quickly be copied many times over by competitors—sometimes in a matter of days or even hours.

Developing an in-depth knowledge of competitors—starting as early as the idea development stage—is an essential component of e-business success. Furthermore, e-businesses should assume that the number of competitors and their capabilities will increase over time, and their planning process should include ideas for adapting to changing competition and access to resources for turning these ideas into action. Small online business operators will eventually discover that while it is important to define, develop, and then stick to one business idea, they must also be flexible so they can compete in the ever-changing and evolving e-commerce industry.

One aspect of analyzing the competition involves thinking about a domain name and researching whether a domain name is available. Section 12.1 covers this in detail.

SELF-CHECK

1. Is it a good idea for a small online business to compete with a major e-commerce site? If not, what would be a preferable strategy?
2. True or false: Selling fad products or services is a smart strategy for a small e-business. Explain your answer.
3. List the five questions that should be researched and answered when developing a new business idea.
4. Is competition a big concern for new online businesses? Why, or why not?

Apply Your Knowledge Select a product or service that interests you and evaluate the value of selling it via a Web site by answering the five questions in Section 3.1.2. Briefly explain why an e-business selling the product or service would or would not be a good idea.

3.2 ANALYZING A BUSINESS IDEA

After developing an idea for an online business—but before investing time and money to get online immediately—it is important to spend some time further researching and evaluating the validity of the idea. Preparation is one of the key ingredients for success, especially in an industry that is changing rapidly as new technological innovations become available. Thus, investing time in advance is as important as investing money later.

The following sections describe three commonly used tools for analyzing new business concepts.

3.2.1 Three-Rings Exercise

The best place to begin gathering feedback about a proposed business is from nearby sources. Be prepared to receive varying opinions—both positive and negative. Use this input as a general gauge of whether to continue reaching out to the next source of information and feedback. Envision this process with the idea at the center, surrounded by three rings from which to collect input. If the closest ring provides mostly positive input, proceed to the next ring. This method is known as a **three-rings exercise** (see Figure 3-1).

Three-rings exercise: A system for evaluating a business idea in which feedback is gathered first from family and friends, then from industry experts, and finally from potential customers.

Ring 1 consists of friends, family, and co-workers. Ask them these questions:

- Have you ever heard of this type of product or service?
- Would you buy this product or service?
- Do you think that the product or service is a good idea?
- What challenges do you think this business will encounter?
- What are the benefits of this product or service?
- Can you envision (the owner) selling this product or service? Why or why not?

In Ring 2, seek input from industry professionals, investors, other entrepreneurs, and organizations that offer support to small businesses. Ask questions similar to those listed for Ring 1. Because of the experience possessed by the people in Ring 2, give their responses more weight. Small-business support resources include:

- **Small Business Administration (SBA) (www.sba.gov):** The SBA, a government-sponsored organization, helps small business owners with loans, navigating paperwork, free seminars, and other services.
- **Small Business Development Center (SBDC) (www.sba.gov/sbdc):** The SBA provides its services through local branches.

Figure 3-1

Three Rings of Decision

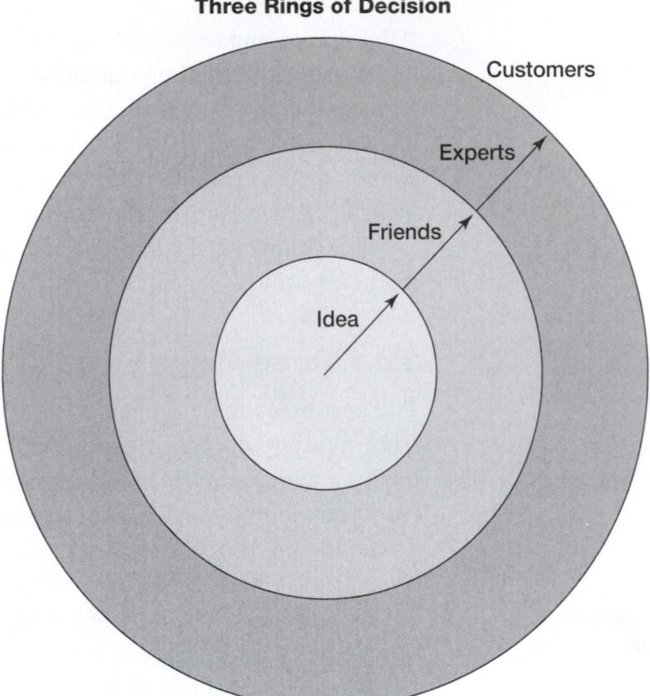

Conduct a three-rings exercise by gathering information first from the people closest to you and then moving outward to other contacts.

- **Chamber of Commerce (www.uschamber.com):** From small towns to large cities, all have local chambers to help owners develop their small businesses.
- **SCORE** (a network of retired executives counseling small businesses) **(www.score.org):** SCORE matches small business owners with business-exec retirees who volunteer their time to help small businesses develop and prosper.
- **Women's Business Center (www.onlinewbc.gov):** The SBA has a special group dedicated to women wishing to create small businesses.

In Ring 3 are potential customers. Ask them these questions:

- Would you use this product or service?
- Have you used a similar product or service?
- How much would you be willing to pay for this product or service?

- How often would you use the product or service?
- Where would you normally go to buy this product or service?
- Would you order the product or service over the Internet?

E-business in Action
Conduct a three-rings exercise.

Receiving a majority of positive feedback from sources in all three rings means that the idea might be worthwhile—or at least there is enough validation to continue to the next phase of the evaluation process.

3.2.2 Conducting a SWOT Analysis

SWOT analysis:
A decision-making tool for business that evaluates the strengths, weaknesses, opportunities, and threats of an idea.

Another popular method for determining the pros and cons of an idea is referred to as **SWOT analysis.** SWOT is short for ***S***trengths, ***W***eaknesses, ***O***pportunities, and ***T***hreats. Companies use this method for several purposes, including as a decision-making tool for product development. The simple process also lends itself to a more thorough investigation of a business idea.

Creating a SWOT chart is simple. On a large sheet of paper, draw a cross to create four separate quadrants. Label the four quadrants *Strengths*, *Weaknesses*, *Opportunities*, and *Threats* as shown in Figure 3-2.

After drawing and labeling the chart, fill in the details. In each quadrant, write the factors that influence or contribute to each of the four SWOT categories for the business idea being evaluated.

Figure 3-2

SWOT Chart	
Strengths	Weaknesses
Opportunities	Threats

A SWOT chart is a valuable tool for analyzing a business idea.

Strengths and weaknesses are considered internal factors that control or specifically contribute (good or bad) to the business concept. Opportunities and threats are external factors that are influenced to some extent by the environment or otherwise outside of a business's control.

After filling in the chart, it is time to analyze the information. Ask the questions in the "Pathway to Doing a SWOT Analysis" box to start developing the SWOT analysis.

PATHWAY TO... DOING A SWOT ANALYSIS

Strengths

- What advantages does the product or service offer?
- Do the owners or managers have expertise in this business or industry?
- Can a patent be obtained to protect the idea?

Weaknesses

- How much will developing the product cost?
- Is getting suppliers going to be difficult?
- Will launching this business require learning the industry from the ground up?

Opportunities

- Does this idea take advantage of a new technology?
- Is this product or service in demand?
- Have changes in policies or regulations made the idea necessary?
- Is this a new product or service?

Threats

- Does the product or service have established competitors?
- Can competitors sell the product or service for less?
- Will changes in technology make the product obsolete?

Use the feedback obtained from informal research (the three-rings exercise) as factors in the SWOT quadrants. Combining other people's opinions with your own provides a more comprehensive—and useful—SWOT analysis.

After completing the categories of the first SWOT analysis, look at which quadrants have identified the most, or most significant, factors. The strengths and opportunities listed indicate the advantages this business might have in the marketplace, and maybe they outweigh the weaknesses and challenges. Perhaps it is possible to see what must be done to offset those disadvantages to make the idea work. Whatever the outcome of the analysis, the process will provide a would-be e-business owner with a better feel for the value of their idea.

E-business in Action
Conduct a SWOT analysis.

IN THE REAL WORLD

"SWOT-"ting at E-Business Ideas

Fabric artist Fran became obsessed with an idea for selling her custom-dyed scarves online—to the point that she seriously considered quitting her job as a teacher to devote her full time and attention to the new venture. Her brother, Joe, a corporate human resources manager, convinced her to hold off on this leap of faith until the two of them could further research and analyze her concept. The first thing Joe had Fran do was conduct a SWOT analysis on the idea. Joe had done SWOT analyses many times in his corporate career, but it was a new—and eye-opening experience—for Fran. The SWOT exercise forced Fran for the first time to list and consider the weaknesses and threats the new e-business faced, including her lack of business experience and much more competition than Fran expected to find. Based on the SWOT analysis, Fran decided to stick with her day job and to continue exploring and refining e-business ideas.

3.2.3 Feasibility Studies

After an idea is approved by three-rings research, and SWOT analysis further indicates it has merit, a business concept must complete one more step for total validation. A **feasibility study** is a formal, written exercise that provides final proof that a business concept is viable.

Feasibility study: A preliminary study undertaken to determine and document a project's viability. The results of the study are used to make a decision whether to proceed with a project.

A feasibility study is an essential exercise that helps entrepreneurs identify an idea that really has the potential to lead to a successful business, as opposed to one with little chance of working out. A well-conducted feasibility study will answer these basic questions:

- Will the product or service work?
- How much will the product or service cost to start?
- Can the idea make money?
- Is the business concept really worth an investment of time and energy?

What sets the feasibility study apart from other evaluation methods? A feasibility study kicks the analysis up a notch. It requires in-depth research to provide more detailed answers to questions in five primary areas.

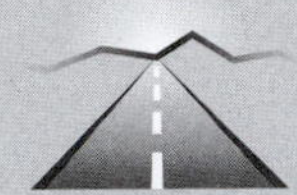

PATHWAY TO... CONDUCTING A FEASIBILITY STUDY

1. The Product and Service
   - What is the product or service?
   - How will customers use the product or service?
   - Where or how will customers buy the product or service?
   - How is the product or service designed?
   - How is the product or service delivered to customers?
   - Has the product or service been tested to determine if it works correctly? (Describe these tests in detail.)
2. The Experience (Including Management Team)
   - Who is the management team?
   - What experience do the owners and the employees have?
   - What are the owner's specific skills and credentials?
   - What are the owner's missing skills or weaknesses?
   - How much time can the owner devote to the business?
3. The Market
   - What is the demand for the product?
   - Who are the customers? (What is the target market?)
   - How big is the market?
   - What is the status of the market? Is the market growing or stagnant?
   - Where and how can the customers be reached?
4. The Competition
   - Who are the primary and secondary competitors? (Describe each in detail.)
   - How do the competitors market their products or services?
   - What makes the potential business different or better than its competitors?
   - Is the product easy to copy? How can copying the product or service be prevented?

5. The Costs

- How much does it cost to make the product or offer the service?
- What other business costs are there?
- What amount of money is needed to start?
- Is there access to funding?
- When will the business make a profit?

E-business in Action → Conduct a feasibility study.

As these questions are being answered, make sure that the answers are supported with detailed research. When the answers are complete, analyze the results in a brief (one or two pages) summary that discusses what has been discovered. The summary should consist of a paragraph for each of the five categories that answer the basic questions. The summary should provide proof of whether the idea is viable. If the feasibility study further validates the idea, it is time to move on to the next piece of the business success puzzle: the customers.

SELF-CHECK

1. Who occupies each of the rings in a three-rings exercise?
2. What four factors are examined in a SWOT analysis?
3. What is a feasibility study? What are the five areas in which it provides analysis?

Apply Your Knowledge Select a niche market served by one or more e-commerce sites. Research these sites and write a brief analysis of this "competition" that could be used in a feasibility study for a new Web site in the same field.

3.3 IDENTIFYING A TARGET MARKET

Marketing: The process of promoting and selling products and services.

Target market: A group of consumers who behave in a similar way and have been identified as potential customers for a firm's products or services.

The concepts of "market" and "marketing" often cause confusion among first-time business owners. While **marketing** is defined as the process of promoting and selling products and services, the first step in effective marketing for any business is understanding its **target market**—a group of consumers who behave in a similar way and are the "target customers" for its products or services.

The average person buys all kinds of goods and services, and as a result they are part of many target markets. While this may have some impact on a customer's buying habits (because most people have only a limited amount of money to spend), a business should only be concerned with why an individual consumer is interested in its products or services. If a business can effectively describe its target customer, it can begin to create promotional efforts that convince them to buy its products or services.

3.3.1 Classifying Customers

During the initial phases of developing a business idea and subsequent efforts to evaluate that idea, it is likely the budding e-business owner has already conducted a fair amount of research into identifying potential customers. Now it is important to further define those customers. The more a firm knows about its target customers, the more easily and cost-efficiently it can market to these customers and build a steady flow of traffic to a Web site.

During this stage of planning, it is essential to describe or segment potential customers. The most common classifications (in descending order of importance) are:

Demographics: Statistical data used to describe a population or groups within it.

Psychographics: The classification of people based on their attitudes or lifestyle choices.

1. **Demographics:** Age, income, gender, and occupation are examples of the statistical data used to describe customers.
2. **Psychographics:** This classification of people is based on their attitudes or lifestyle choices and includes such information as favorite music, hobbies, and other personal preferences.
3. **Geographic preferences:** This points out where people live. The location can include a specific neighborhood, city, state, region, or even country. Customers can also be segmented according to home (or residential) locations versus business locations.
4. **Use-based preferences:** This specifies how frequently customers want or need the product or service.
5. **Benefits:** This describes why customers use the product or service. For example, customers might need it for medical purposes, or customers might receive a luxury benefit, where a product or service is not needed, but choose to invest in the product or service for perceived benefits.

Typically, a target market includes customers described by a mixture of the terms and categories in this list. For instance, a business selling cotton-candy-flavored lip gloss might describe its target market this way:

- Girls
- 10 to 14 years old
- Live at home, in households having a combined annual income of $50,000 or more

- Listen to pop music
- Participate in at least one extracurricular activity per week
- Buy makeup products at least once a month to enhance appearance

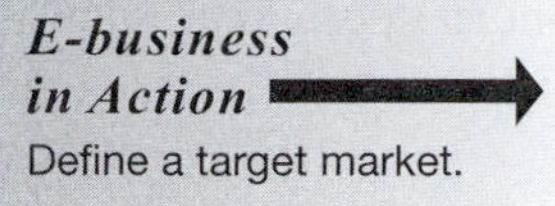
E-business in Action
Define a target market.

Depending on the type of product or service sold, a target market most likely will include a wide mix of customer types—not just one.

IN THE REAL WORLD

Know What's Important to Your Customers

Everything changed when Richard Bradley discovered fly fishing. He left his job of 35 years as a tool and die man in a Long Island emergency vehicle factory. He moved to the Catskills, a mecca for fly fishing. And he began hand crafting high-quality fishing reels. The reels, he says, capture "the spirit of days gone by." Through Bradley's Livingston, New York, storefront and his Web site (www.firbrookflies.com), Fir Brook Flies & Supplies provides discerning customers with reels designed to meet any angler's needs. Bradley offers special finishes, hardware, and custom engraving—all of which have earned him a significant reputation in the field. "Bradley reels will never be mass produced; not now, not ever" Bradley says, "I will not consider it one of my reels unless I make it myself."[2]

3.3.2 Market Research

Conducting the research necessary to describe a target market and determine consumers' needs and preferences requires a commitment of time and effort, though it does not necessarily have to be expensive. While some businesses hire consulting firms to conduct **market research,** a small e-business can turn to a variety of cost-effective methods for gathering information with minimal cost.

Market research: Gathering information about consumers, their needs, and their preferences.

Use Published Market Research

Information from readily available sources is called secondary research and it can be extremely valuable. Cities (or chambers of commerce), states, colleges and universities, the federal government, industry groups, marketing firms, and other entities regularly conduct research that profiles various consumer groups, gathering data on both demographics and buying habits. Much of this information is available free online, or can be obtained on request for little or no cost. Newspapers, business publications, and industry newsletters or magazines are other good low-cost sources for statistics regarding consumers. A business with a larger budget might want to turn to research firms, which charge a fee (ranging from several hundred dollars to several thousand dollars per report) for detailed reports on a specific business sector. Contact companies such as Gartner Group (www.gartner.com) or IDC (www.idc.com) for this type of information.

Survey Potential (Or Existing) Customers

Going directly to consumers for their opinions is called primary research. While a market research firm might charge several thousand dollars to conduct a formal target market study, there are ways to conduct surveys for little or no money. For example, use the power of the Internet and distribute a survey via email to a known selection of potential customers. Or visit a message board or chat room with participants that might be interested in the product or service and invite them to conduct an online "interview." Or conduct a focus group in which a small group of likely customers is gathered together (in person) to complete a survey, be interviewed, or discuss their thoughts about the product.

Observe Competitors' Customers

If potential competitors are already operating online, visit their Web site(s) and explore the pages carefully. (Better yet, become a customer yourself.) You can learn a lot about a business and its target customers by analyzing what it sells and how it markets those products or services. Furthermore, many e-businesses generously share information about their motivation, philosophy, and target customers. Always visit "About Us" or "Company Information" pages first. Businesses that aggressively try to sell online advertising space might go a step further by publishing visitor demographic data, or making it available on request. Contact the Web site as a potential advertiser and ask for the information. Many sites encourage customer communities with message boards or chat rooms for a discussion of the product. Visit those areas to see what customers are saying. It might even be worth contacting customers directly to learn more about them. For competitors with retail locations, visit their stores and observe the customers and their habits in person.

E-business in Action →
Conduct market research.

SELF-CHECK

1. What is a target market? Can a target market contain more than one type of customer?
2. Suggest three low-cost methods for conducting market research.

Apply Your Knowledge Select a product that interests you and that you think could be sold through an e-commerce site. Conduct an online search about the product you have selected and your potential customers. Using this information, write up a description of at least one type of customer in the target market.

3.4 THE VALUE OF A BUSINESS PLAN

A common question from entrepreneurs, especially those starting very small companies, is, "Do I really need a business plan?" Quite honestly, the answer is no. Many entrepreneurs choose not to create written guides for their businesses, and some are doing just fine—but others are struggling.

Starting and managing a business without a business plan is the same as searching for a buried treasure without a map: Although you know that the gold is in the ground somewhere, you end up wasting a lot of time by randomly digging holes in the hope of eventually hitting the jackpot. Effectively, a business plan becomes a new venture's roadmap for success. Without a plan, the odds of success are much lower.

Why, then, do so many people resist using this tool? They resist it for two reasons:

- Creating a business plan involves a great deal of work.
- They don't understand the importance of having a plan.

Section 3.4.1 will explain why having a business plan is a good idea, while the sections that follow will explain exactly what a good plan should contain and how to go about writing one.

3.4.1 What is a Business Plan?

Business plan: A detailed written document that describes all aspects of a proposed business venture.

A **business plan** is a detailed written document that describes all aspects of a proposed venture—its planned activities, projected earnings and expenses, financing needs, management team, marketing plan, even its location. Business plans must follow a relatively standardized format to be effective; Section 3.5 covers the required format and content in detail.

A good business plan should quickly convey to anyone reading it exactly what products or services a firm is going to offer, why people need or want those services, how the firm is going to market itself, and how the firm is going to make a profit from selling its goods or services.

Furthermore, a business plan should attempt to predict the future—to project the results of the first two or three years of a new business, and to cover every possible outcome for the new venture should current conditions change.

This sounds like a difficult task, but it should not be if an entrepreneur has already put the appropriate effort into developing and evaluating their business idea and researching its target market. Starting a business should be approached in a logical step-by-step manner, and creating a business plan is the final step in this process. Anyone who has already researched a concept thoroughly and subjected it to a SWOT analysis and feasibility study (Section 3.2) will find they have compiled good information that simply needs to be applied to the appropriate sections of the plan and developed with additional detail.

3.4.2 Why Create a Business Plan?

By conducting the research necessary to create a business plan, an entrepreneur can build a knowledge base that may be priceless once a firm is open for business. Furthermore, simply formalizing in writing the ideas about what an e-business will look like, how the e-business will operate, and what the goals are is a very valuable exercise. There are four very compelling operation reasons for creating a business plan:

1. **It is easier to secure finances:** This is probably the most common reason for creating a business plan. Bankers or private investors will always ask to see a plan before they lend you money. Lenders have a better chance of protecting (and recouping) their investments when a formal strategy documents projected income and profits. Even self-financed ventures will find a business plan valuable because it forces them to consider how to use the money wisely.
2. **A plan forces critical analysis:** Writing a business plan forces an entrepreneur to honestly evaluate themselves, their ideas, the competition, and their customers to finally determine whether the idea is a valid one. Even if the idea proves to be valid, the planning process should expose weaknesses or threats and allow the owner to correct potential failures before the business even launches.
3. **A plan offers well-defined goals:** Developing a great idea and transitioning it into a viable business opportunity can be challenging. Writing a business plan forces an entrepreneur to fully develop the long-term vision for the product or service, including setting goals—which are called milestones if specific numbers are tied to specific dates on the calendar. Setting milestones gives a new business a tool for evaluating whether it is succeeding or failing in executing its plan.

4. **A plan can provide timeless guidance:** If done correctly, this document provides a concrete plan for operating a business—not only during the startup phase, but also for the next three to five years. Remember that the plan might need occasional adjustments. However, investing the time in advance to create a strong foundation ensures that the owner will have a valuable tool to help make decisions for managing the company.

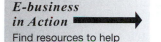

E-business in Action
Learn the value of a business plan.

3.4.3 Getting Help Preparing a Plan

Many people are intimidated about the process of writing a business plan. Fortunately, there are a variety of resources offering help. There are countless how-to books and numerous Web sites offering guidance for writing an effective business plan. For more personalized assistance, contact your local chamber of commerce or a community college business development center for help locating professionals (such as a CPA) or volunteers (from an organization such as SCORE) experienced in developing business plans.

E-business in Action
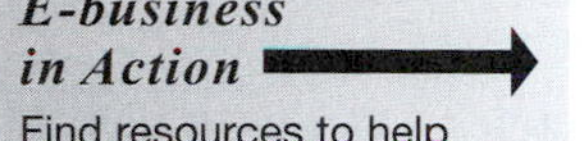
Find resources to help create a business plan.

IN THE REAL WORLD

Finding Help Writing Business Plans

Interior designer Stephanie Mann wanted to write a business plan to help grow her small firm, but she didn't know how to begin. Fortunately, her brother suggested she talk to SCORE, a free, nationwide, small-business consulting service that utilizes the talents of retired entrepreneurs (www.score.org). Mann attended a business plan workshop presented by SCORE and was pleased with what she learned. "I thought the information was very valuable, and I took home materials from the session to put together my business plan." One-on-one sessions with a SCORE counselor provided her with additional assistance. Ultimately, she used her new business plan to grow her client list from 3 to 25.[3]

When writing a business plan, it is desirable to follow an established format (discussed in Section 3.5), and it is wise to use technological tools to help build a plan. The Small Business Administration Web site (www.sba.gov) offers several free and downloadable software programs designed to help create business plans. A variety of commercially available, off-the-shelf software packages designed to assist startup companies in creating business plans are also available. Two popular examples are Business Plan Pro by PaloAlto Software, Inc., and Business Plan Writer Deluxe by Nova Development.

One more option to consider is to hire a professional business plan consultant when you need to secure outside financing. A good consultant can transform the basics of a business idea into a polished document. Remember three important points:

- Hiring a consultant cannot compensate for a poor or poorly developed idea.
- The entrepreneur will still have to invest a lot of time and effort into gathering information to give to the consultant.
- Hiring a consultant is not cheap. Expect to pay anywhere from $1,500 to $5,000 to have a consultant write a plan.

PATHWAY TO... HIRING A BUSINESS PLAN CONSULTANT

When planning to hire a professional to help prepare a business plan, keep the following in mind:

- Look for someone with experience in the same product or service industry.
- Find a consultant who is comfortable with, and knowledgeable of, online businesses.
- Review samples of other business plans the consultant has written.
- Ask for written testimonials and references.
- Get a firm price quote.
- Agree on a reasonable timeline for completing the plan.

SELF-CHECK

1. What is a business plan? Why do some entrepreneurs choose not to create one?
2. Suggest four resources that are available to provide information or help writing a business plan.
3. Give two advantages and two disadvantages involved with hiring a professional consultant to write a business plan.

Apply Your Knowledge Two friends are working to quickly launch an e-commerce site. One of the partners thinks that creating a business plan might be a good idea, the other thinks it would be a waste of time. Briefly explain why creating a business plan before launching the partners' site is a good idea.

3.5 THE ELEMENTS OF AN EFFECTIVE BUSINESS PLAN

A traditional business plan is sectioned into seven or eight major parts. At first, that number of parts might seem a bit overwhelming. Consider, however, that most experts recommend keeping a finished business plan to fewer than 20 pages. Breaking down that recommendation, each section becomes only two or three pages long, which is very manageable.

Each part plays a critical role in your overall plan. Although each section can almost stand alone, the sections work together to present a complete picture, or vision, of the proposed business. Because of that, all of the sections must be included. Depending on the owner's primary reasons for developing a business plan, they can put more effort into appropriate sections. For example, firms seeking outside funding should make sure that the financial section is as thorough and accurate as possible.

The following sections describe the required business plan sections and what they should contain, in the order that each should appear in the plan. Figure 3-3 outlines the eight major parts of a business plan.

3.5.1 Executive Summary

Executive summary: A brief section at the beginning of a business plan that highlights the major points from each of the other parts of the plan.

Although the **executive summary** comes first, it is typically written last. This brief section (a page or two at most) does just what it says: It highlights the major points from each of the other parts of the plan. This page is usually the first one that investors and other advisors read, and how well it is written can determine whether they turn the page or decide that the idea is not worth their time or money.

Figure 3-3

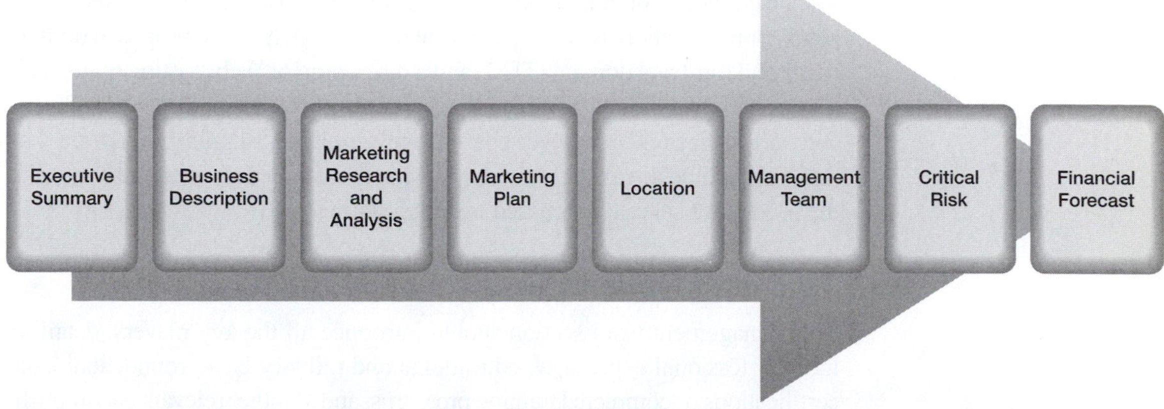

Eight major parts of a business plan.

3.5.2 Business Description

The business description section provides a detailed description of the overall business and its products or services, as well as an overview of the industry. This section should identify the business by name and include a vision statement (or mission statement) that summarizes its goals. The description of the product or service should emphasize its potential and pinpoint exactly what makes it a unique and viable contender in the marketplace.

3.5.3 Marketing

FOR EXAMPLE

See the Toolkit for the marketing section of a business plan for a children's Web site.

The marketing section is important and typically divided into two parts: (1) market analyses and (2) marketing plan. The first part summarizes the research and analysis that has been conducted, including a thorough description of the target market. In addition, there should be a quantification of the market size, an analysis of any trends, and an estimate of the market share that the business anticipates taking. This part should also provide an in-depth view of the competition, including a summary of competitors' weaknesses and ideas for countering their strengths. Much of the information in this section should previously have been gathered during a SWOT analysis, a feasibility study, and other market research efforts (see Sections 3.2 and 3.3).

The second part of the marketing section presents the marketing plan—a description of marketing strategy, pricing, advertising, promotion, public relations, and any ideas for building traffic to the new Web site. Some experts consider the marketing section the most important part of the entire business plan.

3.5.4 Location

The location section is probably more important for a traditional bricks-and-mortar business, but it deserves to be included in an e-business plan as well. The discussion should include the physical location of the business, as well as plans for the location in cyberspace, which should include the proposed domain name and top-level domain (TLD) and a discussion of Web-hosting plans. This section should also detail the business's production needs and costs—hardware, software, office rent, employee costs (wages), utilities, shipping, and more. The result should be a realistic estimate of what it costs to deliver to the consumer the product or service purchased over the Internet.

3.5.5 Management Team

The management team section should introduce all the key players, detailing their professional experience, educational and military background, additional certifications or completed training programs, and all other relevant accomplishments. Whether an e-business is a solo operation or a bigger venture involving several different people, the plan must highlight the expertise and experience that the firm's manager will bring to the venture. Remember to include a copy of the résumé for the owner and every manager and key employee in the firm.

3.5.6 Critical Risks

The critical risks section can be especially intimidating to first-time business owners. It is basically a summary of all the things that can go wrong once the business gets started—sales failing to reach projections, costs of supplies or shipping higher than anticipated, or new competition offering lower prices. What is important about the critical risks section is not just anticipating problems, but also developing potential solutions in advance to ward off crises. The critical risks section will be particularly important to bankers, who might be risk-averse, but most dislike surprises even more. By including critical risks, the entrepreneur proves he or she has knowledge of the business and the market, as well as ideas and tools to make necessary changes.

3.5.7 Financial Forecast

Income statement: A financial statement that shows changes in a firm's financial position over a period of time.

Cash flow statement: A financial statement that shows a firm's net profit after taxes.

Balance sheet: A financial statement that reports a firm's financial position at the end of a period of time.

The financial forecast section should include three-year projections of the business's earnings and expenses. The information should be presented in three important financial documents: (1) the **income statement,** which shows changes in the firm's financial position over the period; (2) the **cash flow statement,** which shows net profit after taxes; and (3) the **balance sheet,** which shows the firm's financial position at the end of the three years. This section should also detail startup costs, plus describe how much money the business will need from outside sources, how the money will be used, and how any loans or other financing will be paid back. Firms seeking outside funding need to provide solid numbers in their financial projections, but need to be careful not to be too conservative, which can scare away potential lenders. Plans being developed only for internal use can be less optimistic and keep profit projections lower.

IN THE REAL WORLD

Learning the Basics of Accounting

Chef and budding entrepreneur Mario had a great concept for an online business selling his specialty Caribbean spice mixes—so good that a local banker told him that a startup loan was practically guaranteed if he could produce a nice business plan to help showcase the concept. One thing scared Mario: numbers. He had no experience in accounting and was intimidated by this part of a plan. Fortunately, the banker friend introduced Mario to a local CPA and the two of them worked on the projected financial statements together. The resulting numbers were as strong as the spices, and a successful e-business was soon funded and launched.

3.5.8 Appendix

The Appendix section is the location for important documents that support the sections of the business plan. This is also where to place copies of loan agreements, patent or copyright documentation, employee contracts, and any other legal documents pertaining to the business.

E-business in Action
Write an effective business plan.

Before writing a business plan, it can be very helpful to review sample plans, particularly those for an e-commerce site. Check out one of the business-planning resource centers on the Web, such as Bplans (www.bplans.com), to locate a sample plan to use as a guide.

3.5.9 Effectively Using a Business Plan

A business plan is important and should be used rather than placed on a shelf to collect dust. Ignoring a plan or forgetting to maintain it is the same as failing to plan. Too many business owners needing a quick source of financing are displeased to find that they have neglected to keep their plan up-to-date. Having to invest the time to redo an outdated business plan—or worse, handing an outdated plan to a banker—can sometimes mean the difference between success and failure.

To ensure that a business plan passes the test of time, consider these suggestions for effectively utilizing a business plan:

- **As reference material:** Refer to the plan often. Reread the original plan regularly to ensure that a new venture is staying on track.
- **As a decision-making tool:** When major operational issues occur or opportunities for expansion arise, turn to the business plan. Decide whether the issue at hand fits into the original goals and timeline before taking action.
- **As a troubleshooter:** When problems surface, minimize frustrations by turning to the plan. Ideally, potential problems and proposed solutions were addressed in the critical risks section. Use these words of wisdom to resolve any problems.
- **As a vision guide:** Once a new business is open, it is easy to lose sight of the overall goals. Concentrating on daily tasks and problems can derail overall progress. Managers should refer to the business plan frequently to refocus their vision from daily details to achieving long-term goals.

On a regular basis—at least annually, but as frequently as every quarter—a new business should formally schedule meetings (or time for a sole proprietor) to evaluate the firm's performance relative to projections in its business plan. If the performance fails to meet the projections, it may mean action is needed to get things back on schedule. It also might mean that there is a flaw in the plan that needs to be addressed. This is the perfect opportunity to update the plan to reflect the new reality of the business and its market.

SELF-CHECK

1. When should the executive summary be written? What is its purpose?
2. What two parts make up the marketing section and what information should each contain?
3. What three documents should be included in the financial forecast section? What information does each provide?
4. How should a business plan be used once a firm is open?

Apply Your Knowledge You are creating a business plan for a Web site that will sell designer hats. Create a short critical risks section, outlining at least four possible risks and potential solutions.

SUMMARY

Section 3.1

- Not all ideas are right for an e-business. Entrepreneurs will have a higher chance of success by focusing on a niche market (rather than going head-to-head with major e-commerce sites) and avoiding fads.
- Succeeding in a niche market requires a business owner to become an expert about their product and target customers.

Section 3.2

- The three-rings exercise is an easy but effective method for evaluating a business idea, conducted by gathering feedback first from family and friends, then industry professionals, and finally potential customers.
- A SWOT analysis considers the strengths, weaknesses, opportunities, and threats facing a business idea, while conducting a feasibility study requires gathering detailed answers to questions in five different categories: products, experience, market, competition, and costs.

Section 3.3

- Identifying a target market requires categorizing and describing potential customers. This information is gathered by conducting market research and a careful analysis of competing Web sites.

Section 3.4

- A business plan is a written document that details all aspects of a proposed venture. Creating a business plan makes it easier to secure outside financing, forces critical analysis, offers well-defined goals, and provides timeless guidance once a firm is up and running.

Section 3.5

- Business plans should follow a relatively standardized format, which includes eight sections: executive summary, business description, marketing, location, management team, critical risks, financial forecast, and appendix (containing important supporting documents).

ASSESS YOUR UNDERSTANDING

UNDERSTAND: WHAT HAVE YOU LEARNED?

Go to **www.wiley.com/college/holden** to assess your knowledge of the basics of planning an e-business.

APPLY: WHAT WOULD YOU DO?

1. Not all business ideas are well suited for small-scale e-commerce sites. Of the following, which would or would not be appropriate for a small e-business? Briefly explain why.
   - A Web site selling collectible figurines whose explosive popularity was launched by a blockbuster summer movie
   - An e-commerce site that sells high-quality, hard-to-get specialty Swedish cooking utensils with a small but growing following in the United States
   - A Web site that sells new and used books at a discount
2. You have been asked to help evaluate an idea for selling gourmet dog treats over the Internet. Briefly outline a plan for conducting a three-rings exercise, suggesting possible survey sources and questions to ask in each analytical ring.
3. With the growing popularity of outdoor cooking, an entrepreneur thought that selling grilling tools online might be a good business idea. Begin a SWOT analysis for this concept by listing at least three factors to consider in each of the categories.
4. You are conducting a feasibility study for a one-person e-business that you are considering starting. Complete the "Experience" section, carefully considering your strengths and weaknesses for such a venture.
5. What are the five categories typically used to describe customers? Provide a sample of data or information that might be included in each category.
6. You are examining the target market for an e-commerce site that will sell lacrosse equipment. Briefly outline a market research plan for the business, describing at least three specific methods and places for gathering information.

7. Assume that you have launched an e-commerce site without creating a business plan. Explain why each of these scenarios might be problematic without a business plan in hand:
   - Six months after starting, you want to make sure that your business is reaching its goals and is on the way to success.
   - You need a bank loan to purchase additional equipment to keep up with an unexpected growth surge.
   - Several minor crises have developed, including a new competitor entering into the market and a sharp increase in the cost of shipping.
8. The "Location" section is an important part of every business plan, even for a home-based venture. Provide a detailed listing of the information that should be included in this section of a business plan for a one-person, home-based e-business.
9. The owner on an e-commerce site selling tie-dyed T-shirts spent considerable time developing a comprehensive business plan. Now that the firm is open for business, offer five ideas for putting the plan to effective use.

BE AN E-BUSINESS ENTREPRENEUR

Developing an E-Business Idea

Select a product related to a hobby or interest of yours and consider creating a Web site to sell that product. (Try to select something that might not normally be sold over the Internet.) Develop the business idea by answering the questions in Section 3.1.2. Based on the answers, briefly explain why this idea would or would not be worthy of further development and analysis.

Conduct a SWOT Analysis

Visit an e-commerce site serving a niche market and assume that you have been asked to analyze the business. Conduct a simulated SWOT analysis on the Web site, including providing answers to the questions listed in Section 3.2.2.

Describe Target Markets

Following the guidelines in Section 3.3.1, write a brief target market description and conduct a basic online search to gather information about likely consumers for each of the following products:

Tandem bicycles
Turkey fryers
Scrapbooking supplies

Starting a Business Plan

The first step in writing a good business plan is to effectively describe the venture. Select a product that interests you and write a brief description section that could be included in a business plan for an e-commerce site that sells the product. Include all the elements mentioned in Section 3.5.2.

KEY TERMS

Balance sheet	A financial statement that reports a firm's financial position at the end of a period of time.
Business plan	A detailed written document that describes all aspects of a proposed business venture.
Cash flow statement	A financial statement that shows a firm's net profit after taxes.
Demographics	Statistical data used to describe a population or groups within it.
Executive summary	A brief section at the beginning of a business plan that highlights the major points from each of the other parts of the plan.
Fad	An intense, widespread, and short-lived enthusiasm for a product or activity.
Feasibility study	A preliminary study undertaken to determine and document a project's viability. The results of the study are used to make a decision whether to proceed with a project.
Income statement	A financial statement that shows changes in a firm's financial position over a period of time.
Marketing	The process of promoting and selling products and services.
Market research	Gathering information about consumers, their needs, and their preferences.
Niche	A small, specialized part of a market.
Psychographics	The classification of people based on their attitudes or lifestyle choices.
SWOT analysis	A decision-making tool for businesses that evaluates the strengths, weaknesses, opportunities, and threats of an idea.

Target market	A group of consumers who behave in a similar way and have been identified as potential customers for a firm's products or services.
Three-rings exercise	A system for evaluating a business idea in which feedback is gathered first from family and friends, then from industry experts, and finally from potential customers.

REFERENCES

1. Ryan McCarthy, "The Next Generation," Inc.com, www.inc.com/30under30/tran.html.
2. Van K. Morrow, "Richard Bradley is a Reel Man," *The Towne Crier,* Mar 10–16, 2004, Volume 14, p. 11.
3. SCORE. "Entrepreneur Grows Her Sales and Finds Success With SCORE," www.score.org/success_w_laimon.html.

TOOLKIT

MARKETING PLAN EXCERPT FROM INTELICHILD.COM

[*Editor note: details for this sample plan are not necessarily correct.*]

4.0 Market Analysis Summary

The InteliChild.com market has been expanding exponentially with the advances of technology in the teaching sectors and the acceptance of technology as a teaching aid. The critical component to our entrance into the market will be approval and support from the school communities—including teachers, the PTA, and special education programs.

4.1 Market Segmentation

Our primary target markets include these four areas:

1. The kids themselves. We include ages 5–9 and ages 10–14 in our market statistics because these are the breakdowns available at **www.census.gov,** and we include only 10% of the total in each category.
2. Parents. We include 10% of the parents, assuming that leads to an average combined income above $100,000. Most of these people live in suburban areas, but the urban upper class is also a major component.
3. Educational institutions for the children of the upper class. This includes day care and private schools. Penetrating this market is excellent because it generates leads to our other targets. We include 107,000 schools in the U.S. in our table.
4. Self-teaching families. There is an excellent group of established customers who teach their children from home. The site will benefit greatly from the time available from this target group.

Market Analysis (Pie)

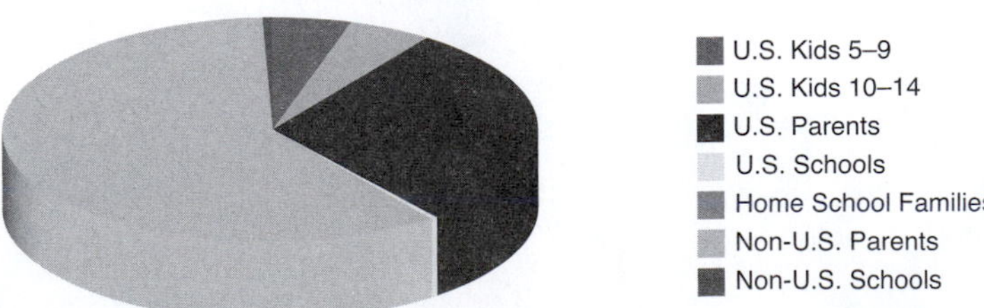

Market Analysis							
Potential Customers	Growth	2000	2001	2002	2003	2004	CAGR
U.S. Kids 5–9	2%	1,994,000	2,033,880	2,074,558	2,116,049	2,158,370	2.00%
U.S. Kids 10–14	2%	1,961,200	2,000,424	2,040,432	2,081,241	2,122,866	2.00%
U.S. Parents	2%	12,000,000	12,240,000	12,484,800	12,734,496	12,989,186	2.00%
U.S. Schools	1%	107,000	108,070	109,151	110,243	111,345	1.00%
Home School Families	40%	5,000	7,000	9,800	13,720	19,208	40.00%
Non-U.S. Parents	4%	24,000,000	24,960,000	25,958,400	26,996,736	28,076,605	4.00%
Non-U.S. Schools	0%	225,000	225,000	225,000	225,000	225,000	0.00%
Total	3.20%	40,292,200	41,574,374	42,902,141	44,277,485	45,702,580	3.20%

4.2 Website Demographics

While we have plans to expand into international territory, our initial launch will target our most important market—the American upper class. We know that most of our clients drive BMW's and have very good taste—they spend money on their children because they can appreciate the technology that we have created. They also generally have high bandwidth connections, and are impressed by first-class design.

4.2.1 Market Needs

The InteliChild.com Web site will have to reflect its product line—simultaneously fun, easy to use, and informative. In order to gain recognition for our site efforts, we are going to have to put together a site that is worthy of attention. The design work should promote the feeling of superior quality. The InteliChild.com attitude will match the company's inherent value drive—parents and educators will feel guilty not buying into these products.

4.2.2 Market Trends

The market for intelligent, technological teaching devices is growing exponentially. The key factors driving this growth are the increase in salaries in the technology sectors, the double-income household, and the loss of leisure time. Hardworking parents are dedicated to giving their children every educational opportunity possible. Our target market's behavioral patterns are changing dramatically as well—research used to happen in many places; now increasingly it happens on the Internet.

4.2.3 Market Growth

The macro-environment is the real reason for the urgency of the InteliChild.com e-commerce project. All trends in our market indicate that a strong Web presence will not be a frivolous extra for the company, but rather, an absolute necessity. As mentioned before, the double-income family in the technological sector is doing their research on the Internet. In order to survive, InteliChild.com must be present as a destination for these search results.

4.3 Industry Analysis

The Web site industry is exploding. Growth is absurd, amazing. We don't have business reasons to detail this situation in this plan; our readers are aware of it.

4.3.1 Industry Participants

This is sample text describing the different companies addressing the same target market. The real plan included details on which companies sell products (toys, books, or games) into this market. It includes who owns them, how much market share they get (according to available information sources), and what we know about their assorted business models.

4.3.2 Distribution Patterns

This is sample text describing the different Web sites addressing the same target market. The real plan included details identifying these Web sites, who owns them, how much traffic they get (according to available information sources), and their assorted business models.

4.3.3 Competition and Buying Patterns

This is sample text describing factors in competition for Web site use by bright children ages 8–14, for sales to their parents and schools. It details information available about the importance of factors such as pricing, shipment, quality, presentation, etc.

4.3.4 Main Competitors

Our competition is the market leader—and their success is a symbol of our potential market. We were pleased to see their Web division spin off to its own company that went public with a tremendous initial offering. The market is too large for them to cover entirely, and as a second-best in dollar market share, with better reviews from the critical industry leaders, InteliChild.com stands in a position to expand our business significantly.

Written with Business Plan Pro, Palo alto Software, www.paloalto.com.

CHAPTER

FINANCING AND LAUNCHING AN E-BUSINESS

Finding the Money, Employees, and Professional Support Needed for Startup

Do You Already Know?

- How to start a business on a tight budget by bootstrapping
- The most common sources of startup financing
- The insurance and taxes required when hiring employees
- What the advantages are of buying an existing Web site

For additional questions to assess your current knowledge on financing and launching an e-business, go to **www.wiley.com/college/holden.**

What You Will Find Out	What You Will Be Able To Do
4.1 Techniques for minimizing the initial investment in starting an e-business	• Calculate the necessary startup costs and launch a business by bootstrapping
4.2 The common sources of financing for a new e-business, including friends, family, and bank loans	• Identify and utilize appropriate sources for financing a new e-business
4.3 When it is right to hire employees, and what insurance and tax requirements and benefit needs come with them	• Hire employees that fit a specific need and fulfill the subsequent insurance and tax requirements
4.4 That there are several advantages, and risks, associated with purchasing an existing Web site	• Evaluate an existing Web site and determine whether purchasing it would be better than starting a new site

INTRODUCTION

A great e-business idea proven by extensive research and supported by a quality business plan still needs money to get off the ground. Realistically, this amount will be in the thousands of dollars, but there are techniques for keeping costs to a minimum. The focus of this chapter's first section is how to calculate the money needed along with ideas for bootstrapping a new business—starting with relatively limited funds. Because even bootstrapped businesses will need cash at some point to ensure their growth and success, the second section will discuss where to get that money. Family, friends, banks, and credit cards are all possible sources, but each has advantages and disadvantages. As e-businesses grow, they may want to turn to specialized financing sources that have become increasingly popular: angel investors and venture capitalists, which have different applications and requirements for small businesses. In addition to cash, many new e-businesses also need help from employees. This is discussed in the third section. Employees should be hired to fill a specific need, and businesses must be prepared to welcome workers by obtaining adequate insurance coverage and filing the necessary tax paperwork. Buying an existing Web site provides an alternative route into e-business for entrepreneurs looking for a faster path to startup. The fourth section evaluates the advantages and pitfalls of this option, and provides sound advice for determining the true value of a pre-existing site.

4.1 LAUNCHING A BUSINESS ON A TIGHT BUDGET

One of the most important choices for new business owners is how to fund their new endeavor. The amount of money available and its sources help define the rules by which a new firm must operate. Consider borrowing $25,000 from a bank. Each month the business will have to come up with enough money to cover that loan payment. If the business cannot keep this commitment, and it is organized as a sole proprietorship, this means the owner is also jeopardizing their personal credit record. On the other hand, if an entrepreneur borrows $5,000 from family members, the entrepreneur might not have to pay the money back right away, but they might be inviting unwanted decision makers into the business.

4.1.1 Calculating Startup Costs

Don't be fooled by all the e-commerce hype about starting an online business for little or no money. Realistically, launching a fully functional e-commerce site requires a financial investment of at least several thousand dollars. A few hundred dollars might allow someone to set up a very basic Web site and have an online presence, but a fully functioning business requires an additional investment in technology, marketing, advertising, inventory, merchant account fees, site-hosting fees, office supplies, labor, and so forth, just to get up and running.

Capital: The money that the owners invest in a business.

Very few businesses become profitable immediately, and many of those that fail do so because there was not enough **capital**—money invested in a business—available. There are two components to estimating startup costs. One is obvious: money to cover equipment and whatever is required to take an e-commerce site live. The other component is money to cover ongoing expenses (rent, salaries, supplies, and so on) until a business is generating adequate revenues to cover those expenses. Most experts recommend that a new business should include in its startup budget enough money to pay its bills for three to six months without using any income.

E-business in Action →
Calculate the startup costs for an e-business.

Consider also whether a business can survive the unthinkable—a server or software crash that shuts down a Web site. Be prepared, financially and otherwise, for any unforeseen problems.

PATHWAY TO... DETERMINING STARTUP COSTS

Not every business has the same startup expenses. The following (listed alphabetically) includes some of the costs to build into a startup budget:

- Accounting, consulting, and legal
- Advertising, marketing, and public relations
- Business plan
- Business travel
- Communications (including telephone and cellular service)
- Computer equipment and software
- Feasibility study
- Insurance
- Interest on loans
- Internet Service Provider (ISP) and Web site hosting fees
- Inventory
- Labor (employees and contractors)
- Market study
- Merchant account fees
- Office furniture, equipment (such as copy and fax machines), and supplies
- Order processing/shipping
- Phone line (toll-free number, where applicable)

- Printing and design for marketing materials, business cards, stationery
- Rent and utilities (such as electricity, heat, water, and sewer)
- Taxes
- Web site design and maintenance

4.1.2 Bootstrapping an E-Business

Bootstrapping: Starting a business with minimal financial resources by working hard, doing without, and keeping costs low.

Just like starting a political campaign, having plenty of money available makes things easier when starting a business. Fortunately, having a lot of money is not a requirement to start an Internet business. Individuals without access to megabucks can always bootstrap their new business. The term comes from the idea of pulling yourself up by your own bootstraps, or making your own way. In the case of financing an entrepreneurial dream, **bootstrapping** is a matter of building a business with minimal resources and making a little money go a long way.

The first rule of bootstrapping is to hang on to other sources of income for as long as possible. In other words, e-business entrepreneurs should plan on keeping their day job. The resourceful individual might design their Web site during lunch breaks or work past midnight to prepare customer orders for shipping. Although keeping a regular job while starting a business can mean a grueling schedule, it provides much-needed financial security in the early stages of building a company.

Another option is to try something in between maintaining a full-time job and starting a business. Many entrepreneurs work part-time jobs at night so that they can dedicate themselves to their new businesses during the day.

E-business in Action →
Launch an e-business by bootstrapping.

What about those all-or-nothing types that want to throw themselves completely into a new business and have the confidence that success (i.e., cash) will materialize? Even they should plan for alternative sources of income. Options include freelance work, short-term consulting jobs, or whatever else it takes to keep money coming in while a new e-business is growing.

4.1.3 Techniques for Keeping Costs Low

Making sure that cash is rolling in to support a new e-business is only the first step in bootstrapping. The second step is learning to conserve cash. Controlling the outflow of money, or how that money is used, is very important. Here are some ways that a good bootstrapper can conserve cash:

- **Become frugal:** Spend only when absolutely necessary, and then buy "on the cheap." Rather than buy brand-new office furniture, find what you need by shopping garage sales, thrift stores, and eBay.
- **Budget wisely:** Create a financial plan that tracks income, expenses, and projected sales. By monitoring the money coming in and going out every day, a business is less likely to get into trouble.
- **Use other people's money:** Rather than borrow money from banks or investors, "borrow" money from suppliers and customers. Negotiate terms with vendors that allow paying for supplies 30 or 60 days out. Then ask customers to pay up front or in "Net 15" days. This strategy allows firms to use their customers' money, rather than cash from the business to pay expenses.
- **Sacrifice for the business:** The cash coming into a business should be just that—money for your business. Using revenues to support a personal lifestyle is a formula for failure. Bootstrappers commonly forfeit luxuries and even downgrade their living circumstances while growing a company.

Barter:
Paying for products and services by exchanging other products or services.

- **Barter to keep costs low:** To **barter** is to pay for products or services without using cash and instead exchange other products or services. This method of conducting business has become so popular that businesses can join formal barter-exchange organizations, such as Southern Barter (www.southernbarter.com). The Internal Revenue Service considers any non-cash transaction as barter and there are a couple of rules to follow to stay legal at tax time. The IRS advises that both parties agree ahead of time on a fair market value for the transaction. That amount should appear as income for both parties when they complete Form 1099.
- **Inspire, don't hire:** The early stages of building a company can be overwhelming, but it is better to resist the temptation to hire employees. Instead, seek people who are willing to work for free. The promise of a job once the company is more stable may be enough to get someone working five or six hours a week right now. Some individuals are willing to work for free in return for a recommendation. Some people design Web sites for free in exchange for using those businesses as client referrals.
- **Use demo software and freeware:** Instead of immediately buying expensive software, use free demonstration (demo) versions that are good for a specified period to defer the investment and prove its necessity. Another option is freeware, software that is distributed at no cost over the Internet. Many of these packages have the same features as a recognizable brand-name product, though most lack technical support, which can be a problem.

PATHWAY TO... FINDING A MENTOR

Hiring a consultant can break the bank before a Web site even goes live. Mentoring is an alternative way to get advice from established professionals that costs nothing. These experts can advise on critical decisions, help networking with other professionals and suppliers, and offer advice on attracting customers. Here are a few steps to follow when trying to establish a relationship with a mentor:

1. Identify a business leader with the appropriate expertise. Search online, check with local member-based business organizations, and ask friends or business associates for suggestions.
2. Call or email the professional and introduce yourself. Briefly explain your situation and specify what you want (candid advice). Offer to buy the person lunch, meet for coffee, or schedule a time for an extended phone conversation.
3. When you get a commitment to spend time together, make the best of it. Be brief, courteous, and attentive—and sell yourself!
4. Take notes. This technique helps you remember any pertinent details, and shows that you're genuinely interested in learning.
5. If all goes well, ask whether you can schedule regular meetings with your mentor. At a minimum, ask whether you can call again if you have more questions.
6. If the meeting doesn't go well, ask whether that person knows someone else who might be willing to advise you. For example, this person might not have time for you or be as knowledgeable as you thought.
7. Send a thank-you note by postal mail or email. Letting people know that you appreciate their time is always worthwhile. Don't forget to include your business card and contact information.

4.1.4 The Advantages of Bootstrapping

Bootstrapping may sound like a risky proposition, but it is quite the opposite. It requires adopting a rigorous thought process that includes detailed and innovative planning. Although bootstrapping may seem painful, the alternative is bringing in other investors or borrowing money. Consider how this approach can positively affect a new business now and down the road.

Maintain Control of Ownership

Keeping full ownership or controlling interest of the business is one of the most important benefits of bootstrapping. The owner makes all the decisions, without having to ask investors, shareholders, or lenders for input. Once the company has grown large enough, the owner can bring in capital by selling shares without jeopardizing this control.

Quick Decision Making

Typically, a bootstrapped organization does not have layers of departments or managers, and there are no outside investors to consult. Quick decisions can be made without getting bogged down by bureaucratic red tape. Offering new products or making significant changes to an e-commerce site quickly provides an important advantage over larger, slow-moving competitors.

Minimizing Risk

Without putting much money on the line, the new business owner's risk is greatly reduced. This also can translate into a significant financial gain because there is minimal initial investment to pay off. The motivating factor of high profits often spurs on success.

Maintaining a Cash-Is-King Mindset

Being frugal pays off now and later. At startup, conservative decisions assist a new e-business in building a positive cash flow. Bootstrapped companies tend to hold on to those same decision-making philosophies in an effort to maintain cash reserves as they expand. This mindset may also help to keep an online business debt free.

IN THE REAL WORLD

A Bootstrapping Success Story

Started with $100, TicketsNow.com is now a major industry competitor. How did this accomplishment come about? After three years of college, Mike Domek ran out of money and enthusiasm for his formal education. Deciding instead to gamble as an entrepreneur, he wrote a personal check for $100 and incorporated his new business. He managed to buy a few office supplies and a two-line phone system, and then converted his one-bedroom apartment to an office. Mike's company specialized in locating premium seating and sold-out tickets for major events, such as rock concerts and sports contests. The business was customer-service intensive, and before long, Mike realized the inefficiency of the business.

(*Continued*)

So, in 1999, he moved the business to the Internet. This strategy gave his customers the option of searching for event tickets themselves and then purchasing them online. Mike was pinching pennies to self-fund growth for the company. The risk paid off. Online-event ticket sales has become a billion-dollar industry. Mike's company is on track to exceed $110 million and has more than 100 employees on its payroll. Even with this success, Mike says that he has held true to many of the original bootstrapping philosophies that got TicketsNow.com off the ground.

SELF-CHECK

1. What two components must be included when calculating startup costs?
2. What is the first rule of bootstrapping? Why is this so important?
3. What are the primary advantages of bootstrapping?

Apply Your Knowledge You are launching an online business on a limited budget. Suggest five specific ideas for minimizing the expenses incurred by the new firm.

4.2 COMMON SOURCES OF FINANCING

As noted in Section 4.1.1, the startup costs for a small e-business will typically run into the thousands of dollars. While bootstrapping can help minimize these expenses, few businesses can be successfully launched without some form of financing.

Personal savings is by far the most common source of startup funds for new businesses, especially sole proprietorships. Most experts stress the importance of the owner investing at least some of their own money in a new venture. In addition to giving the new owner more incentive to work hard and succeed—and avoid losing their savings—financing from savings is cheap and offers more flexibility for a new business. There is no interest to pay and no schedules for repayment. On the downside, putting personal savings at risk can create a serious hardship for some people, especially when an e-business fails.

In addition to savings, there are several other sources for financing a small e-business, which are reviewed in the sections that follow.

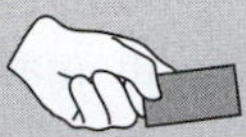

CAREER CONNECTION

With some savings and savvy, a simple idea is transformed into a thriving e-business.

Chris Gwynn had spent a decade working for large companies in the online business industry, but he wanted to start a business that offered more stability and control over his career. After researching various industries and products, he settled on starting Fridgedoor.com, which sells refrigerator magnets. Gwynn started the business as a part-time endeavor in May 1997, while employed by an Internet-based marketplace for industrial supplies. By December 1998, sales had increased enough that Gwynn left his position to work full-time on Fridgedoor.com. Even though the business is based out of his home—spare rooms serve as offices and the basement is the warehouse—it required a significant investment to get started. "I invested my own money," Gwynn explained. "I'd rather not give an exact figure in terms of my investment, but it was over $20,000. Getting a Web site actually created and online is only a small part of the time and financial investment necessary to operate a successful online business."

Tips from the Professional

- Offer high-quality products.
- Provide next-business-day order shipment.
- Give customers a money-back guarantee.
- Include small, personal touches that build customer trust.

4.2.1 Friends and Family

After personal savings, friends and family are the most common sources of startup funds for new small businesses. The simplest method is to simply ask for a loan and the transaction takes place with minimal formalities with Mom or a good friend handing over a check for the necessary funding. The interest on these loans is usually minimal or nonexistent, and the time for repaying the money is often open-ended.

An alternative is to invite friends and family as investors. In other words, they are given a percentage of shares of stock in the business in return for the amount of money they agree to provide. On the upside, that money does not have to be repaid. But if at some point it is preferable for those friends or relative(s) to no longer own a portion of your business, their stock must be repurchased.

Advantages of obtaining financing from family and friends include the following:

- **The money is easy to obtain:** Family and friends already know and trust you and are eager to help. Usually they don't need to be sold on a business idea—let alone shown a business plan.

- **Cash can be obtained quickly:** Unlike going to a bank or venture capitalist, there are few lending steps to complete. Friends and family may be able to access cash quickly for immediate delivery to you.
- **There is a potential large pool of investors:** It is relatively easy to obtain small amounts of money from many different sources. An entrepreneur needing $50,000 can turn to ten friends and relatives investing $5,000 each rather than trying to find one person to contribute the entire amount.

Working with friends and family has disadvantages, too:

- **There can be problems with unstructured terms:** Investments from friends and family tend to be received on an informal basis. That opens the door to uncertainty and inconsistency and big misunderstandings. Be wary of taking on friends and family members as investors without structured, written agreements that clearly define the terms of their investments or the payback terms of loans.
- **You can give up too much stock:** People want to reward those who believe in them, but that makes it easy to give away too much in a small company. Or, if the investors consist of a very large group, the business might have to give up a large block of stock for a relatively small amount of cash. An uneven exchange can put a company in a precarious position as it grows.
- **The business could interfere with relationships:** Taking on a trusted circle of friends or family as investors can lead to heated disagreements, hurt feelings, and a fair share of misunderstandings. Damage to these friendships or relationships with family members is not easy to repair.

4.2.2 Bank Loans

Many banks consider new business loans to be too risky, even when money is not tight. The Small Business Administration is usually eager to help new enterprises obtain bank loans, but competition is keen for the SBA's limited financial resources. Even without SBA support or loan guarantees, it is worth contacting a local bank about a startup loan. Some banks are committed to supporting economic development in their communities, or work with local development organizations to help provide startup funds for new businesses.

IN THE REAL WORLD

SBA Loan Helps Fitness Business Grow

Lisa Druxman had been in the fitness industry for a decade when she created an exercise program called Stroller Strides that she could do with her newborn son. Soon Lisa was teaching the program to other moms, and what started as a part-time business began growing rapidly. Lisa was able to obtain a Small Business Administration guaranteed loan to finance her company's rapid expansion, supported in part by an attractive and effective Web site (www.strollerstrides.com). Thanks to support, business counseling, and financing provided by the SBA, Stroller Strides in now the country's largest and fastest-growing fitness program for the moms of young children.[1]

Before applying for financing, an e-business owner should carefully prepare a loan proposal, including detailed information on the amount of capital needed and how the money will be used. Many banks also require an up-to-date business plan (see Chapter 3 for more information). It also helps if the business owner possesses a good credit history and an above-average personal credit (FICO) score.

Once a business obtains a loan, it will likely have to provide current financial statements on a regular basis. As long as a business is profitable and is making loan payments on time, there will probably be minimal contact with the bank. Short-term loans may require closer bank monitoring.

In addition to traditional bank lending, the following are some loan options that might be available to new online businesses.

Home Equity Loans

With low interest rates and the recent housing boom, banks and other lenders have become creative with borrowing options. Homeowners can "cash out" the equity in their house, use it for other purposes—such as starting a business—and pay it back at a fixed interest rate over 5, 10, 15 years, or more. Another option is to get a home equity line of credit. This provides a fixed amount of money that the homeowner/business owner is approved to borrow, but the money is obtained only as it is needed. Remember, borrowing money against a house is always risky, and many business experts hesitate to recommend this method because of the potential for losing a home when a business fails.

High-Interest Loans

Some specialized lenders finance loans—even high-risk ones for people with a poor credit rating—at high interest rates. These rates are usually similar to or higher than credit card rates. When all other options fail, this method may be a possibility, though it requires extreme caution. The cost of this type of financing is exceptionally high and could prove to be a drain on the cash flow of a new e-business.

Small Business Administration Microloan

The SBA might be a good place to turn for a smaller amount of capital. The federal agency recently introduced the Community Express (or Small Loan) Program for small businesses. The low-interest loans are typically for amounts less than $100,000 and are usually closer to $5,000 or $10,000. No collateral—or even a complete business plan—is needed. However, the loan recipient must participate in a consultation with an SBA-approved technical advisor, and they must have a good credit history. The loans can sometimes be obtained the same day an application is submitted. To locate sources for microloans, contact the state or regional SBA office or visit www.sba.gov.

E-business in Action →
Identify and utilize appropriate sources for financing a new e-business.

4.2.3 Angel Investors

Sometimes a new e-business's financing needs grow beyond what friends and family can provide, and conservative banks might prove to be wary about their risk exposure for an Internet business. In these instances, turning to an angel investor may be the best option. An **angel investor** is an individual, often a retired entrepreneur, who is willing to invest money in startup or young companies. Angels frequently provide loans of $100,000 to $250,000, in the process bridging a funding gap for growing companies that lies between what savings, family, and friends can provide and what venture capitalists are interested in investing.

Angel investor:
An individual, often a retired entrepreneur, who is willing to invest money in a startup or young company.

Angel investors often do not seek an active role in a company. Many simply want to provide capital, although they may seek an advisory role in the company. Conversely, some angels see their investment as a way to stay active in the business world, and they offer their expertise and (more rarely) even labor in addition to their money. These non-monetary resources can be priceless for an inexperienced new business owner, but an overactive angel might be difficult to manage.

One advantage of working with angels is that they are less likely to demand an immediate return on an investment. On the other hand, they often require a fairly large stake in a business to offset their risk. Acquiring money from angel investors is getting tougher. Many expect a startup to have a polished business plan, an experienced management team, and an exit strategy (a way for the angel to recoup their initial investment and then some).

E-business in Action →
Work with angel investors.

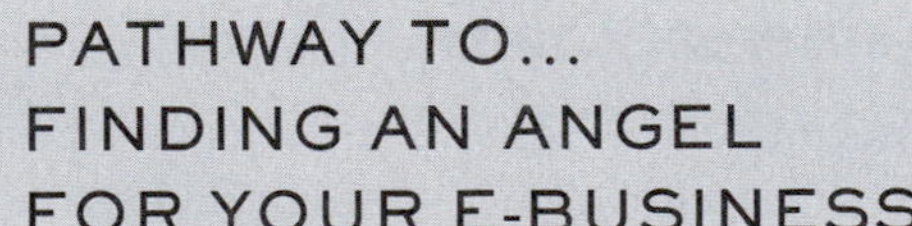

PATHWAY TO... FINDING AN ANGEL FOR YOUR E-BUSINESS

Locating an angel investor often starts by networking with colleagues, friends, and family and asking whether they have any contacts that might be interested. If that doesn't provide any leads, search for angels at the regional or national level. Here are some places to begin a search:

- Chamber of Commerce or other local business-support organizations
- Professional associations (local and statewide) focused on technology
- Accountants, bankers, or attorneys (who often work with or know angels)
- Investment clubs

Online resources for angel networks and entrepreneurs include:

- AngelInvestorNews at www.angel-investor-news.com
- vFinance, Inc. at www.vfinance.com
- NBAI (Network of Business Angels and Investors) at www.nbai.net

4.2.4 Venture Capital

Venture capital: Financing provided by a specialized investment firm that operates with the expectation of high risk and high return on its investment.

Venture capital is financing provided by a specialized investment firm that operates with the expectation of high risk and high return on its investment. Venture capital funding is not the easiest route for securing money for a new e-business. Part of the difficulty can be traced to the dot-com era of the 1990s when millions of dollars were thrown haphazardly into Internet startups and many of these firms failed. In spite of that bursting bubble, venture capitalists are still out in force; getting their money, however, is much more difficult now.

Most experts do not recommend venture capital as a resource for brand-new companies. This type of funding is designed for businesses that need an aggressive (or very large) amount of money to support the next level of business growth. Most venture capitalists are institutional investors (professionally managed funds) that invest anywhere from $500,000 to $10 million or more in a company. Most often, this investment is made in preparation for an initial public offering (IPO) on the stock market, a sale, or a merger with another company.

How does an e-business know whether it is ready to pursue venture capital money? Most venture capitalists generally expect the following from a company:

- **Has already used seed money:** The company should be long past the point of obtaining money from friends and family as part of its startup stage.
- **Has a proven track record:** Investors expect a company to have experience and proof of the underlying business concept under its belt.
- **Has an experienced management team in place:** Being the sole employee of a company is not a good thing when seeking venture capital.
- **Is in a "hot" industry:** Venture capitalists invest in more than a company—they invest in an industry.

- **Is in a high-growth stage:** Securing venture capital means that a company is positioned for significant earnings. A good rule is that the company can achieve annual revenues of $25 million within a five-year time frame.

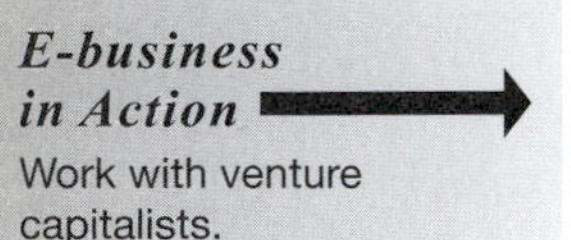
E-business in Action
Work with venture capitalists.

- **Has owners who are willing to relinquish control:** Often, the company founder is replaced as president by an outsider of the venture capitalists' choosing.

PATHWAY TO... LOCATING VENTURE CAPITAL FIRMS

When a firm is ready to contact venture capital firms, two established resources are very helpful for locating firms and determining which firms might be a good match:

- **The Directory of Venture Capital & Private Equity Firms (www.greyhouse.com/venture.htm):** Grey House Publishing offers a hardbound copy and an online database by paid subscription.
- **Pratt's Guide to Venture Capital Sources:** This list of active venture firms, published annually by Venture Economics, includes each firm's location, investment preferences, contacts, and capital pool. For information on subscribing, visit the Web site at www.ventureeconomics.com.

4.2.5 Credit Cards

For better or worse, a credit card is a popular choice for funding a business. More than 80 percent of small businesses have used personal and business credit cards as a source of money, according to the Small Business Administration. Although credit cards may be a quick and easy alternative, they can also be expensive. Some credit cards charge interest at or above 20 percent. In addition, businesses can be assessed large fees for late payments or for exceeding their credit limit. Financial advisors also caution that fully paying down the balance of credit cards can take decades when making only the minimum monthly payments.

The best bet is to use credit cards sparingly and to pay off the balance as quickly as possible to avoid interest charges. Look for cards that offer rewards based on the spending or total balance. Consider moving balances with high interest terms to another card. Also, don't hesitate to call credit card companies to negotiate for a better rate on an existing card.

4.2.6 Other Sources of Financing

Grant:
Monetary award that does not have to be repaid.

Businesses with especially innovative concepts may want to search out grant opportunities. **Grants** are monetary awards that do not have to be repaid. Be wary of Web sites that charge for a list of "free money" resources from government grants. Although legitimate grants are available, there is no reason to pay for information about them: A list can be obtained for free from the Catalog of Federal Government Assistance, at the U.S. government's grant site, www.grants.gov.

Many organizations run contests open to entrepreneurs with distinctive new business ideas. For instance, Visa USA's Idea Happens contest gave $25,000 in seed money to 12 young entrepreneurs who submitted the best ideas for new businesses. Other organizations —such as business magazines, office supply chains, and other large retailers—often sponsor business-plan-writing contests with financial payoffs, or they award cash and prizes as part of their general business contests.

Business incubator:
An organization that supports entrepreneurial development by providing shared resources for businesses at reduced cost.

Business incubators are organizations established to support entrepreneurial development, usually providing shared resources for businesses at reduced (or sometimes zero) cost. Shared resources might mean office space, support staff, or access to volunteer or hired professionals. Although incubators do not traditionally provide startup money (in fact, they usually take a small percentage of stock in exchange for their services), they are still considered an alternative funding source because they provide resources that translate into free investment dollars at startup. Locate technology and small business incubators by contacting the National Business Incubation Association at www.nbia.org.

SELF-CHECK

1. What are the primary advantages and disadvantages of receiving financing from friends and family?
2. What information should be supplied when applying for a bank loan? In addition to payments, what is usually required after the loan has been made?
3. Are venture capitalists a good startup money source? What requirements do venture capitalists have for providing financing?
4. Can a new business be financed with credit cards? If so, what are the rules to follow?

Apply Your Knowledge A friend suggested that an angel investor might be a good source of money for your new e-business. What is an angel investor. What are the advantages, disadvantages, and requirements of working with one?

4.3 HIRING EMPLOYEES

Though one person often can run a simple e-commerce site, it usually takes a larger team to launch a full-featured e-business. Although the goal of hiring additional people is to reduce the owner/manager's workload, the extra responsibilities of supervising those people can become a significant drain on their time. In addition, employees can represent one of the biggest expenses associated with operating a small business. Because of these reasons, new e-businesses should take a very conservative approach to adding employees.

Freelance contractors: Self-employed workers hired under the terms of a contract to provide a service.

Before committing to employees, online entrepreneurs might be better served by first using **freelance contractors**—self-employed people hired under the terms of a contract to provide a service—to perform tasks such as Web programming, graphic design, writing, or marketing. Freelancers offer small businesses flexibility and the ability to hire talented people for a specific short-term project, but they, too, can become a costly option. Because contractors are not employees, it can be difficult to get their full attention or their time specifically when it is needed—leading many firms to consider hiring the help they need.

When the time comes to hire employees, even a very small firm should plan to offer these workers benefits, plus obtain the appropriate workers' compensation insurance. The firm will also have to begin withholding federal and state income tax payments, Social Security taxes, and funds for other benefits, such as health insurance or a 401(k), from their paychecks.

And now the issue of managing people—an online entrepreneur instantly becomes a manager and leader when that first employee walks in the door. The first step, before they ever show up, is to establish employee policies and procedures, put them in writing, and make sure everyone understands them. Inexperienced managers may want to obtain training in guiding employees, which can be frustrating at times, but can also be one of the most rewarding aspects of running a business.

4.3.1 Assembling a Team

When hiring employees, it is important that each employee fulfills a specific need—as opposed to simply bringing in a new employee to share the workload. To that end, the act of hiring should be closely tied to the financial side of the business. Is the company incurring exceptional costs for freelancers or services provided by outside companies that could be managed more cheaply and efficiently by an employee? Or are potential revenues being lost by lack of staffing, for example, by having an in-house customer-service representative to quickly manage problems and maybe even sell additional products to customers? Consult the firm's business plan. It should justify that the effort falls within the guidelines for growth. Then review the budget and confirm the company's ability to manage the added expense.

When it comes time to recruit employees, e-business owners should follow a few simple guidelines during the hiring process:

- Always ask for a résumé, samples of the candidate's work, and three professional references; in terms of references, be certain to follow up on those provided. These documents are especially important when the initial contacts are by email and phone, which is becoming increasingly common.
- Try to hire people who have a passion for computer technology and experience working with computers and the Internet.
- Give special consideration to candidates who respond promptly and courteously to all inquiries. Remember, e-businesses must be focused on serving customers well, and serving them quickly.
- Work ethic and personality are important traits, but it is essential to select people with talents that closely match the business's needs.

If hiring employees the traditional way is too much of a financial burden for a new e-business, there are alternatives to building a team. Many bootstrapped businesses are family affairs, with spouses or children pitching in to share the workload. This can be stressful for some people, but often it is a very successful strategy that is good for both the family and the business. Costs are kept down, unity in purpose (of making a venture succeed) emerges, and future generations of owners or managers are trained so that business can become a long-term family entity.

E-business in Action

Hire employees that fulfill a specific need.

IN THE REAL WORLD

Building an Unconventional Online Team

John Moen knew nothing about computer graphics when he starting his online business, GraphicMaps.com, in 1995—but he did know a lot about maps. His startup was very simple. He taught himself how to create simple Web pages, scraped together $300 to cover initial costs, and took his site live. Not surprisingly, business was slow at first, but it picked up after he started giving away free art and, most importantly, his knowledge of geography. That geographical knowledge led to a second Web site called WorldAtlas.com, which answers questions about geography and generates revenues from banner and pop-up ads directed at the large stream of visitors. Of course, John was not able to answer the thousands of geography questions received every month by himself. For that task, John built an unusual—but appropriate—team of experts: retired teachers. Working from home, these fountains of geographical knowledge log on to the Web site email inbox and quickly research and answer the questions. With the invaluable support of his teacher team, John has more time available to manage his two successful Web sites.

4.3.2 Insurance and Benefits

Perhaps the biggest drawback of starting a new business is giving up all of the benefits an employer would typically provide—and, in turn, having to provide and pay for these same benefits, along with purchasing insurance to protect the company from various calamities. In fact, the insurance requirements for a new business can be quite considerable. The basic business insurance package consists of four fundamental coverages:

1. Workers' compensation
2. General liability
3. Auto (if applicable)
4. Property/casualty

In addition, it is smart to include an added layer of liability protection over those, often called an **umbrella policy,** as well as business interruption coverage. The basic insurance benefit package for employees (and this applies to one-person companies as well) includes three basic items:

Umbrella policy: An extra layer of liability coverage in addition to the basic business insurance policies.

1. Health insurance, including dental and vision-care insurance
2. Life insurance
3. Long-term disability insurance

A small business that is adequately insured against various types of disaster could have monthly premiums anywhere from a few hundred to several thousand dollars, depending on the types of insurance and levels of coverage. Because of this, it is an excellent idea to sit down with a personal financial planner, accountant, or some other impartial person to help define the company's needs before talking to an insurance agent. It is smart to shop around for the best available rates. Keep costs low by avoiding overlapping coverage and keeping deductibles high.

E-business in Action
Fulfill the insurance requirements for a new e-business.

Remember that insurance coverage (particularly when employees are involved) can create a lot of paperwork that must be dutifully completed. It will also create an extra burden on the payroll process by requiring appropriate withholding from employee paychecks.

4.3.3 Employee Forms

When a small business hires employees or contractors (and even when the owner is the only employee), the Internal Revenue Service wants to be in the know—and that involves paperwork. Here are the basic IRS employment forms that every business should be prepared to file:

- **Form W-9:** When a firm hires freelance contractors (non-employees) or consultants to perform work, those individuals must first complete IRS Form W-9. This form provides the information needed to report earnings to the IRS and to generate a Form 1099 that reports their earnings at the end of the year.
- **Form 1099:** If a company hires someone (other than an employee) to do work for them, they need to send a Form 1099 to the employee at the end of the year reporting the amount of money paid. Companies are required to complete this form only if they paid the individual $600 or more. Companies that barter or trade services or products with another company are required to report the value of the trade as income on Form 1099.
- **Form W-4:** All firms with employees must complete Form W-4s to withhold, report, and deposit the correct amount of employment-related taxes. All employers are responsible for withholding money for state and federal income tax, Social Security and Medicare, and federal unemployment taxes.
- **Form W-2:** By the last day of January following the end of each calendar year, companies are responsible for sending this form to employees. A W-2 reports the total income an employee earned during the preceding calendar year, along with the amount of money withheld for various taxes during the year.

FOR EXAMPLE

See the Toolkit for an example of an employee form required of small businesses.

E-business in Action
Fulfill employee tax form requirements.

When hiring freelance contractors, check the IRS definition of what constitutes a contractor versus an employee—the guidelines are relatively strict. For instance, a company that provides workspace and/or a personal computer to a contractor or that requires the person to work a set schedule might cause that contractor to be considered an employee. If that is the case, the company is responsible for withholding taxes from that person. A business can even be fined (and charged interest) if it fails to withhold wages and the "contractor" is later determined to be an employee.

SELF-CHECK

1. What purpose should each new employee fulfill? What documents should be consulted before hiring an employee?
2. What coverage is included in the basic business insurance package?
3. What IRS forms must be filed on behalf of employees and contractors?

Apply Your Knowledge Instead of hiring employees, you decide to get the labor you need by utilizing freelance contractors. What is a freelance contractor? What are the rules for keeping them from being considered employees? What IRS forms must be filed on their behalf?

4.4 PURCHASING AN EXISTING WEB SITE

Securing financing for an online business takes time and persistence, and even then banks and other lenders can be very cautious about giving money to Internet ventures, especially ones that are not yet up and running. And even if financing is not an issue, some would-be online entrepreneurs have more interest in the business aspect of the venture as opposed to the Web site aspect. For these people, building the site, finding a Web host, and so on are just tedious chores on the way to selling products or services. For people in either of these situations, there is another option: Purchase an existing Web site.

4.4.1 The Advantages of Buying an Existing Site

Hundreds of thousands of mom-and-pop businesses have already established a small presence online. Many of these e-commerce sites are doing quite well, while others are struggling or they lack a sense of direction. Sites in those latter categories present an opportunity for an online entrepreneur to get a head start on launching an e-business. There are a number of benefits of purchasing an existing site compared to launching a brand-new business.

Override Startup Costs

Finding an existing online business means not having to worry about all the initial costs and hassles of taking a Web site live. Maintaining or building an existing site is usually cheaper than starting from scratch.

Eliminate Time to Market

Although getting an e-business open can take as little as just a few weeks, establishing that business in the market and gaining a presence in the search engines takes much longer. Buying a ready-made site (even a fledgling one) removes at least some of this concern.

Gain Established Customer Base

The theory "Build it, and they will come" has repeatedly been disproved when it applies to Web sites. Purchasing an online business that has existing customers is a considerable advantage.

Improve Financing Opportunities

Banks and other financing sources are more likely to provide money to purchase or expand a business with strong potential and a proven customer base, as opposed to financing a riskier startup from scratch. A business plan for effectively managing the purchased Web site is a must for convincing financing sources to provide money.

4.4.2 Evaluating a Site's Potential

Buying an existing online business is basically the same as purchasing any other type of business: The buyer must do their homework and determine whether it really is a wise buy. Remember, a successful e-business is much more than just an attractive collection of Web pages. The site should be based on a viable business idea. In fact, it is wise to evaluate the business using the techniques such as the three-rings exercise and SWOT analysis, as detailed in Section 3.2.

The next step is to get as much information as possible from the current owner. Ask for detailed financial statements for as many years of operation as are available and analyze the trends. (Having the statements reviewed by a CPA is another smart idea.) Obviously, a buyer is looking for positive information from these documents (proving the site's ability to make money), but sometimes less-than-stellar financial statements contain hidden lumps of gold. For example, sites plagued by unreasonably high expenses in a category might be turned around by an owner with new ideas or resources that can quickly improve the bottom line by less expensive Web hosting options or a different approach to shipping products.

If the current owner has a business plan, ask to see it. Compare the financial projections to actual numbers. Inquire whether the owner followed their plan closely, and ask where they deviated. Sometimes owners fail to follow their own roadmaps for success, and solutions to existing problems are just waiting to be implemented by a new owner.

E-business in Action →
Evaluate an existing Web site.

PATHWAY TO... ASKING THE RIGHT QUESTIONS WHEN BUYING A WEB SITE

Several important questions should be asked—and answered—before buying an existing Web site. These include:

- Does the purchase include any existing inventory or customer contracts?
- What hardware and software, if any, are included with the sale?
- How many visitors does the site get each day? Ask to see records verifying the number of visitors and other statistics.
- What are the site's popularity rankings in all the major search engines? What, if anything, has the owner previously done to improve the rankings?
- If it is an information product or a service business, can the new owner easily acquire the skills and staff to duplicate it?

4.4.3 Risks of Buying an Existing Site

"Buyer beware" is the best advice for anybody shopping for an existing Web site. In addition to the questions noted in Section 4.4.2, it is essential to ask the current owner why they are selling the site. Some people have valid reasons that have little to do with the health of an e-business—everything from a lack of time (or money) to just being bored with the venture—while others may be trying to escape from a site that is clearly going nowhere. Furthermore, when paying someone for a Web site, make sure that that money is going to deliver something of value in return. For example, ask to see *current* customer records to ensure that the business has an active and committed core of buyers for its products and services. In some cases, digging deeper into a Web site's records will reveal that its true value is minimal. In addition, be on the alert for the following red flags listed in the following sections.

Dormant Sites

A site based on a sound idea and featuring beautiful pages may not be such a great deal if the current owner has suspended operations or even cut back on their activities. A Web site that stops selling products is like a store that closes its doors—customers quickly find other options, and getting them back can be difficult and expensive. Another issue for dormant sites is URL expiration. Ensure that the site's URL is valid and not in danger of lapsing; this is part of the value of an existing site.

Supplier Problems

Sometimes the problems plaguing a great-looking e-commerce site have nothing to do with the site itself, but rather with what it sells. A Web site selling a niche line of products is often dependent on a single supplier or a limited group of suppliers. Before purchasing an existing e-business, ask to talk to the suppliers and make sure the product is available and costs are manageable. Nobody wants to buy a site with nothing to sell, or for which they have to immediately increase prices.

Competition

In the online world, every great idea is almost guaranteed to spawn at least one competitor. Before buying a seemingly successful site, study the competition carefully and inquire to determine whether other new competitors are lurking on the horizon. The last thing an entrepreneur needs is to purchase an e-commerce site, only to discover that Amazon.com is about to launch a beta site selling the same niche products for much less.

Customer Issues

For better or worse, buying a Web site means inheriting its customers, which might also mean inheriting customer problems. A site with a history of poor service is going to have to work extra hard to convince dissatisfied customers that things have changed with new ownership. And how many active customers does the site really have? Ask to review a customer list that includes the buying history to ensure that it is not just a collection of names and addresses of people who purchased one item a few years ago and never came back.

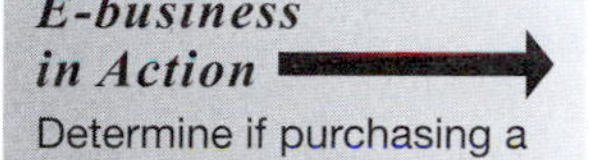

Determine if purchasing a Web site is preferable to starting a new one.

IN THE REAL WORLD

Dig Deep for the Online Dirt

Rob was tired of his corporate sales job and dreamed of running his own online business—a dream that looked attainable when he found a Web site for sale that sold sports collectibles—a passion of his. Cautious by nature, Rob contacted the owner and carefully studied the company and its financial records. He was generally impressed with the numbers, though concerned about a recent drop in revenues. The owner was evasive about the drop-off, explaining his time was consumed by other business ventures. Rob decided to dig a little deeper, visiting sports collector message boards and asking for feedback on the Web site. Rob was shocked to get several angry responses about poor customer service and even allegations of faked sports star autographs. Realizing that serious issues like those could devastate the site's reputation no matter who owned it, Rob wisely decided to keep his day job.

Finally, before buying an existing Web site, it is important to consider one more important question: Could a similar e-business be launched for less money than it would cost to purchase the site? If yes, it might be time to consider going back to the original plan of launching a new e-business from scratch.

SELF-CHECK

1. List four advantages of purchasing an existing Web site.
2. What documents should be obtained when evaluating a site? What specific information should you determine?
3. Why should the suppliers be investigated when considering the purchase of an e-commerce site?

Apply Your Knowledge You learn of a dormant Web site for sale at a bargain price; the pages are attractive and the business model appears sound. What are the major risks of buying this site? What information would you need to clearly evaluate the site's value?

SUMMARY

Section 4.1

- Starting an e-business takes money, and two components must be considered when calculating initial costs: money to cover equipment, fees, and anything else require to get started; and money to cover ongoing costs until the business generates revenue.
- Bootstrapping is an effective technique for launching a new business that basically requires doing as much as possible with minimal money.

Section 4.2

- In addition to personal savings, the most common sources of startup or growth financing for small businesses include friends and family, bank loans, angel investors, venture capitalists, and credit cards.

Section 4.3

- Employees who are hired should fulfill specific needs and be closely linked to an e-business's financial situation. There are other options to hiring employees, including utilizing freelance contractors.
- Hiring employees requires businesses to fulfill a variety of needs, including obtaining insurance coverage, offering benefits, filing appropriate tax forms, and withholding from employee paychecks.

Section 4.4

- Buying an existing Web site can provide a faster and less expensive entry into the e-business world and might be more attractive as a source of bank financing than starting a site from scratch.
- Web sites and their financial and customer records should be carefully evaluated before purchase. There are several risks associated with buying an existing site, including problems caused by dormancy, supplier issues, competition, and customer-related issues.

ASSESS YOUR UNDERSTANDING

UNDERSTAND: WHAT HAVE YOU LEARNED?

Go to **www.wiley.com/college/holden** to assess your knowledge of the basics of financing and launching an e-business.

APPLY: WHAT WOULD YOU DO?

1. Bootstrapping is an effective technique for starting an e-business on a tight budget. List five advantages of employing this strategy. What would be the disadvantages of bootstrapping a new business?
2. Saving money by keeping costs low can mean the difference between success and failure for a new venture. Suggest five specific ideas for saving money while launching an e-business. Research actual costs and estimate the total savings for each idea over one year.
3. You have told a friend with a great e-business idea that you would be willing to invest in his new firm. He says he's not comfortable taking money from family and friends. List five advantages of financing a business this way, and offer three suggestions for avoiding problems.
4. Your e-commerce site was successful in its first year of operation; however, you would like additional financing for expansion. You are intrigued by venture capital. Is it usually a good financing source for a small e-business? List five typical requirements for obtaining venture capital and explain.
5. You need help running an online business and your brother needs a job. He is a hard worker and the two of you get along, but he has no e-commerce experience. Discuss the advantages and disadvantages of hiring him. To what tools would you turn to help evaluate your hiring decision?
6. You are going to interview candidates for the first employee for your e-business. Write five interview questions that you would ask the candidates. What information would you ask the candidates to bring to the interview?
7. You are unsure whether you can afford insurance for your new e-business. What are risks you would face if you failed to purchase at least the basic business insurance package? What are the disadvantages of not offering insurance benefits to employees?
8. An acquaintance offers to sell you their existing e-commerce site for a very low price. Outline a five-point plan for evaluating the value of the site. Explain the key information you hope to obtain with each step.

BE AN E-BUSINESS ENTREPRENEUR

Calculating Startup Costs

Assume you are going to start a simple e-business from scratch, using no existing equipment or materials. Briefly describe the business, then do a rough calculation of startup costs, following the list provided in Section 4.1.1. Research costs that are realistic for the area in which you live. Be generous in your estimates and avoid cutting corners on any expenses.

Bootstrapping a Business

Using your completed exercise in the previous exercise, do a line-by-line review of the costs and suggest methods for reducing—or avoiding—the expenses listed. Be creative (but realistic). What percentage of savings were you able to realize? What other bootstrapping techniques could you employ to improve the financial status of your e-business during startup?

Evaluating Financing Sources

You determine that you need $100,000 to launch an e-business. List five financing sources that you can use in the order that you would use them. Estimate how much money you hope to obtain from each source. List the advantages, disadvantages, and requirements of each source. After reviewing your results, explain why you think it would be a realistic—or unrealistic—plan.

KEY TERMS

Angel investor An individual, often a retired entrepreneur, who is willing to invest money in a startup or young company.

Barter Paying for products and services by exchanging other products or services.

Bootstrapping Starting a business with minimal financial resources by working hard, doing without, and keeping costs low.

Business incubator An organization that supports entrepreneurial development by providing shared resources for businesses at reduced cost.

Capital The money that the owners invest in a business.

Freelance contractors	Self-employed workers hired under the terms of a contract to provide a service.
Grant	Monetary award that does not have to be repaid.
Umbrella policy	An extra layer of liability coverage in addition to the basic business insurance policies.
Venture capital	Financing provided by a specialized investment firm that operates with the expectation of high risk and high return on its investment.

REFERENCES

1. "SBA Success Story: Stroller Strides, LLC," U.S. Small Business Administration, www.sba.gov/idc/groups/public/documents/ca_san_diego/ca_sd_strollerstrides.pdf.

TOOLKIT

Form **W-9** (Rev. October 2007) Department of the Treasury Internal Revenue Service	**Request for Taxpayer Identification Number and Certification**	**Give form to the requester. Do not send to the IRS.**
Print or type See **Specific Instructions** on page 2.	Name (as shown on your income tax return)	
	Business name, if different from above	
	Check appropriate box: ☐ Individual/Sole proprietor ☐ Corporaton ☐ Partnership ☐ Limited liability company. Enter the tax classification (D=disregarded entity, C=corporation, P=partnership) ▶ ------- ☐ Other (see instructions) ▶	☐ Exempt payee
	Address (number, street, and apt. or suite no.)	Requester's name and address (optional)
	City, state, and ZIP code	
	List account number(s) here (optional)	

Part I Taxpayer Identification Number (TIN)

Enter your TIN in the appropriate box. The TIN provided must match the name given on Line 1 to avoid backup withholding. For individuals, this is your social security number (SSN). However, for a resident alien, sole proprietor, or disregarded entity, see the Part I instructions on page 3. For other entities, it is your employer identification number (EIN). If you do not have a number, see *How to get a TIN* on page 3.

Social security number
or
Employer identification number

Note. If the account is in more than one name, see the chart on page 4 for guidelines on whose number to enter.

Part II Certification

Under penalties of perjury, I certify that:

1. The number shown on this form is my correct taxpayer identification number (or I am waiting for a number to be issued to me), and
2. I am not subject to backup withholding because: (a) I am exempt from backup withholding, or (b) I have not been notified by the Internal Revenue Service (IRS) that I am subject to backup withholding as a result of a failure to report all interest or dividends, or (c) the IRS has notified me that I am no longer subject to backup withholding, and
3. I am a U.S. citizen or other U.S. person (defined below).

Certification instructions. You must cross out item 2 above if you have been notified by the IRS that you are currently subject to backup withholding because you have failed to report all interest and dividends on your tax return. For real estate transactions, item 2 does not apply. For mortgage interest paid, acquisition or abandonment of secured property, cancellation of debt, contributions to an individual retirement arrangement (IRA), and generally, payments other than interest and dividends, you are not required to sign the Certification, but you must provide your correct TIN. See the instructions on page 4.

Sign Here	Signature of U.S. person ►	Date ►

General Instructions

Section references are to the Internal Revenue Code unless otherwise noted.

Purpose of Form

A person who is required to file an information return with the IRS must obtain your correct taxpayer identification number (TIN) to report, for example, income paid to you, real estate transactions, mortgage interest you paid, acquisition or abandonment of secured property, cancellation of debt, or contributions you made to an IRA.

Use Form W-9 only if you are a U.S. person (including a resident alien), to provide your correct TIN to the person requesting it (the requester) and, when applicable, to:

1. Certify that the TIN you are giving is correct (or you are waiting for a number to be issued),
2. Certify that you are not subject to backup withholding, or
3. Claim exemption from backup withholding if you are a U.S. exempt payee. If applicable, you are also certifying that as a U.S. person, your allocable share of any partnership income from a U.S. trade or business is not subject to the withholding tax on foreign partners' share of effectively connected income.

Note. If a requester gives you a form other than Form W-9 to request your TIN, you must use the requester's form if it is substantially similar to this Form W-9.

Definition of a U.S. person. For federal tax purposes, you are considered a U.S. person if you are:

- An individual who is a U.S. citizen or U.S. resident alien,
- A partnership, corporation, company, or association created or organized in the United States or under the laws of the United States,
- An estate (other than a foreign estate), or
- A domestic trust (as defined in Regulations section 301.7701-7).

Special rules for partnerships. Partnerships that conduct a trade or business in the United States are generally required to pay a withholding tax on any foreign partners' share of income from such business. Further, in certain cases where a Form W-9 has not been received, a partnership is required to presume that a partner is a foreign person, and pay the withholding tax. Therefore, if you are a U.S. person that is a partner in a partnership conducting a trade or business in the United States, provide Form W-9 to the partnership to establish your U.S. status and avoid withholding on your share of partnership income.

The person who gives Form W-9 to the partnership for purposes of establishing its U.S. status and avoiding withholding on its allocable share of net income from the partnership conducting a trade or business in the United States is in the following cases:

- The U.S. owner of a disregarded entity and not the entity,

- The U.S. grantor or other owner of a grantor trust and not the trust, and
- The U.S. trust (other than a grantor trust) and not the beneficiaries of the trust.

Foreign person. If you are a foreign person, do not use Form W-9. Instead, use the appropriate Form W-8 (see Publication 515, Withholding of Tax on Nonresident Aliens and Foreign Entities).

Nonresident alien who becomes a resident alien. Generally, only a nonresident alien individual may use the terms of a tax treaty to reduce or eliminate U.S. tax on certain types of income. However, most tax treaties contain a provision known as a "saving clause." Exceptions specified in the saving clause may permit an exemption from tax to continue for certain types of income even after the payee has otherwise become a U.S. resident alien for tax purposes.

If you are a U.S. resident alien who is relying on an exception contained in the saving clause of a tax treaty to claim an exemption from U.S. tax on certain types of income, you must attach a statement to Form W-9 that specifies the following five items:

1. The treaty country. Generally, this must be the same treaty under which you claimed exemption from tax as a nonresident alien.
2. The treaty article addressing the income.
3. The article number (or location) in the tax treaty that contains the saving clause and its exceptions.
4. The type and amount of income that qualifies for the exemption from tax.
5. Sufficient facts to justify the exemption from tax under the terms of the treaty article.

Example. Article 20 of the U.S.-China income tax treaty allows an exemption from tax for scholarship income received by a Chinese student temporarily present in the United States. Under U.S. law, this student will become a resident alien for tax purposes if his or her stay in the United States exceeds 5 calendar years. However, paragraph 2 of the first Protocol to the U.S.-China treaty (dated April 30, 1984) allows the provisions of Article 20 to continue to apply even after the Chinese student becomes a resident alien of the United States. A Chinese student who qualifies for this exception (under paragraph 2 of the first protocol) and is relying on this exception to claim an exemption from tax on his or her scholarship or fellowship income would attach to Form W-9 a statement that includes the information described above to support that exemption.

If you are a nonresident alien or a foreign entity not subject to backup withholding, give the requester the appropriate completed Form W-8.

What is backup withholding? Persons making certain payments to you must under certain conditions withhold and pay to the IRS 28% of such payments. This is called "backup withholding." Payments that may be subject to backup withholding include interest, tax-exempt interest, dividends, broker and barter exchange transactions, rents, royalties, nonemployee pay, and certain payments from fishing boat operators. Real estate transactions are not subject to backup withholding.

You will not be subject to backup withholding on payments you receive if you give the requester your correct TIN, make the proper certifications, and report all your taxable interest and dividends on your tax return.

Payments you receive will be subject to backup withholding if:

1. You do not furnish your TIN to the requester,
2. You do not certify your TIN when required (see the Part II instructions on page 3 for details),
3. The IRS tells the requester that you furnished an incorrect TIN,
4. The IRS tells you that you are subject to backup withholding because you did not report all your interest and dividends on your tax return (for reportable interest and dividends only), or

5. You do not certify to the requester that you are not subject to backup withholding under 4 above (for reportable interest and dividend accounts opened after 1983 only).

Certain payees and payments are exempt from backup withholding. See the instructions below and the separate Instructions for the Requester of Form W-9.

Also see *Special rules for partnerships* on page 1.

Penalties

Failure to furnish TIN. If you fail to furnish your correct TIN to a requester, you are subject to a penalty of $50 for each such failure unless your failure is due to reasonable cause and not to willful neglect.

Civil penalty for false information with respect to withholding. If you make a false statement with no reasonable basis that results in no backup withholding, you are subject to a $500 penalty.

Criminal penalty for falsifying information. Willfully falsifying certifications or affirmations may subject you to criminal penalties including fines and/or imprisonment.

Misuse of TINs. If the requester discloses or uses TINs in violation of federal law, the requester may be subject to civil and criminal penalties.

SPECIFIC INSTRUCTIONS

Name

If you are an individual, you must generally enter the name shown on your income tax return. However, if you have changed your last name, for instance, due to marriage without informing the Social Security Administration of the name change, enter your first name, the last name shown on your social security card, and your new last name.

If the account is in joint names, list first, and then circle, the name of the person or entity whose number you entered in Part I of the form.

Sole proprietor. Enter your individual name as shown on your income tax return on the "Name" line. You may enter your business, trade, or "doing business as (DBA)" name on the "Business name" line.

Limited liability company (LLC). Check the "Limited liability company" box only and enter the appropriate code for the tax classification ("D" for disregarded entity, "C" for corporation, "P" for partnership) in the space provided.

For a single-member LLC (including a foreign LLC with a domestic owner) that is disregarded as an entity separate from its owner under Regulations section 301.7701-3, enter the owner's name on the "Name" line. Enter the LLC's name on the "Business name" line.

For an LLC classified as a partnership or a corporation, enter the LLC's name on the "Name" line and any business, trade, or DBA name on the "Business name" line.

Other entities. Enter your business name as shown on required federal tax documents on the "Name" line. This name should match the name shown on the charter or other legal document creating the entity. You may enter any business, trade, or DBA name on the "Business name" line.

Note. You are requested to check the appropriate box for your status (individual/sole proprietor, corporation, etc.).

Exempt Payee

If you are exempt from backup withholding, enter your name as described above and check the appropriate box for your status, then check the "Exempt payee" box in the line following the business name, sign and date the form.

Generally, individuals (including sole proprietors) are not exempt from backup withholding. Corporations are exempt from backup withholding for certain payments, such as interest and dividends.

Note. If you are exempt from backup withholding, you should still complete this form to avoid possible erroneous backup withholding.

The following payees are exempt from backup withholding:

1. An organization exempt from tax under section 501(a), any IRA, or a custodial account under section 403(b)(7) if the account satisfies the requirements of section 401(f)(2),
2. The United States or any of its agencies or instrumentalities,
3. A state, the District of Columbia, a possession of the United States, or any of their political subdivisions or instrumentalities,
4. A foreign government or any of its political subdivisions, agencies, or instrumentalities, or
5. An international organization or any of its agencies or instrumentalities.

Other payees that may be exempt from backup withholding include:

6. A corporation,
7. A foreign central bank of issue,
8. A dealer in securities or commodities required to register in the United States, the District of Columbia, or a possession of the United States,
9. A futures commission merchant registered with the Commodity Futures Trading Commission,
10. A real estate investment trust,
11. An entity registered at all times during the tax year under the Investment Company Act of 1940,
12. A common trust fund operated by a bank under section 584(a),
13. A financial institution,
14. A middleman known in the investment community as a nominee or custodian, or
15. A trust exempt from tax under section 664 or described in section 4947.

The chart below shows types of payments that may be exempt from backup withholding. The chart applies to the exempt payees listed above, 1 through 15.

IF the payment is for . . .	THEN the payment is exempt for . . .
Interest and dividend payments	All exempt payees except for 9
Broker transactions	Exempt payees 1 through 13. Also, a person registered under the Investment Advisers Act of 1940 who regularly acts as a broker
Barter exchange transactions and patronage dividends	Exempt payees 1 through 5
Payments over $600 required to be reported and direct sales over $5,000[1]	Generally, exempt payees 1 through 7[2]

[1]See Form 1099-MISC, Miscellaneous Income, and its instructions.

[2]However, the following payments made to a corporation (including gross proceeds paid to an attorney under section 6045(f), even if the attorney is a corporation) and reportable on Form 1099-MISC are not exempt from backup withholding: medical and health care payments, attorneys' fees, and payments for services paid by a federal executive agency.

Part I. Taxpayer Identification Number (TIN)

Enter your TIN in the appropriate box. If you are a resident alien and you do not have and are not eligible to get an SSN, your TIN is your IRS individual taxpayer identification number (ITIN). Enter it in the social security number box. If you do not have an ITIN, see *How to get a TIN* below.

If you are a sole proprietor and you have an EIN, you may enter either your SSN or EIN. However, the IRS prefers that you use your SSN.

If you are a single-member LLC that is disregarded as an entity separate from its owner (see *Limited liability* company (*LLC*) on page 2), enter the owner's SSN (or EIN, if the owner has one). Do not enter the disregarded entity's EIN. If the LLC is classified as a corporation or partnership, enter the entity's EIN.

Note. See the chart on page 4 for further clarification of name and TIN combinations.

How to get a TIN. If you do not have a TIN, apply for one immediately. To apply for an SSN, get Form SS-5, Application for a Social Security Card, from your local Social Security Administration office or get this form online at www.ssa.gov. You may also get this form by calling 1-800-772-1213. Use Form W-7, Application for IRS Individual Taxpayer Identification Number, to apply for an ITIN, or Form SS-4, Application for Employer Identification Number, to apply for an EIN. You can apply for an EIN online by accessing the IRS website at *www.irs.gov/businesses* and clicking on Employer Identification Number (EIN) under Starting a Business. You can get Forms W-7 and SS-4 from the IRS by visiting *www.irs.gov* or by calling 1-800-TAX-FORM (1-800-829-3676).

If you are asked to complete Form W-9 but do not have a TIN, write "Applied For" in the space for the TIN, sign and date the form, and give it to the requester. For interest and dividend payments, and certain payments made with respect to readily tradable instruments, generally you will have 60 days to get a TIN and give it to the requester before you are subject to backup withholding on payments. The 60-day rule does not apply to other types of payments. You will be subject to backup withholding on all such payments until you provide your TIN to the requester.

Note. Entering "Applied For" means that you have already applied for a TIN or that you intend to apply for one soon.

Caution: *A disregarded domestic entity that has a foreign owner must use the appropriate Form W-8.*

Part II. Certification

To establish to the withholding agent that you are a U.S. person, or resident alien, sign Form W-9. You may be requested to sign by the withholding agent even if items 1, 4, and 5 below indicate otherwise.

For a joint account, only the person whose TIN is shown in Part I should sign (when required). Exempt payees, see Exempt Payee on page 2.

Signature requirements. Complete the certification as indicated in 1 through 5 below.

1. **Interest, dividend, and barter exchange accounts opened before 1984 and broker accounts considered active during 1983.** You must give your correct TIN, but you do not have to sign the certification.
2. **Interest, dividend, broker, and barter exchange accounts opened after 1983 and broker accounts considered inactive during 1983.** You must sign the certification or backup withholding will apply. If you are subject to backup withholding and you are merely providing your correct TIN to the requester, you must cross out item 2 in the certification before signing the form.
3. **Real estate transactions.** You must sign the certification. You may cross out item 2 of the certification.
4. **Other payments.** You must give your correct TIN, but you do not have to sign the certification unless you have been notified that you have previously given an incorrect TIN. "Other payments" include payments made in the course of the requester's trade or business for rents, royalties, goods (other than bills for merchandise), medical and health care services (including payments to corporations), payments to a nonemployee for services, payments to certain fishing boat crew members and fishermen, and gross proceeds paid to attorneys (including payments to corporations).
5. **Mortgage interest paid by you, acquisition or abandonment of secured property, cancellation of debt, qualified tuition program payments (under section 529), IRA, Coverdell ESA, Archer MSA or HSA contributions or distributions, and pension distributions.** You must give your correct TIN, but you do not have to sign the certification.

What Name and Number To Give the Requester	
For this type of account:	**Give name and SSN of:**
1. Individual	The individual
2. Two or more individuals (joint account)	The actual owner of the account or, if combined funds, the first individual on the account[1]
3. Custodian account of a minor (Uniform Gift to Minors Act)	The minor[2]
4. a. The usual revocable savings trust (grantor is also trustee)	The grantor-trustee[1]
b. So-called trust account that is not a legal or valid trust under state law	The actual owner[1]
5. Sole proprietorship or disregarded entity owned by an individual	The owner[3]
For this type of account:	**Give name and EIN of:**
6. Disregarded entity not owned by an individual	The owner
7. A valid trust, estate, or pension trust	Legal entity[4]
8. Corporate or LLC electing corporate status on Form 8832	The corporation
9. Association, club, religious, charitable, educational, or other tax-exempt organization	The organization
10. Partnership or multi-member LLC	The partnership
11. A broker or registered nominee	The broker or nominee
12. Account with the Department of Agriculture in the name of a public entity (such as a state or local government, school district, or prison) that receives agricultural program payments	The public entity

[1]List first and circle the name of the person whose number you furnish. If only one person on a joint account has an SSN, that person's number must be furnished.

[2]Circle the minor's name and furnish the minor's SSN.

[3]You must show your individual name and you may also enter your business or "DBA" name on the second name line. You may use either your SSN or EIN (if you have one), but the IRS encourages you to use your SSN.

[4]List first and circle the name of the trust, estate, or pension trust. (Do not furnish the TIN of the personal representative or trustee unless the legal entity itself is not designated in the account title.) Also see Special rules for partnerships on page 1.

Note. If no name is circled when more than one name is listed, the number will be considered to be that of the first name listed.

Secure Your Tax Records from Identity Theft

Identity theft occurs when someone uses your personal information such as your name, social security number (SSN), or other identifying information, without your permission, to commit fraud or other crimes. An identity thief may use your SSN to get a job or may file a tax return using your SSN to receive a refund.

To reduce your risk:

- Protect your SSN,
- Ensure your employer is protecting your SSN, and
- Be careful when choosing a tax preparer.

Call the IRS at 1-800-829-1040 if you think your identity has been used inappropriately for tax purposes.

Victims of identity theft who are experiencing economic harm or a system problem, or are seeking help in resolving tax problems that have not been resolved through normal channels, may be eligible for Taxpayer Advocate Service (TAS) assistance. You can reach TAS by calling the TAS toll-free case intake line at 1-877-777-4778 or TTY/TDD 1-800-829-4059.

Protect yourself from suspicious emails or phishing schemes. Phishing is the creation and use of email and websites designed to mimic legitimate business emails and websites. The most common act is sending an email to a user falsely claiming to be an established legitimate enterprise in an attempt to scam the user into surrendering private information that will be used for identity theft.

The IRS does not initiate contacts with taxpayers via emails. Also, the IRS does not request personal detailed information through email or ask taxpayers for the PIN numbers, passwords, or similar secret access information for their credit card, bank, or other financial accounts.

If you receive an unsolicited email claiming to be from the IRS, forward this message to phishing@irs.gov. You may also report misuse of the IRS name, logo, or other IRS personal property to the Treasury Inspector General for Tax Administration at 1-800-366-4484. You can forward suspicious emails to the Federal Trade Commission at: spam@uce.gov or contact them at *www.consumer.gov/idtheft* or 1-877-IDTHEFT(438-4338).

Visit the IRS website at *www.irs.gov* to learn more about identity theft and how to reduce your risk.

Privacy Act Notice

Section 6109 of the Internal Revenue Code requires you to provide your correct TIN to persons who must file information returns with the IRS to report interest, dividends, and certain other income paid to you, mortgage interest you paid, the acquisition or abandonment of secured property, cancellation of debt, or contributions you made to an IRA, or Archer MSA or HSA. The IRS uses the numbers for identification purposes and to help verify the accuracy of your tax return. The IRS may also provide this information to the Department of Justice for civil and criminal litigation, and to cities, states, the District of Columbia, and U.S. possessions to carry out their tax laws. We may also disclose this information to other countries under a tax treaty, to federal and state agencies to enforce federal nontax criminal laws, or to federal law enforcement and intelligence agencies to combat terrorism.

You must provide your TIN whether or not you are required to file a tax return. Payers must generally withhold 28% of taxable interest, dividend, and certain other payments to a payee who does not give a TIN to a payer. Certain penalties may also apply.

CHAPTER

5 ACCOUNTING AND TAXES

Keeping Track of an E-business's Numbers and Giving the Government Its Fair Share

Do You Already Know?

- The two most common accounting options are tax year and accounting method
- The legal form of a business affects how it must manage income taxes
- Which employment taxes e-businesses must pay
- How outside professionals can help with accounting and taxes

For additional questions to assess your current knowledge on accounting and taxes for e-businesses, go to **www.wiley.com/college/holden.**

What You Will Find Out	What You Will Be Able To Do
5.1 The options for tax year and accounting method and how to read basic financial statements	• Select a tax year and accounting method; understand balance sheets and income statements
5.2 How each of the common legal forms must manage federal income taxes	• Correctly file and pay federal income taxes for your business's legal form
5.3 Which employment and sales taxes e-businesses might be required to pay	• Withhold and pay taxes on behalf of your employees and determine when to collect sales tax from customers
5.4 That outside professionals can provide essential support for accounting and tax issues	• Identify needs that can be fulfilled by outside professionals and select ones that are a good match for your e-business

INTRODUCTION

Before an e-business starts up, the owner must make some important accounting-related decisions about the company. This chapter's first section offers guidance on this topic, plus provides an overview of how to read the basic financial statements that are important tools for managing a business. Taxes—paying them, collecting them, and staying within the guidelines of the law—deservedly command a lot of attention from small businesses. The second section explains how the legal form of a business affects its federal income tax obligations, how the taxes are paid, and who must pay them. The third section is devoted to employment and sales taxes. Firms with employees must withhold and pay on behalf of their employees a variety of taxes; self-employed individuals have their own requirements. Sales tax must be collected on some transactions, but not all. The fourth section discusses an important resource for e-business—tax and accounting professionals. CPAs, bookkeepers, and other professionals can help keep finances in order as well as provide priceless advice on the complicated world of taxes.

5.1 THE BASICS OF E-BUSINESS ACCOUNTING

Many entrepreneurs freely admit that accounting is not their favorite activity, though some elements of it can be very enjoyable. For example, at the end of every month, there is an opportunity to look at the income statement to see how well a business is doing—on paper, at least. This process is like getting a checkup and viewing a summary of every activity performed during the month, as it relates to the business's bottom line. If all is well, it might be time to pause for a brief celebration before plugging forward along the same path. But if there are problems, an income statement is bound to expose a firm's points of weakness.

Interpreting income statements and other financial statements is just part of the accounting puzzle that new e-business owners must solve. Running a business does not require a degree in accounting—or even any formal training in that field—but there are certain issues with which an entrepreneur should become familiar. In addition, there are some important accounting-related decisions that must be made before startup, which are addressed in the following sections. Fortunately, there are resources, from easy-to-use software packages to accounting professionals, to which e-business owners can turn to help them manage their numbers—and associated tax responsibilities.

Tax year: The defined accounting period used for evaluating a business's financial status and for filing taxes with the Internal Revenue Service.

5.1.1 Tax Year

When starting a new e-business, one of the first things that must be done is to select a **tax year,** the defined accounting period used to provide an annual snapshot of a business's financial status and for filing taxes with the Internal Revenue Service. There are two common options for defining the tax year: the calendar year and the fiscal year.

Calendar Year

This method is defined by that calendar hanging on the wall. The 12 months that are encompassed by this tax year start January 1 and end December 31. A **calendar-year** accounting system follows a month-to-month pattern and then starts all over again on the next January 1.

Calendar year: An accounting schedule using a 12-month period ending on December 31.

Fiscal Year

Although this type of tax year also has a fixed 12-month period, it never ends on the last day of December—any other month, but not that one. For example, a firm could choose to have its tax year run from October 1 to September 30 of the following year. Why adopt this method? For some seasonal businesses, a **fiscal year** provides an opportunity to adapt their accounting and tax schedules to their operational schedule. If the peak sales season is at the end of the year (which is the case for many e-businesses with heavy emphasis on Christmas gift sales), worrying about reporting or paying taxes at the same time can be burdensome.

Fiscal year: An accounting schedule using a 12-month period closing at the end of any month other than December.

Which to Choose?

A calendar year is probably the easiest reporting method to adopt, and a firm does not need IRS approval for this choice at startup. That noted, IRS rules generally require entities whose earnings pass through to shareholders—including partnerships, LLCs, and S corporations—to adopt a calendar year. If a business organized in one of these forms has good reason to think that the calendar year is a problem, or if it is a C corporation or sole proprietorship and simply wants to switch to a different accounting period, the firm must file a request (Form 1128, *Application to Adopt, Retain, or Change a Tax Year*) with the IRS. Unless an IRS code provides for automatic approval, be prepared to pay a filing fee for the change request.

E-business in Action →
Select a tax year.

5.1.2 Accounting Methods

The next decision for a new e-business is to choose the accounting method that will be used to calculate income and expenses. Similar to choosing a tax year, the accounting method must be selected before startup, and the decision does not require IRS approval. And though there are just two commonly used options, IRS rules require certain types of businesses to choose one method or another. And like changing the tax year, it is possible to change the accounting method after startup, but the IRS must provide approval for the change. The two commonly used options are cash basis accounting and accrual basis accounting.

Cash Basis Accounting

Cash basis:
An accounting method that reports income when it is received and expenses when they are incurred.

This is the simplest accounting method, and because of that, many e-businesses choose this system. **Cash basis** accounting requires reporting earnings when they are received (as cash) and reporting expenses when they are incurred. If a check is received, it is noted as income the day it arrives in the mail, even if it is not deposited immediately. If that check subsequently bounces, the income is erased from the books unless the bank eventually pays for it.

The IRS says that a business cannot use the cash method if any of these conditions applies:

- The business is a C corporation with average annual gross receipts of more than $5 million.
- The business is a partnership that has a corporation (other than an S corporation) as a partner, and the partnership has average annual gross receipts of more than $5 million.
- The business is a tax shelter.
- The business has inventory.

Accrual Basis

Accrual basis:
An accounting method that reports income when it is earned (rather than received) and expenses when they are incurred (rather than paid).

In **accrual basis** accounting, revenues are reported when they are earned, rather than when the money (cash) is received. Likewise, expenses are reported as the date owed, as opposed to the date on which they are paid. If a business manufactures items or maintains inventory, accrual basis accounting is considered the best way to provide an accurate picture of financial status from year to year.

The rule that a business with inventory must use accrual basis accounting has some exceptions. A business can use another method if:

- The business is a qualifying taxpayer that passes the gross receipt test (with less than $1 million in gross sales for each year of the test period).
- The business is not a tax shelter.
- The firm is a qualifying small-business taxpayer that passes the gross receipt test (with less than $10 million in average annual gross receipts for each year of the test period).

- The business is not prohibited from using the cash method.
- The firm is an eligible business as determined by the IRS.

The Role of the IRS

IRS rules require businesses to choose an accounting method from two options: (1) cash basis or (2) accrual basis. With IRS approval, a business may change methods after startup. The rules governing accounting methods are somewhat vague and have many exceptions. The best advice is to check with a CPA to determine which accounting method is both allowable and appropriate for a given e-business.

E-business in Action →
Select an accounting method.

5.1.3 The Balance Sheet

No matter which accounting method they use, an e-business's owners and key managers need to know how to make sense of their firm's financial statements. The **balance sheet** is a detailed summary of a business's financial status at a fixed point in time. Most firms create a balance sheet at the end of the tax year (December 31 for those on a calendar year schedule), though it is also common to create and evaluate them more frequently, for example quarterly or monthly.

Balance sheet:
A detailed summary of a business's financial status at a fixed point in time.

A balance sheet is divided into three parts: assets, liabilities, and owner's equity. Furthermore, the balance sheet always balances and is governed by the following equation:

$$\text{Assets} = \text{Liabilities} + \text{Owner's Equity}$$

FOR EXAMPLE
See Figure 5-1 for a sample balance sheet.

To offer a better understanding of the balance sheet, these terms need to be defined and further explained.

Assets

The **assets** are everything of value that a business owns. Assets typically include the following.

Assets:
Everything of value that a business owns.

- **Cash:** Available money in bank accounts
- **Accounts receivable (A/R):** What customers owe a business
- **Inventory:** The monetary worth of whatever merchandise is on hand
- **Fixed assets:** Land, buildings, furniture, and equipment
- **Miscellaneous:** A catchall term for anything that doesn't fit into any other category

Liabilities

The **liabilities** represent all the debts of a business. Liabilities can include the following:

Liabilities:
All the debts of a business.

Figure 5-1

Balance Sheet
Ending December 31, 2005

	2005
ASSETS	
Current Assets	
Cash	$2,500
Accounts receivable	2,800
Inventory	5,500
Total Current Assets	**$10,800**
Fixed Assets	
Buildings	$ 0
Land	0
Furniture and fixtures	1,200
Equipment	7,000
Accum. depreciation	(200)
Miscellaneous	0
Total Fixed Assets	**$8,000**
TOTAL ASSETS	**$18,800**
LIABILITIES AND SHAREHOLDERS' EQUITY	
Liabilities	
Accounts payable	$3,300
Taxes payable	500
TOTAL LIABILITIES	**$3,800**
Net Worth	15,000
TOTAL LIABILITIES & NET WORTH	**$18,800**

A sample balance sheet.

- **Accounts payable (A/P):** What you owe suppliers, vendors, or credit card companies
- **Accrued expenses:** Wages, payroll taxes, and taxes that have been collected but not yet paid
- **Long-term liabilities:** Notes payable to shareholders and the portion of long-term debt (such as bank loans) that is not yet due

Owner's Equity

Owner's equity: The amount of claim the owner(s) can make against the assets of the company.

This is also called net worth or capital. **Owner's equity** represents the amount of claim the owner(s) can make against the assets of the company, or how much they have invested in their company.

E-business in Action
Understand a balance sheet.

When evaluating a balance sheet, it is important to remember the balance sheet equation. Because this statement must always balance, changes in one category must be offset by an appropriate amount in another category. To get a better idea of what a balance sheet should look like, consider the sample shown in Figure 5-1. The total assets are $18,800, the total liabilities are $3,800, and the owner's equity is $15,000. Add the latter two numbers together and the total is $18,800—the balance sheet balances.

5.1.4 The Income Statement

Income statement: A financial statement that summarizes the changes in a firm's financial position over a specified period of time.

Unlike a balance sheet, which looks at a firm's finances at a specific point in time, an **income statement** looks at changes in a firm's financial position over a specified period of time. It provides a quick snapshot of a business's revenues and expenses and provides a measure of how much profit was made, or loss incurred, over that period.

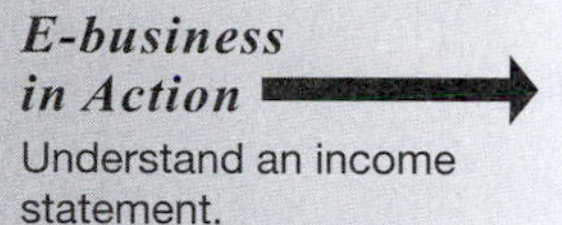
E-business
in Action
Understand an income statement.

Income statements can be created on almost any schedule, but a monthly frequency is probably most useful. That span of time allows managers to quickly spot any unusual fluctuations in sales or expenses and take appropriate action before the problem has become a very expensive one.

Figure 5-2 shows what an income statement looks like.

Figure 5-2

Income Statement (P&L)
For month ended July 31, 2006

			07/31/06
Income:			
Gross Sales:			$9,115.00
Less Returns			(0.00)
Less Other Discounts			(0.00)
NET Sales			$9,115.00
Cost of Goods Sold:			
Beginning Inventory		$500.00	
Add:	Purchases	250.00	
	Freight	50.00	
Cost of Goods Available			800.00
Less:	Ending Inventory	(400.00)	
Cost of Goods Sold			–(400.00)
			$8,715.00

(continued)

Figure 5-2 *(continued)*

Gross Profit (Less)		
Expenses:		
Advertising	150.00	
Amortization		
Bad Debts		
Bank Charges	50.00	
Commissions		
Credit Card Fees	55.00	
Depreciation		
Dues, Subscriptions (Books)	15.00	
Insurance	145.00	
Interest		
Loans		
Maintenance		
Miscellaneous	40.00	
Office Expenses—General	137.28	
Operating Supplies	124.56	
Payroll (Wages & Taxes)	2,800.00	
Permits and Licenses		
Postage	95.00	
Professional Fees	275.00	
Property Taxes		
Rent	650.00	
Telephone		
Landline	289.00	
Cell	150.00	
Training/Workshops	20.00	
Travel		
Utilities	280.00	
Vehicle Expense		
Gas/Mileage	42.14	
Maintenance		
Web Site Fees	355.00	
Total Expenses		5,672.98
Net Operating Income:		3,042.02
Other Income:	0	
***NET INCOME (LOSS):**		**$3,042.02**
*This is pre-tax income.		

A sample income statement.

There are four primary categories on the sample income statement:

- Income
- Cost of goods sold
- Operating expenses
- Net income (loss)

Income

Income:
The sales a business makes during a period.

Sometimes referred to as revenue, **income** represents the sales a business makes during a period. When listed on the income statement, income is adjusted by returns and discounts to determine the net sales.

Cost of Goods Sold

Cost of goods sold:
The cost of merchandise sold during a period.

Cost of goods sold is the cost of merchandise sold during the period. It is computed by first adding the value of the inventory at the beginning of the period to the value of any inventory purchases or shipping costs incurred during that period. Then, the final value of the inventory is subtracted to compute the cost of goods sold.

Operating Expenses

Operating expenses:
The administrative and selling expenses incurred over a period to deliver a product or a service.

Operating expenses include the administrative and selling expenses incurred over the period to deliver a product or a service. Figure 5-2 provides a comprehensive list of various costs that are recorded in this category.

Net income:
The excess income over expenses incurred during a period; also called profit.

Net loss:
When expenses are greater than income.

Net Income (Loss)

Net income is the excess income over expenses incurred during a period—in other words, the profit. If expenses are greater than income, then a business incurs a loss, which is called **net loss.** Calculating net income (or loss) is very simple:

Net income = Net sales – Cost of goods sold – Operating expenses

IN THE REAL WORLD

Using the Income Statement to Track Trends, Good and Bad

Neil's one-man online venture was an exciting experience, but his head was spinning. Admitting a weakness for numbers, he turned to his sister, an accountant, who helped him select and use a simple accounting software package. He entered the daily numbers religiously, but didn't know what to do with the information he accumulated. The next time his sister visited from out of state, she calculated the income statements for the previous few months and reviewed the trends with Neil. The results weren't all positive. While Neil's aggressive marketing efforts had built traffic to the site and sales, he was managing to pay his bills. As his sister quickly pointed out, the reasons why were displayed in black and white on the income statement: Revenues were up, but expenses (particularly advertising and shipping) were up even more. Neil needed to cut costs now or risk failing. Neil made the necessary changes, improved his net income, and started using the income statement to track monthly trends.

Think of the income statement as an essential tool for keeping track of a business; create and review one regularly. It can allow managers to catch mistakes (banking errors, double payment of invoices), identify positive and negative trends, and ensure that an e-business is staying on budget. The information provided can be used to make critical, timely decisions that ensure the success of a venture.

SELF-CHECK

1. What are the two common options for tax year? Do IRS rules require business firms to use one particular option?
2. Explain the difference between cash basis and accrual basis accounting.
3. What formula governs the balance sheet?
4. What are the four primary categories on the income statement?

Apply Your Knowledge In reviewing your firm's balance sheet, you note that cash has increased by $5,000 and accounts receivable by $2,000. Accounts payable has increased by $3,000. All other assets and liabilities remained the same. By what amount would the owner's equity have changed?

5.2 INCOME TAXES FOR E-BUSINESSES

Owners pay income tax on the money their business earns. Almost every type of company has to file an annual income tax return. (The exception is the partnership, which files only an information return.) The important thing to know is that federal income tax is a pay-as-you-go system—the IRS does not want to wait until the end of the year to get its cut of a firm's money. Instead, businesses must pay the amount of taxes that are due every quarter. Because a business does not always know the exact amount to pay in time to file by the IRS deadline (maybe an overdue invoice comes in at the last minute or a refund has to be issued), the tax can be estimated for each quarter and that amount paid.

A business's form of legal organization will have a significant impact on how its federal income taxes will be managed. The following sections detail the IRS requirements for the most common business forms.

5.2.1 Sole Proprietorships

As detailed in Section 2.1.1, a sole proprietorship is a business that is entirely owned by one person—in effect, the person and the business are the same entity. Because of this, the owner is responsible for paying all the business's income taxes, and, in fact, the business taxes are integrated into the owner's individual return. The profits and losses of the business are listed on the owner's personal tax return—Schedule C *Profit or Loss from—Business* and they must also pay a self-employment tax (see Section 5.3.2).

IN THE REAL WORLD

Avoid Using Credit Cards to Pay Income Taxes

A 2007 study by Visa USA revealed that the number of small businesses using credit cards to pay their income taxes had increased by 80 percent over the previous year. Many experts view this as a disturbing trend. Joe Astrachan, director of the Cox Family Enterprise Center at Kennesaw State University, says that the practice suggests small business managers "don't prepare for paying taxes." Instead of pulling out a credit card, it might actually be better to underpay or pay a little late. Why? Credit card interest rates are often higher than the penalties charged by the IRS for late payments. That noted, building a big debt with the IRS can devastate a small business. Possible results include tax liens and a damaged credit history. Ultimately, the best strategy is to plan ahead and budget appropriately for the quarterly IRS payments.[1]

5.2.2 Partnerships and LLCs

Pass-through entities: Legal forms (including partnerships, LLCs, and S corporations) in which income and losses are passed through to the owners, who pay the appropriate income taxes on their personal returns.

Partnerships and LLCs are **pass-through entities,** which means that their income and losses are passed through to their owners. The owners then report the income and losses and pay the appropriate income taxes on their personal returns. The amount of income and loss is proportional to the owner's stake in the business and is called a distributive share.

Even though partnerships and LLCs with multiple owners do not pay taxes directly, they must file Form 1065 *U.S. Return of Partnership Income* with the IRS. This form reports the pass-through amounts to the government. These same amounts are reported on Schedule K-1, which is given to each owner and serves as kind of a W-2 for partnerships.

Once the owners know their pass-through amounts, they can file their taxes. An LLC with a single owner manages its taxes in the same way as a

E-business in Action →
File and pay income taxes in the appropriate manner for your business form.

sole proprietorship, by reporting profits and losses on Schedule C. The owners of partnerships and LLCs with multiple owners report their distributive share of the profits and losses on Schedule E *Supplemental Income and Loss*, which is filed with their Form 1040.

5.2.3 Corporations

C corporations: A business entity that exists separately from owners; responsible for paying taxes and filing returns.

Unlike sole proprietorships, partnerships, and LLCs, **C corporations** exist separately from their owners and thus are responsible for paying their own taxes and filing their own returns. C corporations file Form 1120 *U.S. Corporation Income Tax Return*. Corporations are subjected to rather heavier taxes than other business forms. In recent years, the rate has been 15 percent on the first $50,000 of income, 25 percent on the next $25,000, 34 percent on the next $25,000, 39 percent on the next $100,000, and 34 percent on everything more than $335,000. In addition, shareholders must pay income tax on dividends paid out by the corporation.

S corporations: Like partnerships and LLCs, owners note profits and losses on Schedule E and pay income tax on those amounts.

S corporations are treated as pass-through entities. Like partnerships and LLCs, their owners note their distributive share of profits and losses on Schedule E and pay income tax on those amounts.

Table 5-1 lists the appropriate IRS form to submit when estimating taxes, along with many other forms required by the IRS, according to the type of organization.

Table 5-1 IRS Tax Forms Based on Business Type

Organization Type	*Potentially Liable For*	*Forms Required*
Sole Proprietor	Income tax	1040 and Schedule C1 or C-EZ (Schedule F1 for farm business
	Self-employment tax	1040 and Schedule SE
	Estimated tax	1040-ES
	Employment taxes: Social Security and Medicare taxes and income tax withholding	941 (943 for farm employees)
	Federal unemployment (FUTA) tax	940 or 940-EZ
	Depositing employment taxes	8109
Partnership	Annual return of income	1065
	Employment taxes	Same as sole proprietor
Partner in a partnership (individual)	Income tax	1040 and Schedule E
	Self-employment tax	1040 and Schedule SE
	Estimated tax	1040-ES

SELF-CHECK

1. When must businesses pay their taxes owed to the IRS?
2. How do sole proprietorships manage business income taxes?
3. Do C corporations and S corporations manage income taxes differently?

Apply Your Knowledge An e-business owner told you their business was a pass-through entity? What does this mean? What legal form might their business have? How does the business pay its income taxes?

5.3 EMPLOYMENT AND SALES TAXES

An e-business's tax responsibilities do not necessarily end with filing state and federal income tax returns. A business with employees has a variety of taxes for which it is responsible for withholding and paying to the government. Depending on the physical location of a business, taxes may need to be collected and paid to the city, county, and/or state for the goods and services it sells. Sections 5.3.1 through 5.3.4 examine the issues regarding these tax-paying responsibilities.

5.3.1 Employment Taxes

Whether an online business has just one employee (the owner) or a hundred employees, the business is responsible for paying taxes on behalf of those workers. This responsibility (and its associated paperwork filing) extends to both part-time and full-time workers. These obligations are commonly referred to as payroll taxes. A firm must file withholding forms and submit them with payment to both the IRS and the treasury department for the state in which it is located. The taxes paid on behalf of employees include:

- Federal and state income tax
- Social Security and Medicare taxes (FICA)
- Federal unemployment tax (FUTA)

Calculating the withholding amount can be complicated. Start with the information submitted by employees on a Form W-4 and calculate withholding amounts by using IRS publication 15 *Employers' Tax Guide* (Section 16). It is recommended to consult a **CPA** or **bookkeeper** with withholding experience for assistance in calculating the correct amounts.

Certified Public Accountant (CPA): An accountant that has completed specialized training, has passed exams, is certified, and is well versed in the latest tax laws.

Bookkeeper: A person who manages the recordkeeping activities for a small business, including recording receivables and payables, making deposits, managing payroll, and sending out tax forms.

Once the correct amounts have been withheld from employee paychecks, firms must pay these taxes every quarter. Note that while employees pay their full income tax bill, employees pay only half of what is owed for FICA and FUTA—the employer is responsible for paying the other half of this amount. The IRS requires businesses to file Form 941 *Employer's Quarterly Tax Return* by the last day of the month that follows the end of the quarter. In addition to providing payroll dates, the IRS Web site for small businesses (www.irs.gov/businesses/small/index.html) offers easy access to almost every other type of tax form, as well as an online learning center offering further education about a variety of tax and business startup issues.

There are exceptions to the rule of filing quarterly. A business with employment taxes of $1,000 or less (equal to annual earnings of $4,000 or less) may be eligible to submit payroll taxes annually. The best choice is to check with a CPA to confirm that taxes are being paid properly. The IRS can levy large penalties and interest on small businesses that fail to file their taxes correctly.

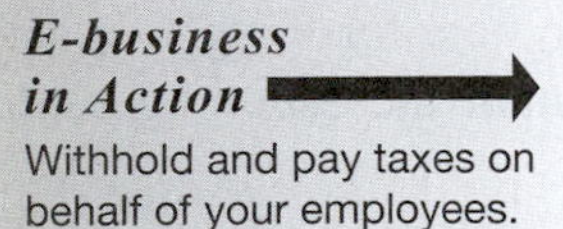

E-business
in Action
Withhold and pay taxes on behalf of your employees.

Electronic filing is an increasingly popular option and a logical choice for an online business. Although the process is fairly easy, some paperwork is involved, which will require some work well in advance of an e-business's start date. To get started with online payments, go to the IRS Web site for small businesses and follow the links to e-file. The necessary documents are Forms 940 and 941.

5.3.2 Self-Employment Taxes

One-person businesses may have an easier time than firms that must deal with the forms, withholding, and payment required for having employees, but that does not mean these sole proprietorships or single-person LLCs are exempt from paying employment taxes. In fact, they must calculate and make quarterly payments of estimated self-employment tax to the IRS in addition to their quarterly income tax payments. **Self-employment tax** is a combined Social Security and Medicare tax that is computed on Schedule SE of Form 1040. It is calculated as a percentage of earnings. As of the 2007 tax year, that amount was 15.3 percent (12.4 percent for Social Security and 2.9 percent for Medicare).

Self-employment tax: A combined Social Security and Medicare tax for self-employed individuals that is computed on Schedule SE of Form 1040.

Self-employed individuals should take special care when preparing their Form 1040. Even though they must calculate and add in self-employment tax on one part of the form, the tax laws currently allow them to deduct one half of this amount on a different part of the form.

FOR EXAMPLE

See the Toolkit for Schedule SE of Form 1040.

5.3.3 Sales Tax

Another e-business tax responsibility is tracking and collecting sales tax from customers and then submitting it to the appropriate state and local agencies. Currently, all states except Alaska, Delaware, Montana, New Hampshire, and Oregon collect sales tax. In addition, several thousand cities, counties, and other local governments also have sales tax in place.

Many e-business entrepreneurs (and consumers) think they can avoid sales tax because they are selling and buying things online. Although federal legislators are debating this issue, for now it comes down to this: A business that sells to people in any state where it has a physical presence (and sometimes that can be the tiniest remote office) must collect tax from customers originating from that same state. The same rule applies to local sales tax—sell a product or service online to a customer in the same city or county and the tax must be collected.

The other issue is that individual states are getting more aggressive about collecting sales tax from Internet-based companies. Yet, a lot of uncertainty remains about how this obligation will be resolved in each state. Maintain current information at both the state and federal levels, and consult with a CPA to stay updated. In addition, the Federation of Tax Administrators Web site has a direct link to the appropriate agency Web sites for each state. To access the site, go to www.taxadmin.org/fta/link/default.html.

Businesses should apply for and obtain a sales tax license before their Web sites go live. As with other types of taxes, most states now offer the option of filing and paying sales tax online, which makes the process quicker and less expensive.

IN THE REAL WORLD

Are Sales Tax Changes Looming?

A 2001 study by the University of Tennessee estimated that the 50 states could soon be losing $45 million per year in sales tax thanks to online purchases. State governments desperately want to get that money, but as of mid-2007 the U.S. Congress had not settled on a solution for the problem. Why not, especially when online retailing giant Amazon.com had stated that it was not opposed to collecting sales tax as long as the system implemented was fair? The problem is twofold: (1) defining "fair" and (2) making things simple. Roughly 7,500 cities, counties, states, and other government authorities collect sales tax. For the system to work, one tax would have to be collected and paid to one authority, which would distribute it to the rightful recipient. Until somebody figures out how to do this (at least one bill pending in Congress offers a solution), online retailers must fall back on the 1992 Supreme Court ruling that said states could require collecting sales tax only from customers in the same state that an e-business is physically located.[2]

5.3.4 Use and Excise Taxes

Use taxes:
Taxes imposed on goods purchased in another state that replaces sales tax that would have been paid if the goods had been purchased in the home state.

Excise taxes:
Taxes imposed on the manufacture, sale, and consumption of various consumer goods and services.

E-business in Action
Collect and pay sales tax when it is appropriate.

There are two other types of taxes that e-businesses might encounter: use taxes and excise taxes.

Use taxes apply to goods purchased in another state—in effect, the state is collecting sales tax that would have been paid if the company had purchased the goods in the home state. Generally a state charges the same rate for its use and sales taxes. Use taxes are commonly enforced more vigorously when a neighboring state has a lower sales tax rate. It is the purchaser's responsibility for filing and paying use tax; generally this can be done online.

Excise taxes are traditionally imposed on the manufacturer and distributor of certain consumer goods; gasoline taxes are a good example. Most e-businesses will only encounter excise taxes when paying their telephone or other communications bills. On the other hand, it is possible that some items sold online might require collection of federal or state excise taxes; the best bet is to research current tax laws and to check with an experienced CPA.

SELF-CHECK

1. What federal taxes must be withheld and paid by employers on behalf of their employees?
2. Under what circumstances would an e-business have to collect state sales tax from a customer?
3. What is the difference between sales and use tax?

Apply Your Knowledge A small business has withheld $71 in federal income tax, $36 in FICA, and $12 in FUTA from the paycheck of one of its employees. How much will be paid to the government on behalf of this worker?

5.4 PROFESSIONAL ACCOUNTING SUPPORT

Accounting and taxes are intimidating topics for inexperienced e-business owners. There are many ways to *not* address these issues. Some entrepreneurs assume that they can just wait until tax time and then have an accountant sort things out. That is often too late to correct serious and expensive problems. Others think they can simply invest in a quality accounting software package and religiously plug in their financial numbers. While accounting software is a great tool, it is not able to answer tough questions about ever-changing tax laws. For these reasons, new e-businesses should consider hiring outside help, even before their Web site goes live.

5.4.1 Accounting and Tax Professionals

An array of tax and accounting professionals are available, but four types are especially suited to meeting the needs of a small business:

- Certified Public Accountant (CPA)
- Enrolled agent
- Tax attorney
- Bookkeeper

Certified Public Accountant (CPA)

Certified Public Accountants, also known as CPAs, have specialized training in accounting, have passed a state-regulated exam, and are recognized by the IRS as a paid preparer for tax returns, meaning that they are authorized to represent a business if it is audited. A typical CPA fully understands accounting methods and is well versed in the latest tax regulations. Additionally, a CPA can legally conduct audits, whereas other accounting professionals cannot.

Enrolled Agent

This type of federally licensed professional understands both state and federal tax laws. In addition to completing an exam issued by the U.S. Department of Treasury, they must also pass a federal background check. An enrolled agent can also gain licensure after having worked for the IRS for at least five years. In the eyes of the IRS, an **enrolled agent** is licensed to prepare taxes, assist in long-term financial planning, and represent a business in the event of an audit.

Enrolled agent: A federally licensed accounting professional that can prepare taxes, assist in long-term financial planning, and represent a business in the event of an audit.

Tax attorney: An attorney who specializes in dealing with issues pertaining to tax law.

Tax Attorney

Most **tax attorneys** do not manage general accounting functions. Instead, they are hired specifically to deal with issues pertaining to the tax law—for example, to manage an IRS audit or to file corporate bankruptcy. Larger corporations might also keep a tax attorney on retainer or hire one in-house; small businesses are less likely to need the services of a tax attorney.

Bookkeeper

A bookkeeper can manage the basic recordkeeping activities for a small business, including making deposits, logging accounts receivable, handling accounts payables, managing payroll, and sending out tax forms, such as W-2s and 1099s. In addition, this person should be comfortable with creating monthly income statements and balance sheets. Bookkeepers have all levels of experience and education and are usually the most affordable form of outside help.

5.4.2 Putting Professionals to Work

Which of the professionals profiled in Section 5.4.1 are most appropriate for keeping an online business in good financial shape? Many small businesses greatly benefit from hiring a bookkeeper. Otherwise, the task of keeping up with bills, taxes, and the daily numbers often falls on the owner, who might already be managing many different jobs in the firm. Depending on their experience, a part-time bookkeeper or a bookkeeping service often can be hired for a fairly low hourly rate. A more experienced person or a full-time, in-house bookkeeper may demand a management-level salary, which might be an excessive investment for a new e-business.

In addition to having a bookkeeper manage the daily financial recordkeeping, it is important to establish a relationship with a CPA or an enrolled agent. This type of professional should be available right from the start to assist a new e-business with the following tasks:

- Set up an accounting system
- Offer advice on the firm's legal organization
- Compile and review financial statements
- Prepare and file taxes
- Assist in long-term financial planning for the business
- Address specific tax-law questions and concerns as they arise
- Ensure that the proper amounts and types of taxes are being filed
- Offer assistance in completing and submitting all quarterly tax documentation and other forms that might be required annually

E-business in Action
Identify needs that can be fulfilled by an outside professional.

Accounting and tax professionals typically charge an hourly rate, which will vary depending on their location, though some tasks (such as tax preparation) may follow a flat fee schedule. If the charges are hourly, clarify in advance for which tasks a business will be charged. For example, some professionals do not charge for questions asked and answered via email, and others do.

5.4.3 Finding and Selecting Professional Support

Accounting professionals can play an integral role in the operations of a small company by serving as trusted financial advisors and helping to

IN THE REAL WORLD

Peace of Mind from Accounting Professionals

Mike had been a midlevel corporate manager for 30 years and thought he had a good understanding of basic accounting. When he accepted an early retirement buyout, Mike used his newfound free time and money to launch a Web site selling the distinctive beer glasses he had been collecting for several years. Despite his business experience, Mike was quickly overwhelmed by the many responsibilities of the new venture and realized he did not know as much about small-business accounting and tax law as he thought. Fortunately, Mike acted quickly, setting up an appointment with a CPA recommended by a friend from his church. The accountant had previously worked with another small online business. He offered Mike considerable advice on his new venture, set him up with a bookkeeping service and accounting software, and kept track of his quarterly tax payments. Feeling secure that this aspect of the business was in good shape, Mike was able to focus on his Web site and marketing efforts.

ensure the success of the venture. It is important to take the time to find and select the best match for a new e-business. Fortunately, there are many places to turn to for help:

- **Referrals:** Ask business peers, friends, and family members whom they use or recommend. Ask for specific information about their experiences and the individual's training or expertise.
- **Local organizations:** Chambers of Commerce and other business associations often make their membership databases available to the public. Although the organizations typically do not endorse one member over another, they can suggest professionals that might be best suited for specific needs.
- **Professional associations:** Industry or professional groups are a terrific place to start a search for a CPA or other accounting professional. Options include: American Institute of Certified Public Accountants, www.aicpa.org; National Association for Enrolled Agents, www.naea.org; and American Association of Attorney-Certified Public Accountants, www.attorney-cpa.com.

After creating a short list of possible candidates, check for proper accreditations and check references. Then schedule a meeting with the candidate, during which several issues are explored.

Experience

Confirm that the person specializes in the appropriate areas of accounting or tax law. Ask what type of work now takes up the majority of the professional's time. Because definitive rules of taxation and the Internet are still somewhat up in the air, it may be difficult to find a professional who specializes in this area. Instead, look for someone who's eager and willing to stay informed on new issues and changes to the tax law.

Availability

A qualified professional often has a waiting list of clients, which might be a problem for a new business needing frequent and speedy assistance. Ask what the person's client schedule is like and ask to see a schedule of a typical workweek. Some eager young professionals make themselves available to answer questions seven days per week.

Firm Size

Size does matter, and sometimes a smaller firm is the better option. Small companies might find themselves at the bottom of the list when a large firm prioritizes its clients. A smaller firm or an independent professional may provide more dedicated attention and be available to answer questions.

Philosophy

Financial advisors are ultimately partners in business and their views should complement the owner's. For example, aggressive risk-taking firms may find that a conservative accountant holds them back—or they might need a conservative outlook as a system of checks and balances.

Work Style

How does the professional interact with clients? Is the professional comfortable simply providing guidance or insist on doing everything and thus billing for time spent? Is the professional comfortable casually answering questions via email or insist on scheduling a formal appointment? There is no correct style, but it is important to choose professionals whose personal style is a good match.

E-business in Action

Select a professional that is a good match to an e-business.

Integrity

Consider the moral values of a financial advisor when choosing a professional to support your business. To protect your company's interests, an accountant must adhere to a code of values. This may be hard to judge during a quick meeting, but trust your instincts to find someone trustworthy.

5.4.4 Accounting Software

In addition to hiring outside professionals, e-businesses will want to acquire tools to keep track of daily financial activities and create simple financial statements. A wide variety of accounting software packages has been developed to support the small-business market. When shopping for accounting software, remember that one size does not fit all. In fact, the choice of software will be determined in large part by a business's anticipated annual revenues and the number of employees it hires. Small e-business startups should focus on entry-level software, such as QuickBooks or Peachtree First Accounting, which generally provide all the functions that most firms will need.

The cost for over-the-counter, small-business accounting packages ranges from $40 to $400 for single users. The price fluctuation depends largely on these factors:

- **Brand:** As with most business products, the price is higher for widely recognized brands. QuickBooks and Microsoft Small Business are a little pricier than the Bookkeeper brand of software.
- **Features:** Price is affected by not only the number of features offered with various accounting software, but also the complexity of those features. Software that easily integrates with an online banking system or that communicates with an online inventory system will be more expensive than a program that tracks invoices and expenses and creates simple reports.
- **Industry:** Some accounting software is designed for a particular type of industry. Buying a package with industry-specific features will push the price to $400 or higher.

Support is another important aspect of accounting software. One advantage of choosing software that has been on the market for a while is that the company is usually capable of providing support, both online and via phone.

Finally, it is important to consider that while accounting software is a valuable tool, the numbers do not enter themselves. Small business owners must either schedule time to manage the daily recordkeeping or find support to keep up with this essential task. Many small firms hire part-time bookkeepers or bookkeeping services to keep up with the daily data entry tasks, even when they utilize in-house accounting software packages.

CAREER CONNECTION

Taking the Headaches Out of Billing for Doctors

Healthcare management professionals Jonathan Bush and Todd Park were interested in running their own medical business when they bought an OB-GYN clinic in San Diego in 1997. Soon they were overwhelmed by the billing problems and associated government red tape. Frustrated, they searched for an Internet-based solution to their problems and found nothing—so they developed their own solution. That solution developed into a company, Athenahealth, now the leading online revenue-management and billing system servicing physicians in the U.S. "We believe passionately that we are on the same mission we were on when we started ... which is to make health care work the way it should," says Park. Bush and Park are pleased with the success of their company, but they are just as proud of how much their business is helping doctors focus on what they do best—heal people. "Billing is killing and frustrating physician practices around the country," explained Park.[3]

Tips from the Professionals

- Believe in your e-business.
- Keep your mission in mind even as your business grows.
- Monitor your business's place in the market.

SELF-CHECK

1. What are four options for professionals to help a small business cope with accounting and tax issues?
2. Where would a new business go to locate accounting and tax professionals?
3. What are the factors that affect the price of accounting software packages?

Apply Your Knowledge What tasks do bookkeepers perform for a small e-business? What are the alternatives to hiring an in-house, full-time bookkeeper? Can accounting software completely replace a bookkeeper? Explain.

SUMMARY

Section 5.1

- There are two options for tax year and two options for accounting method; e-businesses must make their choices before startup. Different types of businesses may be required to select one option over another.
- The balance sheet and income statement are the two basic financial statements with which

every e-business owner should become familiar and use to monitor the status of their venture.

Section 5.2

- Different legal forms require different methods of managing federal income tax. Sole proprietors and the shareholders of pass-through entities (partnerships, LLCs, and S corporations) pay business income tax on their personal returns, but have varying reporting requirements. C corporations must file and pay their own taxes.

Section 5.3

- Firms with employees must withhold and pay, on behalf of those employees, state and federal income tax, Social Security and Medicare tax (FICA), and unemployment tax (FUTA).
- E-businesses are responsible for collecting sales tax on purchases by customers living in the city, county, or state in which the business is physically located, when any of those entities levies a sales tax.

Section 5.4

- The outside professionals that can provide support with accounting and tax issues include CPAs, enrolled agents, tax attorneys, and bookkeepers. Each professional can fulfill a different role for an e-business, and selecting the right professionals should be done with careful consideration.
- Accounting software is a valuable tool for many e-businesses. The cost of different packages will vary widely, based on the features offered.

ASSESS YOUR UNDERSTANDING

UNDERSTAND: WHAT HAVE YOU LEARNED?

Go to **www.wiley.com/college/holden** to assess your knowledge of the basics of accounting and taxes for an e-business.

APPLY: WHAT WOULD YOU DO?

1. Suggest an appropriate tax year and accounting method for the following e-businesses, explaining your reasons for each selection:

- An e-commerce site that sells Halloween decorations and maintains a large inventory
- A Web site owned and operated by two partners that offers online decorating assistance for a modest fee
- An online sporting goods retailer with annual sales of $6 million; organized as a C corporation

2. In reviewing the balance sheet for a friend's e-business, you note the following: The firm owns real estate and equipment worth $100,000; has accounts payable of $30,000 and owes $2,000 in taxes; and has $20,000 of inventory and $25,000 of accounts receivable, with $4,000 in the bank, but owes $50,000 on a long-term loan. Using the form provided in the Toolkit section, calculate the following amounts: total assets, total liabilities, and owner's equity.

3. In reviewing last month's income statement for your new e-commerce site, you discover the following information: sales totaled $5,000 but there were $500 of returns; starting inventory was $6,500, ending inventory was $5,000, and shipping costs totaled $200; and operating expenses were $3,500. What was the net income (or loss)? Suggest any changes that you might make after reviewing this financial statement.

4. An LLC owned equally by four shareholders generates a profit of $124,000. How is this information reported to the government and to the shareholders? How much does each shareholder receive and how does each shareholder pay the taxes on the amount of profit?

5. An e-commerce site organized as a C corporation earned a profit of $120,000. Using rates provided in Section 5.2.3, compute the federal income tax owed on this amount. If the company distributed $50,000 in dividends to its shareholders, would any income tax be owed on the dividends? If yes, who is responsible for paying it? If no, explain.

6. If a sole proprietor earned $32,000 in net income from her e-commerce site, what would she owe in self-employment taxes?
7. A retailer working from home sold a $30 book to a customer living across the street. Both the business and the customer are located in a state with a 5 percent sales tax rate, plus the city sales tax of 2 percent. If the entire transaction took place online, would the customer owe sales tax? If yes, how much? If no, why not?
8. You have limited experience in accounting, and you are concerned about that aspect of your new e-business. Prepare a brief plan describing the type of accounting professionals you would hire. Your plan should include the questions you would ask and the tasks to be performed as contractors or in-house employees.

BE AN E-BUSINESS ENTREPRENEUR

Making Accounting and Tax Decisions

Think up a theoretical e-business scenario—describe a type of product or service that you could sell online. Next, decide which legal form the business will have. Now complete this plan by selecting a tax year and accounting method; justify your decisions. Next, explain how federal income taxes will be paid on the e-business's earnings and which tax forms must be filed. Finally, note whether the firm will have just one employee (the owner) or several. Describe which employment taxes must be paid—and how—for whichever scenario is selected.

Analyzing Balance Sheets

Publicly held e-commerce companies (Yahoo.com, for example) must publish financial statements with their annual reports, which are available online. Access a recent annual report for one of these companies and review the balance sheet. List which company and record amounts for the following: current assets, total assets, current liability, total liability, and owner's equity. Prove that the balance sheet balances by applying the appropriate equation.

Selecting a CPA

Assume that you own and operate a one-person e-business and you are going to interview CPAs. For which accounting tasks are you hoping they can provide help? What specific traits are you going to seek? (These should reflect what you see as your personal style of business management.) Write five sample interview questions that will help you obtain the information necessary to make a good decision.

KEY TERMS

Accrual basis	An accounting method that reports income when it is earned (rather than received) and expenses when they are incurred (rather than paid).
Assets	Everything of value that a business owns.
Balance sheet	A detailed summary of a business's financial status at a fixed point in time.
Bookkeeper	A person who manages the recordkeeping activities for a small business, including recording receivables and payables, making deposits, managing payroll, and sending out tax forms.
C corporations	A business entity that exists separately from owners; responsible for paying taxes and filing returns.
Calendar year	An accounting schedule using a 12-month period ending on December 31.
Cash basis	An accounting method that reports income when it is received and expenses when they are incurred.
Certified Public Accountant (CPA)	An accountant that has completed specialized training, has passed exams, is certified, and is well versed in the latest tax laws.
Cost of goods sold	The cost of merchandise sold during a period.
Enrolled agent	A federally licensed accounting professional that can prepare taxes, assist in long-term financial planning, and represent a business in the event of an audit.
Excise taxes	Taxes imposed on the manufacture, sale, and consumption of various consumer goods and services.
Fiscal year	An accounting schedule using a 12-month period closing at the end of any month other than December.
Income	The sales a business makes during a period.

Income statement	A financial statement that summarizes the changes in a firm's financial position over a specified period of time.
Liabilities	All the debts of a business.
Net income	The excess income over expenses incurred during a period; also called profit.
Net loss	When expenses are greater than income.
Operating expenses	The administrative and selling expenses incurred over a period to deliver a product or a service.
Owner's equity	The amount of claim the owner(s) can make against the assets of the company.
Pass-through entities	Legal forms (including partnerships, LLCs, and S corporations) in which income and losses are passed through to the owners, who pay the appropriate income taxes on their personal returns.
S corporations	Like partnerships and LLCs, owners note profits and losses on Schedule E and pay income tax on those amounts.
Self-employment tax	A combined Social Security and Medicare tax for self-employed individuals that is computed on Schedule SE of Form 1040.
Tax attorney	An attorney who specializes in dealing with issues pertaining to tax law.
Tax year	The defined accounting period used for evaluating a business's financial status and for filing taxes with the Internal Revenue Service.
Use tax	Taxes imposed on goods purchased in another state that replaces sales tax that would have been paid if the goods had been purchased in the home state.

REFERENCES

1. Arden Dale, "Small Firms Reach for Plastic to Pay IRS." *Startup Journal*, www.startupjournal.com/runbusiness/taxadvice/20070615-dale.html?refresh=on.
2. Roy Mark, "Internet Sales Tax Movement Lagging," internetnews.com, www.internetnews.com/ec-news/article.php/3683691.
3. Amanda C. Kooser, "Healthy Profits," Entrepreneur.com, www.entrepreneur.com/worklife/successstories/article81762.html.

TOOLKIT

SCHEDULE SE (Form 1040) Department of the Treasury Internal Revenue Service	**Self-Employment Tax** ▶ **Attach to Form 1040.** ▶ **See Instructions for Schedule SE (Form 1040).**	OMB No. 1545-0074 **2007** Attachment Sequence No. **17**
Name of person with **self-employment** income (as shown on Form 1040)	Social security number of person with **self-employment** income ▶	

Who Must File Schedule SE

You must file Schedule SE if:

- You had net earnings from self-employment from **other than** church employee income (line 4 of Short Schedule SE or line 4c of Long Schedule SE) of $400 or more, **or**
- You had church employee income of $108.28 or more. Income from services you performed as a minister or a member of a religious order **is not** church employee income (see page SE-1).

Note. Even if you had a loss or a small amount of income from self-employment, it may be to your benefit to file Schedule SE and use either "optional method" in Part II of Long Schedule SE (see page SE-4).

Exception. If your only self-employment income was from earnings as a minister, member of a religious order, or Christian Science practitioner **and** you filed Form 4361 and received IRS approval not to be taxed on those earnings, **do not** file Schedule SE. Instead, write "Exempt Form 4361" on Form 1040, line 58.

May I Use Short Schedule SE or Must I Use Long Schedule SE?

Note. Use this flowchart **only if** you must file Schedule SE. If unsure, see Who Must File Schedule SE, above.

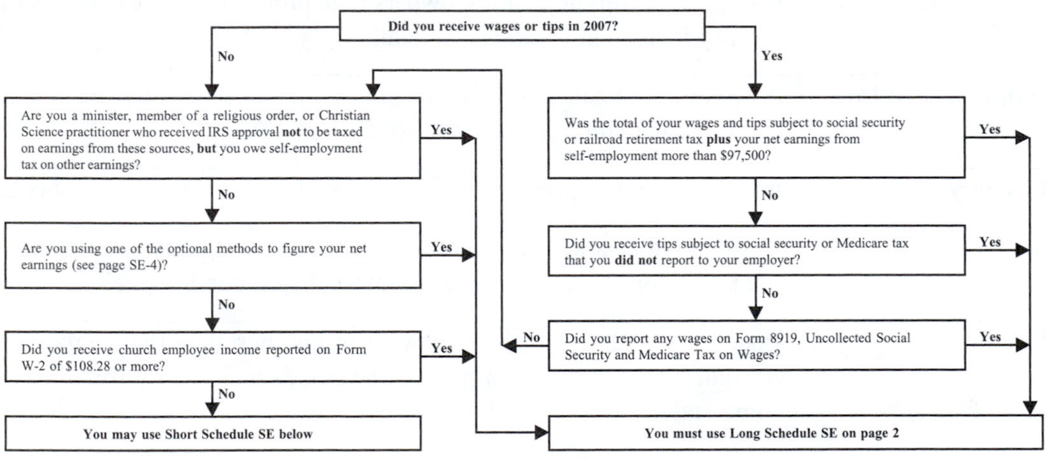

Section A—Short Schedule SE. Caution. Read above to see if you can use Short Schedule SE.

1	Net farm profit or (loss) from Schedule F, line 36, and farm partnerships, Schedule K-1 (Form 1065), box 14, code A	1	
2	Net profit or (loss) from Schedule C, line 31; Schedule C-EZ, line 3; Schedule K-1 (Form 1065), box 14, code A (other than farming); and Schedule K-1 (Form 1065-B), box 9, code J1. Ministers and members of religious orders, see page SE-1 for amounts to report on this line. See page SE-3 for other income to report	2	
3	Combine lines 1 and 2	3	
4	**Net earnings from self-employment.** Multiply line 3 by 92.35% (.9235). If less than $400, **do not** file this schedule; you do not owe self-employment tax . . . . ▶	4	
5	**Self-employment tax.** If the amount on line 4 is: • $97,500 or less, multiply line 4 by 15.3% (.153). Enter the result here and on **Form 1040, line 58.** • More than $97,500, multiply line 4 by 2.9% (.029). Then, add $12,090 to the result. Enter the total here and on **Form 1040, line 58**	5	
6	**Deduction for one-half of self-employment tax.** Multiply line 5 by 50% (.5). Enter the result here and on **Form 1040, line 27** 6		

For Paperwork Reduction Act Notice, see Form 1040 instructions. Cat. No. 11358Z **Schedule SE (Form 1040) 2007**

Schedule SE (Form 1040) 2007 Attachment Sequence No. 17 Page 2

Name of person with **self-employment** income (as shown on Form 1040)	Social security number of person with **self-employment** income	

Section B—Long Schedule SE

Part I Self-Employment Tax

Note. If your only income subject to self-employment tax is **church employee income,** skip lines 1 through 4b. Enter -0- on line 4c and go to line 5a. Income from service s you performed as a minister or a membe r of a religious order **is not** church employee income. See page SE-1.

A If you are a minister, member of a religious order , or Christian Science practitioner **and** you filed For m 4361, but you had $400 or more of **other** net earnings from self-employment, check here and continue with Part I . . . . . ▶ ☐

1	Net farm profit or (loss) from Schedule F, line 36, and farm partnerships, Schedule K-1 (Form 1065), box 14, code A. **Note.** Skip this line if you use the farm optional method (see page SE-4)	**1**		
2	Net profit or (loss) from Schedule C, line 31; Schedule C-EZ, line 3; Schedule K-1 (Form 1065), box 14, code A (other than farming); and Schedule K-1 (Form 1065-B), box 9, code J1. Ministers and members of religious orders, see page SE-1 for amounts to report on this line. See page SE-3 for other income to report. **Note.** Skip this line if you use the nonfarm optional method (see page SE-4)	**2**		
3	Combine lines 1 and 2	**3**		
4a	If line 3 is more than zero, multiply line 3 by 92.35% (.9235). Otherwise, enter amount from line 3	**4a**		
b	If you elect one or both of the optional methods, enter the total of lines 15 and 17 here . .	**4b**		
c	Combine lines 4a and 4b. If less than $400, **stop** ; you do not owe self-employment tax. **Exception.** If less than $400 and you had **church employee income,** enter -0- and continue . . . . ▶	**4c**		
5a	Enter your **church employee income** from Form W-2. See page SE-1 for definition of church employee income **5a**			
b	Multiply line 5a by 92.35% (.9235). If less than $100, enter -0-	**5b**		
6	**Net earnings from self-employment.** Add lines 4c and 5b	**6**		
7	Maximum amount of combined wages and self-employment earnings subject to social security tax or the 6.2% portion of the 7.65% railroad retirement (tier 1) tax for 2007	**7**	97,500	00
8a	Total social security wages and tips (total of boxes 3 and 7 on Form(s) W-2) and railroad retirement (tier 1) compensation. If $97,500 or more, skip lines 8b through 10, and go to line 11 . . . . **8a**			
b	Unreported tips subject to social security tax (from Form 4137, line 10) **8b**			
c	Wages subject to social security tax (from Form 8919, line 10) . . **8c**			
d	Add lines 8a, 8b, and 8c	**8d**		
9	Subtract line 8d from line 7. If zero or less, enter -0- here and on line 10 and go to line 11 . ▶	**9**		
10	Multiply the **smaller** of line 6 or line 9 by 12.4% (.124)	**10**		
11	Multiply line 6 by 2.9% (.029)	**11**		
12	**Self-employment tax.** Add lines 10 and 11. Enter here and on **Form 1040, line 58** . . .	**12**		
13	**Deduction for one-half of self-employment tax.** Multiply line 12 by 50% (.5). Enter the result here and on **Form 1040, line 27** . . . **13**			

Part II Optional Methods To Figure Net Earnings (see page SE-4)

Farm Optional Method. You may use this method **only** if **(a)** your gross farm income [1] was not more than $2,400, **or (b)** your net farm profits [2] were less than $1,733.

14	Maximum income for optional methods	**14**	1,600	00
15	Enter the **smaller** of: two-thirds (2/3) of gross farm income[1] (not less than zero) **or** $1,600. Also include this amount on line 4b above	**15**		

Nonfarm Optional Method. You may use this method **only** if **(a)** your net nonfarm profits[3] were less than $1,733 and also less than 72.189% of your gross nonfarm income,[4] **and (b)** you had net earnings from self-employment of at least $400 in 2 of the prior 3 years.

Caution. You may use this method no more than five times.

16	Subtract line 15 from line 14	**16**		
17	Enter the **smaller** of: two-thirds (2/3) of gross nonfarm income[4] (not less than zero) **or** the amount on line 16. Also include this amount on line 4b above	**17**		

[1] From Sch. F, line 11, and Sch. K-1 (Form 1065), box 14, code B.

[2] From Sch. F, line 36, and Sch. K-1 (Form 1065), box 14, code A.

[3] From Sch. C, line 31; Sch. C-EZ, line 3; Sch. K-1 (Form 1065), box 14, code A; and Sch. K-1 (Form 1065-B), box 9, code J1.

[4] From Sch. C, line 7; Sch. C-EZ, line 1; Sch. K-1 (Form 1065), box 14, code C; and Sch. K-1 (Form 1065-B), box 9, code J2.

Schedule SE (Form 1040) 2007

CHAPTER

6 ONLINE PAYMENTS AND SHOPPING CARTS

Choosing the Tools That Help Money Flow Into an E-Business

Do You Already Know?

- How an online purchase with a credit card works
- The other payment options available to online customers
- Why every serious e-business needs a shopping cart
- The three primary shopping cart options

For additional questions to assess your current knowledge on payments and shopping carts for e-businesses, go to **www.wiley.com/college/holden.**

What You Will Find Out	What You Will Be Able To Do
6.1 How online credit card purchases work and what steps must be taken to accept credit cards	• Accept credit cards by setting up a merchant account; choose a payment gateway
6.2 That there are several alternative payment options, including PayPal, e-checking, and offline payments	• Use PayPal, electronic checking, and other resources to offer multiple ways to purchase products
6.3 What shopping carts are and why they are essential tools for e-businesses	• Select shopping cart features appropriate for your e-business needs
6.4 That shopping cart options include off-the-shelf software, custom programmed carts, or hosted carts	• Select the shopping cart option that best suits your e-business

INTRODUCTION

Like the rest of the business world, running an e-business revolves around bringing in money, though selling products online presents some extra challenges. Instead of customers physically handing over payment, e-businesses must utilize a variety of other options for getting their money. By far the most common is allowing customers to use a credit card. The first section of this chapter explains how online credit card transactions work, and what steps an e-business must undertake to make it possible to accept credit card payments. "Plastic" is not the only payment option for online businesses, as the second section explains. Several alternatives are profiled, including PayPal and electronic checking, as well as mechanisms for accepting traditional offline payments. In addition to accepting payments, another challenge for online businesses is providing an enjoyable purchasing experience that has the familiar feel of shopping in a physical store. Shopping carts, specialized software programs used by e-commerce sites, mitigate this problem. The third section provides a detailed introduction to shopping carts, including a discussion of the many features that e-business owners should consider. The fourth section includes a review of the three primary shopping cart solutions available to e-business owners—off-the-shelf software; custom-programmed software; and hosted shopping carts—and a discussion of the various advantages and disadvantages of the three options.

6.1 ACCEPTING PAYMENTS WITH CREDIT CARDS

It is impossible to sell things over the Internet without a reliable and convenient way to accept money from customers. Fortunately, there are a variety of options, though just like for a bricks-and-mortar store, credit cards are by far the most popular solution. With plastic money now filling the wallets of consumers, most online shoppers expect to be able to pay with credit cards. Fortunately for online merchants, the acceptance and growth of e-commerce have simplified the process of credit card use. In fact, in less than one week, most e-businesses can be ready to accept their first online credit card order.

6.1.1 The Basics of a Credit Card Purchase

Enabling a Web site to accept credit cards is one of the most misunderstood functions of e-commerce. A shopper understands that they have to type a credit card number into a box on their computer screen and then click a "purchase" button. And the customer knows that after a few seconds an approval or denial of the purchase message appears on the monitor. Figure 6-1 provides a simple schematic diagram of how a credit card transaction works.

Figure 6-1

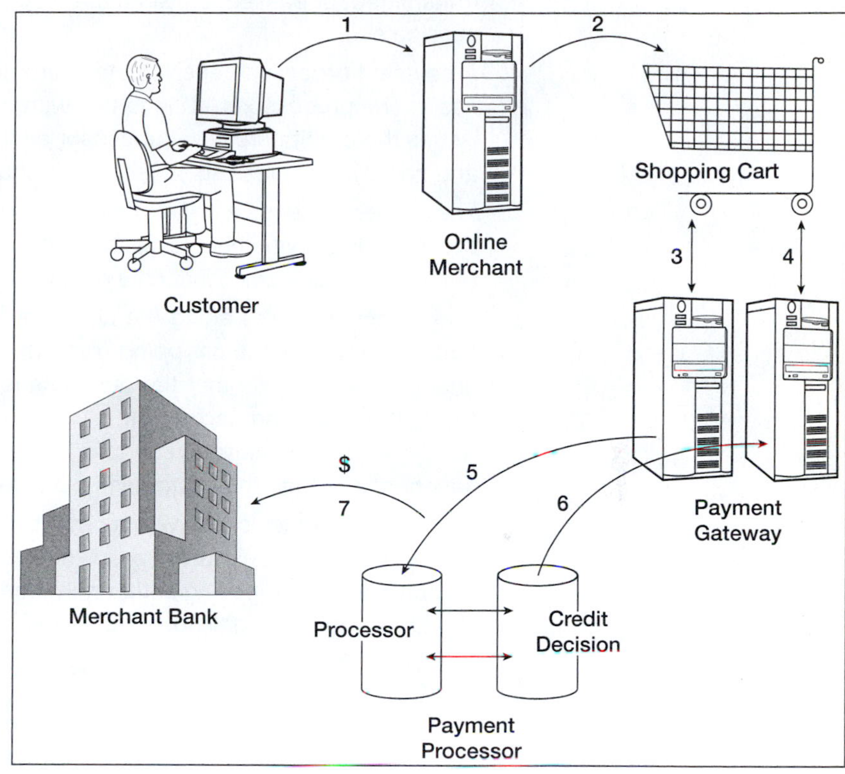

How credit card transactions are processed online.

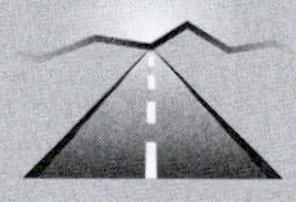

PATHWAY TO... PROCESSING A CREDIT CARD TRANSACTION

Here is how an online purchase with a credit card really works:

1. A customer goes shopping on a Web site and puts products into a virtual shopping cart. When customers are ready to check out, the shopping cart starts the process of completing the sale.
2. The customer pays for the product by using a credit card. The shopping cart program should provide an online form for the customer to complete, including personal information, shipping details, a credit card number, an expiration date, and a verification code from the back of the card.
3. The Web site sends that credit card information to a payment gateway. The gateway is a virtual gate through which information is

transmitted, or passed, between the Web site and a credit card processing site.

4. A payment processor receives the customer's information and verifies it. The processor's job is to talk with the company or bank that issues the credit card. The processor ensures that the card is valid and has enough credit to cover the purchase.
5. The processor sends a credit decision back to the gateway. The processor finds out whether the customer is approved or declined for the purchase and transmits that data right back to the payment gateway.
6. The gateway passes along the approval decision to the shopping cart and finalizes the shopping transaction. The customer gets a final message saying that the purchase is approved (or not). From there, the shopping cart program can provide a receipt, shipping details, and an invitation to shop again. Steps 2–6 take only a few seconds, and then the customer's purchase is complete.
7. While the customer is receiving an approval message, the processor is sending the money to the e-business's bank account. Although this process is happening within milliseconds of the approval process, the money might not be credited to the account for two to three business days.

6.1.2 Securing a Merchant Account

Merchant account: A specialized bank account that allows a business to accept credit cards.

Once an e-business owner has a good understanding of how credit card purchases work, it is time to add credit card functionality to the Web site. The first step is to secure a **merchant account,** a specialized bank account that allows a business to accept credit cards. Resources that offer merchant accounts include banks, direct providers, and third-party agents.

Banks

Most banks now offer e-commerce merchant services as part of their standard small-business service packages. This provides entrepreneurs the convenience of managing their merchant account with the same institution that maintains their checking account. However, be aware of a few things. Banks often:

- Have a more rigid approval process for online businesses because they are still considered high-risk ventures
- Pass the merchant account application to a third-party company for approval (as opposed to processing and managing it internally)
- Increase the costs for a merchant account because the bank is essentially a middleman and gets a commission for referring the account

Direct Provider

Small e-businesses can access many of the same direct merchant account providers that a local bank might use. By going directly to a processor to set up a merchant account, an e-business can cut out some of the initial costs. A merchant account can be set up with one of these processors:

- **Cardservice International:** www.cardservicesales.com
- **Merchant Warehouse:** www.merchantwarehouse.com

Third-Party Agent

Broker:
An independent sales representative who makes a commission from signing up new merchant account customers.

There are two common types of third-party agents. A **broker** is an independent sales representative who makes a commission from signing up new customers. A broker who represents more than one company can help e-businesses compare and find the best rates available. Online services represent another option for finding merchant accounts. Companies that once offered only one service—such as a shopping cart program—are now including bundled access to multiple companion services, such as setting up merchant accounts. When working with one of the larger online services, it is possible to get a better deal on some items. For example, sites like MonsterCommerce (www.monstermerchantaccount.com) have a merchant account program and usually waive setup fees, application fees, and even deposits. They also tend to have higher approval and acceptance rates for online businesses because they target that customer base.

E-business in Action →
Set up a merchant account.

IN THE REAL WORLD

Insider Advice on Choosing a Merchant Account

Aria Financial Corporation (www.Arianet.com) is one of many merchant account providers that specialize in working with online business operators. It boasts an almost 99 percent approval rate for new companies getting started online. According to the company, signing up for a merchant account can be confusing, but the best companies will do a good job of working with an e-business to determine their needs before setting up an account. Most companies have Web sites for completing a prequalification application. A salesperson directly contacts e-businesses that

(Continued)

qualify to determine the needs of the business and process the application. The easiest method is over the phone, even though applications may be acceptable online, via fax, or mail. Aria Financial stresses that online accounts differ from physical or retail accounts; online accounts are considered card-not-present accounts, meaning that the retailer does not have the actual card in hand during the transaction. Card-not-present accounts increase the risk of fraud, which increases the risks and rates for e-business.

6.1.3 Choosing a Payment Gateway

Payment gateway: An e-commerce service provider that communicates to credit card companies, banks, and Web sites, allowing online transactions to take place.

After gaining approval to accept credit cards, an e-business's next action is to choose a payment gateway. The **payment gateway** is an e-commerce service provider that communicates with the credit card companies, banks, and the Web site. Needless to say, the gateway plays an important role in every e-commerce equation.

If an e-business is obtaining bundled services from one source, the merchant account provider might already have a designated gateway—good news because it indicates that a relationship is already established. Alternatively, the provider might have partnerships set up with several gateways. The provider allows the e-business to select a gateway from a list of options.

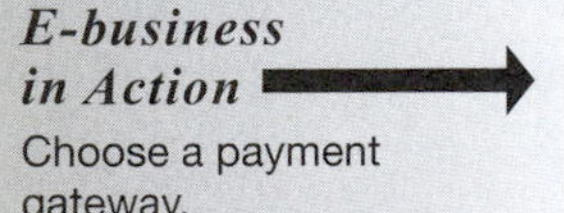

Choose a payment gateway.

Many e-businesses must search for a payment gateway without outside assistance. Hundreds of gateways are available from which to choose. An incorrect choice can halt sales. With good research, an e-business will be able to find the best match for a payment gateway.

PATHWAY TO... CHOOSING A PAYMENT GATEWAY

Look for a payment gateway that meets the following criteria:

- **Diverse:** To be effective, a gateway needs to work with all major credit cards, including MasterCard, Visa, and American Express.
- **Compatible:** One of the most important requirements is that the gateway integrates with a Web site's shopping cart software. Although major gateways are already set up to talk with the majority of off-the-shelf shopping carts, it is wise to verify that the gateway is compatible. Some programming might be required to get the gateway to communicate with the Web site.

- **Pays in a timely manner:** Each gateway has its own rules for when and how to make payments to the e-business's bank. Choose a gateway that deposits money within a few days (as opposed to once a month).
- **Supportive:** As with any service provider, make sure that the payment gateway has customer service support available any time of the day or night.
- **Accessible:** Clients should be able to view the status of their Web site's transactions in an online report, along with other management tools.
- **Feature rich:** Payment gateways have a surprising number of features available, though usually for an additional fee. Recurring billing options, additional payment options, and fraud-protection tools are all desirable features that e-businesses should consider as a Web site grows.

Better-known payment gateways include:

- **Authorize.Net:** www.authorize.net
- **LinkPoint API and LinkPoint Connect:** www.linkpoint.com
- **Plug'n Pay WebExpress:** www.plugnpay.com/webXpress.php
- **Verisign Payflow Link and Payflow Pro:** www.verisign.com
- **WorldPay:** www.worldpay.com/usa/sme/index.php

6.1.4 Fees for Credit Card Transactions

When applying to become an authorized credit card merchant, you should carefully evaluate the real cost of working with various service providers. Although base rates might remain similar, other unexpected fees must be evaluated to ensure your understanding of the many types of fees you may encounter. Nine typical fees include:

1. Application
2. Setup
3. Discount rate
4. Terminal cost
5. Statement
6. Transaction
7. Monthly minimum
8. Charge-back
9. Termination

Application

Some agents charge a nominal processing fee for an application. Expect to pay at least $100.

Setup

A setup fee covers the cost of establishing a merchant account and can range from $200 to $1,000 or more.

Discount Rate

Discount rate: The part of every credit card sale taken by the merchant account provider, typically between 2 and 4 percent.

Each time a customer makes a purchase with a credit card, the merchant account provider takes a part of the sale, called a **discount rate.** The amount varies based on the type of card that is used but is usually between 2 and 4 percent. Many e-business owners think they were promised a lower rate or their contract shows a very low rate. E-business owners should confirm the discount rate and the type of merchant account for which they have contracted to avoid misunderstandings. The account should specify Internet, mail order, or telephone sales. Because these types of transactions do not require swiping an actual credit card, rates for these types of transactions are consistently higher (sometimes by as much as a full point) than those for offline retailers.

Terminal Cost

A small electric terminal or box is required for businesses swiping in credit cards or manually punching in account numbers. The requirement to lease or purchase special equipment may add several hundred dollars to annual costs.

Statement

A monthly statement fee covers the merchant account provider's cost of compiling, printing, and mailing a monthly statement. The average fee ranges from $5 to $15. To possibly eliminate a monthly statement fee, ask the merchant account provider whether online access and printing of monthly statements is available. A printed copy serves as a permanent record. If so, confirm when and how long the online statements are available for viewing.

Transaction

E-businesses pay a small processing fee for each credit card transaction. The nominal amount is usually less than 25 cents per transaction—and, yes, it is in addition to the discount rate.

Monthly Minimum

If an e-business expects to have a limited number of sales (maybe it is a new business or just does not expect much traffic during the startup phase), the merchant account provider might establish a minimum charge level. If sales, number of transactions, or combined discount rate and transaction fees fail to exceed that minimum, the company adds on an additional charge. In other words, the company is counting on an e-business to process many orders so that the merchant account provider makes more money—and the merchant account provider will penalize Web sites failing to live up to their contract.

Charge-Back

When a customer disputes a purchase with the credit card company, the dollar amount of that purchase is taken out of the e-business bank account; this is called a **charge-back.** The merchant account provider may also charge an additional fee for processing a charge-back transaction. Online orders that do not require signatures (or the physical cards to process) are especially susceptible to charge-backs.

Charge-back:
The dollar amount of a sale taken out of an e-business bank account when a customer disputes a purchase with their credit card company.

Termination

Whether an e-business is switching merchant providers or closing the business, the original contract may contain a termination fee, which can be up to $1,000. Before signing any agreement, seek out the clause that specifically explains requirements for canceling the agreement. If early termination is expensive, make sure that a companion clause allows an e-business to upgrade when new features are released. Today's version of the latest and greatest feature can be quickly usurped in a few months. An e-business wants to avoid paying for features that do not keep pace with a growing business.

6.1.5 Preventing Credit Card Fraud

Although all businesses face the increasing problem of credit card fraud, stolen or false credit card numbers and a lack of personal contact can make online credit card transactions particularly vulnerable. Consider the following strategies for preventing credit card fraud:

- Post an anti-fraud policy that warns fraudulent users that systems are in place to monitor all transactions.
- Ask customers for enough information to verify the validity of a card. A name, credit card number, and expiration date are no longer sufficient. For example, more and more merchants now require customers to provide a card's security code.

- If you are suspicious of any charge, contact your merchant bank with the credit card number in question and ask for assistance in verifying the account number and address.
- Be wary of customers that use email addresses from free services such as Hotmail and Yahoo. Such addresses are simple to obtain under a false name. If used for fraudulent orders, tracing these addresses can lead you to nothing.
- Ask customers for shipping and billing addresses. This information can assist credit card issuers when tracking down fraudulent activity.
- Use a phone call or email to contact the customer to confirm the authenticity of an order.
- Be cautious of large or international orders, and send products via a national shipping company that offers tracking on every package sent, eliminating those claims that a package was never delivered.
- Employ a screening service company.

SELF-CHECK

1. What is a merchant account? Where would an e-business go to obtain a merchant account?
2. What do payment gateways do? List five features to consider when choosing a payment gateway.
3. What fees are levied on each individual online credit card transaction?

Apply Your Knowledge Why is it so important for e-businesses to accept credit cards for payment? What are the drawbacks encountered by merchants accepting credit card purchases?

6.2 ALTERNATIVE PAYMENT OPTIONS

Credit cards have a hold on the online shopping market; the majority of customers prefer paying that way. Yet, online security concerns and the demand for flexibility are driving the need for alternative options. E-commerce sites receive a definite benefit when they expand their customers' payment choices. Online stores that offer only credit cards as a payment source get 60 percent of their visitors to purchase something. By having at least four payment options available at checkout, a Web site can increase those customer purchase rates to 80 percent. A variety of alternative payment solution options are available to offer customers.

6.2.1 PayPal

PayPal:
A global service that allows consumers to make Internet purchases without giving their personal financial information to an e-commerce site. Instead they use a PayPal account, funded credit card, check, or bank transfer.

One of the most popular alternatives is allowing customers to pay by using a PayPal account. **PayPal** (www.PayPal.com) is a global service with roughly 100 million users that allows consumers to make Internet purchases without giving personal financial information to e-commerce sites. Customers work exclusively with PayPal—putting money into their account with credit card, check, or whatever method they prefer—and PayPal becomes the financial intermediary for their online transactions. Using PayPal greatly reduces a consumer's risk of online fraud, and it also is a good system for sellers, because PayPal ensures the customer's ability to pay.

PayPal, which is now owned by eBay, found its initial success offering a fast, low-risk method for online auction participants to exchange money. Now all types of e-commerce sites accept payment by PayPal. If an e-commerce site already has a payment gateway, it can add PayPal Checkout Express to its Web site to allow automatic transfer of customers' billing and shipping information stored with PayPal, so that shoppers do not have to reenter information on future visits.

IN THE REAL WORLD

Google Launches Alternative to PayPal

In June 2007, Internet giant Google launched a new service called Google Checkout that some people predicted may lead to the demise of PayPal. While both services offer secure online shopping and refund policies in the event of fraud, they are very different services. Google Checkout lacks many of the features of PayPal; Google Checkout serves primarily as a service for holding and shielding credit/debit card information from sellers. The security is great, but many PayPal users enjoy the ability to transfer money from bank accounts or to wire money to nonusers. Google Checkout offers neither of these features, and for now it is only available for shopping within the United States. That noted, Google has a wide reach and many online retailers undoubtedly will embrace Checkout. In the long run, both services will be very good for e-businesses of all sizes because they will only serve to increase the speed and security of the online shopping experience.[1]

6.2.2 Electronic Checks

Electronic checking, also known as automatic clearing house (ACH) processing, has been in wide use since the mid-1990s (the same time that the use of paper checks peaked), but the method continues to grow in popularity. Data from 2003 and 2004 showed that the use of electronic check payment increased sixfold during those years, reaching 1.25 billion payments.

Electronic checking: A payment system that allows a customer to electronically transfer funds from a personal or business bank account into an e-business bank account.

Electronic checking allows a customer to use funds taken directly from a personal or business bank account. The funds are then deposited directly into the e-business's bank account. For an e-commerce site, the service offers lower processing fees per transaction than with credit cards. The cost can range from 29 cents per transaction to more than a dollar for each electronic check accepted. Increasingly, payment gateways are making electronic check processing available to Web sites. Or e-businesses can offer electronic checking service using a third-party e-check provider, such as Electronic Payment Services' iChex (www.ichex.com) or Pay By Check (www.paybycheck.com).

Before signing an agreement with a third-party electronic check provider, always compare prices. In addition to paying a per-transaction fee, e-businesses are charged a fee for returned checks. They also may be charged activation, monthly service, and integration fees that can cost several hundred dollars. Because of these fees, it is often cheaper to use e-check services offered through a payment gateway.

6.2.3 Offline Payments

An option that is sometimes overlooked by e-businesses is allowing customers to send in payments through a less technically advanced method. Although only a small percentage of shoppers are likely to use these options, using one of these options could be worthwhile. After all, it is certainly not cost prohibitive to extend these offline options:

- **Personal checks:** If speed is not an issue, customers can write and mail a check to an e-business. On receipt of the check, wait until it clears and payment is in the bank before shipping out the merchandise.
- **Bank checks:** These, too, can be mailed after the transaction, though they speed the transaction because there is no need to wait for them to clear before shipping the products.
- **Money orders:** This paper payment system, sold through the U.S. Postal Service (and at other outlets around the world), acts as an alternative to a bank check. Generally, merchants can safely accept a money order and immediately ship products, though money order counterfeiting has become a problem in recent years.
- **Western Union:** This company, which works with local agents, makes it possible for a customer to electronically send payments to an e-business from around the world. Visit www.westernunion.com for more information.

E-business in Action

Offer customers multiple options by offering alternative payment systems.

- **Phone or fax:** Accepting credit card numbers over a phone or fax line—rather than through a Web site—may sound inefficient, but some customers feel safer providing the information this way.

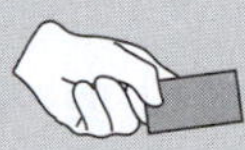

CAREER CONNECTIONS

Even without an emphasis on merchandising, an arts nonprofit benefits from online business transactions.

Douglas Ferrari is the executive director of the Shore Institute of the Contemporary Arts (SICA), a nonprofit arts organization in Central New Jersey (www.sica.org). Ferrari, who always has SICA's mission in mind—to make contemporary art more accessible to the general public—knows that success comes slow and steady. Founded in 2000, SICA opened the doors of its current Long Branch, New Jersey, facility in 2004; the organization's Web site was online in 2005 and receives between 40,000 and 60,000 hits each month.

Although SICA doesn't sell any artwork exhibited at the facility or on its Web site, Ferrari incorporated PayPal into SICA's site in 2006 to facilitate customer services such as memberships and class enrollments. "PayPal makes it easier because people don't have to fill out forms and use the mail," says Ferrari, who chose PayPal because he had an existing eBay PayPal account. The PayPal feature also makes it simple for artists who are entering any of SICA's juried shows and competitions to register and submit entry fees online.

Ferrari plans to pursue other e-business opportunities for SICA, including a shopping cart feature so customers can buy T-shirts, booklets, and other SICA merchandise. "Even if merchandising is not in your immediate plan when you set up with a server, look for a server that utilizes shopping carts, payment gateways, or services such as PayPal," says Ferrari. "It can save you money in the long run."

Tips from the Professional

- Even if you're not ready to sell a product right now, set up your Web site so you can easily do so in the future.
- With any payment service, be cautious of online scams, such as requests to update bank or credit card information.

6.2.4 Other Options

There are other newer payment options, popular with big e-commerce sites, which small e-businesses might want to consider.

Instant Credit

Companies are now providing e-businesses a way to offer customers instant credit terms. Essentially, at the time of checkout, a customer gets approval for the dollar amount of the purchase after an evaluation process that usually takes no more than 15 seconds. Then the customer has a set amount of time to make the payment. If they decide to take the credit offered, the e-business gets the funds immediately. Third-party companies manage everything for these services. One such solution is offered by eCredit.com (www.ecredit.com).

Gift Cards

High-tech versions of the old-fashioned gift certificate have exploded in recent years. Offering gift cards or gift certificates on a Web site is an easy way to extend payment options while increasing sales. An issue to consider: Gift cards can cause some accounting complexities, because while the cash comes in up front, gift cards cannot immediately be credited as a sale. Another issue to consider, gift cards or gift certificates create an immediate liability to account for goods that will be delivered in the future. Get a CPA's advice before offering this option and work out the accounting complexities in advance.

Private-Label Credit Cards

Personalized plastic buying tools have become a hot new trend for retailers and organizations. Private-label credit cards are a great tool for regularly reminding customers about their favorite place to shop online. Now, working with a bank, just about any firm can offer customers a Visa or MasterCard under the company's name. Some companies give users extra incentive for using the cards by offering an extra discount, small rebates on purchases, or special gifts. Contact one of the following financial institutions to learn more about private-label credit cards:

- **Wells Fargo:** http://financial.wellsfargo.com/retailservices/private_label_cc.html
- **CitiCommerce:** www.citicommercesolutions.citi.com
- **CitiFinancial:** www.citifinancialretailservices.com/private_label_credit_cards.php

---

SELF-CHECK

1. Why would an e-business offer multiple options for customer payment?
2. How does a payment service such as PayPal offer customers more security than using a credit card when making an online purchase?
3. Explain how instant credit works.

Apply Your Knowledge A customer wants to make a purchase through a Web site but does not have a credit card. Suggest three alternative options. Explain which is fastest and why.

6.3 AN INTRODUCTION TO SHOPPING CARTS

Shopping carts:
A computer program built into a Web site that mimics the shopping experience in a bricks-and-mortar store, allowing customers to place items in a virtual "cart" and pay at a "checkout."

Shopping carts are computer programs built into a Web site that mimic the shopping experience in a bricks-and-mortar store. As shoppers work their way through an e-commerce site, the shopper places items to buy in a virtual shopping cart with a simple click of the mouse. When the shopper is finished buying, the shopping cart helps them check out. In the process, the shopping cart will do a variety of things, including total the purchases, suggest additional items, figure sales tax (if any), offer shipping options, and compute the delivery costs once an option is selected. The cart also manages the very important payment process, taking the shopper's personal information, along with their credit card number, or arranging an alternative payment system. Good shopping carts will confirm the sale once it has been approved, offer shipping and delivery dates, and even follow up with the shopper at various times after the sale.

FOR EXAMPLE
See Figure 6-2 for examples of online shopping carts.

Does an e-commerce site absolutely need a shopping cart? No. If a Web site sells only a few items, the site may be able to get by using a simple online order form. Shoppers making a purchase can complete the form online, print it, and then fax it to the e-business for processing. Or customers can complete the online form and click "Send" to email the form to the e-business. Either way, the seller must manually process the order and the payment, which is labor intensive. Online order forms also fail to provide a satisfying experience for the customer. Buyers are often left wondering if the seller has received the order, and many are hesitant to transfer their credit card numbers through such insecure environments as fax and email.

Keeping these limitations in mind, it is obvious that any serious e-business needs a shopping cart. Simply put, a shopping cart is an essential tool of e-commerce.

Today's sophisticated shopping cart applications have grown into more than simple shopping baskets for online customers. Many tools may be incorporated into shopping cart programs. An e-business owner's job is to determine what features are needed most right now, and then determine which features are best for the long term. First, determine which tools are available and most important to use. To make this process easier, it is helpful to divide the most sought-after features into four standard categories:

- Back-end management
- Customer-centric
- Integration and maintenance
- Promotion and marketing

Figure 6-2

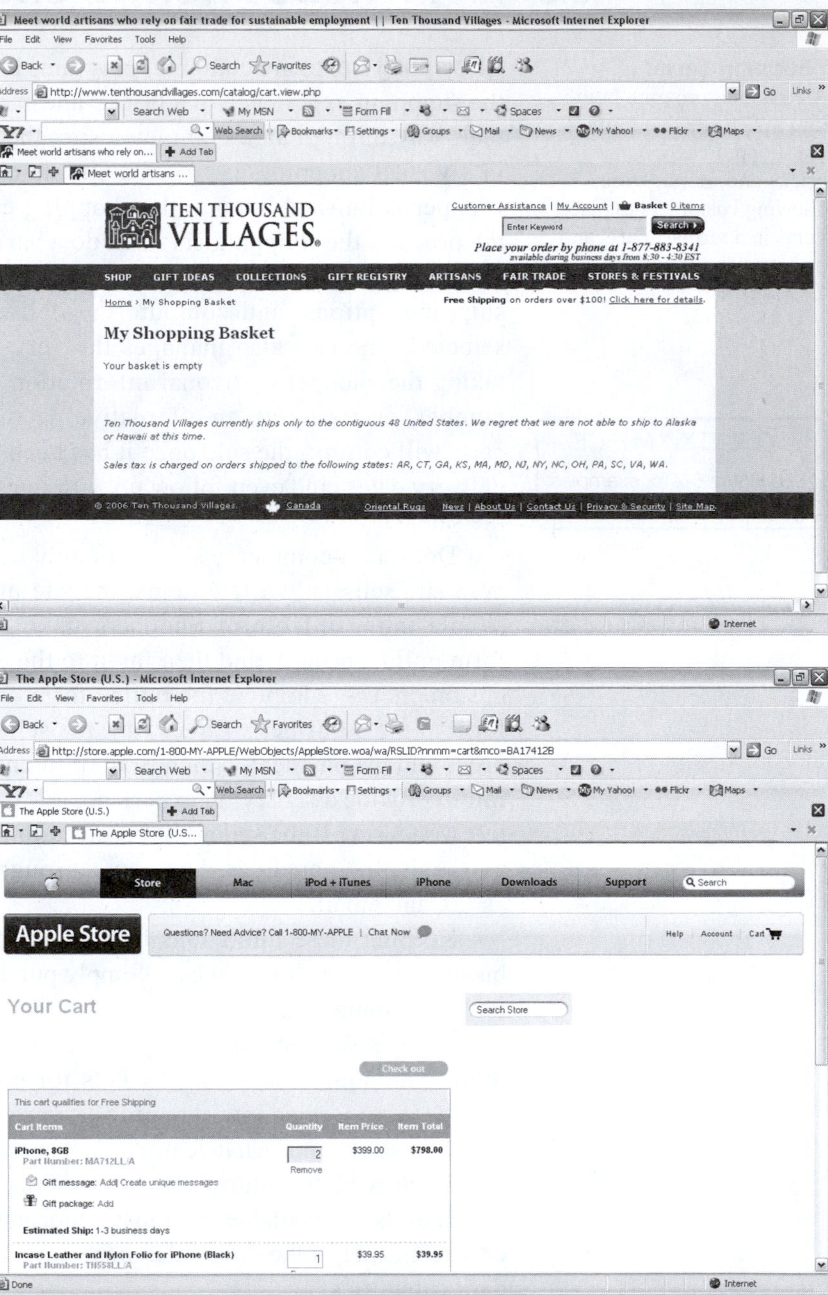

Samples of online shopping carts.

IN THE REAL WORLD

Crafting an E-Business with Shopping Carts and Credit Cards

Carol Jane Rossi loves knitting and crocheting, a passion shared by her sisters, her mother, her grandmother, and her great-grandmother. Rossi decided to take her hobby a step further than her yarn-loving family members by starting a company called J Originals to sell her sweaters, scarves, and other items. Initially, she sold the goods at craft fairs near her Connecticut home. After achieving modest success on the fair circuit, computer-savvy family members helped her expand her operation onto the Internet with JOriginals.com, a very simple Web site. Though her craft fair sales—and reputation—continued to grow, Internet sales lagged. Rossi explains, "At first, I didn't accept credit cards because I didn't have the money to establish a merchant account. I also didn't have a shopping cart application tied into the Web site, which we quickly discovered was holding us back in terms of generating sales based on the level of traffic that was visiting the J Originals Web site." Once Rossi added credit card capability and a shopping cart, J Originals was transformed into a growing and profitable online business.

6.3.1 Back-End Management Features

Each shopping cart program has a set of administration tools. Though the specifics can vary among types of software, ultimately these tools give an e-business owner control of their shopping cart. Here are features to look for in administration tools:

- **Wizards:** Use these tools to customize a shopping cart and integrate it into a Web site. The wizard walks the operator step by step through the entire process; the better the tools the easier the job.
- **Customization:** Having a wide range of customization options is an important feature of shopping cart programs. The more options available with colors and fonts, for example, the more likely that the shopping cart will mesh with and truly feel a part of the Web site.
- **Administrative functions:** Quality shopping carts put control over certain important functions—changing passwords and settings such as font size or number of items to display on a page, for example—exclusively in the hands of the administrator (usually the site's owner).
- **Inventory:** Some shopping carts can be integrated with an inventory system, meaning that it is possible to manage offline stock through the Web site, a very convenient feature.

- **Importing:** Entering products into a shopping cart one by one can be a time-consuming chore. Look for programs that allow importing product numbers and prices from an Excel spreadsheet (or a similar method).
- **Exporting:** Always confirm that product information can be exported from the shopping cart. The export feature is critical if a business switches to a different shopping cart and needs to transfer its inventory.

6.3.2 Customer-Centric Features

What features are most important to customers? When test driving a shopping cart demo, try to view the experience from the eyes of a shopper. Does the cart help process the orders quickly? Does the shopper feel frustrated and abandoned? Features to consider that will benefit customers are:

- **Save settings:** Customers should be able to save products in their shopping carts and then return later to make purchases.
- **Store data:** A high-quality shopping cart will not require returning customers to reenter account information. However, remember that some customers would rather not sacrifice possible security risks in favor of convenience.
- **View order:** Customers should be able to view complete orders as they shop or when they check out. Having to view a series of pages before being able to see total shipping costs, for example, is particularly frustrating.
- **Product views:** Customers cannot touch or feel the products when shopping online—purchase decisions are based on the images and descriptions provided. That is why it is important to use a shopping cart that allows uploading multiple images for one product.

6.3.3 Integration and Maintenance Features

For a shopping cart to work best, the cart must become a seamless part of the overall Web site. If the cart does not work, then a site operator needs to be able to get help—quickly, efficiently, and at all hours of the day or night. Along these lines, consider several critical integration and maintenance factors:

- **Access to support:** When and how is support for the shopping cart available? The best-case scenario is to have access to live support seven days a week. E-businesses that have to wait to get help also make their customers wait, which is a good way to lose them. When shopping for a cart, ask whether there is an extra fee for technical support.
- **Communication with shipping and handling:** Always explore how well a shopping cart can be integrated with major shipping providers (like UPS or FedEx) and how orders are relayed for shipping and handling. Does the software allow the operator to customize how and where the order requests are sent? For example, each time an order request is forwarded

to the shipping department, can a duplicate copy be emailed to another department?

- **Accommodation of other customer accounts:** A shopping cart should have the flexibility to handle all types of orders—from wholesale orders to affiliates. Even if a Web site does not need the flexibility today, it is good to know that the feature is already built into the cart and can accommodate future growth.
- **Integration with your accounting software:** A shopping cart essential is the ability to relay information to an e-business's accounting program. If these two programs cannot function together (or integrate with one another), the e-business owner must enter the data manually into the accounting software.

6.3.4 Promotion and Marketing Features

Of all the benefits a shopping cart can offer, promotion and marketing probably get the least amount of scrutiny before purchase. Most e-business owners should recognize what powerful marketing tools shopping carts are. The following list of functions is a small sample of how a shopping cart can help increase sales:

- **Product reviews and ratings:** Feature additional information on product pages to increase credibility and boost the potential for purchase.
- **Coupons:** Set up coupon codes to be entered by customers at the time of purchase.
- **Free-shipping option:** Offer free shipping as a marketing special, which can be an important competitive advantage during busy shopping seasons.
- **Gift certificates:** Another great seasonal (or year-round) tool is to offer the option of purchasing and using gift certificates, or virtual gift cards.
- **Discounts:** Set up different types of customer groups (such as wholesale or frequent buyer) to give a discount based on buying behavior. Or offer limited-time discounts by product.
- **Cross selling:** Suggest similar or complementary products that customers may like when they view certain products or check out.
- **Upselling:** Offer an incentive to purchase more products through upselling—for example, "Buy one, get one at half price" or "Buy two and get one free."
- **Survey tools:** Find out what customers are thinking by displaying a brief survey before checkout or when a customer abandons a shopping cart (leaving your site without a purchase).

E-business in Action

Select a shopping cart with the appropriate features for your e-business.

- **On-site search capability:** A good search tool helps customers easily find products based on several search criteria, such as brand name, category, or generic product name.
- **Search engine friendliness:** Use the shopping cart built-in features to better market products in the major search engines.

SELF-CHECK

1. How do customers purchase products from Web sites that do not employ a shopping cart? What issues does an e-business face when not using a shopping cart?
2. List three desirable back-end management features and explain why each is valuable to an e-business owner.
3. Why is integration such an important topic when evaluating shopping carts?

Apply Your Knowledge List five features to look for in a shopping cart program that could help to increase sales. Explain how to use each feature you listed.

6.4 EXPLORING SHOPPING CART SOLUTIONS

Naturally, marketing features and administrative tools are not the only features to consider when selecting a shopping cart. A more important decision is how the cart is delivered and set up for use. Three primary options for shopping cart software for e-businesses are (1) buying off-the-shelf software, (2) hiring a programmer to create a custom-built shopping cart package, and (3) using a hosted solution, where the e-business pays a fee to access the host server.

The first two options require installing and managing software on the site's server. The following sections explore all three options.

6.4.1 Off-the-Shelf Software

Before so many hosted shopping carts flooded the market, off-the-shelf software was the best bet for a quick, inexpensive solution. It still is a good option for many e-businesses. An off-the-shelf shopping cart allows an e-business to add the software to its own server. Many Web developers pursue this option and then become resellers of their particular shopping cart programs.

An advantage of using an off-the-shelf type of shopping cart is that an e-business is not tied to a specific Web host. This makes switching Web hosts simpler, though the importing and exporting tools found in most shopping carts make this issue less of a concern. Other advantages include control and price. For larger stores, the price issue is particularly important. Whereas a hosted shopping cart that supports 1,000 products might cost $199 per month, the 1,000-product ceiling may become a problem for fast-growing e-business sites. It sometimes makes sense to make a higher initial investment in off-the-shelf software in return for the freedom of offering an unlimited number of products.

Depending on the shopping cart, the price for the software can range anywhere from $399 for a basic program to more than $5,000 for a more dynamic product. When purchasing a shopping cart, technical support may or may not be included in the price. It is not unusual to be required to purchase a separate technical support package. Also, make sure that the cart is compatible with the e-business's preferred payment gateway. If not, extra programming—and extra cost—may be required to enable the software to communicate with the gateway.

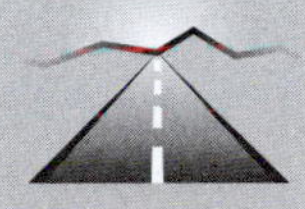

PATHWAY TO... FINDING SHOPPING CART SOFTWARE

Numerous companies sell off-the-shelf shopping cart solutions. Some of the most recognized providers are:

- **Miva Merchant (http://smallbusiness.miva.com):** Offers all-in-one products such as online storefronts and individual tools such as shopping cart systems.
- **X-Cart (www.requestsoftware.com):** One of the leading shopping cart providers.
- **ShopFactory (www.shopfactory.com):** Also provides the ability to create ready-to-go storefronts with shopping cart systems included (or sold separately).
- **ShopSite (www.shopsite.com):** Offers shopping cart systems at various price points for all sizes of business.
- **PDG (www.pdgsoft.com):** Shopping cart systems with built-in search engine capabilities.

6.4.2 Custom-Designed Shopping Carts

E-businesses that cannot find a shopping cart that perfectly fits their needs have another option: Custom design—or hire someone to program—a shopping cart that is unique to their needs. The obvious advantage of this option is that an e-business can get a program that meets their specifications in every way. The biggest disadvantage is cost. For online entrepreneurs who also happen to be programmers, creating their own shopping cart might be an obvious and inexpensive course of action. Or, if a business can find someone to do the job inexpensively, having a custom shopping cart programmed may be the same price or less than an off-the-shelf or hosted solution.

The previous scenarios are the exception rather than the rule. Hiring someone to program a custom shopping cart can become expensive fast. Some programmers charge a minimum of $15,000 for this type of project, and that amount will quickly be exceeded when adding beyond-the-basics features. Another problem is that a customized solution can be difficult to integrate with payment gateways, often requiring additional coding. Perhaps the biggest drawback is the limitation on support and ease of scalability. Each time the e-business hits a snag, it has to go back to the developer for help. As needs change or new features are desired, the software developer must be called, which can get expensive.

For large enterprises, the cost of changes may be small deterrents. Small online businesses will usually find their money and time better spent elsewhere. E-businesses that decide to delve into a custom-designed shopping cart should review the steps in the "Pathway to Creating a Custom-Designed Shopping Cart."

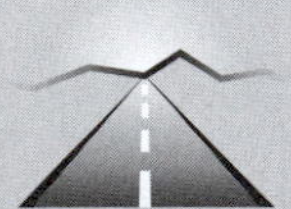

PATHWAY TO... CREATING A CUSTOM-DESIGNED SHOPPING CART

- **Bid and Quote:** Get at least three bids before selecting a developer. Then ask for a final quote delivered in writing before the project begins. Provide each prospective programmer with the same list of specifications when they develop the bids.
- **Define the Support:** Discuss what type of setup and ongoing support are available, including when support is available and how soon a support issue will be addressed. (Support might be available only during weekdays, and it might take three business days to process a request.) The cost of the support should also be included in the final quote.
- **Determine the Timeline:** Be specific about the time involved for any type of software development project. Set a series of targets, or objectives, that should be completed by a specific date. A specific timeline ensures that the project stays on track.
- **Get the Details:** The more details offered, the better. For example, find out how many programmers typically work on a project. More programmers can result in faster delivery, but can also add to the overall cost.

6.4.3 Hosted Shopping Carts

Hosted shopping carts have become an extremely popular option for e-businesses. In this scenario, the shopping cart software is maintained on a remote server by a company specializing in the services. E-businesses pay a fee to use the software and the server space required for storing product information. This strategy offers four specific advantages:

- **Cost:** A hosted solution is a more affordable option than in-house shopping cart software, especially for a first e-commerce endeavor. For a small monthly fee (as little as $10), an e-business can get immediate access to an extensive set of shopping cart features.
- **Simplicity:** Because most hosted shopping carts integrate easily into existing Web sites, they are usually easy to implement.
- **Support:** Hosted sites typically include good customer and technical support. Support hours for hosted solutions are usually around-the-clock, a real asset knowing that e-business problems may be encountered both day and night.
- **Flexibility:** Hosted shopping carts rarely require a long-term commitment, meaning that it is possible to test the service for a relatively short time to see if desired results are delivered. As long as the shopping cart has a good exporting feature, products can be moved to another cart that is a better fit.

Some terrific hosted shopping carts are available, each with different features. Your time is well spent investigating and locating a perfect fit. Three popular hosted shopping carts are described in this section.

1ShoppingCart

1ShoppingCart (www.1ShoppingCart.com) has been around for a long time and has a large fan base. The various plans support as many as 10,000 products and a host of marketing features. Four short-term plans, ranging from $29 to $79 per month, and annual accounts, which run $299 to $799, are available.

- **Autoresponder:** Not a shopping cart, just the ability to respond to email queries.
- **Starter:** A basic shopping cart system, lacking the tools to analyze sales.
- **Basic:** A shopping cart system plus simple email marketing tools.
- **Professional:** A complete shopping cart, autoresponders, email marketing tools, and affiliate tracking software. Available on a 30-day trial for only $3.95.

GoECart

Like 1ShoppingCart, GoECart (www.goecart.com) provides several different hosted shopping cart plans, with monthly or annual terms. The least expensive plan—Silver—allows up to 100 products, and costs $124.95 for setup and $79.95 per month. The most expensive plan—Platinum—allows unlimited products, and costs $1,999 for setup and $199.95 per month. GoECart includes almost all its features with each plan, so there is no need for an e-business to sacrifice marketing tools just because it maintains a small product line.

IN THE REAL WORLD

Hosted Cart is the Perfect Solution for Men's Clothier

SuitYourself.com is the online sales arm of the highly successful Fairfield Men's Store. Owner Naresh Mansukhani sells a varied array of high-quality men's fashions out of his bricks-and-mortar location in Connecticut, but he has also maintained a presence on the Web since 1993. "It still remains more of an informative site than a sales tool," Mansukhani explained. "But it gives us great satisfaction that at least we are able to share our philosophy with the rest of the world." For several years, SuitYourself.com used a custom shopping cart, but in 2002 it shifted to a hosted solution, GoECart.com. The hosted shopping cart proved a better match for a business that placed greater emphasis on its physical store, but still desired a highly professional and functional online presence. "GoECart was exactly the solution we were seeking. . . . Our company got a full-featured storefront and technical support for a great price," Mansukhani said.

ProStores

ProStores (www.prostores.com) is backed by eBay. Not surprisingly, it offers the standard shopping cart features and then some. In fact, ProStores ranges somewhere between a stand-alone shopping cart and a full storefront solution. ProStores integrates seamlessly with eBay stores and connects to other shopping sites, such as Google's Froogle.

ProStores has an unusual pricing structure, with four options ranging from $6.95 to $249.95 per month. The lower-end solution is the Express cart, which has minimum features and allows only ten products. On the other end of the equation is the Enterprise option, supporting an unlimited number of products and an extensive line of tools. The main drawback of the ProStores Express plan is that PayPal is the only payment option. In addition, all plans have a successful transaction fee added on to the monthly charges, which can quickly add up.

E-business in Action

Select the shopping cart option that best suits your e-business.

SELF-CHECK

1. Compare the advantages of off-the-shelf shopping cart software and a hosted solution.
2. Why would an e-business find it worthwhile to invest in custom-programmed shopping cart software?

Apply Your Knowledge Explain why choosing a hosted shopping cart solution may be the best option for a small e-business being launched on a very tight budget. Discuss any disadvantages of employing this strategy.

SUMMARY

Section 6.1

- Accepting credit card payments is essential to the success of most e-businesses. Enabling credit card transactions requires obtaining a merchant account and choosing a payment gateway.
- E-businesses must pay a variety of fees to allow accepting credit card purchases, including a discount rate (typically 2 to 4 percent of each sale) and a flat fee for each transaction.

Section 6.2

- Beyond credit cards, there are a variety of alternative payment options, including PayPal, electronic checking, and offline payments. By offering at least four options at checkout, a Web site can increase customer purchase rates (typically 60 percent to 80 percent).

Section 6.3

- Shopping carts are computer programs built into a Web site that mimic the shopping experience in a bricks-and-mortar store, allowing shoppers to place items in a virtual "cart" and accepting payment at the "checkout." Shopping carts are an essential tool for every serious e-business.
- When evaluating shopping carts, e-business owners should consider the features in four different categories: back-end management, customer-centric, integration and maintenance, and promotion and marketing.

Section 6.4

- Two options for businesses that want to maintain their own shopping carts are off-the-shelf software and custom-designed packages. These are good options for firms offering large numbers of products and desiring highly customized shopping carts.
- Hosted shopping carts are maintained on a server owned by another firm, and access is provided for a fee. Low cost and simplicity are among the advantages of this increasingly popular option.

ASSESS YOUR UNDERSTANDING

UNDERSTAND: WHAT HAVE YOU LEARNED?

Go to **www.wiley.com/college/holden** to assess your knowledge of the basics of online payments and shopping carts for an e-business.

APPLY: WHAT WOULD YOU DO?

1. A customer makes an online purchase using a credit card. Briefly explain the roles played by the shopping cart and payment gateway in making the transaction possible.
2. A new e-business owner established the necessary accounts to accept credit card payments. The application fee cost $150 and setup cost $300. Over the course of the first year he averaged 100 transactions per month, each generating about $50. The owner's discount rate was 2 percent and he also had to pay a 10-cent fee per transaction. At the end of the first year, what was his total cost for accepting credit cards? Figuring all charges, what was his actual per-transaction cost the first year?
3. Outline five measures an e-business owner should take to help prevent credit card fraud?
4. A Web site gets 120 visitors per day and each purchase averages $50. If the site offers a single type of payment source—credit cards—statistics say that 72 of those people will make purchases. How much revenue does the site generate each day? If the site adds three more payment options, the purchase rate increases to 80 percent. How many purchases are made each day? How much revenue is generated each day? Over one year, how much extra revenue is generated by offering more payment options?
5. An e-business accepts payments by credit card, e-checking, and PayPal, but wants to expand its options to increase sales. Create a list of five other payment alternatives, listing the major advantages and weaknesses of each new option.
6. A friend with a simple e-commerce site has seen his/her business stagnate, but is not convinced a shopping cart is needed. Create a list of ten specific ways that a shopping cart can improve sales.
7. People often focus on the sales and customer-oriented advantages of shopping carts, but shopping carts offer other benefits to e-business owners. Discuss some of the shopping cart features that can improve the operations of an online business.

8. Explain the advantages and disadvantages of all three shopping cart options with respect to each of the following considerations: cost; technical support; number of products offered; customization; and integration into the Web site.
9. In comparing two hosted shopping carts, an e-business owner notes that the two hosted shopping carts offer similar features, but have very different pricing structures. Solution 1 costs $500 to set up and $75 per month. Solution 2 costs only $99 to set up and $50 per month, plus charges a 10-cent fee per transaction (the e-business owner averages 500 transactions per month). Analyzing costs for one year, which solution appears to be a better deal? What appears to be a better solution over five years?

BE AN E-BUSINESS ENTREPRENEUR

Offering Varied Payment Options

Studies have shown that the payment options offered by an e-business can have a dramatic impact on its sales. Noting that the point of selling is making it as convenient as possible for customers to hand over money, develop a payment option plan for a Web site that sells decorative ceramic planters. Provide at least five distinctive options. Discuss what steps must be taken to make each option available, the approximate costs of providing each option, and any special rules that must be set up for each option.

Evaluating Shopping Cart Customer Features

Select two e-commerce sites that each employ full-featured, though distinctively different, shopping carts. Tour both sites thoroughly to evaluate the purchasing experience as a customer. Select five customer-oriented features that are important to you and then compare/contrast these features in each site, noting positives and negatives. Explain which site provides a superior customer experience, and suggest how the inferior site can adjust its shopping cart to improve customer appeal.

KEY TERMS

Broker An independent sales representative who makes a commission from signing up new merchant account customers.

Charge-back The dollar amount of a sale taken out of an e-business bank account when a customer disputes a purchase with their credit card company.

Discount rate The part of every credit card sale taken by the merchant account provider, typically between 2 and 4 percent.

Electronic checking A payment system that allows a customer to electronically transfer funds from a personal or business bank account into an e-business bank account.

Merchant account A specialized bank account that allows a business to accept credit cards.

Payment gateway An e-commerce service provider that communicates to credit card companies, banks, and Web sites, allowing online transactions to take place.

PayPal A global service that allows consumers to make Internet purchases without giving their personal financial information to an e-commerce site. Instead they use a PayPal account, funded credit card, check, or bank transfer.

Shopping cart A computer program built into a Web site that mimics the shopping experience in a bricks-and-mortar store, allowing customers to place items in a virtual "cart" and pay at a "checkout."

REFERENCES

1. Elsa Wenzel, "Shopping PayPal or Google Checkout," C/NET Reviews, http://reviews.cnet.com/4520-3513_7-6553495-1.html.

CHAPTER 7

PRODUCTS, INVENTORY, AND FULFILLMENT

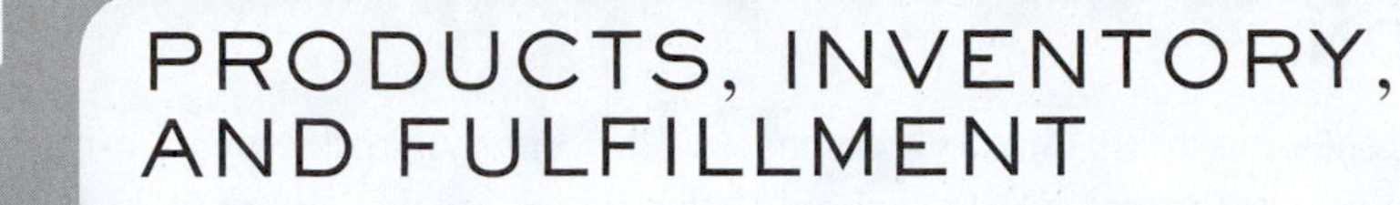

Deciding What to Sell, How Much to Charge, and How to Get Products to Customers

Do You Already Know?

- Where to find products for selling online and how to price them
- How to build and manage inventory for an e-business
- The different fulfillment options available to online businesses
- The best strategies for shipping products to customers

WWW For additional questions to assess your current knowledge on products, inventory, and fulfillment for e-businesses, go to **www.wiley.com/college/holden.**

What You Will Find Out	What You Will Be Able To Do
7.1 What makes a good product and how to determine the price for a product	• Manufacture or buy goods to sell online and price them appropriately
7.2 That there are several strategies for building and managing inventory	• Select a suitable inventory management strategy and maintain the right number of products for sale
7.3 How customer orders are fulfilled and the two primary options for completing this process	• Fulfill customer orders in-house, or outsource the function to an appropriate fulfillment house
7.4 The various options for shipping products to customers	• Offer customers multiple shipping options, set up accounts with shipping companies, and deliver overseas orders

INTRODUCTION

The majority of e-businesses are built on the model of selling tangible products through a Web site. Though the transactions take place electronically, they involve real products—items that must be created or purchased by an e-business, priced to earn a profit, stored, and then packed up and shipped out to the customers that buy the products. This chapter examines all of these different phases of product management, starting in the first section with selecting appropriate products to offer for sale online and pricing them in such a way to make the desired profit. The second section reviews different inventory strategies and discusses how many products an e-business should offer, which are dependent on its business philosophy and other factors. The third section covers how once customers buy products, those orders must be fulfilled—picked, packed, and shipped. There are two primary options for this function: (1) keep the job in-house or (2) outsource it to a specialized fulfillment house. Shipping products to buyers is an important topic for e-businesses. The fourth section offers advice on the options to offer customers, establishing accounts with shipping companies, and shipping products overseas.

7.1 SELECTING AND PRICING PRODUCTS

A natural choice for making money online is to sell a product. Whether selling uniquely crafted items or buying and reselling goods on the Web, selling a tangible product over the Internet has proven to be a successful online earnings model ever since e-commerce began taking off in the early 1990s.

With tangible goods, the question of making a profit can be captured in a simple four-word phrase: "Buy low, sell high." As entrepreneurs have known for thousands of years, to make money, a product must be sold for more than it costs. An e-business owner must project how much will be spent acquiring (or producing) and selling the product and at what price the product can be reasonably sold in the marketplace. The positive difference between the cost and the revenue is called the **profit.**

Profit:
The money left over after all costs are paid.

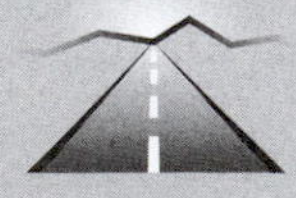

PATHWAY TO... DETERMINING WHETHER A PRODUCT WILL GENERATE A PROFIT

Before spending any money on a product, answer seven basic questions to help project a product's potential profit:

1. What is the cost of producing or purchasing the product?
2. How much is the overhead—the cost for utilities, rent, salaries, transportation, and other costs?

3. Can the product be priced so that it covers all costs and still remain competitive with similar products?
4. Will added shipping costs diminish the competitive price point?
5. What volume of products should be sold each month to reach the desired profit margins?
6. How much traffic (how many visitors) must be driven to the site and converted to customers in order to reach sales goals?
7. How much must be spent on marketing to attract the desired level of traffic?

When developing a list of products to be sold online, tabulate the projected expenses, estimate the income, and carefully consider whether or not the business plan can work successfully. If the potential profit is not enough to at least cover immediate needs, make adjustments before startup. Possible adjustments include finding additional products, raising prices, or reducing expenses. Even after making necessary changes, it still will be apparent that the success of product-based revenue models will be largely dependent on the products themselves—thus the need to choose the inventory wisely.

7.1.1 Manufacturing and Selling Your Own Goods

Creating goods and selling them online is generally the most successful e-business venture in terms of sheer profit margin. Creative and enterprising entrepreneurs can sell their own work on e-commerce sites, on auction sites such as eBay, and on Web sites that have been set up to market a particular type of item (such as ArtQuest, www.artquest.com, where artists can list their own works for sale). All kinds of custom-made items can be sold online, ranging from delicately smocked dresses for children to custom-designed iPod skins. However, a few characteristics give some items an advantage over other items, including:

- **Product quality:** Without exception, consumers expect a product worthy of its price tag. Entrepreneurs who create their own products have complete control over product quality. Designs should be finished and the workmanship should be at a high level before any product is put up for sale.
- **Originality:** If a handmade product is a unique twist on a mass-marketed product, the product can be very successful. Internet shoppers are always looking for products that are unique or different from the items available in most retail stores.

- **Fitting a niche:** A handmade product may not be completely unique, but may still be part of a specialized, hard-to-find group of products (such as personalized cell phone cases or cases for fountain pens). Narrowing a product's appeal is a good way to increase revenue potential.
- **A built-in customer base:** A product, such as woven altar cloths for churches, may be designed to appeal to a specific group of people. Having a clearly identifiable existing customer base that can be marketed to makes selling a product much easier.

E-business in Action
Manufacture goods to sell online.

IN THE REAL WORLD

A Painter Who Is Also a Successful Online Entrepreneur

Marques Vickers is an artist whose life has been dramatically changed by the Web. "I can clearly say that Internet access enabled me to pursue my present course even if it meant shifting directions," Vickers declares. He uses his self-named Web site, www.marquesv.com, to sell his own paintings, sculptures, and photography, as well as his books on buying and marketing fine art online. He first went online in November 1999 and his various Web sites (he owns more than 20 domain names) receive anywhere from 25,000 to 40,000 visits per month. Vickers' initial objective was to create a personalized around-the-clock presence for his work, but the Web site has proven to be a very profitable tool for selling his creations. In fact, Vickers has recently relocated from his original base in California to a new home in the south of France. His e-business required considerable work to begin, but now operates smoothly and is fairly inexpensive to maintain. What are Vickers' expenses for Web hosting and Internet access? Only about $29 per month.

7.1.2 Buying and Reselling Goods Online

Outside of creating and marketing handmade goods, there are many other options for making money online by selling products. In fact, the overwhelming majority of online entrepreneurs are people who buy tangible goods at low prices and sell them online for a profit. These products can either be sold directly through an entrepreneur's own Web site or through a third-party Web site.

Selling directly online means that customers come directly to a business's Web site to buy an item. The marketing, publicity, and fulfillment are all under the entrepreneur's control. Selling directly requires substantial effort, but can potentially be very rewarding. Entrepreneurs with little selling experience may want to allow other Web sites, such as eBay, to market their products. Such third-party Web sites bring in customers and provide systems for creating sales descriptions and receiving payments. In return, the host Web site takes fees for its services. This process allows entrepreneurs to avoid much of the work associated with selling directly online.

No matter what method is used to sell goods, a source must still be found for the merchandise. Many people who sell online begin by cleaning out their closets, their garages, and their attics. They sell off the extra merchandise in their own homes and the homes of friends and relatives. Others scour flea markets, estate sales, garage sales, secondhand stores, dollar stores, and many other marketplaces, looking for goods they can sell online. This method can be used to make part—sometimes all—of their income.

One problem with the reselling strategy is the amount of time spent searching for and transporting the items to sell. Another problem is overcoming difficulties encountered while building sufficient inventory to earn a profit from online sales.

Many e-businesses follow the methods employed by most traditional retail stores—buying their inventories wholesale from manufacturers or distributors. Buying **wholesale** means purchasing products at a discounted price and then reselling them at a marked-up price. The wholesale strategy is effective because it offers greater control over product supply and costs, but it offers other challenges.

Wholesale:
Products that are purchased at a discounted price and then resold at a marked-up price.

For example, entrepreneurs are responsible for ensuring that the following tasks are completed:

- **Purchase inventory in bulk:** To get a discount, large quantities of units usually must be purchased.
- **Warehouse the inventory:** Entrepreneurs are expected to store the inventory they purchased, possibly for several months. Space must be found in homes, or warehouses must be rented. Because online merchants tend to buy larger quantities of merchandise at wholesale prices than they do at flea markets, warehousing can be an expensive proposition.
- **Ship the products to customers:** Packaging and shipping must be handled for each item sold, either by hired employees or by the entrepreneurs themselves.
- **Handle returns and exchanges from customers:** If a customer is unhappy with a product or the item is damaged, the product has to be shipped back and dealt with accordingly.

Among the biggest drawbacks of buying wholesale is that the initial cash commitment is high. Storing all the products can be difficult. A garage or spare bedroom might suffice for a while, but eventually other storage space may have to be rented. The additional overhead expense can cut profitability considerably.

When merchandise is purchased from a wholesaler, some form of proof the merchandise is being purchased for a business and not for personal use is typically required. Wholesalers may ask for a state-issued reseller's certificate or a federal tax ID number. If the wholesaler does not require these items, the wholesaler may not truly be charging wholesale prices.

E-business in Action →
Purchase goods to resell online.

7.1.3 Pricing Online Products

After deciding what products or services the business will be selling, the prices of the merchandise must be determined. Researching similar products may have provided an idea of what items will have the best chance of selling. However, no matter how trendy or in-demand the products are, setting the wrong prices can keep the products from being sold. This section examines a sampling of successful pricing strategies and important pricing considerations.

The following factors are the most powerful in influencing what price to assign to a particular item:

- **Cost:** How much it costs (expenses) to create or purchase the product before reselling it to customers.
- **Demand:** Determined by the number of customers who are seeking out the product—either because the product meets a need or the customer simply desires it.
- **Competition:** How many competitors are offering the same, or a similar, product, and at what price?
- **Market position:** The customer perception of a particular product. For example, an upscale store might purposely employ higher prices while a low-cost, warehouse-style store might employ a more competitive pricing strategy.
- **Profitability:** How much money does an e-business want to make on each item sold after all expenses associated with selling the item are considered?

Product pricing is one of the most critical business decisions. All the advice and pricing models offered in textbooks or by economists can be confusing. Keep it simple. The basic price should primarily be determined by the cost of the product being sold. The basic price incorporates every expense associated with an item, including the wholesale price paid (the raw costs of materials to make the product), overhead costs, and shipping costs to deliver the product to the customers.

Fixed costs:
Costs, such as rent, which do not fluctuate. Often called overhead.

Variable expenses:
Costs that may fluctuate periodically.

Pricing floor:
The lowest price that should be charged for a product.

Costs or expenses that do not fluctuate are called **fixed costs** and are often considered as overhead (such as rent). Expenses that might change periodically are **variable expenses.** The price of the product should cover all variable expenses, and help contribute toward fixed costs.

After the cost of what is being sold is understood, pricing decisions can be made. Two common pricing strategies are:

- **Cost-plus:** Totaling the costs of the expenses associated with the product and then adding an amount desired as profit. The resulting dollar amount represents the **pricing floor,** or the lowest price that should be charged.
- **Value-based:** With this strategy, a price is set that reflects the highest amount customers are willing to pay for the product. Unlike the cost-plus method, the value-based method considers market conditions, such as demand, competition, and the perceived benefits (or value) of a product's features.

For example, if the cost for selling a coffee mug is $4.50, should it be sold for the same price? No, a respectable profit must be made. That amount depends on how much is desired—within reason, of course. If it is decided that $5.50 must be made on every mug, the price is set at $10.00 per item. This is an example of cost-plus pricing.

E-business in Action →
Establish appropriate prices for online goods.

Using value-based pricing, a higher price might be set based on consideration of other factors. For instance, how much are customers willing to pay for a coffee cup? In other words, what cost does the market bear? The next consideration is to find out what competitors are charging for similar products. If $9.99 is the top price on other sites, it may be unreasonable to expect to set a much higher price.

SELF-CHECK

1. When selling custom-made products online, what four characteristics give products an advantage in the marketplace?
2. What are the primary advantages and disadvantages of buying products wholesale and reselling them online?
3. Which factors are the most powerful in influencing pricing?

Apply Your Knowledge An e-business owner determines the need to charge $20 for baseball caps to make a desired profit, but discovers that a competitor is charging $18 for the same product. Discuss the risks of pricing the caps at either $18 or $20. Which option is the best?

7.2 BUILDING AND MANAGING INVENTORY

Choosing the best products and prices is certainly an important factor in starting any new online business, but another issue must also be considered: How much inventory should be kept on hand? In other words, how many different products should be available for sale? The answer depends on not only the type of products being sold but also the type of business strategy being implemented.

Online shoppers are accustomed to a nearly endless array of choices because they can easily jump from one Web site to another. These customers are also quick to make a decision about whether a site's inventory meets their expectations. To keep the attention of most online shoppers, it is necessary to have a clear strategy for what type of—and how much of a—product is offered.

It is unnecessary to carry thousands, or even hundreds, of products to find success online. However, there are three important factors to consider when deciding on how much inventory to maintain, as well as some distinct online inventory strategies, each with its own advantages and disadvantages.

7.2.1 Factors Affecting Inventory Management

When building an e-business, a variety of decisions must be made, including determining how much inventory (number of different products) to maintain. Sometimes, real-world issues, including budgets and product availability, overwhelm the ideal scenario. In such cases, a business should forget idealism and develop an inventory plan that falls within the boundaries of what is realistic and offers the best chance to make the desired profit by considering several factors.

The Amount of Money Available

A budget always goes hand in hand with how much inventory is maintained at any given moment. E-businesses can buy their products wholesale, buy the supplies to make their own creations, or even purchase the rights to resell products. No matter the strategy employed, most businesses will have a set budget for buying materials or completed products to sell. What a business can afford usually determines the number of items an e-business offers for sale on its Web site, and what it maintains in inventory to cover projected sales.

Shopping Cart Limitations

Depending on the type of shopping cart system employed, an e-business might be limited in the number of items it can carry. This, too, can be a budget issue. Many shopping cart programs escalate in price based on the number of products offered. If an e-business can only afford the shopping cart version for up to 25 products, for example, it makes it easier to narrow down how much inventory to maintain.

The Number of Products Available

A particularly important issue to consider for products that are custom-made to order is the number of products available. The time required for manufacture—or the availability at different times of the year—might force an e-commerce site to maintain limited supplies of some products. Businesses uncomfortable with the idea of a slimmed-down inventory might want to consider stocking up on inventory before officially launching their e-commerce site, or before offering new items for sale.

7.2.2 Strategies for Inventory Management

There are numerous options for managing inventory, but three common—and very different—strategies are frequently employed by e-businesses:

- Low-price strategy
- Being all things to all people
- Niche strategy

Low-Price Strategy

Competing based on price can be difficult, but it is a popular inventory strategy for some e-businesses. Entrepreneurs whose customers primarily use price to decide whether or not to buy should use the following techniques:

- **Provide many choices:** The customers are looking for good deals, and might not even have a specific item in mind when they are shopping. Having a variety of choices makes it more likely that the customers will find something to buy.
- **Change products often:** Even if a site does not get large volumes of traffic, returning customers expect a revolving inventory. If the customers discover that the inventory of a site remains constant after several return visits, the customers will stop returning altogether.

Being All Things to All People

The second strategy is a popular option for many first-time online entrepreneurs. The Web site offers a little bit of everything, until the business owner gets a better idea of what actually sells. This trial-and-error method of offering a chaotic variety of products can be cumbersome, but effective.

To reduce stress and quickly find the best products to retain, use the following techniques:

- **Keep products in limited supply:** When offering a large variety of products, maintain a relatively low level of inventory on all products to keep expenses down and storage issues to a minimum.
- **Rotate featured products often:** Highlight different products daily or weekly to find the customers' preferences. Featuring or spotlighting select items helps to quickly narrow down what products the customers respond to most.
- **Track results to learn inventory needs:** Maintaining detailed sales records is essential to determine what type of products customers respond to most. With reliable information about customer buying habits, it is possible to begin scaling down the number of products and adjust inventory to provide a better selection.

Niche Strategy

Specializing in one field usually leads to the best inventory strategy—and provides the most likely chance for success when building an online business. Consider the following advice when building inventory to serve a niche:

- **Offer a select number of products:** Focus on the quality or uniqueness of the products rather than on mass quantity. In addition to stocking relatively few items, it is also possible to keep relatively low levels of stock—as long as a steady supply of new items is being added to the online store.
- **Become an authority on the product:** By managing a single type of product, it is also possible to build a large body of knowledge about this area of interest. Customers may be just as likely to seek out the site for the expertise offered as for the product offered. Narrowly focused but authoritative sites can afford to keep inventory levels low and demand a premium price for products. Authoritative sites may charge a finder's or consultant's fee to assist customers in locating rare and/or desirable items not maintained in inventory.

E-business in Action
Select a suitable inventory management strategy.

IN THE REAL WORLD

Don't Forget Inventory When Starting Up

Lucky and Jinele Boyd, co-founders of MyTexasMusic.com, understand that it is easy to overlook inventory and order processing when starting an e-business, but now they understand just how important these topics are. Lucky advises entrepreneurs to have a "big vision" when creating e-commerce sites, which means having sufficient inventory to meet demand. The entrepreneur should also have efficient processes in place for picking and shipping orders when the e-business goes live. Most e-business owners firmly believe that having too many items for sale is preferable to not having enough, even if it strains the budget. The key in e-commerce is to keep people from having to wait too long for their purchases. Jinele Boyd says that MyTexasMusic treats every order with urgency and tries to ship the same day the order arrives. Another tip is to personalize each order. "We hand-write a note inside every box," Jinele boasts. "People tell us how amazed they are that a 'real person' handled their order."

7.2.3 Maintaining Inventory

Shoppers on the Web want things to happen instantly. If shoppers discover that an e-business is out of stock of an item they want, they are likely to switch to another online business instead of waiting for the first business to restock the item. With that in mind, owners should obey the basic principle of planning to be successful: Instead of ordering the bare minimum of an item, owners should make sure that there is extra stock. Too much inventory initially is better than running out in the future.

Owners should rely on software or management services to help keep track of inventory. Another useful strategy—but one that requires familiarity with databases—is recording initial inventory in an Access or SQL database. A database requires manual input of sales, which keeps business owners aware of the number of units left. Owners can also connect their sales catalogs to their databases by using a program such as Adobe ColdFusion, which can update the database as sales are being made. However, it may be necessary to hire someone with Web programming experience to initially set up the system.

No matter what strategy an e-business owner employs, two basic questions should always be answered:

- **How many items are in stock right now?** Always maintain enough stock not only for everyday demand, but also for sudden increases in demand (for example, demand resulting from holiday season buying).
- **Is it time to reorder?** Establish reorder points at which supplies should be automatically reordered (for example, when only a certain amount of inventory remains).

E-business in Action →
Maintain the appropriate inventory of products for sale.

SELF-CHECK

1. What real-world issues can affect inventory management?
2. What are the key elements of inventory management for an e-business employing a low-price strategy?
3. What tools should e-businesses employ to manage inventory?

Apply Your Knowledge Explain how an e-business focusing on a specialty niche would manage its inventory differently from one that is trying to "be all things to all people."

7.3 SUCCESSFUL FULFILLMENT STRATEGIES

Setting up an online business can be full of excitement and milestones. The true payoff, though, is best realized when that first payment rolls in for a product sold online. That event provides validation for why the e-business was created. Even though getting the money provides great satisfaction, it is important to remember that the transaction is not yet completed.

Fulfillment: The practice of delivering a product to a buyer after payment has been received; also known as filling the order.

After the payment has cleared, e-businesses still need to manage one critical area of the sale: fulfillment. **Fulfillment** is the practice of delivering the product to the buyer after payment has been received—filling the order. In a retail store, fulfillment is easy: Hand the customer a shopping bag with the purchase and the receipt, and the customer walks out the door. In an online business, other steps are needed to fulfill an order, and with advances in Internet technology and shipping services, achieving the fulfillment goal is easier than ever.

Outsourcing: Paying another company to manage some aspect of a business's functions, for example, fulfillment.

Planning for order fulfillment does not start when payment is received. This section discusses the elements that can affect fulfillment, starting with how an e-business is set up. There are a variety of strategies for storing, organizing, and shipping products. In some cases, the best step you can take is to pay another company to manage shipping and other fulfillment functions—a strategy called **outsourcing.**

7.3.1 Fulfillment Basics

The moment that an e-business receives payment, the clock begins ticking and the customer is eagerly awaiting the item they have purchased. Online sales present tremendous challenges. The Internet offers a sense of immediacy in offering customers the ability to quickly find and purchase items from the comfort of their homes, but the system also has a built-in waiting period while the product is picked, packed, and shipped. This waiting period only intensifies customer feelings about their online purchase. A customer who experiences a bad fulfillment process will remember nothing else about a business, even if the Web site is well designed and the ordering process easy.

Effective fulfillment is all about establishing systems that are in place before the first order is received. First, consider how the business has been set up, and how work flows during a typical day. Then lay out everything so that the basic operations and daily tasks can be completed with the minimum amount of time, effort, and cost.

PATHWAY TO... PLANNING YOUR DAILY FULFILLMENT WORKFLOW

To help plan the daily workflow, first ask these questions:

- Does the business operate from home or from a dedicated office space?
- Will the business buy products for resale and store them?
- Will the business ship out products itself or outsource this task?
- Is the online business required to work in conjunction with a physical store?
- How many employees need access to the merchandise and system?

Second, track the flow of one item offered for sale:

1. Get the product in stock.
2. Prepare the product for sale.
3. Store the product while it is for sale.
4. Pack the product after it is sold.
5. Ship the product out after it is packaged.

Think about when and where these events take place to help plan the business setup and the daily workflow.

Space is an important consideration for fulfillment functions. Home-based businesses might need to borrow a spare bedroom for storage and shipping, while firms using a rented office might need to pay for more space to manage storage and shipping functions.

Timing is also important, especially when having to coordinate pickup schedules with shipping companies. Establish a cutoff time for same-day order fulfillment and be conservative. It is better to underpromise and overdeliver than to consistently miss deadlines and disappoint customers.

The key is to set up a model that fits the size and structure of the e-business, but also to be flexible enough to handle changes. There is no reason for a part-time e-business selling 20 items per month to buy an expensive software inventory program. Likewise, as volume grows, it is not realistic to expect to run a multi-million-dollar venture with a pencil and pad of paper. Also, choose a system that makes it easy to track inventory and orders at any point in time—to quickly determine if products are in receiving, on the shelf, being packed, or en route to the customer.

7.3.2 In-House Fulfillment

Many small businesses manage their own fulfillment, which means packing and shipping their own products and sending the products out the door. Doing so allows these businesses to control the quality of shipments so that they know their customers are being served. Typically, doing so makes sense: Because the inventory is on-site, orders can be packed at the source and sent out rather than relayed to some distant warehouse.

To set up an in-house fulfillment model, first determine the amount of inventory needed. Second, calculate the amount of space required to store inventory. The tasks of estimating order volume, inventory levels, and storage requirements continue on a regular basis after the e-business goes live. It is better to estimate on the high side and have extra inventory in stock, rather than running out and disappointing new customers.

Maintaining enough space to house adequate inventory is important. Different models, both in-house and outsourced, allow e-businesses to hold more products than their current available space.

Relationships with vendors help determine the amount of space required. Businesses that receive shipments in batches must have enough space available to take in a shipment and hold it until sales are made for the product. Vendors that can ship items in a just-in-time approach can reduce space requirements. In **just-in-time (JIT) inventory management,** vendors deliver their products just before an e-business needs them for listing or shipping out. In effect, the vendor takes on the warehousing function. However, a JIT strategy has some risks. If a just-in-time vendor is late with a shipment, an online business may find itself with nothing to send out to customers.

Just-in-time (JIT) inventory management: An inventory system in which vendors deliver their products just before a business needs them for shipping out.

If the warehouse space required is more than the available space, moving is not necessarily the best option. Instead, either consider renting temporary storage, or renting dedicated warehouse space for inventory. A JIT strategy requires keeping some sample products close at hand, for taking photographs, writing descriptions, or expediting shipping to preferred customers.

After resolving the issue of space, think about labor: Who will pack and ship the products? The number of orders to be packed and shipped helps determine fulfillment worker needs. A business packing only a few orders a day may simply need some of the owner's time, or a single employee, to manage the task. As the number of orders continues to grow, e-businesses should consider hiring dedicated employees to perform the fulfillment to maintain consistency and quality in this very important function.

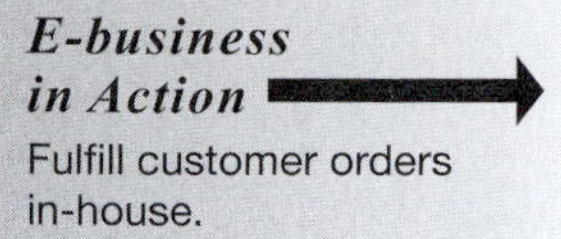

Fulfill customer orders in-house.

IN THE REAL WORLD

Recognize the Advantages of Handling Fulfillment Yourself

Christian Girts, the founder and owner of fly-fishing equipment e-tailer AnglersVice.com, is a believer in handling fulfillment himself. Girts offers a wide array of products, but he warehouses everything in his 700-square-foot basement. Why? "This allows us to ensure that all orders are processed within 24 hours or less," Girts explained. "I have learned to avoid using drop-shippers and maintain my own inventory. If you use a drop-shipper, you're giving up product control. That can hurt your business." Furthermore, Girts advises e-business owners to carefully research their suppliers before selecting them. "Ensure that inventory will be available to you when you need it, and that your suppliers have no qualms about working with an online merchant."

7.3.3 Outsourcing Fulfillment

Most people have a passion for the businesses they want to create, happily nurturing their dreams of turning a business idea into reality. Few business owners dream, however, of running a shipping-and-warehouse operation. Therefore, many business owners choose to outsource their fulfillment operations to someone else in order to focus on aspects of their business. Contrary to popular belief, businesses do not need to be a Fortune 500 corporation to outsource fulfillment. Small businesses around the world have successfully outsourced the fulfillment process thanks to fulfillment houses.

Fulfillment houses: A business that specializes in packing and shipping other business's goods.

Fulfillment houses are businesses whose sole job is packing and shipping other people's goods. By grouping multiple clients' shipping operations, a fulfillment house can employ fewer people to manage the volume of goods than individual companies that hire their own staffs. These fulfillment companies often feature state-of-the-art, computerized, inventory management systems and train employees to achieve optimum efficiency.

Outsourcing companies also offer specialized and enhanced services in three other areas that affect e-businesses: customer service, reporting, and scalability.

Customer Service

Fulfillment houses typically employ their own customer service teams to manage customer calls or emails—for example, order status inquiries or special handling or shipping requests. Fulfillment houses can greatly benefit growing e-businesses, which frequently find themselves overwhelmed with customer service issues and hiring and training staff to handle this function.

Reporting

As an e-business grows, the owner needs to keep track of how many orders go out for each product line, and then analyze that data. Most fulfillment houses have a tracking and reporting capability built into their systems to be able to deliver reports that allow customers to plan for their next phase of business.

Scalability

Scalability refers to allowing an e-business to periodically grow or shrink—in terms of employees, space utilized, or materials consumed—depending on current needs. Scalability is a particularly important issue for seasonal businesses, including those that must build inventory to satisfy Christmas season demand. Businesses that manage this issue in-house may have to rent temporary warehouse space or use temporary workers (or hire, then lay off "permanent" staff). Fulfillment services provide an alternative option. Utilizing the fulfillment house's larger base of shared resources, small e-businesses can grow quickly to accommodate short-term needs, then shrink accordingly when business slows.

7.3.4 Choosing a Fulfillment House

Many outsourcing companies specifically target small-business accounts, especially online businesses. Outsourcing companies know that by pooling inventories of several small businesses, a smaller team of trained personnel can manage the accounts in one warehouse. In other cases, your outsourcing partner can be a similar business that has its fulfillment processes perfected and has decided to use that expertise to make money for other companies by solving their fulfillment headaches.

When searching for a fulfillment partner, keep these three guidelines in mind:

1. **Establish a budget:** Knowing what it can afford is essential for every e-business before they start researching outsourcing options. The budget should always factor in savings in employee labor, but also transportation costs for shipping goods to the fulfillment house—which can be substantial if it is located a long distance from the e-business or its suppliers.
2. **Shop around:** Always get two or three estimates. Get a feel for the service levels each company offers, and see whether a high-service, high-price company is willing to match a competitor's lower price.
3. **Factor in all the costs:** Not all price quotes show the total cost. Some low-price quotes actually require a large investment of time and money on the e-business's part.

When looking for a fulfillment house, vendors, manufacturing partners, and even fellow business owners are all good places to get referrals. It is possible to simply turn to the Internet and search out an option, but it pays to get a firsthand evaluation of the company from a current or past customer.

Other outsourcing fulfillment options are shipping companies, which are increasingly involved in all aspects of fulfillment. UPS Logistics, for example, helps businesses around the world coordinate their supplies, orders, and product flow.

After finding the right outsourcing partner, create an agreement to define the terms of the relationship. Important terms to specify include service level and the rate of customer response. E-businesses also need to establish how quickly the company will ship products, what materials will be used in packing them, and how quickly the shipping company will respond to customer requests.

E-business in Action →
Select an appropriate outsourcing option for order fulfillment.

7.3.5 Working Efficiently with Outsourced Fulfillment

After selecting and negotiating an agreement with a fulfillment house, it is important to do more than just sign the contract and begin transferring inventory. The two partner companies need to talk about how their relationship will work and their expectations for each other. Even though the e-business has hired the fulfillment house to do "all the work," they still need to provide three items: inventory, order information, and payment.

Inventory

Most fulfillment houses take on an e-business's inventory and warehouse it at their location. Decide how much inventory to transfer, when to do it, and when and how replacement inventory should be received. Make sure to count the inventory before it leaves, and double-check the inventory list after it arrives. Some fulfillment companies provide the trucks and labor to move inventory; others require their customers to make the arrangements.

Order Information

When orders are placed, use a reliable and automated way to get that order information to the fulfillment house. Orders can be transferred individually as they are received, or in batches once or multiple times during the day. In some cases, fulfillment companies also operate the order collection—the order goes directly from customers' computer screens to the fulfillment company's database. If the fulfillment house is taking orders, request detailed reports with all the customer information transmitted during the sale. Remember, customer orders are the building blocks for a customer list that helps e-businesses thrive.

Payment

Fulfillment houses do not pack and ship orders out of the goodness of their hearts—they need to be paid. Options for managing this cost are:

- Build the extra cost into the shipping charge, and have that money transferred each time the company fills an order.
- Have the company prepare invoices for one or two months' worth of orders. Most e-businesses will be required to pay a retainer to cover initial orders.
- If the company is taking orders and payment, the company can keep its portion of the shipping amount and pay the e-business for the goods it ships out.

Periodically, a fulfillment house sends a report detailing the activity performed. Examine the report carefully. Not only should this report offer an overview of the flow of business, but should also reveal the quality of the fulfillment house's work. Simply compare ship dates to the times orders were received to calculate how quickly the company is processing orders.

As inventory drops at the fulfillment house, there must be a trigger to prompt the transfer of more inventory and avoid supply on hand reaching zero. Many fulfillment houses can calculate this number by using sophisticated computer tracking systems that monitor shipment levels and predict how long it takes to ship all inventory in their possession. The fulfillment house usually factors in time to cover unexpected delays in inventory transfers or unusual changes in orders.

7.3.6 Taking the Drop-Shipping Approach

Drop-shipper: A wholesaler that is paid by an online merchant to ship a product to a customer.

Another way to outsource fulfillment is to use a drop-shipper. Unlike a fulfillment house, which ships the goods owned by you to your customers, a **drop-shipper** owns the products and pays you a sales commission. A drop-shipper is basically a wholesaler who ships directly to your customers; such companies typically service several retailers.

Drop-shipping has the advantage of saving an online business the expenses associated with inventory, storage, handling, and distribution—this can make it a good alternative for online businesses getting established on a tight budget. However, that freedom from inventory expenses comes at a cost, cutting about 10 percent off your margins. And with many products on the Internet, the difference between making money and going out of business may be a matter of only a few percent.

SELF-CHECK

1. How does a fulfillment house assist an e-business other than inventory storage and shipping?
2. What are the basic rules when shopping for a fulfillment house?
3. List and explain three items an e-business must have in place to supply their fulfillment house?
4. Provide one advantage and one disadvantage to using a drop-shipper as a means of outsourcing fulfillment.

Apply Your Knowledge Compare and contrast five major issues to consider when evaluating in-house versus outsourced fulfillment.

7.4 SHIPPING PRODUCTS

Customers that order online want to receive the merchandise quickly. Many options are available for shipping those products, but often customers expect to decide which option is the best. Some are willing to pay extra to get their order faster. Other customers often have a favorite shipping carrier, or a carrier that they refuse to use.

When those same people hear the words "Shipping and handling," they usually envision an e-business performing these basic steps:

1. Pull an item off the shelf.
2. Put that item in a box.
3. Add packing material.

4. Seal the box with tape.
5. Add the recipient's address and the return address to the box.
6. Ship the box.

These steps demonstrate the basic flow of the shipping process, but there are many ways to make this process happen. E-businesses handling their own shipping can take advantage of some existing systems to make the process easier.

7.4.1 Offering Multiple Shipping Options

In the end, the best way to keep customers happy is to offer them multiple shipping options. Multiple options can mean offering variety in:

- **Shipping carriers:** Including FedEx, UPS, DHL, or the U.S. Postal Service.
- **Shipping methods:** Each carrier typically offers various shipment speeds on a sliding price scale—for example, Next Day Air, 2nd Day Air, or Ground. It usually is not difficult for e-businesses to pass along all these options to their customers.
- **Order mixing:** A customer who orders multiple items can select which items get which kind of shipping. For example, a customer who orders a heavy computer system and a light book about computers can have the book delivered to start reading the next day, and have the heavy computer system delivered by ground in two weeks.

When customers are offered these options, the e-business (or its fulfillment house) must be ready to use each service whenever it is needed. Companies must have access to current shipping rates for all carriers and methods to be able to maintain accurate price quotes on all weights and sizes. Shopping carts must also be updated with the same shipping information.

The rewards of these efforts are best expressed in terms of customer satisfaction. Giving customers shipping choices is like giving them product choices. Customers feel more in control of the shopping experience and believe that a business is willing to cater to their needs. Often, an online business charges a flat fee for the lowest shipping rate and slowest delivery service. Although that strategy may work for some customers, it misses the customers who need items immediately or by a guaranteed date.

E-business in Action →
Offer customers multiple shipping options.

The best example of the power of multiple shipping options is Amazon.com. To spur sales, it offers free shipping for customers spending at least $25, and it ships the items by U.S. Postal Service Ground Mail. However, customers can specify all or part of their orders to be sent a certain way, and they can pay the appropriate rate for faster shipping, such as Next Day or 2nd Day Air.

IN THE REAL WORLD

Don't Give Away E-Business Profits with High Shipping Costs

Marcia Collier, an eBay Power Seller, remembers how shipping was managed during the early years of e-business. Sellers would scavenge used cardboard boxes and other shipping supplies, and customers would hardly bat an eye. But things have changed—buyers demand a highly professional approach to online shopping, meaning that e-businesses need to buy quality supplies and offer multiple shipping options. Even with the bar raised to high levels, e-businesses can find ways to save money. Collier recommends buying items like packing tape and bubble mailers in bulk. Shopping for the best price on boxes is also a good idea—or use one of the many free boxes and envelopes provided by the U.S. Postal Service for shipping products by Priority Mail. Package insurance is another necessity that many sellers neglect, but it can be expensive. Collier suggests using a private parcel insurance company (such as U-PIC, www.u-pic.com) to save up to 80 percent on what major carriers charge.[1]

7.4.2 Establishing Accounts with Carriers

Delivering online orders has become big business for shipping companies. Therefore, carriers are fighting to keep customers by virtue of their service—and adding new features and adjusting prices whenever necessary to succeed. Shipping companies usually cater to higher-volume customers, but also to online businesses that produce a steady, predictable stream of shipments in smaller quantities. In fact, online businesses setting up accounts with multiple carriers often have negotiating power for better rates and services.

To sign up for a business account, choose one of these methods:

- Contact the company by phone and work with a sales representative to set up an account.
- Go to a shipping company's Web site and look for a business account link for the appropriate forms to complete.
- Go directly to a shipping company's office and ask to speak to a representative to set up an account.

PATHWAY TO... SETTING UP A SHIPPING ACCOUNT

Shipping companies will ask questions to gauge the prospective level of shipping. Be prepared to answer the following:

- How many packages will be shipped in an average week?
- What is the average size and weight of typical packages?
- Are customers in the United States, or will there be a mix of domestic and international packages?
- What is the expected percentage breakdown of various options—Next Day, 2nd Day, or Ground?

When setting up a shipping system from scratch, make estimates based on research and by talking to similar e-businesses. Although companies are rarely bound by these numbers, a starting point to set up an account is required.

Ask about rates and price breaks for certain shipping levels. There may be a discount tier within easy reach. Hitting a sales goal is easier if the goal is measurable.

E-business in Action
Set up accounts with shipping companies.

An account with a shipping company is typically free of monthly charges, unless a special service is provided. The company keeps a payment method on file so that an e-business can accrue shipping charges and make one monthly payment, rather than paying every time they ship a package. After signing up for an account with a shipping carrier, always review the monthly bill. Never assume that a carrier automatically screens the bill or provides notification for overcharges.

CAREER CONNECTION

An online power-tool supplier takes advantage of e-business resources to get the job done.

Mark Lauer is president of Pennsylvania-based General Tool & Repair, Inc., a power-tool supplier that expanded its business by adding an e-commerce site (www.gtr.com). Now the company receives 10 to 40 online orders each day and generates monthly revenues of $35,000–$45,000 through its Web site. Credit card verification and order processing are major functions for the online business, but General Tool & Repair has software—and operational rules—to make the jobs easier and to minimize problems. A program called Authorizer checks the shipping address against the address of the credit card owner to make sure the order is legitimate and that the item can be shipped. If the program notes a problem, then the customer is emailed to make sure the purchase is legitimate or to explore shipping options. Lauer also notes that the company accepts credit card numbers through a secure server, but does not process the orders online. Processing credit cards offline allows time to make sure that the item is in stock before charging a customer's account. Typically, the order is processed and shipped out the day after the order is placed. Lauer estimates that the Web site replaces 50 salespeople. "This is all business we never had until two years ago, so it's basically all extra sales," he notes happily.

Tips from the Professional

- Add e-commerce to your business.
- Increase efficiency by utilizing e-business software.
- Consider the benefits of offline credit card processing.

7.4.3 International Shipping

The Internet, fax and data lines, and cell phones have allowed online businesses to reach millions of new potential customers. Shipping companies have responded by improving international shipping capabilities, which gives e-businesses more options for servicing their customers.

The only shipper that reaches most countries in the world is the U.S. Postal Service (USPS). When selecting USPS economy or ground service, the package reaches its destination in an average of three to six months, with no tracking capability. The USPS also offers air-mail service, which takes at least a week to reach its destination country. Although the USPS offers insurance for packages to most countries, it typically does not provide any tracking capability. The only service it offers that guarantees a tracking number and insurance is its Global Express Air Mail service, an expensive option. To see a list of countries and services that the USPS delivers to internationally, go to www.usps.com/business/international/welcome.htm.

Other shipping services—for example, UPS, FedEx, or DHL—use some form of air courier, which can be expensive for heavy items. Although these services automatically issue tracking numbers, in some cases their tracking capabilities end when the packages enter their destination countries. Each country also places specific limits on package weight and dimensions. Consult each company's Web site for information about country-specific limits.

Regardless of the shipper you choose, all international shipments require a customs form to document the following information about an item:

- The country of origin
- The quantity
- A description
- The value of each product in the package

Shippers such as UPS and FedEx incorporate the customs form information into their label-creation process so that when you create your label, the appropriate shipping documents are created alongside it. The USPS uses two customs forms, which can be completed by hand or online:

1. **Green (Form 2976):** For packages that weigh less than 4 pounds
2. **White (Form 2976-A):** For packages that weigh more than 4 pounds or have insurance

E-business in Action →
Efficiently deliver overseas orders.

In some cases, the destination country also requires a certificate of origin or a signed affidavit that certifies the origin country of an exported item. Some countries also require that the goods be inspected by an independent, third-party organization and a certificate of inspection included with the label and customs forms. For more detailed information on how to send large shipments overseas, consult the International Chamber of Commerce Web site (www.iccwbo.org).

SELF-CHECK

1. What information is required for an e-business to set up an account with a shipping company?
2. What shipping option serves the greatest number of countries outside the U.S.? What is one significant weakness of using this option?

Apply Your Knowledge Knowing that customers prefer "multiple options" for shipping, summarize what options a customer-friendly e-commerce site should offer for shipping purchases.

SUMMARY

Section 7.1

- Selling handcrafted items online offers tremendous profit potential, but the goods must be of very high quality, be original, fill a niche, and have a built-in customer base to be successful.
- Most Web sites selling tangible goods buy items at wholesale from manufacturers and distributors and resell them at an appropriate markup. The wholesale strategy is effective but requires a high initial investment and the ability to warehouse the products.
- Product pricing is a critically important business decision that is influenced by a number of factors, including cost, demand, competitors' pricing, market position, and profit requirements.

Section 7.2

- Inventory management strategies will be affected by a number of factors, including finances, shopping cart capacity, and product availability. Most small e-businesses successfully utilize a limited inventory strategy, but large inventory strategies are also an option.

Section 7.3

- Fulfillment is the practice of delivering a product to a customer—picking, packing, and shipping. E-businesses can choose to manage this function in-house or outsource it to a specialized fulfillment house.
- Outsourcing fulfillment can offer a variety of benefits for e-businesses, including improved customer service, detailed reporting, and scalability to accommodate seasonal changes in business.

Section 7.4

- Customers expect e-businesses to offer a variety of shipping options, including a choice of delivery companies, speeds, and prices. Accounts must be established before startup to ensure that shipping works efficiently starting with the first order.

ASSESS YOUR UNDERSTANDING

UNDERSTAND: WHAT HAVE YOU LEARNED?

Go to **www.wiley.com/college/holden** to assess your knowledge of products, inventory, and fulfillment for an e-business.

APPLY: WHAT WOULD YOU DO?

1. The owner of an e-business selling decorative cell phone covers finds a supplier that sells the covers wholesale for $5 each. To make an appropriate profit, the e-business must mark up the price 80 percent for resale—what is that price? The supplier offers a 5 percent discount for buying in greater quantities, but the e-business's cost increases by five cents per phone cover to pay for extra storage. Would this be a good deal? Why?
2. An online entrepreneur selling homemade candles is trying to develop a price for her top-of-the line product. Each unit costs $7 to manufacture and carries $3 of fixed costs. The owner's goal is to earn a 30 percent profit on each sale, though she has discovered that customers would be willing to pay $15 for this type of candle. What price would she set for the candle using a cost-plus model? What about a value-based model?
3. An e-business owner wants to launch a Web site selling sports collectibles, but is unsure whether to sell items from all kinds of sports or just from tennis, a niche he knows very well. Describe which inventory strategy the e-business owner would employ for each of these options. List and explain the advantages and disadvantages of each strategy for a small e-business.
4. A friend selling knitting supplies online is unsure of how often to replenish inventory. Briefly describe a plan that could be used to track inventory and determine when it is time to reorder. Explain the tools and techniques that would make the job easier.
5. You are worried about needing to rent larger, more expensive warehouse space for your e-business, but you have heard that just-in-time inventory management might be a solution to your problem. Define just-in-time inventory management, explain how it might solve warehousing problems for small businesses, and suggest the risks of employing this strategy.

6. A friend planning to sell unique tools and hardware online does not want to manage warehousing and shipping for his small business, but believes that outsourcing will cost too much. Convince your friend to seriously consider the outsourcing option by detailing at least five advantages of outsourcing fulfillment as opposed to keeping it in-house.
7. What are the major challenges that must be effectively managed for an e-business that chooses to work with an outside fulfillment house?
8. An entrepreneur planning to use a Web site to sell documents and photographs autographed by famous people has neglected the topic of fulfillment in their business planning. Describe the steps the entrepreneur must undertake to ship standard 8 x 10 photographs. What materials will need to be purchased? What shipping options should be offered?
9. An e-business owner is exploring expanded marketing to foreign countries, but is worried about shipping costs. Explore the U.S. Postal Service Web site (www.usps.com), and determine what it would cost to ship a two-pound package, dimensions 9 × 12 × 3 inches and value of less than $100, from your home zip code to Paris, France, using three speeds of services. Summarize the cost and expected delivery time for the three options.

BE AN E-BUSINESS ENTREPRENEUR

Exploring the Basics of Fulfillment

Fulfillment sounds like a simple process, but it actually requires e-business owners to set up a smoothly working system—filled with numerous details—to consistently deliver products to customers. To learn more about this process, detail the life cycle of a coffee mug that will be sold online while a business manages it before, during, and after it is sold. At each step, list the specific requirements that a business must satisfy to complete the step in terms of space, manpower, supplies, and services.

Examining Shipping Options

The bulk of the orders shipped out by your e-business can fit in a 9 x 12 x 4-inch cardboard box and weigh less than two pounds. Orders have a value of $50. Visit the Web sites of three different shipping services and calculate the cost of shipping a package from Chicago (zip code 60605) to Los Angeles (90001) using three different speeds of service. Compile a table that summarizes the delivery time and price for the different carriers.

KEY TERMS

Drop-shipper	A wholesaler that is paid by an online merchant to ship a product to a customer.
Fixed costs	Costs, such as rent, which do not fluctuate. Often called overhead.
Fulfillment	The practice of delivering a product to a buyer after payment has been received; also known as filling the order.
Fulfillment house	A business that specializes in packing and shipping other business's goods.
Just-in-time (JIT) inventory management	An inventory system in which vendors deliver their products just before a business needs them for shipping out.
Outsourcing	Paying another company to manage some aspect of a business's functions, for example, fulfillment.
Pricing floor	The lowest price that should be charged for a product.
Profit	The money left over after all costs are paid.
Variable expenses	Costs that may fluctuate periodically.
Wholesale	Products that are purchased at a discounted price and then resold at a marked-up price.

REFERENCES

1. Marcia Collier, "The Hidden Costs of Shipping Products," Entrepreneur.com, www.entrepreneur.com/ebusiness/ebaycenter/ebaycolumnist/article175082.html.

CHAPTER

8 MARKETING AN E-BUSINESS

Advertising and Promoting an Online Brand

Do You Already Know?

- What a brand is and how to create one
- The most popular options for online advertising
- How to use newsgroups and Internet mailing lists for promotion
- What blogging and podcasting are

For additional questions to assess your current knowledge of marketing for e-businesses, go to **www.wiley.com/college/holden.**

What You Will Find Out	What You Will Be Able To Do
8.1 Techniques for branding an e-business and developing a marketing budget	Create an e-business brand; develop a marketing budget
8.2 The four popular options for online advertising	Advertise an e-business using banner ads, pop-up ads, search-engine ads, and classified ads
8.3 How to use newsgroups and Internet mailing lists for promoting e-businesses	Promote an e-business in newsgroups; compile and send promotional materials to an Internet mailing list
8.4 That there are several creative, low-cost options available for promoting e-businesses	Promote an e-business with newsletters, blogging, podcasts, automated techniques, offline advertising, and press releases

INTRODUCTION

"Build it and they will come," was a great line in the classic baseball movie *Field of Dreams,* but it has no standing in the competitive online business world. Every new e-commerce site also needs an aggressive and effective marketing strategy if it wants to succeed. This chapter provides an overview of the steps needed to get started, and the many great options available for promoting an e-business. The first section introduces the concept of the brand and explains how an e-business should go about developing one. In the second section, the all-important topic of budgeting for a marketing program is discussed, including a review of methods for deciding how much money to spend. The third section provides an overview of online advertising, with an introduction to four popular types of ads: banner ads, pop-up ads, search-engine ads, and classified ads. Newsgroups and Internet mailing lists provide unique opportunities for highly targeted e-business marketing. In addition to discussing strategies for exploiting these opportunities, this chapter explains the important distinction between using "opt-in" mailing lists and sending out "spam." The fourth section reviews creative and cost-effective promotional strategies available to e-businesses. These include electronic newsletters, blogs, podcasts, automated marketing tools, offline advertising, and press releases—all potent tools for attracting new customers and holding onto existing ones.

8.1 MARKETING BASICS: BRANDING AND BUDGETING

In the early days of the Internet, entrepreneurs could build a Web site, get mentioned in the right places, and instantly receive a stream of customers, whether they sold sweaters or homemade apple butter. There was not much competition, and a hungry audience would soak up whatever they could find. Web sites and online commerce companies now sell everything that is legal (and a few things that aren't), and there is enough competition to last a long time. The days of building a Web site and receiving instant traffic are mostly over; now marketing is an essential part of the e-business equation. This section explains the first steps in developing a marketing strategy—branding and budgeting—to get the word out to the masses.

8.1.1 Creating a Brand

To get noticed, an e-business needs to have a basic marketing strategy. The strategy defines and drives its marketing efforts—regardless of what those efforts are. Sending out the right message at the start is always important to prevent wasting funds and avoiding customer confusion.

Brand:
The message that a company portrays in everything it does, from communicating about the business, to acting a specific way, to providing value through products and services.

The first step in any marketing strategy is to create a brand for the business. A **brand** is the message that a company portrays in everything it does, from telling people about the business, to assuring customers of reliable, dependable service, to providing value through products and services. A brand is not one piece, but rather an overall sense that customers and the general public get when they think of a business. A brand is the successful combination of a memorable logo, a catchy slogan, and actions that back up the claims a business makes about itself. These individual elements all influence how customers view a business—but no one element is the brand. Rather, the brand is the overall impression that customers have of a business.

What kind of brand should an e-business develop? Every e-business will be different depending on its mix of products and services, but consider the following points when developing a brand for an online business:

- **Competitive prices:** Because online businesses do not have to pay for expensive retail space, they can offer lower prices than their offline competitors. As a result, many e-commerce sites promote their price advantage in their brands.
- **Convenience:** A huge advantage for e-businesses—online customers can shop from the comfort of their homes, any time of the day or night.
- **Customized service:** Even though e-businesses rarely develop a face-to-face relationship with their customers, the ease of online communications frequently benefits service offerings. As a result, e-businesses are often able to satisfy each customer's specific request or match people with similar interests—another possible component of brand development.

Although many more examples exist, the lesson is that e-businesses have many compelling options when developing a brand.

To jump-start the e-business brand-development process, take a sheet of paper and write down the Web site's name and URL. Next, list 25 to 50 keywords that can be used to classify or describe the e-business and what it offers. While doing this, imagine someone looking for the business or its products using an Internet search engine. What keywords or search phrases would they use?

Next, write 25-word, 50-word, and 75-word descriptions of the site and what it offers. Choose the wording carefully so that the descriptions catch the attention of readers, tell what the online business is all about, and encourage readers to visit the site. Be as specific as possible when writing the descriptions.

The information developed by these exercises will prove important for several reasons. For example, a company logo or slogan might incorporate some of the stronger keywords or phrases that are developed. The keywords will be used when registering the site with search engines. The descriptions and keywords can be used to write advertising copy, press releases for announcing the site to the media, or messages to targeted mailing lists.

For a brand to be effective, the words generated by the exercises and conveyed to the world must also be backed up by actions. If a Web site promises low prices, the e-business should make an effort to keep prices low. If it promises top-notch customer service, then it must be attentive to the needs of its online shoppers. When the shopping experience matches the words describing an e-commerce site, an e-business can be confident that shoppers will embrace their brand.

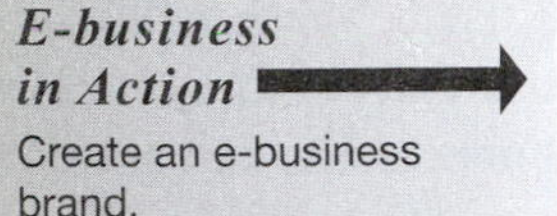

E-business in Action
Create an e-business brand.

IN THE REAL WORLD

The Power of Word of Mouth Marketing

When 27-year-old Rob Kalin conceived Etsy—an online marketplace for buying and selling all things handmade—few people could have predicted the level of success he'd achieve with the venture. Kalin, a painter and photographer, needed a way to sell his creations online; eBay and other sites sold too many types of goods and just didn't fit the bill. So with the help of two friends, Kalin launched Etsy's Web site (www.etsy.com) in June 2005, just three months after coming up with the idea. Today, Etsy has 45 employees, offices in Brooklyn and San Francisco, and approximately 550,000 registered users. Like eBay, much of Etsy's revenues come from its minimal listing fees and sales commission; to date, nearly $10 million worth of handmade goods has been sold on the site. Perhaps most impressive is how much of Etsy's marketing is based on creative word of mouth marketing. Etsy encourages staffers to spread the good word—"Buy, Sell, and Live Handmade"—by participating on blogs and forums, as well as by using email lists and social networking sites.[1]

8.1.2 Marketing Budgets

The sections that follow show that there are many different ways to advertise and promote an online business and its brand. To generate an ongoing flow of traffic (comprised of potential new customers as well as returning customers), e-businesses need to invest time and money into advertising, public relations, and promotion. Simply running a few banner ads or sending out an occasional press release will not be enough to keep a business thriving. E-business marketing demands creativity, time, financial resources, and the willingness to experiment in order to determine what works best for a particular type of business.

How much money is the right amount to spend on e-businesses marketing? There is no single correct answer to this question, but there are four methods for establishing an appropriate marketing budget:

- **Percentage of sales:** A simple way to establish a promotional budget is to select a percentage of actual or projected sales. Traditional businesses often budget between two and 20 percent of their sales to marketing; 5 percent is a common figure. New online businesses often budget much more—50 to 60 percent of revenues is not unheard of—but this can create a significant financial strain.
- **What is affordable:** E-businesses on a tight budget may be better off estimating promotional expenses based on available funds, at least until cash flow increases. The problem with this approach is that marketing is viewed as an expense rather than as an investment.
- **Watch the competition:** "Keeping up with the Jones's" is a common strategy in business as well as life. In tough competitive environments it may be important to match competitors dollar for dollar so as not to lose precious customers and sales. "Keeping up with the Jones's" is also a good way to spend too much money too quickly, so expenditures must be monitored carefully.
- **Setting objectives:** Advertising experts advise using objective-based budgeting for marketing: set a goal and a timetable and fund it appropriately. Small firms should use this approach cautiously; it is easy to quickly become overextended.

Even e-businesses with plenty of cash and generous marketing budgets should utilize the many free or low-cost promotional opportunities available on the Internet, such as banner exchanges, participation in newsgroups, blogging, and opt-in mailing lists. Remember to keep free or low-cost opportunities in perspective. Free promotional efforts alone are rarely adequate for developing a full-scale successful marketing program. Furthermore, some of these opportunities often require a significant time commitment and other investments to be fully exploited (such as hiring designers or writers, or buying a mailing list). Budget accordingly when using "free" promotional methods.

E-business in Action
Develop an e-business marketing budget.

SELF-CHECK

1. What is a brand? Are an attractive logo and a catchy slogan enough to promote a brand? What other elements are needed?
2. List three benefits that an e-business might promote as part of its brand identity.

3. What are four common methods for setting a marketing budget? What are the disadvantages of each?

Apply Your Knowledge Your e-business sells custom desktop photo frames and you are developing a brand identity. To start the process, make a list of 25 keywords that might apply to the Web site and write a 25-word description of the e-business and what it offers.

8.2 E-BUSINESS ADVERTISING

Once a basic brand has been developed, it is time to share it with the world. For online businesses, it is both logical and relatively easy to promote that brand online through advertising. Billions of dollars are spent each year on Web advertising (just look at Google's growing numbers), and the numbers increase each quarter. Online advertising speaks to a captive audience because the advertising is part of the screen, built into the Web page in a variety of ways. In addition, online advertising offers a better chance of having the right ad stare the right customer in the face, because the medium allows effective targeting of who receives which ad.

The following sections review four popular options for online advertising: (1) banner ads; (2) pop-up ads; (3) search-engine ads; and (4) classified ads. All offer distinct advantages (and disadvantages). A smart marketing strategy for an online startup might test all four options to determine the effectiveness of each one.

Banner ad:
A rectangular advertisement that displays basic information about an e-business and takes the customer to the Web site when they click on the ad.

8.2.1 Banner Ads

In many ways, **banner advertisements** are like the traditional print ads purchased in local newspapers. Most are simple, rectangular spaces containing a limited amount of promotional information about an e-business. Banner ads differ from print ads in one important respect: The ads are interactive. An interested viewer simply has to click on the banner to be instantly taken to the Web site being advertised.

> **FOR EXAMPLE**
> See Figure 8-1 for sample banner ads provided by Google.com.

In some limited cases, e-businesses can place a banner ad on another Web site for free. Most of the time, however, a fee is charged to place a banner ad—much in the same way that a business must pay to place a print advertisement. In fact, selling banner ad space has become a major revenue stream for many Web sites.

Many e-businesses successfully use banner ads as part of their marketing strategy. The banner ads are especially effective promotional tools when:

- They are visible for a long period of time. However, running ads for long periods can be very expensive.

Figure 8-1

Google AdWords

It's All About Results™

Contact Us - Help

AdWords Home

AdWords Support

Overview

- AdWords Advantages
- Program Comparison
- Success Stories
- News and Updates
- Demos and Guides
- Industry Research
- Inside AdWords Blog

Getting Started

- Editorial Guidelines
- Step-by-Step
- Tips for Success
- Account Navigation
- Keyword Tools

Google AdWords Image Ad Formats

Image Ads | Video Ads

Leaderboard (728 x 90)

View examples of placement

Banner (468 x 60)

View examples of placement

Small Square (200 x 200)

View examples of placement

Square (250 x 250)

View examples of placement

Medium Rectangle (300 x 250)

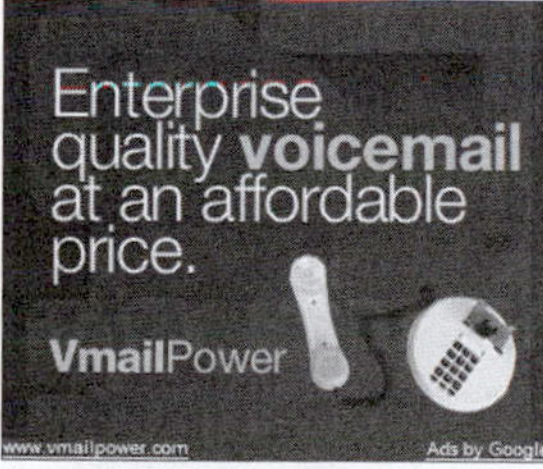

Enterprise
quality voicemail
at an affordable
price.
VmailPower
www.vmailpower.com
Ads by Google

View examples of placement

Large Rectangle (336 x 280)

Not a Green Thumb?

Get advice from gardening experts.

Green Garden Gifts

www.greengardengifts.com Ads by Google

View examples of placement

Skyscraper (120 x 600)

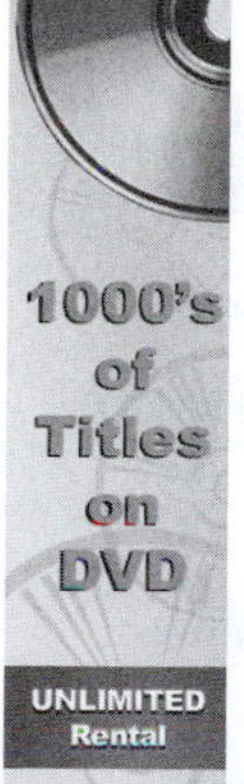

1000's
of
Titles
on
DVD
UNLIMITED
Rental
www.nolimitdvd.com
Feedback - Ads by Google

View examples of placement

Wide Skyscraper (160 x 600)

View examples of placement

©2006 Google - AdWords Home - Terms and Conditions - Privacy Policy

Sample banner ads from Google.com.

- They are placed on high-traffic Web sites, which can also be expensive, because high-traffic Web sites usually charge more to host banner ads.

Banner ads differ from other Web-specific publicity tactics in one important respect: Banner ads publicize in a one-to-many fashion rather than in a one-to-one fashion. Banner ads broadcast the name of an organization indiscriminately, without requiring the viewer to have to choose to find out about a site by clicking a link (though this option is available).

In general, Web sites have three methods of charging for banner ads:

Cost Per Thousand (CPM): A banner ad charge determined by the number of people who visit the Web page on which the advertisement appears.

Click-through Rate (CTR): A banner ad charge determined by the number of viewer clicks that prompt a link to the advertiser's Web site.

Cost Per Click (CPC): A banner ad charge system in which the advertiser determines how much is paid for each click on their ad or keyword. Different advertisers wanting to use the same ad space or keywords bid against each other.

- **Cost Per Thousand (CPM):** The charge is dependent on the number of people who visit the Web page on which the advertisement appears. The more traffic a Web site gets, the higher the ad rate will be. In the CPM method, payment is dependent on the number of *views* an ad receives.
- **Click-through Rate (CTR):** A click-through occurs when a viewer clicks on an advertisement that links to the advertiser's Web site. Using the CTR method, the billing comes after all the click-throughs have been tallied.
- **Cost Per Click (CPC):** CPC is similar to CTR in that the advertiser pays when someone clicks a link that takes the person to the Web site. The main difference is that in the CPC model, the advertiser determines how much is paid for each click. The CPC system is used for both banner and search-engine ads. Different advertisers wanting to use the same banner space or keywords bid against each other, offering a certain price per click. The high bid gets the ad. E-businesses using this system should make sure that they do not have to pay for repeat visits, only for unique clicks on an ad.

E-business in Action →
Promote an e-business with banner ads.

Because of the substantial investment involved in positioning banner ads, it is important that the people who view the advertisement are interested in the goods being offered. Here, again, keywords are very useful in determining which Web sites to advertise with.

8.2.2 Pop-Up Ads

Pop-up ad: An ad consisting of a window that pops up on a user's screen whenever the user visits the advertised Web site or one on which ad placement has been purchased.

Pop-up ads are another popular form of online advertising. Pop-up ads are a window that pops up on users' computers whenever the user visits the advertised Web site or one from which an ad has been purchased. The window, which looks like it appears out of nowhere and sometimes makes a "pop" sound, covers the user's screen and demands attention. Sometimes the window contains an ad, though the ads often ask the consumer for information. The three main types of actions for pop-up advertising are as follows:

- **Pops up:** This most common type of ad window appears when a page is viewed and pops atop the desired page. The ads work best when the content is related to the page opened: Subscribe to a (related) newsletter, buy the book, attend the seminar, or other supplementary information.
- **Pops under:** When a Web page is opened, a new advertising window is opened underneath the primary viewing window. The new window is often unrelated to the main Web page. The content is only visible when the user specifically tries to close it, or closes or minimizes the other window(s) on top of it.
- **Pops on top:** These ads, also called interstitials, totally replace the desired content. The ads must be viewed for a period of time and then closed before the desired content may be viewed. Online magazines often use interstitials to force readers to deal with advertising before continuing with a story being read.

Reasons for using pop-up ads:

- **Larger.** Pop-up ads can occupy an entire window and provide a more detailed, complex offer with the ample space provided.
- **Effective.** More screen space leads to greater success. A 2003 study by the New Architect revealed that pop-up and pop-under ads had more than twice the click-through rate of banner ads.
- **Better convey brand.** With the entire screen available, e-businesses can include the full brand image they are trying to portray to customers.

Reasons for not using pop-up ads:

- **Not everyone likes them.** Many online users despise this type of ad, which might undermine their willingness to visit a Web site employing them.
- **Dangers of overuse.** Displaying a pop-up ad on a Web site home page is expected (or at least tolerated). But redisplaying the ad on every page slows user movement, and can alienate potential customers.
- **Technology issues.** Because the technology creates an extra window, pop-ups can cause user confusion and sometimes affect other software.
- **Blockable.** Browsers often offer a "no pop-up" option that many Web surfers gladly use. As a result, businesses that rely only on pop-up advertising could miss a large portion of the customer population.
- **Divert focus.** Diverting attention from a main product with an in-site pop-up can inadvertently hurt sales.

E-business in Action
Promote an e-business with pop-up ads.

8.2.3 Search-Engine Ads

If an entrepreneur was building a new gas station, would the entrepreneur be better off placing the station on a rural country road or on a freeway off-ramp? The answer is simple: The freeway off-ramp—the entrepreneur would want to position the business where the most customers were located. The best businesses in the world cannot succeed if their customers cannot find them, which is why location and access are so important. In a similar way, e-businesses need to position themselves where the traffic is, and nowadays most people find Web sites through search engines. Therefore, advertising on a search-engine page will deliver "drive-by" traffic.

Search-engine ad: An advertisement tied to specific keywords in a search engine. When selected keywords are typed in a search box, an appropriate ad is displayed.

One big benefit of search-engine advertising is that it allows targeting consumers who identify their interests with their keystrokes. **Search-engine advertising** works like this: Products or Web sites are tied to specific keywords. Someone types those keywords in the search box, and an appropriate ad is displayed. Suppose that a potential customer is searching Google for a specific brand of golf clubs. If a business sells that brand of products, their ad appears next to the search results. Because the ad is targeted only to people who demonstrate that interest (by typing), the rate of return is higher than a generic ad to an untargeted audience.

Although Google and Yahoo! are the two biggest companies in search-engine advertising, they are by no means the only game in town. Table 8-1 shows a list of major companies that offer search-engine advertising.

E-businesses with products or services that appeal to a certain niche audience should identify news or portal sites that cater to the same interest area. Many specialty portals and news sites offer search-engine advertising opportunities. Although some of these Web sites outsource their advertising to companies like Google or DoubleClick, many are still open to some partnership or direct-pay arrangement for advertising.

The leader in search-engine ads is Google AdWords, which offers e-businesses an opportunity to create their own ads and bid on keywords that trigger the display of those ads. When a Google user types these keywords

Table 8-1 Search-Engine Advertising Companies

Company	*Service URL*
Google AdWords	adwords.google.com
Yahoo! Overture	searchmarketing.yahoo.com
Looksmart Advertiser Solutions	search.looksmart.com
Miva Pay-per-click program	www.miva.com/us
Enhance Enhance Interactive	www.enhance.com

during a search, the ad appears on the right side of the results screen in a "Sponsored Links" box.

Google tracks the number of times an ad is clicked, and bills based on the quantity. Like other similar services, AdWords allows an e-business to set a budget for a given period of time and pay only for the ads it can afford. When the budget is depleted, the ad stops appearing. Advertisers also have the option of running more than one ad and targeting customers based on territories such as cities or countries.

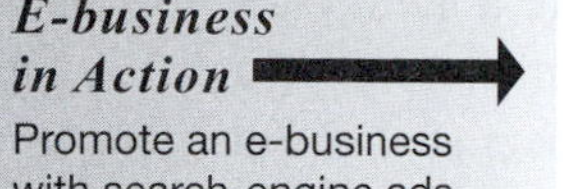

Promote an e-business with search-engine ads.

8.2.4 Classified Advertising

Classified ad: A simple text-based ad that is organized by category.

A **classified ad** is a simple (usually) text-based ad, organized by category—in other words, classified. The ads are often overlooked for online advertising, in part because some people consider them "old-fashioned." Newspapers (and some magazines) have traditionally made a lot of money on classifieds, but these print media sources have been forced to give up a large portion of the classified ad market to the Internet. The Internet is a great venue for classifieds, offering sellers the ability to post ads quickly and change the copy frequently and cheaply. For shoppers, online classifieds are easily searched. Rather than spending precious time scanning multiple pages and small print, online shoppers can simply type a keyword or two into a search engine and immediately get the ads that interest them.

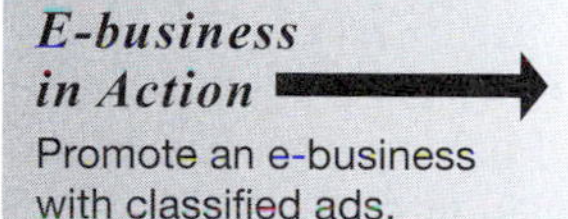

Promote an e-business with classified ads.

E-businesses have discovered that focused classifieds for a specific product or service can be a very effective and cost-efficient way to attract

FOR EXAMPLE

See Figure 8-2 for an example of a typical ad on craigslist.com.

Figure 8-2

Your Family Deserves Healthcare. Let Us Help You Afford It!

Reply to: serv-8061845@craigslist.org
Date: 2007-12-11, 9:58AM MST

Are You Risking Your Health Due To High Insurance Costs?

- *Plans To Fit Any Need.*
- *Lowest Rates.*
- *Simple Application.*

Visit us at this address: ***health.leaderhealth.com***

Location: Denver/Boulder

it's ok to contact this poster with services or other commercial interests

PostingID: 8061845

A sample of a typical ad from craigslist.com.

customers. Classified ads are also inexpensive to create and easy to place using email. Many sites offer inexpensive online classifieds, and many are focused on specific products or services—for example, sites for selling used cars, for listing available apartments, or for selling products related to hobbies. There are also venues—such as AOL Classifieds and craigslist—that offer free online classifieds. Also, newspapers are a great place for online classifieds because many have started posting print classifieds online for no extra charge. The online strategy helps newspapers stay competitive with the Internet, and offers the advertiser highly desirable access to two different markets for one price.

SELF-CHECK

1. What are the three common billing strategies for banner ads and how do they differ from each other?
2. What are the key disadvantages of pop-up advertising?
3. How do search-engine ads work? Why are search-engine ads so effective?
4. Why are classifieds so well suited to the Internet?

Apply Your Knowledge Your e-business marketing strategy includes testing all four of the popular online advertising options. Each strategy has some risks. List one to consider for each type of ad and explain how you will minimize the potential negative impacts.

8.3 MARKETING TO NEWSGROUPS AND MAILING LISTS

Many areas of the Internet can provide entrepreneurs with direct access to potential customers as well as a chance to interact with them. Two useful places to market directly to individuals are newsgroups and Internet mailing lists. Both are highly targeted and offer unprecedented opportunities for niche marketing. Using newsgroups and Internet mailing lists requires creativity and time, but the potential returns are significant.

The first step for any e-business planning to utilize newsgroups and mailing list is to develop a brief target customer profile. Second, the e-business owner should join and participate in lists and newsgroups that cater to customers that meet the profile. For example, an e-business selling sports memorabilia online should join newsgroups started by sports fans.

8.3.1 Newsgroups

Newsgroups are popular forums for computer users to communicate on the Internet. The exact structure varies somewhat from group to group, but Microsoft's definition is still the most useful explanation:

Newsgroup:
A collection of messages posted by individuals to a news server; a dedicated computer maintained by a company, group, or individual for storing the messages.

> *A **newsgroup** is a collection of messages posted by individuals to a news server. News servers are computers maintained by companies, groups, and individuals, and can host thousands of newsgroups. You can find newsgroups on practically any subject. Although some newsgroups are monitored, most are not, and messages can be "posted" and read by anyone who has access to that group. There are no newsgroup membership lists or joining fees. Your Internet Service Provider must have a link to a news server for you to set up an account with that news server. . . . After you set up an account, you can read and post messages on any of the newsgroups stored on that news server. When you find a newsgroup you like, you can "subscribe" to it. . . . Newsgroups can contain thousands of messages, which can be time-consuming to sort through. Many newsgroup readers have a variety of features that can make it easier to find the information you want in newsgroups.*

Newsgroups can provide numerous promotional opportunities for online businesses. An Internet newsgroup is similar to a public bulletin board or discussion group that focuses on a specific topic or caters to a specific audience. Anyone can start a newsgroup or participate in the "conversation" happening there.

Some newsgroups are moderated, which means someone acts as a gatekeeper and reads and sometimes edits each text message posted to a newsgroup to ensure that the material is relevant. Unmoderated newsgroups often get cluttered with spam and other messages that have no relevance to the newsgroup's main topic. The difference between a newsgroup and an online chat forum is that newsgroups do not happen in real time.

Newsgroups have evolved over the years. Today, online services such as America Online, Yahoo!, and Google all have their own special interest groups open to people who want to join. Becoming active in special interest groups can be a great way to reach your target audience.

Because newsgroups cater to very specific audiences and focus on particular topics, becoming an active participant in newsgroups will allow an e-business owner to reach potential customers with specific interests. To effectively use newsgroups, it is important to consider "netiquette" and avoid posting messages in the interactive discussion that are blatant ads for a product or service. Instead, by becoming active in the conversation, an e-business owner can mention their online business as a resource and answer questions from others.

There are literally thousands of different newsgroups in existence, and new newsgroups are created daily. Some newsgroups have thousands of active participants who generate dozens or perhaps hundreds of messages per day, whereas others are less busy.

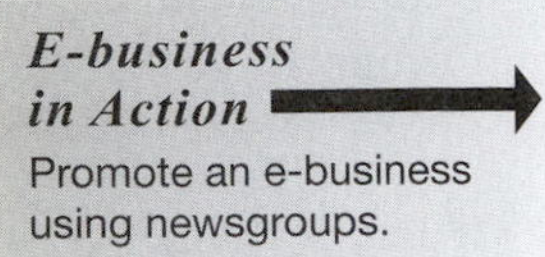

Promote an e-business using newsgroups.

To obtain a complete listing of Internet newsgroups, visit www.cyberfiber.com or use the newsreader software provided by Internet service providers or email and news reader software (such as Microsoft Outlook Express).

8.3.2 Internet Mailing Lists

Internet mailing list: A group of people with similar interests who discuss their favorite topics via email.

Internet mailing lists are similar to newsgroups, except that messages posted to a mailing list are automatically sent to an email inbox. Internet mailing lists involve groups of people discussing one of their favorite topics via email. On AOL, this service is called Groups@AOL (keyword: My Groups).

The mailing-list format lends itself to calm, mature discussion, where relationships between the list members grow and deepen over an extended period of time. Most Internet experts feel that the mailing-list format is the most civilized type of online community. Another common type of Internet mailing list is the newsletter or announcement format, where a single writer (the list owner or moderator) broadcasts a periodic email to a willing audience (and the audience does not participate directly).

There are several free or inexpensive services to help companies establish an Internet mailing list to communicate with clients or customers. For example, Yahoo! Groups (http://groups.yahoo.com) hosts alumni groups and support groups, plus groups for sports fans, small-business operators, and thousands of other organizations and interests. Using other services, e-businesses can establish and manage an "opt-in" Internet mailing list. Many ISPs and Web site–hosting companies offer economical, email list managers to online business operators.

Online businesses can also establish one-way, email-based communication with clients, customers, or anyone else using an Internet-based mailing list. There are several ways online businesses can communicate with existing and potential customers on their mailing list:

- Distribute a company newsletter (see Section 8.4.1 for more information).
- Send out new product announcements or press releases.
- Email special offers or online coupons.
- Provide additional product information to existing customers (for example, user hints, product upgrade announcements, or suggested additional products).

When using Internet mailing lists and email as a marketing tool, it is important that the people receiving promotional emails have requested the

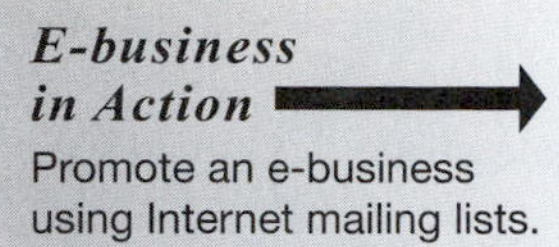
E-business
in Action
Promote an e-business using Internet mailing lists.

information by subscribing or opting into the email list. When someone provides their email address in order to be included, they are opting in and requesting that the information be emailed to them. When someone decides they no longer wish to receive the information via email, they need a way to "opt-out" or unsubscribe to the list.

8.3.3 Spam

Spam:
Unsolicited emails sent en masse to promote a product or service.

Spam filter:
Software programs that block unwanted spam.

Carefully managed opt-in/opt-out customer-friendly mailing lists are not the only Internet marketing tool. Another is mass email or **"spam."** The concept of instantly sending thousands or millions of promotional email messages to people on the Internet is very appealing because the cost associated with doing this type of mailing is extremely low. The problem is, many people dislike receiving unsolicited advertisements by email. Furthermore, spam has built a well-deserved negative reputation because it is frequently used by companies pitching cybersex, gambling, pyramid schemes, or scams. In response, software companies offer a host of **spam filters,** programs designed to block unwanted spam.

The spam world offers no shortages of providers, and its low costs are very tempting. There are a number of online companies that specialize in sending mass emails very inexpensively. There are also several different software packages that enable users to gather email addresses and quickly send junk email to the lists gathered. Even if these approaches are inexpensive and somewhat effective, e-business owners trying to create a reputable business should question whether this is the best approach.

Alternative approaches to email marketing exist that allow quick list building but avoid some of the problems of spam. Some companies, such as PostMaster Direct (www.postmasterdirect.com), develop lists of email users who specifically request information on specific topics of interest to them. E-businesses can purchase or rent these targeted email lists and send these people email for much less money than it would cost to send a mass mailing via the U.S. Postal Service. They also can take heart in knowing that the users should have interest in their products and a history of asking for information on related subjects.

No matter how a list is built, e-businesses that choose to use some form of email to communicate with customers or potential customers must be professional and respectful. In particular, the subject line should clearly state the content of the message so that the recipient can quickly choose to read the message or delete it. Some companies use misleading message subject lines to get people to read their messages. Although this might get someone to open the message, it can also create a sense of resentment. Email can be an effective promotional tool, but everyone in the online world loses if companies simply use the medium to harass recipients.

SELF-CHECK

1. What is a newsgroup? What are two appropriate strategies for marketing an e-business to a newsgroup?
2. What are the advantages of working with Internet mailing lists? What types of marketing materials can be sent to the list?

Apply Your Knowledge Spam has given email marketing a bad reputation that is often undeserved. Explain the important differences between marketing to an Internet mailing list and sending out spam.

8.4 CREATIVE PROMOTIONAL STRATEGIES

While online advertising is especially effective for promoting an e-business brand, it also can be an expensive option, especially for new and small-scale operations. Fortunately, the Internet is a realm of endless possibilities and creative solutions. As a result, e-business owners have many exciting alternative strategies available for promoting their brand and their products. Some ideas utilize the latest technologies, while others are simply an application of good old common sense. Most importantly, many of these strategies are easy and inexpensive to implement and will help diversify an e-business's marketing strategy and attract new customers.

IN THE REAL WORLD

Revoltionary Marketing Strategy

The revolution began in 1991 in a Princeton dorm room with two friends, a simple idea, and a box full of worms. The two friends were Tom Szaky and Jon Beyer, both students at Princeton, and the idea was to take waste (a la university dining halls), process it (here's where the worms come in), and turn it into a useful product—a powerful organic plant food that is the foundation of their groundbreaking company, TerraCycle (www.TerraCycle.net). Today the plant food is mass-produced and bottled directly in used soda bottles. TerraCycle products can be found online as well as at Target, Wal-Mart, and Home Depot, and sales are expected to jump to $10 million next year.[2] The company's hip Web site takes a fresh approach, drawing customers in with video tips, surveys, contests, and other interactive elements. TerraCycle's founders use their campaign against waste as a part of their marketing strategy; in fact, they have teamed up with yogurt and drink pouch manufacturers to put together "brigades" of container and pouch recyclers (participants can raise funds for their favorite charity by helping TerraCycle collect what might otherwise end up in a landfill). The company's Bottle Brigade recycling program has already rescued and reused more than two million soda bottles.

8.4.1 Newsletters

The goal of every e-business is to have traffic on their Web site and to have customers buy something. The customer visit and sale are important achievements, but what the e-business really needs is a repeat customer. Studies have shown that working to get an existing customer to return to a site is as much as six times more effective than working to get a brand-new customer. How to attract repeat customers is an important consideration for new e-businesses working with limited resources.

Newsletter: An electronic communications tool, often distributed by email, containing articles and other information promoting an e-business and its products.

Existing customers often need a little extra encouragement to come back, and one of the best tools for encouraging them is a **newsletter**—basically an electronic version of the paper communications tool sent out by churches, schools, and countless other organizations. Most newsletters are a combination of articles and information, with reviews of specific products, sales events, or company news. Having a regular newsletter that customers can subscribe to offers e-businesses many benefits:

- **Communicate with customers.** Newsletters give e-business owners the opportunity to share information about the business and what products or services are offered. Although most people have trained themselves to skip over pure advertisements, reading stories or tips can break down customer defenses so that they listen and find out more.
- **Share information.** The products e-businesses sell have a specific use, so helping customers use the products more effectively provides added value. For example, a Web site that sells cooking supplies could send out a newsletter that includes recipes and describes how its products help make different foods. The key to newsletters is carefully balancing information with promotional material. Too much promotion, and a newsletter simply becomes a sales flyer and people stop reading it.
- **Build a connection.** If customers become accustomed to receiving a regular newsletter that they find helpful, they build a connection in their minds that the e-business is a trusted source. The customer might think,

"Oh, yeah, that's the company that puts out the Top 10 Tips that I read every week. Those people know what they're talking about, so I'll use them to order my next batch of supplies."

- **Build a community.** E-businesses that cater to a specific interest group will quickly understand that belonging is as important as buying for many of their customers. Giving customers a voice in newsletters will help them feel like they are part of something important, and their loyalty will grow. Plus, customers may start providing a significant portion of the newsletter content with short articles, comments, or reviews, and will take some of the workload off the e-business owner.

Creating a newsletter does not have to be a large and complex project full of deadlines and drama. Newsletters do, however, demand some planning, consistency, and guidelines to be effective. Several questions, outlined below, must be answered before launching an e-business newsletter.

Who Will Write the Newsletter?

Many business owners think that their job is to create each newsletter and develop all its content. That may be both unrealistic and unwise, especially if the business has staff to help out. Owners may want to write a column, but it is a good idea to have different people contribute other parts of the newsletter. It also may be a good investment to hire a freelance writer to create parts of the newsletter. As noted earlier, customers are also a good source of material, whether they are contributing articles, providing product reviews, or simply asking questions.

What Will the Newsletter Cover?

A newsletter needs to provide different, fresh, and relevant content every time. Stay current on pertinent issues by reading newspapers, magazines, and press releases to help generate ideas. News stories from other sources can only be reprinted with the publisher's consent. Quotes or statistics can be pulled from articles, as long as the source is cited.

How Frequent Will the Newsletter Be Released?

Any schedule is acceptable—weekly, monthly, or quarterly, for example—as long as it is consistent. Readers lose interest with late or varied schedules, so choose a publishing time that is manageable without much stress. The release day is also an important consideration. Some companies target the day of new product releases to send out their newsletters. For example, a Web site selling CDs might send out a newsletter every Tuesday, because that is when new music typically hits retail stores.

What Format Should the Newsletter Have?

There are a multitude of computer programs for designing newsletters, although they can be presented in only two main formats:

1. Plain-text has words and Web links but no graphics. Although plain-text newsletters can be read by anyone and are quick to send and receive, they look plain.
2. HTML has words, graphics, and design formatting to look exactly like a Web page. HTML newsletters can be very attractive, but cannot be interpreted by every email system and can take a long time to show up on-screen.

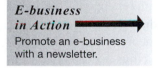

E-business in Action
Promote an e-business with a newsletter.

Be smart and create two different versions and ask readers during the sign-up process which version they prefer to receive.

How Should the Newsletter Be Distributed?

Email is the standard method, but be alert for possible pitfalls. Once a customer list grows beyond a few dozen people, the Internet service provider should be consulted to ensure that they do not stop distribution when they see the increased traffic. Most ISPs are very wary of spam, either coming in or going out. Accordingly, a newsletter should be emailed only to people who have specifically requested it.

If an ISP is unwilling or unable to manage a large-scale newsletter distribution project, it may be time to contract with a specialized company to manage newsletter distribution. Specialized companies have computer systems to manage the newsletter mailing, plus they can manage the mailing list, adding new subscribers or deleting the email addresses of customers who opt out of the mailing. Table 8-2 lists a few of these companies.

Table 8-2 Email Newsletter Distribution Services

Name	*URL*
Constant Contact	www.constantcontact.com
JangoMail	www.jangomail.com
Novo Solutions	www.novosolutions.com
Delivra	www.delivra.com
EXMG	www.exmarketing.com

8.4.2 Blogging

Blog:
Short for Weblog. An online digital diary or forum where text, photos, and other material can be posted and made available to the public.

One of the newer trends for communicating online is through the use of blogs. A **blog** (short for Weblog) is an online digital diary or forum where anyone can write anything and make it available for the Web-surfing public. By mid-2005, there were more than nine million blogs online with new ones being launched daily. Celebrities, politicians, business operators, hobbyists, families, and writers use blogs to reach out to the general public (or a specific audience) and share thoughts and ideas.

Although blogging has become especially popular as a way to keep in touch with friends and family, online business owners have also discovered that blogging can be a powerful marketing and promotion tool. It is a great way for an e-business to communicate directly (yet informally) with current and potential customers, keeping customers up-to-date regarding new products or other developments. Furthermore, blogs are good tools for creating a two-way dialogue with customers: People reading a blog can post their own comments, ideas, and suggestions for others to read. Many e-businesses use blogs instead of emailed newsletters.

Blogs are versatile and easy-to-use tools. They can include graphics and photos in addition to text. Blogs can be part of a company's Web site, or established on a separate site. Blogs can be created in less than a few hours, though they require an ongoing time investment to post new entries and keep the content fresh. Best of all, most of the popular blog hosting/publishing services are free to use and require no programming.

Google operates one of the most popular blogging services, called Blogger.com, a free service. Other blogging services include Square Space (www.squarespace.com), Type Pad (www.typepad.com), and Blogomonster (www.blogomonster.com). Another way to add a blog to an existing Web site is to use the blogging tools offered by www.wordpress.org or www.moveabletype.org. Also, companies using Web site–creation software or a turnkey site development solution will find that they usually have blogging capabilities already built into their system.

Blogs are a great tool for enticing people to return to an e-commerce site. The best way to do this is to frequently update the blog with news or information of interest to your customers. Possible e-business blog topics include:

- Information about the company's day-to-day operations
- Details about product/services, including previews of new products
- Announcements about sales and special promotions
- Practical tips and strategies for using products or services

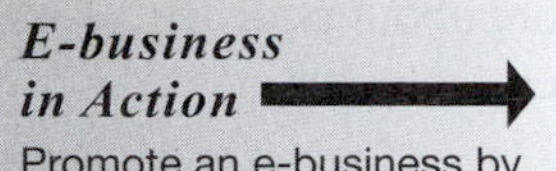
E-business in Action
Promote an e-business by blogging.

- Answers to questions from customers
- Testimonials from customers
- Useful and interesting industry news

IN THE REAL WORLD

An Unconventional Approach to Online Music Marketing

Back in the late 1970s and early 80s, the British rock group, Gang of Four, was ahead of its time. Today, Gang of Four bassist Dave Allen continues on the same path, but with a different venue—an online music company. Allen, who has years of experience in all areas of the music industry, has been heavily involved in Internet strategy since 1994, working for companies such as eMusic.com (the first pay-for-download music service) and Intel. After moving to Portland, Oregon, Allen and business partner Ned Failing started their online music label, Pampelmoose. The partners were well aware of the problems facing the record industry—an alarming drop in album sales in the face of surging digital sales. Their solution was to use the Internet to market new music. Like a conventional record label, Pampelmoose offers services such as studio production, distribution, and promotion; the company also offers Pampelmart, an online store where bands can sell their goods. Allen credits his blog, which replaced the company's e-business page in 2005, for much of the business's success; monthly visitors, who are looking for Allen's take on music, Portland, and pop culture, have increased from about 30,000 per month to 142,000 per month. Some are even buying merchandise. "A blog is a useful vehicle for pointing people at your product," says Allen. "It's the retail store window, if you will." [3]

8.4.3 Podcasting

Podcast:
A recorded audio program available online for download in a file format that can easily be transferred to an MP3 player.

Podcasting has become almost as popular as blogging when it comes to "broadcasting" information. A **podcast** is a recorded audio program—a full-length radio show, for example—that is made available online for download in a file format that can easily be transferred to an Apple iPod or compatible MP3 player.

Online businesses can use a podcast to tell people about their products and how to best use them, and to offer audio tutorials, testimonials, and other information. Take time to listen to podcasts produced by other companies and determine how they are creating original audio content to promote their company and products. To learn more about podcasting as a marketing tool and listen to thousands of different samples, visit any of these sites:

- www.podcast.net
- www.podcastalley.com
- www.ipodder.org
- www.odeo.com
- www.podshow.com

A basic podcast can be created on a personal computer by connecting a microphone and utilizing specialized recording software. The method is inexpensive and easy, though quality podcasts with outstanding content will obviously do a better job of selling products. For more information about producing podcasts, the following Web sites will be helpful: www.gopodder.com; www.castblaster.com; and www.easypodcast.com. In addition the Apple Web site (www.apple.com/podcasting/) offers information about the various iPod MP3 players and related technology, plus information about podcasting, including a useful tutorial.

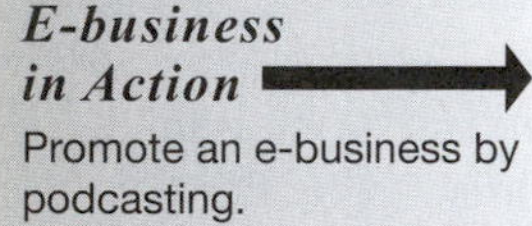
E-business in Action
Promote an e-business by podcasting.

8.4.4 Automated Marketing

The Internet has elevated customer expectations on how quickly they receive information. Many customer questions require contacting an e-business, usually by email, for an answer. But how long will it take to get them an answer? Small e-businesses may be overwhelmed by customer inquiries and take many hours or even days to send out replies. Customers who do not receive a prompt response to their questions often get frustrated and leave in search of another e-business from which to purchase. And what about simple marketing processes like sending out email offers? Will a one-person operation have time to complete even these basic marketing tasks?

By setting up automatic processes, e-business marketing campaigns can operate 24 hours a day, every day. And with automation managing the more routine tasks, owners are free to manage important business functions. Here are tools e-businesses can use to automate the marketing process:

Autoresponder: A software tool that automatically generates an email response based on an incoming request.

- **Autoresponders:** A software tool that automatically generates an email response based on an incoming request, such as when someone joins a newsletter mailing list. An autoresponder can add the name to the database and send that person a welcome message and maybe even an introductory newsletter issue. Be careful not to overuse autoresponders; customers can be quickly turned off by too many form letters.

Tickler:
A reminder, an offer, or an update directed to a customer that is automatically distributed by email.

- **Ticklers:** Automatic reminders, offers, or updates distributed by email sent to customers every few weeks with contact managers such as ACT! or Salesforce.com. Include a variety of offers in a tickler to slowly but surely encourage contacts to visit the Web site and make a purchase.
- **Archived information:** Sometimes, the best way to help customers is to enable them to help themselves. E-businesses should dedicate a portion of their Web site to hold all marketing information. Put the most frequently asked questions in this help section, and make sure that it is accessible from any page of the Web site. Try putting the marketing material in different formats to appeal to different customers. A brochure can be turned into an audio file sales pitch, or a PowerPoint presentation can be transformed into a downloadable video file, for example.

E-business in Action →
Promote an e-business with automated marketing techniques.

8.4.5 Offline Advertising

Online businesses should remember that all marketing does not need to be done online. In fact, a good e-business marketing plan should include a component of non-Web promotion to drive customers to the Web site. For example, any traditional communication on behalf of an e-business should reference the online store and Web address. Offline media that can be used to advertise and spread the word about online businesses include:

- **Business cards:** Add the Web site address, email address, and Web site slogan to business cards, along with the business's name, address, and phone number.
- **Company letterhead or stationery:** All letters—whether a response to a request for information or a thank-you note to a customer or vendor—should include a Web site address as part of the letterhead.
- **Business flyers and brochures:** Many e-businesses will find value in creating and printing a supply of brochures that explain the business. Brochures can be handed out at meetings or public events and should include the company logo and Web site address.
- **Catalogs:** Printed catalogs often encourage customers to browse and shop. Even some of the biggest e-businesses, from Dell to eBay, now send out printed catalogs to remind people of the goods at their online sites.
- **Company vehicles:** Company trucks or vans should remind passersby about the online business with whom they are associated.

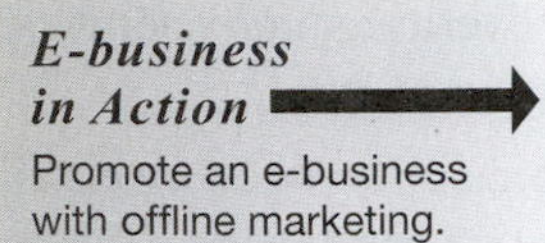

Promote an e-business with offline marketing.

- **Boxes:** One way that Amazon distinguishes itself is by plastering the Amazon logo on its customized boxes and mailers. Not only do customers know instantly that their orders have arrived, but anyone around them is also gently reminded of the Amazon brand—a good strategy for any business.

8.4.6 Press Releases

Press release: A short document that is designed to make a newsworthy announcement about a business to the media.

A **press release** is a document (usually between 500 and 1,000 words) designed to make a newsworthy announcement about a business to the media. A press release is a key tool for public relations professionals. A press release answers the basic questions on the minds of reporters who may be interested in reporting on the topic of the press release—who, what, when, where, why, and how. E-businesses may want to send out press releases at startup, or when hiring new personnel, releasing new products, or making a significant upgrade to their operations.

Once a press release is written, the goal is to get it into the hands of interested editors, reporters, and journalists. Press releases can be sent to the media via U.S. mail, fax, or email. Media contact lists can be created by reading bylines in newspapers and magazines, or by purchasing a media directory.

Broadcast Interview Source (www.expertclick.com) publishes a variety of media directories that list the contact names, phone numbers, addresses, fax numbers, and email addresses of writers, reporters, producers, editors, and radio/television hosts. The Gebbie Press's All-In-One Directory (www.gebbieinc.com) lists contact information for more than 25,000 media people from TV and radio stations, newspapers, magazines, African American and Hispanic media, news syndicates, networks, and AP bureaus.

Consider including the following when compiling a list of media outlets to send press releases to:

- Television shows (especially those that cover your industry)
- Radio stations (especially those focusing on news and talk shows)
- Newspapers
- Magazines and trade journals
- Newsletters
- Online publications (including popular blogs)
- The Webmasters at sites in similar interest areas
- Special-interest groups or clubs

Press releases are a powerful way to reach potential customers. To generate the best possible publicity, make sure the press releases contain only

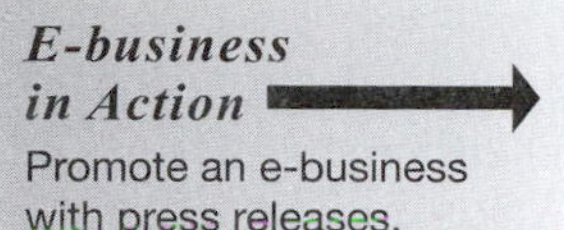

newsworthy information the media would be interested in covering. When promoting a product, the press release should discuss what the product is, why there is a need for it, and why, for example, a magazine, newspaper, or radio or TV station's audience would be interested in it. The press release should position the executives within the company as experts in their field, who are available to be interviewed.

E-business
in Action
Promote an e-business with press releases.

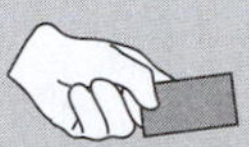

CAREER CONNECTION

The Great Holtzie takes on the world of entertaining children with laughter and an aggressive approach to Internet marketing.

In early 2007, Adam Holtz, a Philadelphia area recruiter, decided to change careers and do something that would make him happy—entertain kids. Six months later, The Great Holtzie, as he's known to his young fans, has become the area's hottest children's comedian, thanks largely to his presence on the Internet. Within a month of starting the business, Holtz had his Web site online. "I knew that the Web site was going to be important," Holtz says, "so along with refining my act, I concentrated on getting the site up and running right away."

After seeing what his competition's sites were like (most seemed to cater to kids), the 38-year-old Holtz decided he'd try a different tactic—create a smart, hip site that would appeal to the aesthetics of adult women, the moms who are booking the parties. Holtz bartered with a friend to design a site (thegreatholtzie.com) that matched his approach to comedy: no clown makeup, costumes, or gimmicks. Soon after, Holtz spent $200 for Internet optimizing, achieving exactly what he wanted—when someone searches for a "Philadelphia birthday entertainer," The Great Holtzie's name comes up near or at the top of the search results.

Holtz also takes advantage of alternative online marketing strategies, such as press releases, articles, mailing lists, and craigslist.com. The Great Holtzie even has a MySpace page where he's created a network of potential customers. But this aggressive approach to Internet marketing doesn't cost a fortune. Holtz spends no more than $300 a month for marketing on Google, Yahoo!, and some Philly area Web sites. The investment has paid off; about 75 percent of his business comes from online sources.

At the moment, Holtz's site is all about selling the service, but he foresees a time when he may sell T-shirts or videos or incorporate a way that customers can pay for shows through the site. In the meantime, the Great Holtzie's enthusiasm grows with each gig. "This is a total dream come true," he says.

Tips from the Professional

- Do your research. See what your competition is doing, especially on the Internet.
- Figure out what your competition is doing wrong and correct it in your own business.
- Be aggressive!

SELF-CHECK

1. Explain four benefits of creating and sending out an electronic newsletter to a mailing list of existing and potential customers.
2. How can automated marketing tools help a small e-business stay connected to its customers?
3. List five methods for promoting an online business offline.
4. What is the purpose of a press release? List five places that an e-business could send one.

Apply Your Knowledge Your e-business sells wildlife art prints; your Web site includes a link to a blog that you update weekly. Write a short (two or three paragraphs) sample blog entry that connects with customers and promotes the business.

SUMMARY

Section 8.1

- The first step in any e-business marketing strategy is to create a brand, the message that the company portrays in everything it does. Every firm will have a different brand depending on its mix of products (or services), but it is logical to consider the many advantages of the online experience when developing a brand.
- E-businesses should develop an appropriate marketing budget by employing one or more of the following methods: as percentage of sales; determining what is affordable; following the competition; or setting objectives.

Section 8.2

- There are four types of online advertising that are commonly employed to promote an e-business: (1) banner ads, (2) pop-up ads, (3) search-engine ads, and (4) classified ads. A smart marketing strategy for a new e-business might include testing all four options to determine their effectiveness.

Section 8.3

- Newsgroups and Internet mailing lists take time and creativity to utilize, but both consist of highly targeted customer groups that offer rich opportunities for different types of niche marketing.
- Email promotions must be used with great care. Ideally, email promotions should be sent only to recipients who "opt in" to receive a promotion. A mass emailing to an untargeted list is called spam and is frowned upon by the online community.
- An informative, regularly published newsletter is an excellent tool for building a strong relationship with existing and potential customers.

Section 8.4

- Blogging and podcasts are just two of the relatively new methods available for promoting e-businesses using emerging Internet technology. Other creative marketing efforts include using automated customer contact tools, offline advertising, and sending out press releases.

ASSESS YOUR UNDERSTANDING

UNDERSTAND: WHAT HAVE YOU LEARNED?

Go to **www.wiley.com/college/holden** to assess your knowledge of the basics of marketing for an e-business.

APPLY: WHAT WOULD YOU DO?

1. Choose 25 keywords to describe the brand of an e-business that sells high-end, all-natural, organic cosmetics.
2. Describe three characteristics of an effective pop-up ad.
3. A friend who has launched a Web site to sell bowling equipment is considering the benefits of search-engine advertising. Choose five keywords that should appear in the ad.
4. E-business entrepreneurs need to utilize all available marketing opportunities. List three free options for online marketing.
5. Assume that you're marketing a new line of custom fishing lures. Identify three newsgroups to target.
6. Discuss how often an e-newsletter from an online pharmacy should be distributed. Explain your reasoning. Describe the potential scope of the content.
7. Explain how, if at all, a blog would serve the following two online businesses:
   - a local health food store
   - a national sporting goods supplier
8. You're looking for ways to market your online specialty wine-distribution company. How could automated marketing benefit your business without adding to your workload?
9. Which forms of offline advertising would most benefit the wine-distribution company from the previous question? Explain your choices.

BE AN E-BUSINESS ENTREPRENEUR

Branding Basics

Like any business, an e-business needs a clearly defined brand to set it apart from the competition. Compose a statement describing the brand of the following types of consumer goods:

- Gently used designer handbags
- Geneology/family tree kits
- Vegetarian cookbooks

Comparing Advertising Approaches

Conduct an online search for vintage T-shirts. Compare the advertising approaches of two different T-shirt businesses, noting how each company uses banner ads, pop-up ads, and search-engine ads differently. Determine which e-business uses these techniques most effectively.

Developing a Marketing Strategy

You've decided to add rebounders, or mini exercise trampolines, to your e-business that sells children's sporting goods. Visit other Web sites to evaluate what, if any, competition exists. Develop a strategy for advertising and marketing your rebounders. List in order of priority the four online means of advertising you would pursue.

KEY TERMS

Autoresponder	A software tool that automatically generates an email response based on an incoming request.
Banner ad	A rectangular advertisement that displays basic information about an e-business and takes the customer to the Web site when they click on the ad.
Blog	Short for Web log. An online digital diary or forum where text, photos, and other material can be posted and made available to the public.
Brand	The message that a company portrays in everything it does, from communicating about the business, to acting a specific way, to providing value through products and services.
Classified ad	A simple text-based ad that is organized by category.
Click-through Rate (CTR)	A banner ad charge determined by the number of viewer clicks that prompt a link to the advertiser's Web site.
Cost Per Click (CPC)	A banner ad charge system in which the advertiser determines how much is paid for each click on their ad or keyword. Different advertisers wanting to use the same ad space or keywords bid against each other.
Cost Per Thousand (CPM)	A banner ad charge determined by the number of people who visit the Web page on which the advertisement appears.
Internet mailing list	A group of people with similar interests who discuss their favorite topics via email.
Newsgroup	A collection of messages posted by individuals to a news server; a dedicated computer maintained by a company, group, or individual for storing the messages.
Newsletter	An electronic communications tool, often distributed by email, containing articles and other information promoting an e-business and its products.
Podcast	A recorded audio program available online for download in a file format that can easily be transferred to an MP3 player.
Pop-up ad	An ad consisting of a window that pops up on a user's screen whenever the user visits the advertised Web site or one on which ad placement has been purchased.
Press release	A short document that is designed to make a newsworthy announcement about a business to the media.

Search-engine ad	An advertisement tied to specific keywords in a search engine. When selected keywords are typed in a search box, an appropriate ad is displayed.
Spam	Unsolicited emails sent en masse to promote a product or service.
Spam filter	Software programs that block unwanted spam.
Tickler	A reminder, an offer, or an update directed to a customer that is automatically distributed by email.

REFERENCES

1. Kerry Miller, "Etsy: A Site for Artisans Takes Off," BusinessWeek.com, www.businessweek.com/smallbiz/content/jun2007/sb20070611_488723.htm.
2. "Catching Up with the 2006 30 Under 30 Alumni," Inc.com, www.inc.com/30under30/2007/catching-up-with-the-2006-alumni.html.
3. Marc Hogan, "From Rock Star to Entrepreneur," BusinessWeek.com, www.businessweek.com/smallbiz/content/jan2007/sb20070116_568424.htm?chan=search.

CHAPTER

EFFECTIVELY USING SEARCH ENGINES

Using Google, Yahoo!, and Other Sites to Increase E-Business Visibility

Do You Already Know?

- How search engines work
- How to sign up with different search-engine sites
- The difference between <META> tags and keywords
- Where to look to find out what search engines know about Web sites

For additional questions to assess your current knowledge on using search engines to promote e-businesses, go to **www.wiley.com/college/holden.**

What You Will Find Out	What You Will Be Able To Do
9.1 How search engines work and how to increase a site's visibility in the search-engine rankings	Use search engines to build traffic to an e-commerce site with keywords and other tools
9.2 How to sign up with several popular search engines and determine when to pay for search services	Register a site with Google, Yahoo!, and other services; determine when it is appropriate to pay for improved results
9.3 How to use <META> tags and keywords to attract potential customers	Place <META> tags and keywords appropriately to improve search-engine rankings
9.4 How to determine the method used by search engines to rank Web sites; how to monitor competitor rankings; and how to build links to improve a Web site's search-engine rankings	Determine how Yahoo! and Google rankings are assigned; monitor competitor rankings; build links to improve rankings

INTRODUCTION

Search engines and Web portals are the first places that most Internet users go when they are looking for something on the World Wide Web. Because of this, working with search engines—and improving search-engine rankings—is a major component of the marketing efforts for most successful e-businesses. The first section of this chapter begins by explaining how search engines work and how e-businesses can use basic tools of the search business—keywords and <META> tags—to get search engines to notice their Web pages. The second section explains the basic steps for signing up with Google, Yahoo!, and other major search engines and discusses when it may be smart to pay for listings instead of accepting what is delivered for free. An in-depth review of visible search tags—keywords—and invisible ones—<META> tags—follows in the third section, with instructions for creating search tags, placing search tags, and organizing Web pages for the greatest impact on search results. The final section explores the all-important topic of search-engine rankings: monitoring and managing rankings, evaluating competitors' rankings, and techniques for building links that will help improve a site's rankings.

9.1 AN INTRODUCTION TO SEARCH ENGINES

Search engine: A specialized Web site in which a visitor types keywords into a box and receives a list of links to other sites that match those keywords.

Web portal: A Web site that offers a broad array of information, services, and links related to a single topic.

A **search engine** is a specialized Web site in which a visitor types keywords into a box and is rewarded with a long list of links to other sites that match those keywords. Some of the most successful Internet business ventures—Google and Yahoo! quickly come to mind—were built on attracting visitors with their powerful search engines. The huge visitor counts enabled the diversification of their businesses to offer a multitude of information and services—news, sports, shopping, email, and much more. Search-engine sites that embrace the diversified format are called **Web portals.** The broad-scope Internet giants are not the only search engines or portals available. Other numerous sites with powerful search capabilities, as well as information, services, and links, cater to very narrow areas of interest.

Internet search engines are free to use, and companies such as Yahoo! sell online advertising and sponsorships to generate revenue. Advertising on a popular search engine or Web portal is an ideal way to reach large numbers of Internet users and target specific audiences. Virtually all search engines are searchable by keyword or phrase; but like the Yellow Pages, are also divided into categories, allowing customers to pinpoint links that lead to topics of interest. A visitor may visit an e-business by chance after conducting an Internet search seeking a business-related topic.

Because search engines and Web portals are generally the first place Web surfers go to find what they are looking for online, one of an e-business owner's first steps in promoting their Web site should be ensuring that the site is prominently listed with popular services. Simply being listed with a search engine, however, is not enough. When a visitor sees a list of possible links after a search query, a Web site needs to be one of the first on that list to help ensure that the visitor will actually visit the site. With so many Web sites available and so much competition, obtaining a top listing is not always an easy task, yet it is an essential one.

9.1.1 Search-Engine Optimization

Search-engine optimization: The process of obtaining a prominent listing placement on a search engine, Web directory, or information portal.

Getting noticed by search engines is far from being a passive process. The process of obtaining a prominent listing placement on a search engine or Web portal is called **search-engine optimization.** Understanding how these services work and how to obtain a desired placement is a skill that requires a significant, ongoing time commitment. Each search engine is slightly different in terms of layout and design. Pinpointing exactly how and where a Web site should be listed on each of the popular Web directories requires research.

Many third-party services can be hired to assist e-business owners in listing their Web sites with the search engines to achieve prominent placement. Search-engine listing and optimization services charge a fee, but the assistance provided can save an e-business owner valuable hours. Results are not instantaneous, even when using a third-party service. After a Web site is registered with a search engine, unless it is a paid placement, several days or weeks may lapse before a listing appears.

E-business in Action →
Use search engines to build traffic to a site.

No matter the type of online business, focusing on search-engine optimization and achieving good placement on services such as Google or Yahoo! will drive traffic to a Web site. After listing with a Web site, an owner can better utilize the power of search engines, Web directories, and information portals by taking advantage of the paid advertising and paid placement opportunities available. Using advertising opportunities ensures that when a visitor uses a search engine and enters a search phrase or keyword that is relevant to a Web site, a link to that Web site appears.

9.1.2 How Search-Engines Work

Each search engine uses different methods (which are usually kept secret) to compare information against similar sites to develop the all-important rankings that are delivered to users. E-businesses that figure out how the search engines work are the ones that are continually near the top of the rankings; other businesses, despite well-designed and informative Web sites, remain buried on the 10th or 20th page of results. A few years ago, human intervention could elevate worthy sites to the top and achieve featured placement. Today the placement process is much more computerized, giving owners the ability to learn and utilize the ranking system.

Keyword: Specific word that is tied to a particular subject; what is typed into a search engine's "search" box.

The words entered into a search engine typically are not ordinary words. They are **keywords,** or specific words that are tied to a particular subject. When keywords are entered into a search engine, the engine searches through its database to find sites that mention those keywords and returns those sites in a specific order. The database is made up of countless entries of different Web pages that were gathered by either computer programs (known as bots or spiders) or human editors.

The search engine does not analyze entire Web pages by comparing every word on a page to the keyword(s) specified. Instead, the search engine examines notes, or a shorthand summarization of that page. These notes are taken from elements such as:

- The name of the Web site and particular Web page
- The words used in the title (or head) of the Web page
- The first paragraph or two of the Web page
- The words assigned by the Web page to represent the title and description (by using <META> tags, which are introduced in Section 9.3.1)
- The Internet links present on the Web page
- The words used by other Web pages that offer a link to the Web page

E-business in Action → Utilize keywords to increase site traffic.

The first page of the search results contains Web pages that include the search term. The most effective place to put an important keyword is in the site's URL, but this is not always feasible. Often it is necessary to put the keywords in <META> tags or in the headings and initial body text of a Web site. Sites are not limited to a single keyword. Sites can have multiple keywords or even phrases consisting of several keywords. However, it is easier to promote a handful of keywords or phrases than to try to offer everything to everyone. Accordingly, e-businesses must learn to home in on the most important words or phrases that customers will use when they search for products.

9.1.3 Getting Noticed by Search Engines

Increasing a Web site's visibility on search engines involves knowing the rules the engines use and ensuring that that site follows those rules. Search engines do not base their rankings solely on keywords. If they did, a Web page that mentions the same word a thousand times would be at the top of their rankings. Instead, search engines also look for references, or how many other Web sites offer a link to a given Web page. The more links that point to a particular page, the higher that page appears on the search-engine rankings. This is especially true for Google. The reasoning is that if other Web sites are all pointing their visitors to a particular page, that page must have more relevant content than other, nonlinked pages.

To be noticed by a search engine, it is necessary to have other Web sites link to a Web page. Greater weight is given to a Web page whose referring links use the main keywords for that page in the text for that link. For example, when promoting a Web page for an e-business called "Arctic Technology Solutions," the best URL for getting noticed by a search engine is www.arctictechnologysolutions.com. The chances of being noticed are increased if leading IT consultants link to the Web site, especially if they build the link this way:

<a href=http://www.arctictechnologysolutions.com> Talk to Arctic Technology Solutions! </a>

Notice that the clickable text that points to the Web site contains the same keywords as the URL. The search engines get a double message that the Web site contains the text "Arctic Technology Solutions" because their computer programs read the keywords in both the HTML command and the clickable-text words.

Search engines do not work solely by paid advertisements and computer programs that automatically scour Web pages. The human factor still plays a role. Yahoo!, one of the first search engines, originally compiled its directory of Web sites using live employees. Today, Yahoo's Web directory is harder to find than originally (dir.yahoo.com). However, editors still index sites and assign them to a New Additions category, which includes sites that are especially unique or interesting in the editors' perspective. Human editors are rarely coerced to index specific Web sites. However, making a Web site unique, interesting, and content rich can help a business appear in directories and search results, which, in turn, often leads to an increase in paying customers.

E-business in Action →
Increase Web site visibility.

Having a site added to the Yahoo! Directory greatly increases that site's visibility. However, Yahoo! charges a $299 fee for businesses to be included. A better strategy is to focus on free directories, such as MSN and Google, to improve visibility.

IN THE REAL WORLD

Small-Town Christmas Retailer Keeps Up with the Times

Looking for holiday decorations? Do what millions of customers do and try Bronner's, the world's largest Christmas retailer, in Frankenmuth, Michigan. What began in 1954 as Wally Bronner's small-town storefront has grown and evolved into a Christmas empire consisting of

(Continued)

IN THE REAL WORLD (Continued)

stores, catalogs, and a Web site. The store, which has moved from its original location, is a major attraction, featuring more than 50,000 trims and gifts, including Christmas ornaments, Santa suits, artificial Christmas trees, Christmas lights, nativity scenes, Christmas decorations, collectibles, and more. In an effort to reach an even wider customer base, Bronner's began in 1991 to distribute more than three million catalogs each year. And in 1996, Bronner's went online with its Web site (www.bronners.com), which offers approximately 3,000 items for purchase. Throughout its history, Bronner's has been family-run and focused on customer service and loyalty. To ensure quality, the company's call center, catalog and Web site fulfillment, and shipping are all done in-house.

SELF CHECK

1. What is a search engine? How do search engines differ from Web portals?
2. What are two primary tools that search engines use to rank Web sites?
3. Are search engines always determined by computer? Explain.

Apply Your Knowledge You hope to improve your Web site's search-engine rankings by making better use of keywords. List five elements on your Web site that would be a good source of keywords.

9.2 SIGNING UP WITH SEARCH ENGINES

In order for search engines to list a Web site, the site must be registered with each engine individually. When visiting any search engine, look for a link that says "Suggest a URL," "Add a URL," or "How to Suggest a Site." Clicking on such a link will provide details on how to proceed with a free Web site listing. Each search engine follows a slightly different process for site submissions.

Although registering a site on each of the various search engines and keeping the listing current can be a time-consuming process, it is worth taking the time to personally ensure that a site is listed with at least the top ten search engines. For a relatively small fee, e-businesses can hire a company that will register a URL with hundreds of search engines, Web portals, and directories.

The cost of hiring a company to register a Web site can range anywhere from a flat, one-time fee of about $50 to several hundred dollars per month. The least-expensive service offers search-engine submission only, whereas the more expensive services actually conduct search-engine optimization and take steps to ensure that a site will receive prominent placement with each popular search engine. The registration process can take anywhere from several days to several weeks to begin seeing listings appear on the various search engines, so be patient. By contrast, paid advertisements and sponsored links on the search engines appear almost instantaneously (see Section 9.2.4).

PATHWAY TO... ADDING A WEB SITE URL TO GOOGLE

1. Go to www.google.com/addurl.html. Google's Add Your URL to Google page appears.
2. **In the URL box, enter the full address of the Web site's home page.** Remember to add the http://. Only include the home page name unless it is not index.html, index.htm, or default.html.
3. **In the Comments box, enter a one-sentence keyword description of the Web site.** Limit comments and keywords found on each subcategory page. Use the keywords with which the Web site should be closely identified.
4. **Type the squiggly word shown in the box that is displayed.** Google adds a special "human detector" on this form to distinguish between humans completing the form and special software programs that do it automatically. Software programs cannot analyze this box because all they see is the generic name for the graphic. Only human eyes can interpret the letters that are shown.
5. **Click the Add URL button.** By clicking the Add URL button, you send Google all the information provided. Eventually a Googlebot will be sent to the Web site's home page. From there, the Googlebot follows the links to read every page it can find and stores the results.

9.2.1 Google

Google sends its own programs, known as Googlebots, around the Web looking for new sites to add to its index. An e-business does not need to wait and hope that a Googlebot will magically land on a new Web site, especially during the critical startup phase. Instead, new e-businesses should complete Google's simple, one-page Web form that identifies sites for its software programs to analyze.

9.2.2 Yahoo!

The roots of Yahoo! are in its category search, not just a general search. Every category has an index page that contains lists of Web sites that belong to that category. Each index page also points to subcategories, each of which has its own index page. As Yahoo! has grown and acquired other Internet companies, from Overture to Flickr, it has maintained the category approach to organization and accepts submissions for its general search.

The Yahoo! submission process is still in human hands. The editors scan these submissions and decide what to include and where to include it, which is one aspect that sets Yahoo! apart from the other search engines. Unfortunately, to guarantee that a URL submission is reviewed by Yahoo! editors, e-businesses must pay.

9.2.3 Other Search Engines

E-business owners have no assurance that submitting Web addresses to—and even getting picked up by—Google and Yahoo! is all that is required to get noticed by search engines. After all, who uses the other, smaller search engines? The answer is that big search engines such as Google and Yahoo! do. By increasing a Web site's listings in all the smaller search engines, a site can get more customer referrals, which in turn leads to higher rankings on the Big Two search engines. See Table 9-1 for a listing of smaller search engines.

FOR EXAMPLE

See Figure 9-1 for Yahoo's page for submitting a Web site for free.

Figure 9-1

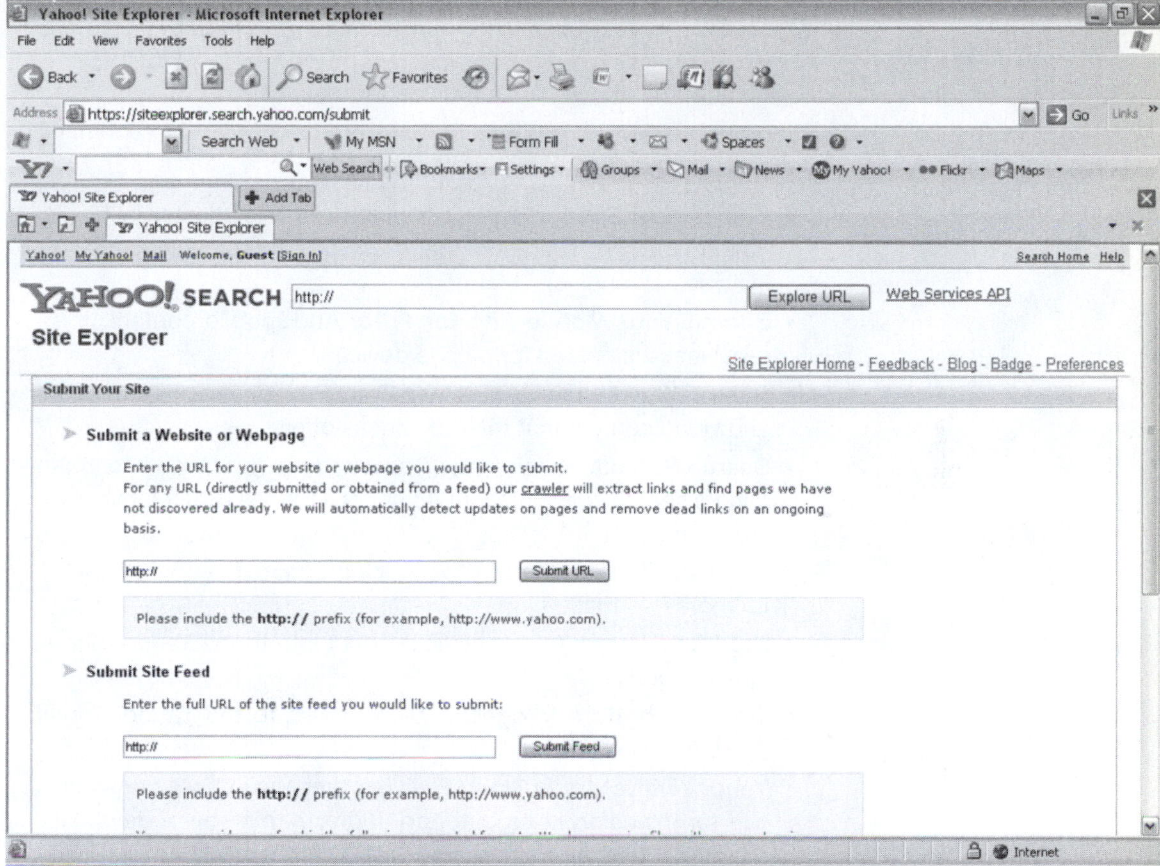

Yahoo's page for submitting a Web site for free.

Accordingly, e-business owners should research customer visit logs to identify which search engines the customers are using. Then take the steps necessary to be indexed by those search engines, many of which are free.

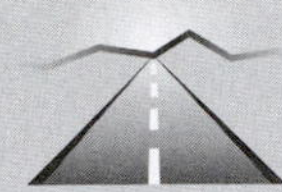

PATHWAY TO... ADDING A WEB SITE URL TO YAHOO!

1. Go to http://search.yahoo.com/info/submit.html.
2. **Choose the type of content to be submitted.** Yahoo! offers many ways to submit site content to its engine:
   - **Submit Your Site for Free:** Submit the Web site address (although Yahoo! does not guarantee that it will look at it or include the site in its search engine).
   - **Submit Your Mobile Site for Free:** Add mobile content, if an e-business is geared for mobile devices.
   - **Submit Your Media Content for Free:** Provide images and audio and video content that the e-business offers.
   - **Search Submit:** Allows e-businesses to put their Web site in the Yahoo! search index in about 48 hours. (The fee is $49 for the first Web site.)
   - **Sponsored Search:** A cost-per-click program. (See Section 8.2.1 for more information.)
   - **Product Submit:** Add specific product info to the Yahoo! Shopping directory.
   - **Travel Submit:** Add specific travel deals to the Yahoo! Travel Deals section.
   - **Yahoo! Directory Submit:** Ensures that Yahoo! will consider a site for inclusion in its category index within seven days. Remember, there is no guarantee that a Web site will be approved and added—only a guarantee that it will be reviewed. (Submitting for free carries no guarantees.) The cost for this program is $299; if a site is accepted, there is an annual $299 fee to continue inclusion.
   - **Yahoo! Standard:** Submit a site for category inclusion in the Yahoo! main directory.
3. **Enter the URL of the Web site being submitted.** Regardless of the type of content being submitted, the last step is entering the URL. Click Submit URL, and the address is sent to Yahoo! for inclusion in its next robot search of the Internet.

Table 9-1 Free Search Engine Submittal Pages

Company	*Submission URL*
MSN Search	http://search.msn.com/docs/submit.aspx
AltaVista(Yahoo)	http://addurl.altavista.com/addurl
Beamed	www.beamed.com/search/AddURL.html
FindRex	www.findrex.ca/admin/submit.html
SearchIt	www.searchit.com/addurl.htm
InfoUSA	http://dbupdate.infousa.com/dbupdate/index.html

Many medium-size search engines—like Ask.com, Lycos, and Looksmart—have their own ways of accepting submissions (mainly by paid inclusion), and some have no manual submission process any more. Search engines rise and fall in popularity, just like the results they display, so e-businesses should be alert for flourishing search programs and to get listed on them as quickly as possible.

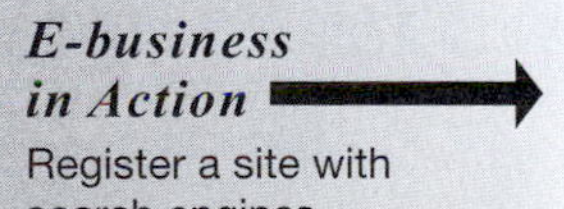

E-business in Action
Register a site with search engines.

Many third-party companies offer, for a price, guaranteed submissions to hundreds, or even thousands, of search engines. The reality is that many of the links that are offered are no longer valid because companies get absorbed or go out of business. The Internet is an extremely dynamic business environment, so be wary of promises that cannot be kept. And while some companies offer decent service for maintaining a presence on lesser-known search engines, e-businesses are smart to manage their position on the larger search engines themselves.

9.2.4 Paying for Listings

The placement that will bring in the most traffic is at the top of the first page of a set of search results, or in a column at the side of the page. A more effective tool is to use color to highlight the site name and URL. However, the only way to get such preferential treatment is to pay for it. A growing number of online businesses are paying search engines to list their sites in a prominent location.

Listing with search-engine sites is growing more complex all the time. Many sites are owned by other sites. Products can also be listed on shopping aggregation sites. E-business owners can make consolidation of search sites work to their advantage by carefully selecting a few search services, which then leads to listings on many other sites.

IN THE REAL WORLD

Cultivating Success with Search-Engine Marketing

Lars Hundley, who in 1998 started his first online store, Clean Air Gardening, has received substantial publicity because of energetic marketing and good use of search-engine resources. "I use Yahoo! Search Marketing (also known as Overture) and Google AdWords. I also sometimes use shopping aggregation sites, such as Yahoo! Shopping, Shopzilla, and Shopping.com." Hundley uses a variety of search-engine placement tools. He says, "I also use tools, such as Wordtracker and the Overture search term Suggestion tool, to make sure that I use important keywords in all my product descriptions. I always try to name and describe things in the words that people are searching for, and I think that really pays off over time." In addition to search-engine marketing, Hundley uses his journalistic experience to write and distribute press releases and pitch articles to magazines, such as *U.S. News and World Report* and *This Old House.* He also sends out an email newsletter every two weeks to a list of 10,000 subscribers. Hundley's multifaceted marketing efforts must work: He reports that Clean Air Gardening brought in gross revenues of more than $1.5 million in 2006.

Yahoo! is a notable search engine because its search results mix organic results and paid listings, and the paid ads appear at the top, along the right, and at the bottom of a results page. Paying for Yahoo! Search Marketing (http://searchmarketing.yahoo.com) will not guarantee a business being listed in the Yahoo! directory, but it does ensure some measure of certainty that a Web site will at least appear in search results on the site. What sets Yahoo! Search Marketing apart is that an editorial team reviews a site's keywords and ads. Google AdWords' listings are also reviewed thoroughly, but the results come back in a matter of seconds and appear to be automated. Yahoo! Search Marketing originally used Google's search technology, but developed its search marketing system based on companies like Inktomi and Overture, which it began purchasing after 2002.

To improve a Web site's chances of appearing in the Yahoo! directory, an e-business owner should do three things:

1. **Make the site interesting, quirky, or otherwise attention-grabbing.** This makes it more likely to stand out from the multitude of new Web sites and gain the attention of a Yahoo! editor.
2. **Try to apply to the main Yahoo! index.** There is no penalty for applying, and the potential benefits are great.
3. **Try a local Yahoo! index.** Major areas around the United States and other parts of the world have their own Yahoo! indexes. Go to http://yp.yahoo.com/yp/states.html to browse by city. Find the local index most applicable and apply it as described in the previous step. The chances of being listed locally are much greater than on the main Yahoo! site.

One way of improving a listing on Yahoo! is by paying to become a sponsored Web site, which can cost anywhere from $25 to $300 or more per year. A sponsored site is listed in the Sponsored Sites box at the top of a Yahoo! category. The exact cost is dependent on the popularity of the category. Owners should consider options other than Yahoo! as well. Several Web-based services are trying to compete by providing their own way of organizing and evaluating Web sites. Two alternatives are Best of the Web (http://botw.org) or the guides employed by About.com (www.about.com).

E-business in Action
Determine the necessity of paying for search-engine listings.

SELF CHECK

1. What is an alternative strategy to having an e-business register with search sites themselves? Explain the disadvantages.
2. List and explain the advantages to paying for improved results on a search-engine site. Explain the disadvantages.

Apply Your Knowledge You run an e-commerce site that sells unique sports-team caps. Knowing that Yahoo! editors influence search rankings, suggest three ways to grab their attention and improve the site's search rankings.

9.3 <META> TAGS AND KEYWORDS

An e-business may use different methods for incorporating keywords into Web pages to make sure that those keywords will be viewed as the most relevant and important words representing the page. For example, keywords should appear in multiple locations so that the search-engine bots know that those keywords represent the content of a Web site. The best locations are not always obvious. Consider a Web page offering viewers the 100 greatest uses for a ball-peen hammer. An inexperienced Web page manager may simply use the words "ball-peen hammer" repeatedly in the body of the Web page, but there are many superior locations than the body of the Web page to consistently attract the attention of search-engine bots. Some locations are invisible to the Web visitor—and others are hiding in plain sight.

9.3.1 What are <META> Tags?

HyperText Markup Language (HTML): A computer language used to create World Wide Web pages.

<META> tag: Computer code, usually invisible to a Web page viewer, that defines the name, purpose, author, and date of a Web page. Search engines read this tag to catalog Web pages more efficiently.

Web pages are built using a computer language called **HyperText Markup Language,** or HTML. Many commands identify Web page information. For keyword purposes, the most important tag to use in a Web page is **<META> tag,** which is usually invisible to a Web page viewer. The <META> tag is hidden in the computer code for the page. It defines the name, purpose, author, and date of a Web page. Search engines read the tag to catalog Web pages more efficiently.

Two types of <META> tags are important for search-engine optimization: (1) A short, text-based Web site description (usually one or two sentences) created by the Webmaster for a site; (2) A detailed list of keywords and search phrases (one or two words) that the Webmaster can relate directly to the site. Search-engine bots are interested in knowing what information is assigned to <META> tags. Bots take that information with a grain of salt, however, because they know that <META> tag info is being written by a biased source—namely, the author of the page. Nevertheless, the <META> tag information is added into the formula for reading and interpreting Web pages.

During the Web site design process, defining <META> tags for every Web page on the site is important. Designers commonly forget these optional tags because the tags do not affect the performance of the Web page on the server. Web sites lacking <META> tags end up being categorized by search engines based on the first few words found on a site. The search engine will then automatically attempt to choose keywords for a site—keywords that may not always be beneficial and can even prevent potential customers from looking at a site.

The <META> tag is specific to only the individual Web page where the tag resides. Therefore, the information in the <META> tag for a home page is (and should be) completely or significantly different from an interior Web page that focuses on one product line. It should also be remembered that <META> tags are not a guaranteed solution for getting a site to the top of a search-engine list.

9.3.2 Creating <META> Tags

For each Web page, insert at least two <META> tags into the HTML for the page. More options are available, like defining the author of the page or the last revision date of the Web page. Although it may be desirable to define the fields for other reasons, the tags are not as helpful for targeting search-engines. <META> tags should be part of the head of each Web page, instead of the body section.

The syntax of a <META> tag works in two parts: The type of <META> tag is defined by assigning a name, then assigning the content for that <META> tag. For example, assigning the keywords Arctic, Technology, and Solutions to a <META> tag would look like this:

```
<META name="keywords" content= "Arctic, Technology, Solutions">
```

The two <META> tags that should be included on every page are the keywords and description. For added effect, some people repeat their keywords as part of their descriptions. The search engines, though, are reading the <META> description and looking for context. A long list of keywords in the <META> description tag does not improve search results. Creative integration can help efforts. A Web site selling gourmet artichoke sauces, for example, may create <META> tags that look like this:

```
<META name="keywords" content="Gourmet, Artichoke, Sauces">

<META name="description" content="Our gourmet chefs have picked
the freshest artichokes to create gourmet artichoke sauces sure to liven up
any artichoke recipe!">
```

Notice the repeated use of the targeted keywords as part of the context of a readable, legible sentence. Although the <META> description tag does not have a hard limit, using more than one or two sentences is counterproductive. Overloading the description tag waters down results to the point that the search engines do not know any more what is particularly meaningful.

Keywords, like Web page addresses, are frequently misspelled. E-business owners should be sure to include several variations on keywords that might be subject to errors: for instance, Mississippi, Misisippi, and Mississip. Capitalization is less important, however, because more searchers ignore capitalization and only insert lowercase letters.

The Internet is a global phenomenon, so the audience is not restricted to one region or country. Similarly, keywords should not be restricted to one particular language. It is possible to define an attribute of the <META> tag known as lang (short for language). The search engines implement a filter if they see the lang defined and then assign the correct keywords to the specified language in the Web surfer's preferences. An e-business selling soccer jerseys and sweaters to Americans, Britons, and Spaniards might create <META> tags that look like this:

<META name="keywords" lang="en-us" content="soccer, jersey, sweater">

<META name="keywords" lang="en" content="football, jersey, jumper">

<META name="keywords" lang="es" content="futbol, Jersey, sueter">

Another valuable addition to the HTML tag is the ALT attribute. This attribute is assigned to image files that are loaded into a Web page. The **ALT attribute** is a description of a graphical image that is displayed on the Web page if the Web browser cannot load the image properly on the screen. Because search engines cannot read text that is part of a graphical image, they read the ALT attribute, if it is defined, and give it some weight. Like the <META> tag, the optional ALT attribute is easily forgotten when a Web site is being designed, but it offers a tremendous additional opportunity to promote keywords.

ALT attribute: A description of a Web page graph stored in the code and read like a <META> tag by search engines.

E-business in Action →
Place <META> tags to improve search engine rankings.

9.3.3 Visible Keyword Tags

Although search engines rely on HTML commands like <META> tags to gain an understanding of the purpose of a Web page, their computer programs are more interested in discovering the "natural" meaning of a Web page. The computer programs interpret the text that is visible on the page to understand what the page is conveying to users. Therefore, e-businesses need to make sure that the keywords that best identify their Web page are clearly used in visible—but not always obvious—locations.

- **Page name:** Every Web page is simply a file containing HTML commands and text, and each file must have a name. The last three or four letters of the filename after the period (known as the extension) must be *htm* or *html* because of Web standards. Everything before the period in the filename is completely up to the author, and should logically describe the purpose of the page. A page set up to sell tennis equipment, for example, should not use an abstract filename, like order.html. Instead, name this page tennis.html or tennis-equipment.html. When designing a Web site for optimal search-engine recognition, avoid Web pages offering two or more categories of products. Instead, divide the product lines and dedicate a single page for each one.

- **Page title:** Every Web page on a site should have a title, regardless of the purpose of the page. This valuable space is selected by search engines. The worst thing a page designer can do is leave an empty title. The second-worst thing is use a vague or meaningless title, like "Welcome to my Web site!" or "Stuff for you." Make sure that each title includes the important keywords for that page.
- **Page headings:** Just like human eyes read headlines quicker than any other text on a page, computer programs read headlines and assign a greater weight to them than to the body text on a page. Be more specific in the headings than in the title—just keep the headings focused on the page content, not on the overall site.
- **First sentence:** The first sentence on the page is typically a summary or overview of what the page offers. Because some search engines do not index an entire page of text, make sure that the first sentence clearly explains the page's purpose.
- **Text inside links:** Search-engine bots are hungry for Web links, so make sure that any clickable text contains the right keywords for that link. The bots assign weight to those keywords because they are being referenced by the link.

By adding keywords in page names, page titles, page headings, first sentences, and text inside links, the e-business should also incorporate the same keywords into the flow of text that is easy to read. Keywords should form complete sentences. Search-engine bots notice context, so any out-of-place lists of keyword lists are flagged as nonessential.

Any valuable keywords should appear as text only (not graphics) on a Web page. Search-engine bots cannot scan the contents of a graphics file—only the text that is in the HTML file (or the ALT attribute for an image). For example, when using graphics for a navigation menu or header, complement that menu with a text menu at the bottom of the page to emphasize keywords as clickable text and improve a site's ranking.

Keyword density:
The number of keywords on a page multiplied by the number of times each one is used.

One additional factor important to maximizing a site's presence in search engines is **keyword density:** the percentage of words on a page that match a specified set of keywords. High keyword density often correlates to high value to search-engine users. Increasing keyword density (using fewer keywords more often) is a way to gain a good search-engine ranking (see Section 9.4). Increased keyword density will lead to a better ranking than using many keywords fewer times.

E-business in Action
Use keywords to improve search-engine rankings.

CAREER CONNECTION

An entrepreneur reaps the rewards of a technological update.

Megan Duckett is owner and founder of Sew What?, a California-based custom theatrical drapery company. Duckett, who was working for a rock concert staging company by day, started off sewing stage props for clients at her kitchen table. She decided to start Sew What? (sewwhatinc.com) a year later in 1992, after her part-time sewing business gradually became more profitable than her job with the staging company. Today, Sew What? designs, manufactures, and installs theatrical drapery and stage curtains for entertainment events and theatres as well as major touring acts such as Madonna, Sting, the Dave Matthews Band, and Rod Stewart.

Although Sew What? has experienced tremendous growth—it now has 33 employees and a 15,000-square-foot building in Rancho Dominguez, California—it wasn't that long ago that Duckett felt her business had stalled. She had cornered the highly specialized entertainment market in southern California, but she wasn't getting anywhere building a customer base elsewhere. "The biggest challenge for us has always been reaching new customers," says Duckett. Only 20 percent of Sew What's customers were in states other than California, and they'd only had two international clients. "I knew there was a bigger world out there, but I didn't know how to make them aware of our company," she says. Her solution: to pay for a professional redesign of the Web site and have it optimized. It didn't take long to see results, with a 45 percent increase in revenue and a dramatic shift in customer demographics; in 2006, the percentage of Sew What's customers that were from out of state rose to 66 percent.

The company doesn't put much money into online or offline advertising. Duckett attributes the success to the new site and the technology that went into it to make it more effective on the Internet.[1]

Tips from the Professional

- Pick the right search-engine optimization specialist and be willing to stay involved with the process from start to finish.
- Let your passion for your product show in every piece of literature, correspondence and advertisement.
- Only risk what you are willing to lose.[2]

9.3.4 Strategic Page Design

A Web site is a collection of Web pages that make up an overall e-business. Therefore, every Web page representing the business should be well defined and serve a specific purpose. Create well-defined Web pages that make sense to both users and search-engine bots.

Keep the following four rules in mind when constructing Web pages for an e-business:

1. **One page, one focus:** If one Web page has two or more product lines, break up that page so that each line is on a separate page. A category index

page can be used to optimize the business's overall mission, allowing each product page to be a launching pad for that subset of the business.

2. **Define the page:** Be certain that all definitions, tags, and keyword mentions are at the top of the HTML source code for a Web page. Several search engines limit the number of characters per page that they accept. Avoid losing out by placing comments or JavaScript code first.
3. **Think about keyword density:** Focus each Web page to target a select group of keywords and phrases. This technique increases the weight of each of these phrases more than when trying to use every keyword in every page. When the same words are used repeatedly, search engines see this density of words and assign greater weight to the few words that are used than does an average Web site that tries to be popular for every popular keyword.
4. **Put away the bells and whistles:** A Web page that excessively uses elements such as graphics, animation, and video or audio files on the same page as valuable product information should separate the extra features into a separate section of the Web site. An alternative is to create two versions: one with just text and basic graphics, and the second with all multimedia elements. Remember that search-engine bots, as well as customers, will stop searching when a page is slow to load because of excessive graphics, animation, video, and/or audio files.

SELF CHECK

1. What is a <META> tag? What are the two types of <META> tags that are important for search engines? What information does each type contain?
2. How do keywords differ from <META> tags?
3. List three rules of page design that will help improve attractiveness to search engines.

Apply Your Knowledge Your Web site sells custom-made turquoise jewelry. Brainstorm three strong keywords that will appeal to search engines and suggest three places to use each keyword. Write the suggested text containing the keyword for each location.

9.4 SEARCH-ENGINE RANKINGS

Although Web pages might last forever in a search engine's database, the Web site's importance or relevancy does not carry over. As Web site owners try to determine ways to improve their positions in search-engine results, search engines update their systems and algorithms to reduce the effect of specific tricks that become popular.

Keyword spamming: Hiding paragraphs of keywords by matching the keyword text color with the color of the page background.

One such practice is **keyword spamming.** Web site owners hide paragraphs of targeted keywords by matching the color of the keyword's text with the color of the Web page background. For example, the owner of a Web site using a white background puts in a block of keywords using white text. These keywords are invisible to customers browsing the Web site because the white text does not show up on a white background. The spiders that download the information from the Web page can see the keywords, however, and they assign weight to those keywords regardless of relevance. Search engines now compare the colors used and eliminate those keywords, even if the colors being used are slight variations of each other.

E-business owners need to stay up-to-date of the changes the search-engines make to their programs, and then update their Web sites accordingly to take advantage of whatever the new rules enforce. The last thing an e-business needs is to optimize a Web site based on one set of rules and then have the site ignored because the rules changed.

A variety of Web sites provide news, updates, columns, and information about major and secondary search engines:

- **SearchEngineWatch.com:** The site's tag line is: "The source for search-engine marketing," and many users agree. The company uses a variety of mechanisms—like news articles, blogs, discussion boards, and a marketplace for vendors of search-engine optimization (SEO) products—to spread the word about search-engine marketing. It offers a wide variety of free content and a reserved Members section (which has premium articles written by experts), an extensive archive of information, and a private newsletter. It even sponsors the Search-Engine Strategies Conference and Expo, in different cities around the world, to promote the same concepts as the site.
- **SearchEngineForums.com:** This site offers discussion areas that cover everything from general search engines (like Google or Yahoo!) to specific topics such as link building. It has a number of discussion boards—including a section dedicated to building, hosting, and maintaining Web sites—that provide much-needed help for online-store professionals.
- **AnitaSearch blog:** Anita Cohen-Williams runs MySearchGuru.com, a site that helps companies update their Web sites for search engines by offering low-cost solutions like optimization and search-engine submissions. Cohen-Williams now operates her own blog at Blogger, where she references the most current tools and news being used in the search-engine optimization field. Her blog is located at http://anitasearch.blogspot.com.

9.4.1 Monitoring and Managing Rankings

The key to monitoring and managing search-engine rankings is to avoid trying to be in the top spot. Considering the enormous amount of new information that becomes indexed every day—not to mention the constant updating of search-engine algorithms—e-business owners can waste a lot of time trying to stay on top.

Most people who are presented with multiple pages of search-engine results typically skim the first page and try a few links. A few of them then go to the second page and try more links. After the second or even third page of results, however, if the destination sites are not close to what the user is looking for, that person typically enters a new string of keywords, gets a different set of results, and tries again. Considering this scenario, a good strategy is to establish two goals:

1. To consistently achieve a position among the first page or two
2. To retain a ranking that is high enough on the list that it appears on competing Web sites

Achieving these goals first requires that an e-business gain an understanding of what the search engines know about their Web site, which is not as difficult as it sounds. Search engines provide a growing number of tools that offer a window into their databases and reveal what they now know about a given Web site. The following sections briefly describe how to learn more about Google and Yahoo! rankings.

Yahoo!

As one of the oldest search engines on the Internet, Yahoo! has built an extensive database structure of the Web, which is classified by category and subject as well as by the links that point to the page. Yahoo! uses all that information and its own algorithms to construct search results. For e-business owners desiring a better understanding of what information is used to determine their ranking, Yahoo! offers the Site Explorer tool, which shows all the information it has gathered about a specific Web site. Follow these steps to use Site Explorer:

1. Go to http://siteexplorer.search.yahoo.com.
2. Enter the URL of the Web to be analyzed and click the "Explore UR" button.
3. View all the pages in that Web site, displayed in their natural search order.
4. Click the Inlinks button to see how many Web sites offer links to the specified domain, a very valuable piece of information.

Google

One way that Google decides how to order its search engine is by assigning every Web page a specific PageRank. The term PageRank was invented by the Google founders to represent the popularity of a Web site, from 0 to 10, based on the number and quality of other Web sites that offer links back to the Web site in question.

The patented PageRank algorithm ranks Web pages by using a vast link structure to indicate the value of a page. Google PageRank interprets a link from Web Site A to Web Site B as a vote for Site B (from Site A). PageRank then looks at the quality of Site A, the voter, and other factors of both pages to determine an ultimate rank.

Google offers a way for Web site programmers to search its database with an automatic query and return the PageRank value for any submitted URL. For a quick way to find out the Google PageRank for a Web site, go to one of these sites:

E-business in Action →
Determine how rankings are assigned.

- http://google-pagerank.net
- http://rankwhere.com/google-page-rank.php
- www.urltrends.com

9.4.2 Watching the Competition

No analysis of Web site search-engine rankings is complete without looking at the competition. Most e-businesses have more than one competitor, and smart companies are always trying to figure out how to steer customers away from the other sites and to their site. An important aspect of the competitive struggle is staying on top in search-engine rankings. Typically, customers link to the first Web site that pops up on a search list. Sometimes that chance click is all it takes to lock up a loyal long-term customer.

When considering the competition, it is important to recognize the difference between two types of competitors:

Indirect competitor: A competitor that sells some of the same products, but has a broader or different overall focus.

Direct competitor: A competitor that is a similar size, caters to the same target market, and offers a similar product mix.

1. **Indirect competitor:** Sells some of the same products, but its overall focus is broader or very different. This category includes the online retail giants that offer a huge mix of products. Indirect competitors do not warrant as much scrutiny.
2. **Direct competitor:** Businesses that are a similar size, cater to the same target market, and offer a similar (or almost identical) product mix. These competitors must be carefully monitored.

The best way to learn about e-business competitors is by going online. Go to the competition's Web site to analyze their page design and find out what it offers to customers. Then take the analysis deeper and answer five questions about competition:

1. What keywords are used in their Web site names?
2. What keywords appear in their Web page titles and headings?
3. What <META> keywords and descriptions are used? (In the Web browser, choose View Source to see the HTML source code.)
4. How many other links point back to their Web sites?
5. What is their Google PageRank?

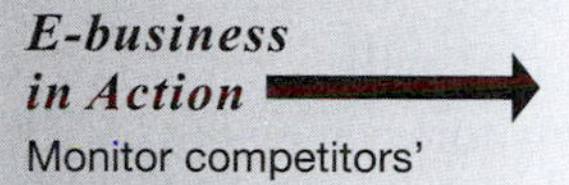
E-business in Action
Monitor competitors' Web sites.

While reviewing competitors' Web sites, note the techniques utilized to attract the attention of search engines. Then check out their search results on multiple search engines. If the competing site gets consistently higher rankings, figure out why and adopt—and improve upon—techniques that seem to work well. When reviewing competing sites, do not copy any information from those sites. The original content of all Web sites is protected by copyright. Although it is acceptable to analyze, utilize, and adapt similar techniques or concepts, it is illegal to plagiarize text or reuse a site's graphics or photos without permission.

IN THE REAL WORLD

Fresh Ideas about Online Organic Foods

Jasch and Kathleen Hamilton, the founders of Diamond Organics, believe that everyone, not just top chefs, should have access to top-quality organic and gourmet foods (www.diamondorganics.com). They started Diamond Organics in 1990, in California's Monterrey County. The company, billed as the nation's premier source for farm-fresh all-organic food with guaranteed overnight nationwide delivery, comes up at or near the top of any Web search for organic food delivery. The company has twice outgrown its distribution center and can now ship more than 2,500 orders per day. Since 1996, the number of all-organic products the company carries has quadrupled, its catalog has increased from 24 to 84 pages, and it has developed and expanded a Web site to include an online store that now accounts for more than 40 percent of sales. To stay at the top, much of the company's marketing is focused on the Internet, with online advertising and email newsletters.

9.4.3 Building Your Own Links

Some Web site owners have decided that if they cannot get other Web sites to offer a link to them, then they need to build their own links. The sole purpose of some Web sites is to serve as part of a network to promote a central site. When visiting referral sites, it is obvious in some cases that they are built for only one reason—to fool search engines by building links. Accordingly, search engines have adapted their rules, and many ignore sites whose only purpose is to link somewhere else.

The right way for e-businesses to create their own network is to build a series of targeted, focused, content-rich sites that each feed into one primary e-commerce business. For example, for an e-business that sells pet supplies, rather than add original content solely to the main e-commerce site, the company can instead set up targeted Web sites featuring dogs, cats, birds, fish, gerbils, and hamsters. The targeted Web sites' content should each provide authoritative information that will allow them to build a loyal following of visitors. Enthusiastic visitors can be directed to the main e-commerce site when they are ready to make a purchase.

An example of other, simpler strategies for building links is to identify content sites in the same interest area (though it is smart to avoid potentially competitive e-commerce sites) and suggest cross-promotion programs. In addition to exchanging links with the partner, the two sites may actually want to swap or share content. Building a small network of several linked partner sites not only will help improve search-engine rankings, but also increase the number of new visitors.

E-business in Action →
Build links to improve search-engine rankings.

Another strategy is to offer selected products for sale on sites like eBay, then linking from the sale listing to a pure content site with nothing for sale. In turn, the content site links back to the main e-commerce site. Some sales sites have restrictions on linking that may not allow such an arrangement, so remember to ask before setting up a questionable link.

SELF CHECK

1. Why must e-businesses continually monitor their search rankings, along with the methods employed by search engines?
2. What are two realistic goals to set when monitoring and managing search-engine rankings? Why is it not better to try to rank No. 1?
3. What is the difference between direct and indirect competitors? Which type of competitor deserves the most attention when analyzing search-engine rankings? Explain.

Apply Your Knowledge Your e-commerce site sells gardening tools. Briefly describe how (and why) you can set up a network of content sites to improve the main site's search-engine rankings. Provide specific examples for the content sites.

SUMMARY

Section 9.1

- Search engines and Web portals are generally the first place people go when looking for something on the Internet, making prominent placement on these services essential for e-businesses. The process of improving placement in search results is called search-engine optimization.

Section 9.2

- Different search engines employ different strategies to determine rankings, though most commonly they analyze the keywords embedded in a site and quantify the number of links from other sites.
- Registering a new Web site with Google, Yahoo!, and other search engines is the first step for inclusion in their searches, but this process alone will not guarantee high rankings. Sometimes it is necessary to pay a search site to improve performance in their rankings.

Section 9.3

- <META> tags are hidden in the code and invisible to the viewer, but contain important information about the Web page and are used by search engines in determining rankings.
- Keywords are visible tags that are analyzed during the search-engine ranking process. Keywords should appear in elements such as the page name and title, the first line of text, and page links.

Section 9.4

- The ranking techniques used by various search engines are always evolving, and e-business managers must stay up-to-date about changes and adapt their Web sites to maintain high rankings.
- A smart strategy for monitoring and managing search-engine rankings is to consistently stay in the first two pages of rankings and stay ahead of key competitor rankings.

ASSESS YOUR UNDERSTANDING

UNDERSTAND: WHAT HAVE YOU LEARNED?

Go to **www.wiley.com/college/holden** to assess your knowledge of effectively using search engines for an e-business.

APPLY: WHAT WOULD YOU DO?

1. A friend has launched an online business selling hand-knitted baby blankets. Her startup funds are limited, but how would you convince her that search-engine optimization is worth the investment?
2. For a dog-walking/dog-treat business called Treats and Trails, determine which ten keywords will best ensure the site's visibility on search engines.
3. Suggest the type of links that would help get the Treats and Trails Web site noticed by search engines.
4. E-businesses should consider registering with both the Google and Yahoo! search engines. List five other search engines that should be utilized. Explain the benefit of listing with small and mid-size search-engines.
5. Compare both a keyword <META> tag and a descriptive <META> tag for a Web site that sells handmade jewelry made from sea glass.
6. An e-business needs to make sure that the keywords that best identify its site are placed properly. Go to the home page of Turner Classic Movies (www.tcm.com) and identify three locations where keywords should appear on a Web site. Give your choices for five effective keywords.
7. Evaluate a Web site of your choosing for its use of keywords. Determine whether the site follows the suggested rule of using fewer keywords more often, rather than using many keywords fewer times.
8. Monitoring a Web site's page ranking is important for any business. Draft a memo to your e-business's staff explaining how to check your site's ranking with Yahoo!
9. Assume you've launched a Web site that sells organic gourmet coffees. Conduct an Internet search to identify a direct competitor as well as an indirect competitor.

BE AN E-BUSINESS ENTREPRENEUR

Getting Noticed on the Internet

You're about to launch a Web site selling hot sauces. Compose both a <META> keyword tag and a <META> descriptive tag for the business's site. Outline the steps you would take to optimize your presence on Google and Yahoo!

Matters of Smart Design

Conduct an Internet search to find a Web site that follows the rules of strategic design outlined in Section 9.3.4 of this chapter. Describe how the site follows three of the rules.

Dueling Web Sites

Choose two competing Web sites (www.lowes.com and www.homedepot.com, for example). Determine the Google page rank for each, then conduct a brief analysis of both sites:

- What keywords are used in the Web site names?
- What <META> keywords and descriptions do the sites use?
- What links point back to the Web sites?

Choose the site that you believe is most effective and explain your choice.

KEY TERMS

ALT attribute A description of a Web page graph stored in the code and read like a <META> tag by search engines.

Direct competitor A competitor that is a similar size, caters to the same target market, and offers a similar product mix.

HyperText Markup Language (HTML) A computer language used to create World Wide Web pages.

Indirect competitor A competitor that sells some of the same products, but has a broader or different overall focus.

Keyword A specific word that is tied to a particular subject; what is typed into a search engine's "search" box.

Keyword density	The number of keywords on a page multiplied by the number of times each one is used.
Keyword spamming	Hiding paragraphs of keywords by matching the keyword text color with the color of the page background.
<META> tag	Computer code, usually invisible to a Web page viewer, that defines the name, purpose, author, and date of a Web page. Search engines read this tag to catalog Web pages more efficiently.
Search engine	A specialized Web site in which a visitor types keywords into a box and that receives a list of links to other sites that match those keywords.
Search-engine optimization	The process of obtaining a prominent listing placement on a search engine, Web directory, or information portal.
Web portal	A Web site that offers a broad array of information, services, and links related to a single topic.

REFERENCES

1. Karen E. Klein, "How SEO Upped the Revenues," Businessweek.com, www.businessweek.com/smallbiz/ content/jul2006/sb20060705_363880.htm?chan=search.
2. Interview with Megan Ducket of Sew What? Inc., WorkHappy.net, www.workhappy.net/2006/07/interview_with__1.html.

CHAPTER

10 E-BUSINESS CUSTOMER SERVICE

Providing an Online Shopping Experience that Will Guarantee Repeat Visits

Do You Already Know?

- The important differences between traditional and online customers
- The common strategies for providing customers information online
- How to effectively use email as part of customer service
- How to provide live support to customers

For additional questions to assess your current knowledge on customer service for e-businesses, go to **www.wiley.com/college/holden.**

What You Will Find Out	What You Will Be Able To Do
10.1 How online customers differ from traditional customers and what unique needs they have	Provide customer service options that meet the unique needs of online shoppers
10.2 That there are a variety of creative solutions for providing information to online customers	Use FAQ pages, electronic newsletters, and RSS feeds to provide information to existing customers
10.3 How to effectively use email to communicate with, and provide information to, online customers	Make effective use of email with autoresponders, signature files, fill-in forms, and other tools
10.4 That there are a variety of advanced strategies for providing information and service to online customers	Use live support, discussion groups, and other tools to enhance customer service

INTRODUCTION

At face value, it would appear that the online shopping experience is naturally impersonal and lacking in opportunities to connect with someone at the other end of the connection. Yet, correctly implemented and managed, online customer service should be anything but impersonal. In fact, one of the strengths of online shopping is the opportunities it offers for superior service compared to bricks-and-mortar retailers, whether that service is delivered in the form of ample and easily accessed product information or a quick response to questions. The first section of this chapter discusses strategies for servicing online customers—which starts with understanding the difference between them and traditional customers, and also what exceptional demands they naturally bring with them when visiting a Web site. The second section talks about information—in particular, about creative solutions for delivering it to customers. The lesson conveyed is that increasing the outward flow of product information will minimize the inward flow of customer questions and problems. Email remains one of the most important uses of the Internet, and is very much the case for the world of e-commerce. The third section goes beyond the obvious, explaining different ways to use email to service customers' needs as well as deliver essential information to them. The fourth section explores advanced customer service strategies, including methods for automating customer service functions that keep shoppers happy and reduce an e-business owner's workload; effectively using newsgroups for customer service functions; and keeping international shoppers' needs in mind when developing a customer service program.

10.1 UNDERSTANDING AND SERVING ONLINE CUSTOMERS

Many first-time e-business owners start their ventures with a number of preconceived notions about customers and how to keep them happy. Many of their assumptions about customers, though, are based on the traditional bricks-and-mortar retail experiences. Some of the basic customer-service concepts that work in a traditional retail store still apply online, but many do not. Therefore, one of the first things that a new e-business owner needs to do is understand the needs and desires of their Internet customers. A logical first exercise in this process is to compare the motivation and desires of traditional versus online customers. Next, online entrepreneurs must develop an understanding of the basic expectations that their customers will bring with them to the Web site. Finally, e-business owners must interpret the common behavioral patterns of their typical customer, then further reinforce those patterns to increase both customer purchases and the customers' rate of return to the Web site for future shopping trips.

10.1.1 Traditional Versus Online Shoppers

Traditional and online shoppers have some similar characteristics, but the reasons a customer buys from a retail location can be very different from how, why, and when customers choose to shop online. To convince customers to buy their goods, owners must get to know their customers—both online and off. This chapter explains the differences between offline and online customers and how both can be accommodated.

Once accidental or happenstance, most online shopping is now purposeful. Customers are making a conscientious decision each time an online purchase is made. The reasons for shopping in a real, bricks-and-mortar store are very different from the reasons for shopping online. For example, customers showing up in a physical retail store expect the following features:

- **Security:** Customers may think that shopping in a retail store is more secure than giving out credit card information on a Web site.
- **Guaranteed delivery:** Sometimes, purchasing a product is a time-sensitive issue. If customers need to receive an item by a certain time or date, shopping online may become an afterthought. This need-it-now mentality is especially true during a holiday rush.
- **Instant gratification:** Waiting for a product to ship is not every customer's idea of shopping. Sometimes, customers need or want an item immediately, and shopping in a store gives that instantaneous gratification.
- **Loyalty:** Customers are familiar with a store and feel a connection. They often translate familiarity into a perceived relationship with the owners and employees, and these customers are quite loyal to the store.
- **Service:** Having access to personalized service is positive for many traditional shoppers. These customers typically believe that shopping in a store is the only way to get that level of assistance.
- **Only option:** Some customers simply do not consider other buying alternatives. They may think in-store shopping is the only option because they are not comfortable or familiar with the Internet, do not have online access, or just are not aware that the option to shop online exists with a particular store.
- **Trying before buying:** Some customers need to see, touch, or try on products before making a buying decision. Internet shopping does not satisfy these customers' needs.
- **Avoiding extra charges:** Shipping cost is the main factor working against online shopping. Many customers decide to shop offline simply to avoid getting additional shipping and handling fees added to their purchases.

In comparison, customers have the following expectations from an online store:

- **Research capabilities:** Shopping online provides the opportunity for detailed research before making a final purchasing decision. Shoppers can read product reviews, get customer feedback, compare brands, and then make a purchase—all in a matter of minutes. Research shows that male customers are especially prone to do a little digging before they start buying online.
- **Hard-to-find items:** An item may be out of stock in a store, or it may not be available locally at all. Shopping online provides access to products that are not otherwise readily available.
- **Niche/specialty items:** Customers are frequently attracted to online stores because those stores provide access to specialty items, including vintage goods, collector's items, or other types of exclusive or niche products.
- **Convenience:** Customers enjoy the flexibility that comes with virtual shopping—knowing the store is never closed.
- **Value:** Although shipping costs may be of concern to an in-store shopper, an online buyer may factor in such things as the cost of gasoline and time.
- **Price:** Comparing prices and finding the best deal online is easy today. The ability to obtain prices for specific products is the main reason many customers shop online.
- **Extended inventory:** Retail stores traditionally have limited shelf space. On the other hand, a Web site can virtually house an unlimited number of products—the choice selection is typically better than traditional bricks-and-mortar locations. Products can even be ordered and shipped from a manufacturer or supplier. Because many Web shoppers believe that they have access to a wider product selection online, e-commerce stores are often their first stop for shopping.

10.1.2 Offering Superior Online Customer Service

At the heart of the difference in shopping online, as opposed to in a store, is the level of customer service. Top-notch online support is one of the single most influential factors in whether customers return to buy again. A high level of service is particularly important online because customers have limited ability to interact with products. Customers depend on the Web site to provide as much information about a product as possible in order to make an immediate buying decision. If there is not enough detail on the Web site or a customer has an unusual question, then the customer must have the ability to get answers quickly. If those answers are lacking, the customer will not hesitate to visit other sites.

Fortunately, offering exceptional customer service online is relatively easy. The technology is readily available, and is affordable. Here are a few of the ways to reach out to customers:

- **Email:** One of the easiest ways to provide customers with information about products is to correspond via email. E-businesses should post a customer service email address throughout their Web site, then respond to queries in a timely manner—in less than 24 hours. Use an automated responder to automatically generate a return email that notifies customers that their message has been received and when they should expect to get a response.
- **Phone:** All e-commerce sites should post a direct phone number so that shoppers can access immediate support. If the line does not offer 24-hour support, clearly state customer service's normal operating hours. Toll-free numbers are preferable, though businesses are charged for each call they receive, which can become expensive.
- **Live chat:** Although some online shoppers like the anonymity that the Internet provides, many more demand instantaneous support, such as that found in a store. To answer that need, consider offering "stand-by" customer support representatives through live-chat technology. This tool enables customers to immediately connect to a person who can answer their questions (either through an instant messenger–style format or audio over the computer). See Section 10.4.1 for more information on this option.

10.1.3 Satisfying Customer Demand for Information

Savvy Web shoppers are spoiled by the amount of information they can find at the stroke of a key, but too much information can actually overwhelm customers and distract them from purchasing. Thus the challenge is to anticipate what information a shopper really needs (and wants) to know about a product and then provide that info (and only that info) in a succinct and accessible manner. The following list gives some of the most sought-after product information:

- **Product descriptions:** All details need to be made available to a customer. The information should be offered in layers. In other words, give a brief description of the product, but then give customers the option to click a link for more details. For example, listing the color and style of a coffee table is wonderful, but omitting the dimensions can prevent a customer from purchasing a table.
- **Photographs:** Because the customer cannot physically hold the product, the customer needs to be able to see it from every angle—or even from

the inside for some products. Like text descriptions, a good strategy is to offer photographs in layers. Display a large, pleasing, overall view of the product with the ability to click links to see different angles or close-up views of critical details.

- **Similar or companion products:** Provide suggestions and links to products that support or work well with the target item. Customers appreciate being told that a certain item will not work unless they also purchase a cable or other part that is not included. Protective (specialized covers), maintenance (cleaners, for example), or informational (how-to books) products should be suggested to customers to enhance their shopping experience.
- **Reviews:** Customer reviews came into vogue after Amazon.com made them popular. Providing easy access to reviews by experts or other credible sources (such as magazines) is also a hot demand from online customers.
- **Delivery options:** Customers need to fully understand the different methods of delivery that a site offers. The information includes the provider of the service (the U.S. Postal Service, UPS, Federal Express, or some other shipping company), the delivery options (for example, Express or Ground), and the cost. Customers also want access to a shipping number with a direct link to track the delivery status of their purchase.
- **Contact information:** Customers want to be able to find a phone number and email address and to receive a response when they use them.
- **Return policies:** People seldom ask about return and exchange policies before making a purchase at a bricks-and-mortar store. The customer does not think about these policies until he is back at the store, standing in line to return the item. Online shoppers, though, usually want this information before they make that final purchase. Especially when buying clothing or perishable items, customers want to be reassured that they can get a fair deal if something goes wrong when they receive the products.

IN THE REAL WORLD

Lowe's Builds an Online Presence

Lowe's Home Improvement (www.lowes.com) has been in business for more than 60 years, helping customers "improve the places they call home." With more than 1,450 stores in 49 states—and about 150 new stores built in 2007 alone—Lowe's has a substantial bricks-and-mortar presence. The retailer's online presence continues to grow as well; the site offers features such as a gift advisor and gift registry, the ability to view local ad circulars, and free shipping on certain orders. Interactive guides and how-to videos are offered on a variety of subjects, from getting organized to building a deck to planning a kitchen makeover. The Web site's friendly, uncluttered design reflects Lowe's focus in its retail stores on female consumers, who, according to the company's extensive research, are involved with or responsible for many home-improvement decisions.

10.1.4 Special Demands of Online Customers

Customers shop online for many reasons, but another underlying difference between real and virtual shoppers is that online customers have great expectations for an e-commerce site. All customers are particular and demanding, but the Internet has increased these tendencies, and online stores must perform to the raised expectations. E-businesses can go above and beyond the normal service levels to keep their customers happy.

Stay Open All Night

Most customers expect an online store to be open 24 hours a day, seven days a week. Although it appears easy, running a 24/7 store involves work.

- **Customer support:** Can customers contact a business in the middle of the night and expect to get an answer, or will prospective buyers receive help only during normal business hours?
- **Routine maintenance:** Maintenance includes anything from a server going down (and the store being temporarily offline) to a glitch in the payment gateway provider that prevents credit cards from being processed. When a business is open around the clock, a back-up plan is helpful for all the things that could go wrong off-hours. Customers are not too concerned with those problems—customers can go to a competitor's site to get what they want.

To ensure an online store is always open and fully functioning, many e-businesses use a third-party, 24/7, site-monitoring service.

Offer a Variety of Payment Options

Accepting multiple forms of payment is an absolute necessity online. Customers may be more forgiving when they shop in a bricks-and-mortar retail location because they can use cash, credit, or a check. Most Web site transactions involve paying by credit card, but many customers prefer different options—in part because of security concerns—and will seek out e-businesses that offer the choices they want. Refer to Section 6.2 for a detailed discussion of online payment options.

Provide a Wide Array of Products

Virtual inventory is a big component in e-commerce, whether all products are stored in a warehouse behind a retail location or are drop-shipped from a supplier. Customers want a business to provide a large selection, including everything available in a retail location. In addition, customers expect an e-business to be well stocked—at all times. If a product is on back order or temporarily out of stock, customers expect to be told before they start the checkout process.

Be Ready to Perform During the Holiday Rush

Having a return policy clearly accessible is certainly a plus during a busy holiday season, but that is just the bare minimum. Keep in mind that customer expectations peak at holiday time. And not just at Christmas; most businesses have a seasonal period when demand peaks. The seasonal rush can be prepared for in the following ways:

- **Offer expedited deliveries.** A delivery company may not have a problem with rush delivery, but owners need to make sure that they can get the items packed and out the door to meet the hectic pace.
- **Extend delivery times.** Again, owners need to manage those very last-minute orders that arrive the day before (or the day of) the major holiday. Whether or not they can extend their delivery times often depends on whether they have enough help behind the scenes to keep filling those orders.
- **Stock up on inventory.** Nothing is worse than running out of a hot item and finding out that more cannot be obtained until after the holiday. Owners may want to go a little heavy on their inventory or to alert their suppliers to the potential of increased demand.
- **Increase service reps.** Customers rarely hesitate to ask for help when it comes to holiday shopping.

Although the busiest retail season is typically November and December, some other holiday periods also drive sales. According to recent research, online sales also increase during Valentine's Day, Easter, and Mother's Day (to name a few).

Be Flexible—Online and Off

Businesses with both online and offline locations are in a unique predicament. The good news is that the two complementary retail outlets offer the opportunity to increase sales. The bad news is that customers rarely see a distinction between the two sides of the business and expect it to be more accommodating.

For example, customers who buy from the Web site may want to return the item to the physical store. E-businesses either need to offer this option, or if not, make the policy clear at the time of purchase. Similarly, customers that see a special deal online expect to get the same price in the physical store.

E-business in Action → Provide special customer service options to online customers.

As long as customers have plenty of options for shopping in all locations, online/offline businesses may have a distinct advantage in the marketplace. For example, Lampsplus.com includes a store locator feature that helps customers get information about any of its many bricks-and-mortar locations on the West Coast. Each location page includes a detailed map and store phone number, along with a photo of the actual store.

SELF-CHECK

1. List three strategies for maximizing communications opportunities with online customers.
2. Describe five types of information that should be readily available on all e-commerce sites.
3. Explain three ways that online retailers can maximize customer service (and sales opportunities) during holiday seasons.

Apply Your Knowledge You are opening an e-commerce site in conjunction with your preexisting retail gift shop. Discuss the differing demands of online and offline customers with regard to each of the following topics: security, delivery time and expense, inventory, price, and customer service.

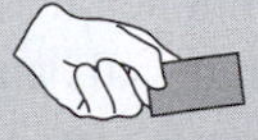

CAREER CONNECTION

One of America's "coolest" entrepreneurs stays focused by listening to customers.

Harvard graduate Marc Katz left the financial world of Wall Street to do something "entrepreneurial and meaningful" with his life. Katz and two friends fine-tuned their ideas and started CustomInk.com, a "design online" custom printing service, in March 2000. CustomInk allows anyone to design their own professionally screen-printed T-shirts, embroidered caps, or any of over 150

(Continued)

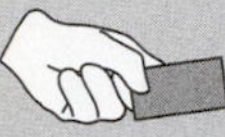

CAREER CONNECTION *(Continued)*

other products using a simple Web browser. The company, based in Tysons Corner, Virginia, has received rave reviews: Inc. magazine touted CustomInk as one of the fastest-growing private companies in the country; Inc.com named Katz, in 2006, as one of "America's Coolest Young Entrepreneurs," and Washingtonian magazine named CustomInk (for the second time) one of the best places to work in the Washington, D.C., area. High praise, indeed, but for Katz and company, there's an even more important statistic: CustomInk's customer satisfaction rating is 99 percent. In fact, in 2002, CustomInk made a bold—and unheard of—move by streaming all customer feedback, uncensored and unedited, on its home page.

"When we started the business, our goal was to make the whole process customer-friendly and efficient," says co-founder Dave Christensen. "And as the business keeps growing, we continue to innovate and improve that process." A team of professional artists reviews every order to ensure quality, and "Inkers," as staffers call themselves, are available to provide friendly assistance over the phone. In 2007, after receiving many requests from customers, the company launched a new service called CustomInk Singles that lets people design and order single shirts for individual use or gifts, as opposed to having to order in bulk.

CustomInk continues to grow, now delivering about five million custom shirts a year. "We are proud of the growth we have achieved over the past few years," says Katz. "We have a great team of people here who really care about providing customers with an amazing experience." [1]

Tips from the Professional

- Get a close adviser who has good entrepreneurial experience and is someone you trust.
- Listen to what your customers have to say.

10.2 SHARING PRODUCT INFORMATION ONLINE

Customer satisfaction is all about expectations. If customers get what they expect (or more than they expect), they will be satisfied. Proper communication with customers is the key to setting their level of expectation. Providing more information in the beginning results in fewer phone queries and complaints later. Traditional businesses used printed materials such as pamphlets and brochures to describe available products and services. Today, however, obtaining information online is the method of choice for many consumers—even when the customer is planning to purchase through a bricks-and-mortar retail outlet.

Online communications are much cheaper than printed materials. A 1,000-word description of a new company's products and services formatted to fit on a 4 x 9-inch foldout brochure would cover several panels and take hundreds of dollars to print. By contrast, putting the same description on a few Web pages online, or distributing to subscribers using email, would require only minimal cost.

Online publishing also has the advantage of easier updating. When adding new products or services, printed materials require an entirely new print run to update the information. With online materials, it only takes a small amount of time and effort to change the contents or the look.

Email is probably the most common way for customers to communicate with e-businesses; this important topic is explained in detail in Section 10.3. The following sections offer three other customer communication strategies that when used effectively can provide shoppers with enough information that they will not need to contact a Web site by email to get their questions answered.

10.2.1 Frequently Asked Questions (FAQs)

Frequently Asked Questions (FAQs): A page generally presented in question-and-answer format covering topics of high interest to customers. Each brief answer provides essential information about the business or its products.

A set of **Frequently Asked Questions,** or **FAQs,** is a familiar feature on many online business sites—so familiar that most customers expect to find an FAQ page on every business site. Even the format of FAQ pages remains relatively constant from site to site, and the predictability is an asset. FAQ pages are generally presented in question-and-answer format, with topics appearing in the form of real questions that have been asked by other customers—or at least have been designed to resemble real questions. Each question has a brief answer that provides essential information.

However, simply having an FAQ page is not enough. The page must be comprehensive and easy to use. One technique that keeps an FAQ page from getting too long or confusing is to list all the questions at the top of the page, which allows readers to jump to a specific question that relates to them by simply clicking a hyperlinked item.

It helps to have more than one perspective when writing FAQs. Inviting visitors, customers, family, and friends to develop questions about the business is a useful tip that ensures an FAQ page is relevant to all users. Most users are looking for information about the following topics:

- **Contact information:** Is it possible to reach the business quickly by mail, fax, or phone, and what hours is the business available?
- **Instructions:** Are there detailed instructions available about a business's products and services? If so, where?
- **Services:** Is there a return policy?

Figure 10-1

Randomshirts.com :: FAQ's - Microsoft Internet Explorer

http://www.randomshirts.com/store/pages.php?pageid=7

HOME OF THE $10 TEE!

Randomshirts.com

Pick a Category: $10 Tees, Softees, Girls Only, Winter Wear, Shane&Shane, Posters, Clearance

Other Stuff: Custom Orders, Tavin Videos, MySpace, Contests

About Us | Mission | FAQ's | Team Random | Contact
Wish list | Gift Certificates | Special Offers | Affiliates
Orders history | Returns | Bonuses
Log In :: Register

20% off Sale! Now through Dec 24th 20% off EVERYTHING!!

Randomshirts.com :: FAQ's

FAQ's

SHIPPING

We have hired a shipping company named Fulfill Plus, based out of Houston, TX to do our shipping. They're much better at it than us. However, In order to offer our shirts at such a low cost to you, we have to keep a limited amount of shirts in stock. So, we ask that you allow 1-2 weeks for shipping, giving us enough time to make the shirt if we don't have it in stock. Due to the nature of this system, we do not offer any faster/expedited shipping as of right now.

We ship USPS and UPS to ship our shirts, depending on which method you choose during checkout.

We DO ship to APO addresses via USPS.

It's really as easy as baking a tasty cookie...you know...the kind that you just take out of the package and slap on the cookie

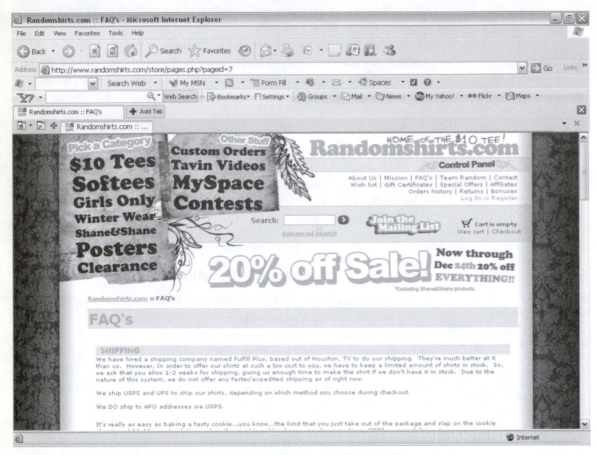

An excerpt from Random Shirts e-business's FAQs.

FOR EXAMPLE

See Figure 10-1 for an excerpt from an e-business's FAQs.

E-business in Action

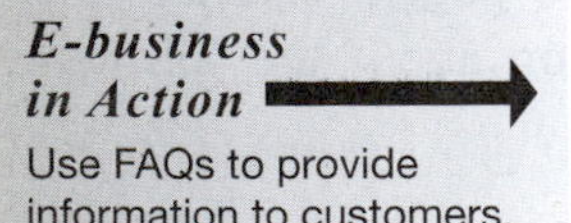

Use FAQs to provide information to customers.

- **Sales tax:** Is sales tax added to the on-screen cost?
- **Shipping:** What are the shipping options?

The page does not have to be called Frequently Asked Questions, either. For example, the retailer Land's End (www.landsend.com) uses the term "Fact Sheet" for its list of questions and answers. Whatever the page is called, however, it should be updated regularly. Customers are often discouraged by outdated FAQ pages. Owners should check to make sure all questions match currently offered products and services.

10.2.2 Online Newsletters

Sharing information with customers and potential customers through a downloadable or emailed newsletter is a great way to build credibility for a business. Owners should consider producing a regular publication that is offered for download on the Web site or sent out to a subscribing mailing list to improve customer service and promote the business. Benefits of newsletters include:

- **Customer tracking:** Subscriber email addresses can be added to a mailing list also used for other market purposes, such as promoting special sales items for return customers.
- **Low-bandwidth:** A newsletter does not require much memory. Newsletters are useful for businesspeople that receive their email via mobile devices (laptops, smartphones, and PDAs) specifically designed for sending and receiving email.
- **Timelines:** Breaking news can be added to an electronic newsletter faster and more easily than it can be put in print.

Most newsletters are created by typing the contents in plain text (ASCII) or HTML format. HTML can include headings and graphics that show up in programs that support HTML email messages. If plain-text format is used, it should be formatted with capital letters, rules consisting of a row of equal signs, hyphens, or asterisks, and blank spaces to align elements.

Portable Document Format (PDF): An electronic publishing format that keeps images, typefaces, and other layout features intact and allows viewing with Adobe Reader software, no matter what program was used to create the document.

One other possible format for a newsletter is Adobe's **Portable Document Format (PDF),** which enables an owner to save a publication with images, special typefaces, and other layout features intact. No matter what format the newsletter was originally created in, users only need the Adobe Reader software—which is widely available and free to download—to view a PDF file.

Sending the publication at night and sending it in stages (to only a certain number of subscribers at a time) are two techniques that can help a publication to reach a large number of subscribers quickly and reliably. Hiring a company, such as SkyList (www.skylist.com), to do the day-to-day mailing list management—such as keeping track of customers who have subscribed or unsubscribed—can also help save valuable time.

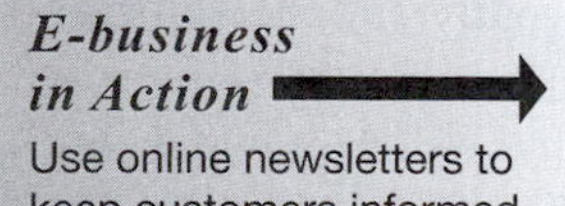

E-business in Action
Use online newsletters to keep customers informed.

10.2.3 RSS Feeds

Newsletters and hyperlinks are quickly becoming outdated. Today, RSS feeds have become a preferred option for sharing information with customers. RSS stands for "Really Simple Syndication." Although sending an RSS feed of a Web site or eBay listing sounds complicated, it is actually quite easy.

RSS feed: A system for converting the contents of a Web page to an extensible markup language (XML) file so that the file can be read quickly using an RSS reader software program.

RSS feeds are a way to convert the contents of a Web page to an extensible markup language (XML) file so that it can be read quickly by anyone with an RSS reader software program. People subscribe to an RSS feed and receive it every time a site's contents are updated. RSS is widely used by bloggers. Business owners can capture an RSS feed of their online sales and offer it to subscribing customers, which is easy for owners selling through an eBay store:

When turning a catalog listing into an RSS feed, each listing needs a standard description: a listing title, a description, and a hyperlink. Each item is then formatted as such:

```
<item>
<title>Model 101 Widget</title>
<description>Check out the Widget 101, the latest and greatest widget
offering ever!</description>
<link>http://www.mywidgetcatalog.com/widget101.html</link>
</item>
```

E-business in Action →
Use RSS feeds to provide information to customers.

The formatting should be checked at a site, such as Feed Validator (feedvalidator.org), before subscribing to an RSS reader. A list of potential RSS readers can be found at searchenginewatch.com/show Page.html?page=2175281. Copy the feed to the reader and distribute it.

10.2.4 Blogs and Podcasts

Blogs:
Short for Web log. An online digital diary or forum where text, photos, and other material can be posted and made available to the public.

Podcast:
A recorded audio program available online for download in a file format that can easily be transferred to an MP3 player.

Section 8.4 discussed creative ideas for marketing e-businesses that are equally effective as customer service tools. Two of the most effective high-tech tools for communicating with existing customers are (1) **blogs,** short for (Web log), an online digital text diary, and (2) **podcasts,** a recorded audio program that can be downloaded to a PC or MP3 player for listening at the consumer's convenience. Both technologies offer the ability to create a personalized, entertaining, and informative one-way dialogue between an e-business and its shoppers that can greatly enhance customer service. For example, an e-business owner that maintains a regularly updated blog may want to use the space to discuss issues of special concern to regular customers. Topics may include the limited availability (or new shipments) of popular items, the last day to order a product to receive it during the holiday season, or even the business's return policies. A creative strategy for using podcasts may be to create a mix of unique content interlaced with quick reminders of customer service options and policies.

The key to using blogs and podcasts is to be both entertaining and informative while providing basic information. How many customers are going to devote precious time to reading or listening to a dry discussion of customer policies? But if they get laughs, music, interviews, or special information in addition to those policies or product updates, the customers may become loyal, informed, and happy.

SELF-CHECK

1. Why are "Frequently Asked Questions" pages so important?
2. What are two possible ways to distribute an electronic newsletter?
3. What are the advantages of using RSS feeds?

Apply Your Knowledge You are developing an FAQ page for your Web site that sells gifts and gadgets for golfers. Write five sample questions and answers for the page.

10.3 EFFECTIVELY USING EMAIL FOR CUSTOMER SERVICE

Being anonymous is not a good strategy for e-business owners. Customers do not always need to be able to reach someone at all hours of the day, but they need to believe that they can receive attention at any time of the day or night. Providing top-notch customer service via email is one way to achieve this goal.

Many Web hosting services give subscribers more than one email inbox in each account, allowing e-businesses that take advantage of this option to set up multiple emailing addresses. For example, one address can be used to communicate with customers personally, while a second can be used for general queries. Email addresses can also be set up that respond to messages by automatically sending a text file.

The following sections discuss methods that will help e-businesses make the greatest customer service impact with email.

10.3.1 Effective Email Strategies

Today, most people have an email account. However, e-business owners must be more aware of email features than the average person. The more that an e-business owner can discover about the technical points of email, the better they are able to serve their customers. Several ways to utilize email for business publishing and marketing go beyond simply sending and receiving messages.

Autoresponder: Software that sends automatic replies to customer requests for information, or responds after a customer has subscribed to an email publication.

Setting Up Autoresponders

Autoresponders (sometimes called mailbots) are software programs that can be set up to send automatic replies to requests for information about a product or service, or to respond to a customer action, such as subscribing to an email publication. Though somewhat impersonal, the effectiveness cannot be underestimated. Even if a full response will not be sent for a while, these automated communiqués at least let customers know that their email has been received and that the information requested is forthcoming. The automatic responses can be provided either through an individual's email program or through a Web host's email service. Web hosts usually allow a user to purchase an extra email address that can be configured to return a text file (such as a form letter) to the sender.

E-business in Action
Make effective use of autoresponders to communicate with customers.

Quoting

Quoting: An email feature that allows a user to copy portions of the message to which they are replying.

Responding to a series of questions is easy when using **quoting,** a feature that allows a user to copy portions of the message to which he or she is replying. Quoting, which is available in most email programs, is particularly useful for responding to a mailing list or newsgroup message because it indicates the specific topic being discussed. To show the difference between the new email message and the quoted material, it is customary to put a greater-than character (>) in the left margin next to each quoted line. Editing the original message is acceptable, but it is considered polite to type the word <snip> when cutting something out.

Attaching Files

A quick and convenient way to transmit information from place to place is to attach files to a document or file along with any email message. Attaching files allows the inclusion of any material to which an owner has access; the included material appears as a separate document that recipients can then download to their computers. On most email clients, attaching a file only requires clicking a few buttons.

Attachments can become quite large without the proper compression. Compressing a lengthy series of attachments by using software, such as StuffIt or WinZip, conserves bandwidth and allows users to send multiple attachments to individuals whose accounts do not accept multiple attachments.

10.3.2 Signature Files

Signature file: A text statement that software automatically places at the bottom of email messages.

One of the easiest and most useful market tools on the Internet is a **signature file,** or a text blurb that a system appends automatically to the bottom of email messages and newsgroup postings. Signature files can be edited by the user to tell readers something about the business, or to provide company contact information. To create a signature file:

1. Open a text-editing program.
2. Press and hold down the hyphen (-) key or the equal sign (=) key to create a dividing line that separates the signature from the body of the message. Do not make this line too long or it may run onto another line—30 to 40 characters is best.
3. Type the information that will appear in the signature, pressing Enter after each line. Good information to include is name, job title, company name, email address, and Web site URL. Three or four lines is the typical length.
4. Choose File->Save.
5. Enter a name for the file that ends in the extension .txt.
6. Click the Save button.

E-business in Action
Use signature files to transmit information to customers.

The process of making the signature file appear automatically varies between email software packages, though the process is usually quite simple.

10.3.3 Easy-to-Use Fill-In Forms

Online fill-in forms are a unique use of email that can give customers a means to provide feedback and essential marketing information, like where customers live, their age, and their interests. Customers can also use forms to ask questions about an e-business, its products, or even orders they have placed on the Web site. Fortunately, unlike the older, paper-based forms, online forms are quick to complete and can be responded to almost immediately, making them valuable to customers.

Forms consist of two parts, only one of which is visible on a Web page:

1. The visible part includes the text-entry fields, buttons, and check boxes that an author creates with HTML commands.
2. The invisible part of the form is a computer script that resides on the server that receives the page. This script, typically written in a programming language, such as AppleScript, or C11, processes the form data that the reader submits to a server and presents that data in a format that the owner or operator of the Web site can read and use.

When customers connect to a page that contains a form, they complete the visible fields and click a button to transmit the data from the remote computer to the Web site. A computer script called a Common Gateway Interface (CGI) program receives the submitted data and processes it so that it can be read. The CGI may email the data or present the data in a text file.

CGI programs can also be created to prompt a server to send users to a Web page that acknowledges receipt of the forms—a nice touch that customers are sure to appreciate.

Writing the scripts that process data is generally the province of Webmasters and computer programmers, but many Web page programs (such as FrontPage or Dreamweaver) offer tools that allow e-businesses to create forms and scripts that process the data. Creating their own form gives an e-business owner more control over the content and appearance of the forms.

FOR EXAMPLE

See Figure 10-2 for an online customer service form.

A description of the form and any special instructions should be added at the top of the Web page. Copyright and contact information should be included at the bottom of the page, following the pattern of other pages on

Figure 10-2

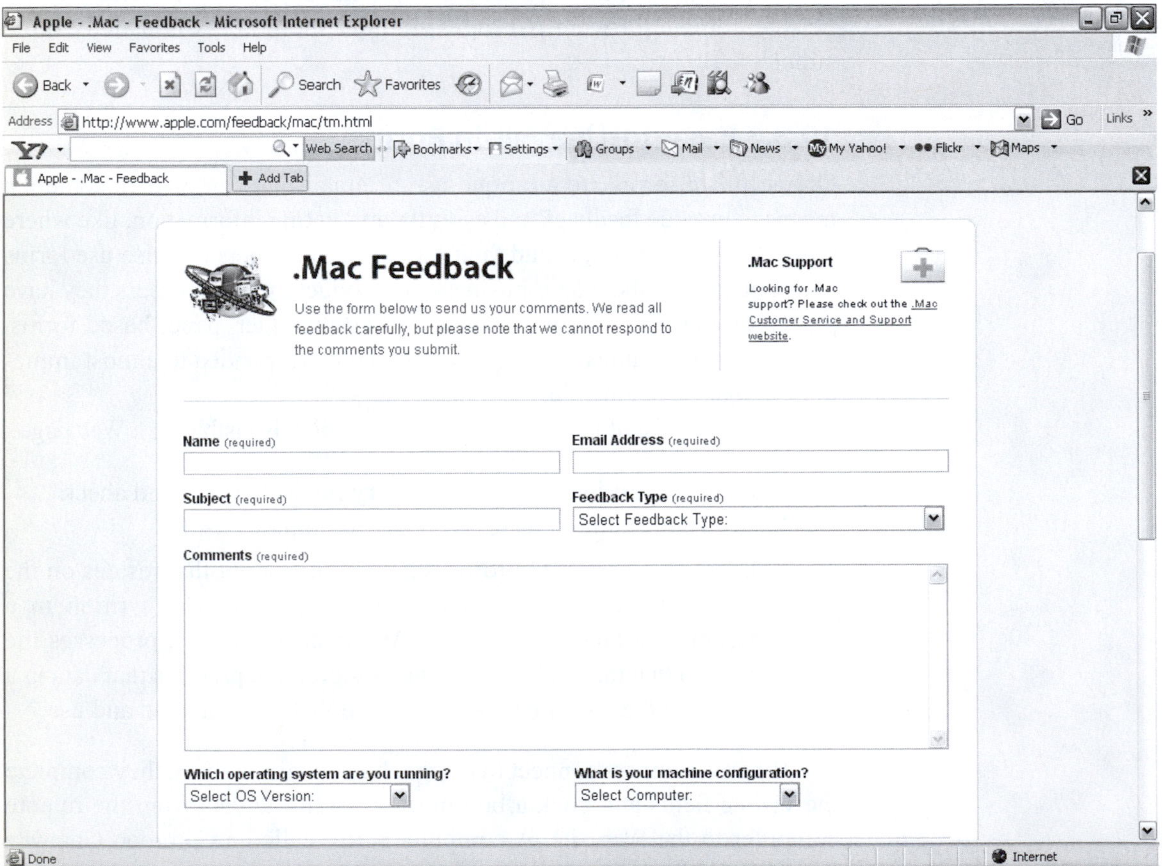

An online customer service form.

IN THE REAL WORLD

Cowgirl-Style Customer Service

The Cowgirl Company's skincare products are inspired by the spirit of the cowgirl, but the company doesn't expect its customers to actually ride horses or wear boots. Anyone who's looking to nourish and protect their skin from the damaging effects of stress and the elements will do. The company was founded in 1994 by Donna Baase, a licensed esthetician and teacher in the natural body care industry. Baase, who lives in Colorado, created the original Cowgirl Cream skin treatment using natural oils and indigenous plants of the West. The company went online with its Web site in 1999 (www.cowgirlskincare.com); today over 20 percent of its sales come from the Internet. The company uses its attractive Web site to draw in new customers with features such as skincare tips and recipes; customers can also join the "Cowgirl Club," which entitles them to enter contests, submit their Cowgirl testimonials, and receive information on Cowgirl news and specials. Though the company plans to look for ways to keep the Web site fresh and appealing, it continues to use other methods of increasing site traffic, such as direct mail.[2]

E-business in Action
Use fill-in forms to gather customer information.

the site. The form can be edited later by using the Forms submenu option, if necessary, including changing questions asked and modifying the background color of the form.

SELF-CHECK

1. How can autoresponders be used to improve customer service?
2. What can be used to minimize the size of email attachments?
3. Describe three ways that e-businesses can use fill-in forms for communicating with customers?

Apply Your Knowledge The owner of an online store selling running shoes and clothing is looking for an easy, inexpensive way to share simple information with customers. Write sample text for three signature files that could be used to accomplish this goal.

10.4 ADVANCED CUSTOMER SERVICE STRATEGIES

In the past, people often went to the market on a daily basis. The shopkeeper often set aside items based on their customers' individual tastes and needs. Often, transactions were accompanied by friendly conversations about family, politics, and other neighborhood gossip. Good customer service can make online customers feel like they, too, are shopping at a caring business. The following sections reveal some strategies for improving customer service and making customers feel like part of a community.

10.4.1 Live Customer Support

On the Web, as in real life, people like a prompt and personalized response. E-business owners are challenged to provide live customer support on their Web sites. This can be done using real-time (or near real-time) Internet technologies, such as chat and message boards. The online auction giant eBay, for example, has a New Users Board where beginners can post questions for eBay support staff, who post answers in response. **Chat** is another immediate sort of customer service in which individuals type messages to one another in **real time,** as it is happening.

Chat:
An Internet communication system in which individuals type messages to one another in real time.

Real time:
Occurring in the same time frame experienced by people.

E-business in Action →
Use live support to enhance the customer service experience.

LivePerson (www.liveperson.com) provides a simpler alternative that allows small businesses to provide chat-based support. LivePerson is software that enables an owner to see who is connected to their site at any specific time and allows a visitor to chat with them. Chat-based support allows the business's employees to personally guide customers through the process of making a purchase. To use LivePerson, an owner must first install the LivePerson Pro software on their own computer (not the server that runs the site). LivePerson Pro is free for the first 30 days and $99.99 per month thereafter.

10.4.2 Discussion Groups and Newsgroups

A small business can turn its individual customers into a cohesive group by starting its own discussion group or newsgroup on the Internet. Discussion groups work particularly well to promote a particular type of product or in a provocative or even controversial area of interest. There are three kinds of discussion groups:

1. **A local group:** Some universities create discussion areas exclusively for their students. Other large companies set aside groups that are

restricted to their employees. Outsiders cannot gain access because the groups are not on the Internet, but rather on a local server within the organization.

2. **A Web-based discussion group:** Use Web page-layout software to create a discussion area on a business Web site. Users can access the area from their Web browsers without using special discussion-group software. Alternatively, Yahoo! offers a service for creating Web-based discussion groups.
3. **A Usenet newsgroup:** Individuals are allowed to create an Internet-wide discussion group in the alt or biz categories of Usenet without having to go through the time-consuming application and approval process needed to create other newsgroups.

Usenet is a system of communication on the Internet that enables individual computer users to participate in group discussions about topics of mutual interest. Internet newsgroups have a hierarchical structure: Most groups belong to one of seven main categories (comp, misc, news, rec, sci, soc, and talk), the name of which appears at the beginning of the group's name. For example, a group may be called rec.food.drink.coffee.

Another popular category is alt, which currently means alternative (it originally meant anarchists, lunatics, and terrorists) and is a catchall category in which anyone can start a group. The first step in creating an alt discussion group is going to Google Groups (groups.google.com) or launching a Web browser's newsgroup software.

To find out how to start a group in the alt category, go to Google (www.google.com), click Groups, and search for the How to Start an Alt Newsgroup message. Follow the instructions contained in this message to establish a newsgroup. The process involves:

1. Writing a brief proposal describing the purpose of the desired group, and including an email message where people can respond with comments. The proposal also contains the name of the group in the correct form (alt.groupname.moreinfo.moreinfo). Keep the group name short and professional.
2. Submitting the proposal to the newsgroup alt.config.
3. Gathering feedback on the proposal via email.
4. Sending a special control message to the news server that gives access to Usenet. The exact form of the message varies from server to server. Consult the ISP on how to properly compose the message.
5. Waiting a few days or weeks as news administrators (the people that operate news servers at ISPs around the world) decide whether to adopt the request and add the group to their list of newsgroups.

E-business in Action →
Use discussion groups and newsgroups to enhance customer service.

IN THE REAL WORLD

Sharing an Interest with Customers

A common thread among many successful entrepreneurs is that the owners have a passion for their product. Joan and Bill Keller, the founders and owners of Letravelstore.com, are no exception. After meeting in college in 1973, the pair traveled through Mexico, Belize, and Guatemala. In 1976, the two married and started Le Travel Store in San Diego, selling luggage, travel gear, travel books, and maps. The store was designed as a place for people just like themselves—independent, international travelers. More recently the Kellers added a Web site, which is a reflection of the couple's storefront. The site offers the same high-quality travel products as well as extra Web features such as insightful top-ten lists (for traveling boomers, on-her-own travelers, student travel, tropical travel, and so on) and information on the latest travel gadgets. Like the store, the site is a place where customers can think about the next destination; for added inspiration, the Kellers also post their personal travel logs from far-away places like Morocco, Argentina, and Finland.[3]

10.4.3 International Service

The beauty of the World Wide Web is that it is truly a worldwide phenomenon. An e-commerce site originating in the United States is undoubtedly going to attract customers from other countries, which is one of the great advantages of doing business on the Internet. However, making a Web site available for viewing overseas is a lot simpler than selling products and effectively serving customers outside the United States. E-business owners planning to market their products globally should be prepared with an appropriate product support system.

Language is probably the biggest barrier to overcome, but U.S.-based companies have an advantage in that English is spoken throughout the world. That noted, it is essential that any text—especially purchasing instructions and product descriptions—is written both clearly and simply. Furthermore, attention must be paid to avoid any culturally biased language or ideas. Maybe more important than words are clear images and easy-to-follow diagrams for describing products and the buying process to customers with a less-than-fluent grasp of English. The best strategy for handling questions from foreign customers is to provide enough basic, easy-to-follow information so their questions are answered in advance. Unless you have phone operators fluent in multiple languages, customer queries by email should be encouraged. Email queries will allow e-businesses an opportunity to translate the text, consider the question, and send an appropriate response. Numerous sites are available that provide free and easy-to-use translation tools for a variety of languages.

Before making a big push for global customers, Web entrepreneurs should realistically consider the vast cultural differences that may render Web sites that are effective in the United States relatively worthless in other parts of the world. Customers in Asia, for example, have very different tastes from those in the United States. In Asia, Web sites tend to place more emphasis on color and interactivity. A Web site that may work well in the United States by looking clean and well organized may have to be replaced with the seemingly more chaotic blitz of characters and options that are often found more compelling in Asian markets. Can a U.S.-focused Web site effectively cater to a global target market? If not, is the e-business willing to make an investment to customize their site? Both questions should be carefully considered and the potential reward realistically estimated before investing scarce resources in what could be a risky venture.

SELF-CHECK

1. What is live customer support? How can live customer support be used to provide enhanced customer service?
2. How can e-businesses use discussion groups to enhance a customer service program?

Apply Your Knowledge Your Web site potentially may have a customer base in England. What customer-service related barriers should be considered? What should be explained on the Web site for customers in England?

SUMMARY

Section 10.1

- One of the first steps in developing an effective e-business customer service program is understanding the significant differences between traditional and online customers.
- The Internet may have an advantage over traditional retail outlets in delivering exceptional customer service. To be effective, e-businesses must provide multiple avenues for communicating with customers, and publish easily accessed information about their products and the shopping experience.
- Online shoppers have exceptionally high expectations for the Web sites from which they buy, including being open 24 hours per day, offering multiple payment options, and supporting shopper demands during the holidays.

Section 10.2

- Sharing information online is cheaper and more flexible than the traditional method of publishing a printed brochure or catalog. A variety of creative methods for sharing electronic information includes FAQ pages, newsletters, and RSS feeds.

Section 10.3

- Email is an effective way to communicate with customers, though there are tools for enhancing the back-and-forth flow of information, including autoresponders, attached files, signature files, and fill-in forms.

Section 10.4

- Several advanced strategies for enhancing customer service include providing live, real-time support using chat programs or message boards; providing customer support through Internet discussion groups; and customizing Web sites to provide information and support for global shoppers.

ASSESS YOUR UNDERSTANDING

UNDERSTAND: WHAT HAVE YOU LEARNED?

Go to **www.wiley.com/college/holden** to assess your knowledge of the basics of customer service for e-businesses.

APPLY: WHAT WOULD YOU DO?

1. For reasons such as security and familiarity, some consumers are still not comfortable about shopping online. Explain three ways that online retailers can offer customer support to make an online shopping experience more approachable.
2. A friend who runs an e-business selling bird feeders has resisted the idea of an online newsletter. Describe the potential benefits of such a service.
3. Explain how a blog or podcast would be an effective customer service tool for the following e-businesses:
   - Dating service
   - French language school
   - Wedding planner
4. You've decided to start up an eBay store selling used books. The venture would be part-time, however. What's the best way for you to handle any email inquiries that might come in while you are at your full-time teaching job?
5. Describe how a Key West fishing guide's Web site could utilize a fill-in form feature. What information would such a form request from its customers?
6. Conduct an online search to find a camera repair service. List five ways the site offers assistance to its customers. Compare the site's customer service features to that of a direct competitor.
7. Explain how live customer support would benefit the customers of an online photo service.
8. An e-business that sells teaching aids for parents who home school their children receives dozens of email inquiries and questions about home-schooling each day. What feature could the company add to its Web site to bring those customers together for a shared dialogue.

9. A Web log can be used both as a marketing tool and as a way to enhance customer service. Find two unrelated companies that use a blog and discuss how each are used as part of an approach to customer service. Compare the two, taking into account the entertainment and information offered on each.

10. A travel e-business that specializes in planning golf vacations has plans to offer its trips to customers around the globe. Explain two considerations of such a move.

BE AN E-BUSINESS ENTREPRENEUR

Providing Product Information

Evaluate a retail Web site that you've used in the past 12 months based on the kind of product information that is available to customers:

- Product descriptions
- Photographs and images
- Customer reviews
- Delivery options
- Contact information
- Return policies

Discuss which areas require improvement and outline how to get the job done.

Customer Satisfaction in a Crunch

A company that sells homemade peanut brittle experiences a busy season from mid-November to New Year's. Outline the steps the company should take to ensure continued customer satisfaction during this period.

Creating an Effective FAQ

Outline the information that should be included on the Frequently Asked Questions page of a professional organizer's Web site.

KEY TERMS

Autoresponder Software that sends automatic replies to customer requests for information, or responds after a customer has subscribed to an email publication.

Blog	Short for Web log. An online digital diary or forum where text, photos, and other material can be posted and made available to the public.
Chat	An Internet communication system in which individuals type messages to one another in real time.
Frequently asked questions (FAQs)	A page generally presented in question-and-answer format covering topics of high interest to customers. Each brief answer provides essential information about the business or its products.
Podcast	A recorded audio program available online for download in a file format that can easily be transferred to an MP3 player.
Portable document format (PDF)	An electronic publishing format that keeps images, typefaces, and other layout features intact and allows viewing with Adobe Reader software, no matter what program was used to create the document.
Quoting	An email feature that allows a user to copy portions of the message to which they are replying.
Real time	Occurring in the same time frame experienced by people.
RSS feed	A system for converting the contents of a Web page to an extensible markup language (XML) file so that the file can be read quickly using an RSS reader software program.
Signature file	A text statement that software automatically places at the bottom of email messages.

REFERENCES

1. "Inc. Recognizes Ink... that's CustomInk.com.," Business Wire, http://findarticles.com/p/articles/mi_m0EIN/is_2005_Oct_20/ai_n15725010.
2. "Establish an Email Strategy," Smallbusinessschool.org, http://smallbusinessschool.org/webapp/sbs/sbs/index.jsp?page=http%3A%2F%2Fsmallbusinessschool.org%2Fwebapp%2Fsbs%2F100%2F146%2Ftranscript10.jsp.
3. "Invite Customers to Create Content," Smallbusinessschool.org, http://smallbusinessschool.org/webapp/sbs/sbs/index.jsp?page=http%3A%2F%2Fsmallbusinessschool.org%2Fwebapp%2Fsbs%2F100%2F146%2Ftranscript10.jsp.

EQUIPMENT, SOFTWARE, AND WEB HOSTING

Effectively Equipping an E-Business for Online Success

Do You Already Know?

- Which personal computer (PC) features are most desirable for use with an e-business
- Which software packages e-businesses should purchase
- The disadvantages of using an Internet service provider (ISP) to host a Web site
- What high-performance features must be considered when selecting a Web host

For additional questions to assess your current knowledge on equipment, software, and Web hosting for e-businesses, go to **www.wiley.com/college/holden.**

What You Will Find Out	What You Will Be Able To Do
11.1 The desirable features that must be evaluated when selecting PCs and other office equipment	Choose an appropriate PC, basic office equipment, and Internet connection for a new e-business
11.2 The basic software that should be purchased by e-businesses and the features to consider before buying	Select a Web page editor, Web browser, email package, and other essential software for running an e-business
11.3 What features are most desirable in choosing an ISP and why ISPs might be a good option for hosting	Select an ISP and determine if it is also a viable option for hosting a Web site
11.4 The features to consider when selecting a host and what alternative server options are available	Select an appropriate Web host and hosting plan; evaluate the viability of alternative server options

INTRODUCTION

Many e-businesses get started on a single personal computer, and it is possible that one PC might remain the heart and soul of a small online firm long after startup. Yet for most e-businesses, it is limiting to think in terms of one particular computer. A full-featured small business usually needs multiple computers and a variety of office machines, as well as a full suite of software, a good connection to the Internet, and a quality Web site host to ensure success. This chapter will explore these topics in detail, providing direction that will help any e-business to equip itself appropriately. Begin with a good computer. The first section outlines the basic features that a well-equipped PC should possess, and weighs the pros and cons of selecting a desktop or notebook system. This first section also discusses other must-have pieces of office equipment (with ideas for doing more with less), and outlines options for connecting to the Internet once computers and other equipment are in place. The second section focuses on software, profiling all the major types of programs that e-businesses should consider purchasing, including Web page editors, Web browsers, and email packages. The third section explores Internet service providers (ISPs). While some Internet connections come hand-in-hand with an ISP, others do not. Furthermore, some small e-businesses will find that they should look seriously at using ISPs to host their Web sites. Most e-commerce firms will find that their Web sites need to be served by a dedicated Web-hosting service. The high-performance features that Web hosts should offer are explained in-depth, and an introduction to service plans and contracts is presented. The fourth section discusses alternative host-server options for obtaining expanded storage space, improved customer access, and more control over Web sites.

11.1 BASIC OFFICE EQUIPMENT

Becoming an information provider on the Internet places an additional burden on a computer and peripheral equipment. E-business owners can spend hours online every day. The better a computer system is, the better able it will be to handle key tasks, everything from downloading emails to scanning documents to taking and uploading digital photographs. This section introduces many upgrades that e-business owners may find useful to improve existing hardware configurations.

Two general principles apply when assembling equipment and software for an online business:

1. Search the Internet for what is needed, because most businesses can find nearly all their inventory online—and at a good price.
2. Take the time to get all the facts before purchasing, including detailed information on warranties and technical support. Regarding the latter, make sure that any vendor provides phone support 24 hours a day, seven days a week. Also ask how long the typical turnaround time is in case any equipment needs to be serviced.

Business owners purchasing a large amount of new hardware and software should update their business insurance. Send the insurer a list of the new equipment and verify that the new items are covered. If not, the policy may need a rider to cover the new equipment, or they may have to purchase a policy specifically for computer-related items.

11.1.1 Choosing a PC

The personal computer is the heart and soul of every e-business because all the company's valuable data resides on it and it is the primary means of communicating with the outside world. Will an existing PC be adequate for the new online venture, or is it time to upgrade or buy a new system? If a new system seems to be the way to go, what is the best way to invest the new business's dollars wisely?

The cost of purchasing a computer can be outrageously low—as little as $299. But what does a buyer get for that price? That off-the-shelf computer for $299 is probably a stripped-down model, maybe not much more powerful than that old machine it is replacing. Remember to look beyond processor speed; assessing a PC's capabilities means considering its various types of memory, video and networking cards, and other features. Yes, computers become "obsolete" quickly (as new, faster processor chips are developed), but a well-equipped PC should be able to shoulder the load for a few years.

With the PC market so competitive, e-businesses should be able to assemble a powerful system at an affordable price and with a good warranty and technical support as part of the package. While e-business owners may be tempted to build their own computer, doing so is not feasible since technical support will not be available for the finished product.

General terms that are important to understand when purchasing a new computer include the following:

Gigahertz (GHz): Units of measurement indicating how quickly a computer's central processing unit (CPU) performs functions.

Random Access Memory (RAM): Memory that a computer uses to temporarily store information needed to operate programs; expressed in billions of bytes, or gigabytes (GB), or in megabytes (MB).

- **Gigahertz (GHz):** This unit of measurement indicates how quickly a computer's processor can perform functions. The central processing unit (CPU) of a computer is where the computing work gets done. In general, the higher the processor's internal clock speed, the faster the computer.
- **Random Access Memory (RAM):** The memory that a computer uses to temporarily store information needed to operate programs. RAM is usually expressed in billions of bytes, or gigabytes (GB), or megabytes (MB). The more RAM a computer has, the more programs it can run simultaneously.
- **Synchronous dynamic RAM (SDRAM):** Many ultrafast computers use some form of SDRAM synchronized with a particular clock rate of a CPU so that a processor can perform more instructions in a given time.

- **Double data rate SDRAM (DDR SDRAM):** A type of SDRAM that can dramatically improve the clock rate of a CPU.
- **Auxiliary storage:** Refers to physical data-storage space on a hard drive, CD-RW, DVD, or other device.
- **Network interface card (NIC):** A necessary hardware add-on for a DSL modem user or for those expecting to connect their computer to a network. Having a NIC usually provides an operator with Ethernet data transfer to the other computers. (Ethernet is a network technology that permits an operator to send and receive data at very fast speeds.)

The simplest way to determine the best PC system for an e-business is to follow these general guidelines:

1. Decide how the computer will be used. Be specific about the type of activities, such as accounting, word processing, database management, or digital photo storage.
2. Identify the specific software applications that will be used for each activity. Determine recommended system requirements, including available memory and processor speed.
3. Match the software requirements with a PC, and allow room for expansion and upgraded programs. Look closely at not only the processor but also the hardware and other features:
   - **Hard drive space:** Buy as many gigabytes (GB) as possible; at this writing, 200–250 GB drives are common.
   - **Memory capacity (RAM):** Major manufacturers of PCs for small businesses equip their PCs with a minimum of 2GB RAM up to 4GB dual-channel DDR2 SDRAM from 667 MHz to 800 MHz. E-business owners should purchase as much RAM as the budget allows, with space for adding additional memory as the business prospers.
   - **CD-ROM RW or DVD-RW** (allows saving data to a disk).
   - **Networking card** (preferably wireless-ready).
   - **Monitor** (with option for a flat-panel monitor, which requires less space on the desktop): Focus on resolution, size, and refresh rate.
   - **Keyboard and mouse** (wireless, ideally).
   - **External hard drive** for backup.
4. Compare the support service and warranties. Be sure to find out whether support is free and, if yes, for how long. Extended warranties, which are similar to buying insurance, are often a good investment.

IN THE REAL WORLD

Setting Up Shop at Home

When Robert Woltz, CEO of Medical Solutions International (MSI), acquired the staffing service in 1991, it began losing money because of the high overhead costs of its corporate office setting. But Woltz wasn't going to give up on his investment in MSI, which places nursing professionals in hospitals around North America, England, and Ireland. Woltz made the bold decision to run the business out of his Tempe, Arizona, home. The change to a lower overhead—including five full-time staffers that are based out of home offices around the country—"flipped us," Woltz says of the company's recovery.

After three years of having the business at home, the Woltz household is a technological wonder. The main office, with two computers, is located in the living room, and the den, which serves as the recruiting office, houses a high-speed duplex color printer (to save money on brochure printing). The laundry room holds five servers. Woltz realizes that the technology costs are worth it. "Without the technology, you could try it, but it wouldn't succeed," he says.[1]

11.1.2 Desktops Versus Notebooks

Notebooks used to be considered a luxury item, something that only well-heeled corporate travelers could afford to lug around. And lug was the operative word—even a modestly outfitted notebook could give its owner a good workout.

Times have dramatically changed. Technology has shrunk both the size of the components required to run a high-powered notebook and the cost. Now it is possible to assemble a portable system that rivals a great desktop PC for only a slightly higher price. Some people like notebooks because they occupy so little space on top of a desk. For others, portability is paramount. Anybody facing the prospect of even occasional business travel should seriously consider a notebook. That way, e-business owners can leave home and know they have the tools in hand to help correct any problem that might crop up on their Web site or back in the office.

Online entrepreneurs planning to equip their firm with multiple PCs should plan on buying at least one notebook. Bootstrappers confined to purchasing just one PC should consider these factors before they decide on a desktop or a notebook:

- **Budget:** Desktop computers can be bulky, but they are packed with options at rock-bottom prices. Comparatively, you pay for the convenience and small size that a notebook offers—though in recent years prices for the portable models have fallen sharply.

- **Convenience:** Putting a price tag on convenience is difficult. If computers need to be toted from room to room or from city to city, a notebook is the only option and usually worth any premium price they command.
- **Capability:** Any application that can be run on a desktop can be run on a notebook, and high-capacity hard drives are the norm in portables. One downside is that notebook screens may not be best for graphics intense applications. When in the office, notebooks can be connected to a larger monitor, though that adds to the cost of the system.
- **Comfort:** Some users have trouble adjusting to the compact keyboards, touch pads, and smaller screens on notebooks (although notebooks are available with larger screens). In the office, notebooks can utilize wireless add-ons: keyboard, mouse, and stand-alone monitors.

11.1.3 Other Must-Have Equipment

Office equipment and computer peripherals—copiers, printers, scanners, and more—used to cost several thousand dollars each. The big, clunky pieces of equipment filled the office and needed frequent servicing and messy powders and inks to keep running. Both the size and the prices of office equipment have dropped tremendously, and maintenance is much simpler. More importantly, technology has pushed the development of all-in-one items such as combination fax/copier/printer/scanners that provide small firms multiple functions for one low price.

When evaluating equipment needs, think about the functions that must be fulfilled on a daily basis instead of thinking about an office as a growing collection of machines, cartridges, and cords.

Printing

Although email now dominates most correspondence, e-businesses still need to print invoices, offline marketing materials, and hardcopies for files. The two primary options are laser printers (which use a laser to draw the images) and inkjet printers (which spray ink on the page). A laser printer is designed for more demanding, high-volume print jobs. An inkjet is usually more affordable and offers superb quality for a small office. Great inkjet printers can now be purchased for $100 or less, but compare ink cartridge requirements before buying: A year of ink can cost much more than the original printer. Consider the number of pages printed per minute (ppm) and whether or not your business will print in black and white only, or black and white and color.

Faxing

Sending or receiving a facsimile (fax) is still a necessity, even with the explosive use of email, but this should not require a big investment. Rather than purchase a separate fax machine, consider obtaining fax software that turns a PC into a fax machine, or sign up for a Web-based fax service (such as eFax.com) and receive faxes as attachments to email. All-in-one machines with fax capability are another cost-effective option. Business owners who use a fax machine and who have a busy stream of fax traffic may want to dedicate a phone line to the fax to avoid tying up a phone line that customers may want to use for voice calls.

Copying

Having access to a small copier can be a good investment for many offices. A business that has a high volume of copying should look at a dedicated, copy-specific machine with features such as duplexing (printing on the front and back) and collating. Smaller quantities can be handled by other strategies, such as all-in-one printers, or even using a scanner-printer combination. Most scanners now come with built-in software that allows one-touch color copying.

Scanning

Scanners, which are particularly useful for working with photos and other images, also offer quick conversion of images or documents into digital formats. In this state they can be manipulated, printed, stored, faxed, or emailed. There are three common types of scanners:

- **Flatbed:** The most common model and the most versatile, operates like a photocopier for scanning paper and photos.
- **See-through vertical:** This scanner style is often recommended for use with digital photography because of its quick scan time and ability to fully display images as they are scanned.
- **Sheet-fed:** Not very versatile, but valuable for scanning large volumes of individual pages or photographic prints at high speeds.

Photography

Many businesses might not immediately think of a camera as must-have equipment, but digital cameras have become one of the most powerful tools in the e-business world. Being able to quickly snap a good picture of a new product and post it online makes the digital camera a serious moneymaker for many businesses, especially ones that make use of eBay and other auction sites.

Digital cameras have become very affordable, with prices falling and available **megapixels** (the measure of maximum photo resolution) rising. Megapixels are calculated by multiplying the number of pixels in an image—for example 1,984 vertical pixels × 1,448 horizontal pixels equals 2,872,832 pixels, or 2.9 megapixels. The higher the resolution, the fewer photos a camera can store at any one time, but the better the quality.

Megapixels: The unit of measure for digital photo resolution, which is calculated by multiplying the number of vertical pixels by the number of horizontal pixels.

When purchasing a digital camera, look for the following features:

- The ability to download images to a computer via a FireWire or USB connection
- Bundled image-processing software
- The ability to download image files directly to a memory card that can be easily transported to a computer's memory card reader
- A macro function that enables a user to capture close-up images
- An included LCD screen that lets the pictures be seen immediately

11.1.4 Connecting to the Internet

Considering the variety of Internet service choices available, now is certainly a great time to start an online business. Firms can select a plan that truly meets their needs without being too great a strain on the budget. Though saving money is a good thing, online businesses should not skimp on their Internet service. After all, it—along with Web site hosting—is the backbone of every e-business.

Dial-up

Using a dedicated phone line and modem, dial-up was once the most common method of accessing the Internet. The technology is now considered quite limiting, especially for e-businesses, with its poor modem-transaction quality and slow 56 Kbps connection speed. At that speed, Web pages will load slowly and large downloads can literally take hours. Although an ISDN (Integrated Services Digital Network) connection was once viewed as ultrafast at 128 Kbps, that is no longer the case, either. The advantage that remains for both dial-up and ISDN is price. They provide a cheap alternative for accessing the Internet; dial-up providers often charge $10 per month, or less, for service. However, unless an e-business owner is located in a rural area where there are no other options, dial-up should not even be considered, even at that low price.

Broadband

Broadband: A term that refers to any high-speed Internet connection, usually cable or DSL.

Broadband is where e-business owners want to be when it comes to their Internet connections. The term refers to any high-speed Internet connection, and current commonly available technologies allow download speeds as high as 8 Mbps, 142 times faster than standard 56K dial-up. Broadband works by carrying many different channels of data over a single wire, or source. As a matter of fact, the continued growth in e-commerce is credited to the ever-expanding number of consumers who have access to a broadband connection in their homes, which has significantly increased speed to make shopping online faster and easier. With a large number of homes (in the millions) expected to add broadband over the next few years, experts predict that online business will continue to boom.

Two common broadband options are:

DSL (Digital Subscriber Lines): A high-speed Internet connection using a normal phone line and a digital modem.

1. **DSL: Digital Subscriber Lines** provide a high-speed connection using a normal phone line and digital modem capabilities. Special equipment allows phone lines to be used simultaneously for accessing the Internet and for regular voice communication. Although DSL systems might advertise maximum download transfer rates as high as 7 Mbps, the reality is that most users experience much slower rates (1.5 Mbps is common) and upload is often limited to around 896 Kbps. However, that is still fast enough to get the job done. Unfortunately, some phone companies have been slow to establish DSL access to all areas. In terms of price, DSL charges often range from $25 to $50 per month depending on the speed of service available and whether it is bundled with phone service.
2. **Cable:** Cable television companies have jumped onto the high-speed Internet bandwagon in a big way by adding technology that sends Internet service into homes on the same communication lines that deliver TV programming. Cable Internet is typically faster than DSL—up to 14 Mbps in some areas, and 8 Mbps download capability is very common. However, cable modems use shared bandwidth, whereas DSL uses dedicated bandwidth, which means that bandwidth is shared by multiple users on the same cable loop. If all cable users are online at the same time, a slowdown occurs. A shared network is also associated with a higher security risk, though how much risk is debatable. Cable pricing tends to be somewhat higher than DSL, especially for the very high-speed options; $40 to $80 per month is typical. Some companies offer discounts for bundling TV and the new voice-over-Internet phone services.

IN THE REAL WORLD

Utilizing Startup Resources

College roommates Jamee Kunichika and Sherilyn Luke had an idea for a product, but one with the potential for being a tough sell. The idea was simple, but unconventional: liquid toilet odor deodorizer. The two had been intrigued by a Japanese product, but both felt that they could greatly improve on the packaging and scent. After spending a year researching and refining their idea, Kunichika and Luke launched POOF (www.Poofdrops.com), a pocket-size bottle of a fresh-scented

(Continued)

IN THE REAL WORLD (Continued)

deodorizer. To cover the startup costs of equipment and supplies, the pair invested $25,000 each and then took a loan of $50,000 from the Small Business Administration; two years later, Kunichika and Luke are each earning between $40,000 and $50,000 a year from the part-time venture. The two, who received guidance from the Small Business Development Center, believe that being able to utilize a one-stop warehouse and fulfillment shop (Shipwire) has been key to POOF's success.[2]

SELF-CHECK

1. Compare the advantages of desktops and notebooks.
2. List three functions to be fulfilled in a typical office, and specify two equipment options for fulfilling each need.
3. What are the two common options for broadband Internet service? What are the advantages of each option?

Apply Your Knowledge You want to buy one new desktop system to start a new e-business. Researching online, list the ideal technical specifications for a Windows-based system that will be running Microsoft Office, QuickBooks Pro, and Adobe Dreamweaver.

11.2 ESSENTIAL SOFTWARE

One of the great things about starting an Internet business is the Internet software. Online programs are inexpensive (sometimes free), easy to use and install, and continually updated. Although most business owners begin with a basic selection of software to find information and communicate with others in cyberspace, the following sections describe a variety of program types that may be helpful in creating an online business.

11.2.1 Web Page Editors

Web page editor: A program that allows creating and editing the HTML content that makes up a Web site.

There are many **Web page editors**—programs that allow business owners to create and edit the HTML content that makes up their sites. Many user-friendly, inexpensive programs include Macromedia HomeSite, Microsoft FrontPage Express, and BBEdit for Mac users. To determine the best Web page editor for your e-business without hiring a consultant, utilize the Web page editor page located at http://webdesign.about.com/od/htmleditors and complete the questionnaire at the lower left of the page. A list of the majority of Web page editors is included on this site with links in which to investigate each product.

The advanced programs described here go beyond the simple designation of Web page editors. They not only allow users to edit Web pages but also help them to add interactivity to their sites, link dynamically updated databases to those sites, and keep track of how a site is organized and updated. Some programs (notably FrontPage) can even transfer Web documents to a Web host with a single menu option. Easily transferring Web documents to a Web host increases time available to concentrate on other areas of the business.

Dreamweaver

Dreamweaver is a feature-rich, professional Web authoring tool by Adobe. Dreamweaver's strengths are not so much in the basic features; rather, Dreamweaver excels in producing Dynamic HTML (which makes Web pages more interactive through scripts) and HTML style sheets. Dreamweaver has ample FTP (File Transfer Protocol) settings and gives users the option of seeing the HTML codes they are working with in one window, and seeing the formatting of the Web page in a second, WYSIWYG (What You See Is What You Get), window. The latest version is a complex and powerful piece of software. It is available for both Windows and Macintosh computers.

Microsoft FrontPage

Microsoft officially discontinued FrontPage at the end of 2006, when Microsoft introduced Expression Web; however, FrontPage continues to be widely used. FrontPage is a powerful Web authoring tool that has unique e-commerce capabilities. In FrontPage, a Web site can be visually organized. The main FrontPage window is divided into two sections. On the right is the Web page currently being edited, and on the left is a tree-like map of all pages on the site showing which pages are connected by hyperlinks.

Microsoft Expression Web

Expression Web is a user-friendly yet powerful editor that has strong support for Cascading Style Sheets (CSS), a technology that allows the formatting of multiple Web pages consistently by using standard commands that all Web browsers can interpret. Expression Web includes Dynamic Web Templates—sets of Web pages that have master areas that appear on each Web page; make a change to the master area, and the change is carried out through the whole site.

Adobe GoLive

GoLive, a highly popular Web page tool, is an especially good choice for users who want to exert a high level of control over how their Web page looks. GoLive helps make use of the latest HTML style-sheet commands that precisely control the positioning of text and images on a page. GoLive (available for Macintosh OS X versions 10.2.8 to 10.4 and Windows XP and 2000) is especially well integrated with Adobe Photoshop and Illustrator, two popular and sophisticated graphics programs. Users can even create Web pages that are especially formatted for wireless devices, such as personal desk assistants (PDAs) and Web-enabled cell phones.

11.2.2. Web Browsers

Web browser: Software that allows users to view and navigate the World Wide Web.

A **Web browser** is the software that allows Internet users to travel from site to site. The Web browser is the primary tool for conducting business online. Users enter a site's address, or URL (Uniform Resource Locator), and the browser displays the site or page on the computer screen.

Microsoft Internet Explorer remains the dominant browser, with the majority of computer users relying on it. Apple's Safari is the dominant browser among the growing population of Mac computers. Netscape Navigator, at one time the most popular browser, is still considered a viable alternative to Internet Explorer and also works on Mac OS and Linux systems. Mozilla's Firefox Web browser is rapidly gaining in popularity. Mozilla's increased security and wide variety of user-friendly features—plus that fact that it's free—make it an increasingly popular choice for users on a variety of platforms.

Keep in mind that a browser is typically included when purchasing a new computer, although which browser is employed varies with the operating system. Users can always download a different browser for their computer or update an older version of an existing browser. Start downloading the browser of your choice by going to these Web sites:

- Microsoft Internet Explorer: www.microsoft.com
- Mozilla Firefox: www.mozilla.org
- Netscape Navigator (Version 9): www.netscape.com/ns8

Never assume that just because a Web page works fine with Internet Explorer it will function the same way with another browser. Smart e-business owners will make all the major browsers (and even some minor ones) available on their desktop. This will allow them to regularly check for consistency among Web page views displayed with different browsers. For example, Internet Explorer may display a Web page in a slightly different way than Firefox. The difference may be subtle, or it may cause the loss of pertinent product information or graphics. Making Web pages work with all browsers is a good way to make sure all customers are able to make the purchases they desire.

11.2.3 Email

Email is a painless way to communicate with customers, vendors, and employees. Unfortunately, the popularity of this communication tool has led to a bigger problem: How do people keep up with, sort, store, and reply to all these messages? And, what's the best way to combat spam, viruses, and other harmful or annoying applications that are unwelcome additions to an inbox?

Users can resolve these issues by finding a good email program. In addition to acting as an organizer and system for filtering junk mail, an email system should be simple to use and pack a few added features.

The following email programs are all good options:

- **Thunderbird:** The email program designed by Mozilla automatically detects and sorts junk mail. Packed with features, Thunderbird also offers an enhanced three-column view of email. Download Thunderbird for free at Mozilla.org (www.mozilla.org/products/thunderbird).
- **Eudora:** The latest version of Qualcomm's Eudora features ScamWatch, which identifies and protects against illegal email schemes. There are three levels of Eudora, including a free version with limited features built-in and paid advertising. The Pro edition costs $49.95. Choose the Eudora that's right for you at www.eudora.com.
- **Outlook or Outlook Express:** Microsoft created two versions of its email messaging system. Outlook Express, the simpler version, often comes free with new PCs. Outlook or Outlook Express is functional for use at home or in a small business. Outlook offers much greater capabilities and is a better choice for most businesses. It can be purchased separately, but is also bundled with the Microsoft Office package.

11.2.4 Other Essential Software

Most businesses require some robust software programs to manage core business activities, such as generating printed letters and invoices, juggling finances, designing marketing pieces, and making sales presentations. The choice of business software is almost endless, but some basic packages should be purchased, installed, and learned before startup.

New computers often come loaded with basic software packages, such as Microsoft Works. Many of these inexpensive, all-in-one packages are limited in their capabilities; e-businesses are advised to spend money to buy full-featured packages for some functions. The following sections describes some core software packages every e-business should consider:

Word Processing

Working with documents, either creating or reading them, is standard procedure in business. Therefore, a powerful word processor is a very good investment. Microsoft Word is the most widely embraced word processing package; WordPerfect is also popular. Free, open-source word processors are perfectly suitable, though they lack the support provided by purchased packages.

Graphics and Image Editing

Graphics software is a necessity for any business working with images, for everything from creating logos to manipulating digital photos. Adobe Photoshop is the most powerful image editing package, though it is a richly featured program that can be a challenge to master. Other programs, such as Adobe Illustrator or Corel Draw, come in handy for creating electronic artwork.

Accounting

Good accounting can make or break a business, and keeping track of business financial information—payroll, invoices, and profit-and-loss statements—requires specialized software. Popular products include Quicken, QuickBooks Pro, Peachtree Accounting, and Microsoft Money. This is a good investment, even when using an outside bookkeeping service; many business owners have been taken for large sums of money because they have not monitored their finances along the way.

Document Viewing

Portable document format files (PDFs) preserve all the layout attributes of graphics-intensive files, including text formatting and photos, no matter what software was used to create the files. They are commonly used for a variety of purposes by online businesses. PDF files can then be viewed, printed, or searched using free Adobe Acrobat Reader software, available for download at www.adobe.com. The more robust Adobe Acrobat is a for-pay package that allows users to do many more things with PDFs, including appending comments and even editing text. Microsoft Office 2007 includes the capability to save files in Portable document format (PDF).

File Compression

Sending or receiving large files via the Internet is easier using a file-compression package, such as WinZip (Windows) or Stuffit (Mac), which shrinks a file down to a manageable size before attaching it to an email. Recipients open the files effortlessly using free file expansion software. Both utilities are affordable and can be downloaded and tested for free for a limited period.

Presentation

This type of software allows users to create a professional presentation by using text and graphics and by applying special effects to the content. Microsoft PowerPoint is by far the most popular presentation package. Microsoft PowerPoint is easy to use and allows creating individual slides that can be viewed one by one or run in sequence as a slide show. Keynote is a Mac-only alternative.

Movie and Audio Players

Video and audio clips are now an important part of the daily Internet experience. Seeing and hearing clips requires a software viewer or player. Users are urged to maintain a selection of viewers so that they have players to manage any file format encountered. Microsoft includes Windows Media Player with Windows, and Apple ships QuickTime Player with Macs; cross-platform versions of both packages are also available. RealPlayer, which also works on multiple platforms, is another highly recommended no-cost package (www.real.com/freeplayer).

SELF-CHECK

1. What functions do Web page editors perform? Do all e-businesses need one? Explain why or why not.
2. Why would an e-business need additional Web browsers beyond what is preloaded on a new PC?
3. What features should a powerful email program offer?
4. What is PDF and how is it used? Why?

Apply Your Knowledge Develop a list of software packages that you would deem essential when starting a new business. Research online, select actual products, and determine prices for each. Calculate the total cost. Explain whether or not your choices would be a reasonable investment for a new business. If not, recommend options for saving money.

11.3 INTERNET SERVICE PROVIDERS

Internet service provider (ISP): A company that provides customers access to the Internet.

An **Internet service provider (ISP)** is a company whose purpose is to provide customers access to the Internet. Section 11.1.4 discusses connecting to the Internet, and it may seem obvious that once an e-business chooses a connection to the Internet they will have also chosen an ISP; that is not always the case. While dial-up and cable connections go hand in hand with a specific ISP, DSL service—provided by phone companies—requires signing up with a separate ISP.

Web-hosting service: A company that stores Web site files on a specialized computer (called a server) and makes the files available on the Internet.

Not to be confused with an Internet service provider is a **Web-hosting service**—a company that stores Web site files on a specialized computer (called a server) and makes the Web site files available on the Internet. ISPs and Web hosts are different services, but many ISPs also serve as Web hosts. Some e-business experts believe that e-businesses should avoid using Web-hosting services offered by ISPs, but for small firms looking for a place to store a modest e-commerce site, that may not be true. In fact, one of the best places for a first-time e-business owner to turn for Web hosting is to their ISP.

The following sections briefly review basics to consider when selecting an ISP, and offer an analysis of choosing an ISP for Web hosting versus working with a dedicated Web-hosting business. Working with dedicated Web hosts is detailed in Section 11.4.

11.3.1 Selecting an ISP

E-businesses using a dial-up or DSL Internet connection will need to carefully explore ISP options. Not all ISPs are created equal. In general, the provider that offers the least expensive pricing with the fastest connection will be the best, but four important questions should be asked:

- What types of connections are offered?
- How many dial-up numbers do they have?
- What is the access range (only local coverage, or regional and international cover as well)?
- What type of tech support is offered? Are phone calls or email inquiries accepted at all hours of the day or only during certain hours? Are personnel always available on call or are clients sent to a phone message system?

Bigger does not necessarily mean cheaper or better, however; many regional or local ISPs provide good service at rates that are comparable to the giants such as Verio or EarthLink. A good place to look for ISPs is The List (www.thelist.com). The site lists about 8,000 ISPs and can be searched by area code or by country code, or it can be focused on the United States or Canada.

11.3.2 Using ISPs for Web Hosting

Businesses that are searching for an ISP that also offers a Web-hosting account should be on the lookout for some particular features.

- Look for an ISP that does not limit the number of Web pages that can be created.

- Find an ISP host that offers at least one email address with each account and that allows the addition of other email addresses for a nominal fee.
- Ask about pricing, which is usually set at a monthly rate for a maximum amount of storage space. Pricing can be expensive for large sites, but ISPs are often very affordable for small sites. For example, a rate of $14.98 per month for 2GB of Web site space is very reasonable.

Before committing to using an ISP for Web hosting, it pays to explore services offered by a dedicated Web-hosting company. There are significant differences between putting a Web site on an ISP server and putting it on a server dedicated to Web hosting. Consider:

- **Domain names:** Web-hosting services allow users to choose their own domain names, whereas an ISP may not. Or some ISPs will require users to upgrade to an expensive business account in order to obtain the vanity address.
- **Access speed:** Limited bandwidth is an issue with many ISPs, which are primarily focused on delivering Internet service to individual users. Low bandwidth can mean slow-loading Web pages, frustrated customers, and lost sales.
- **Security:** Web hosts typically offer better Web site backup and security systems than ISPs.
- **Space:** While ISPs may be fine for small Web sites, a growing e-business may find their server storage limits (or increased charges) a serious impediment.
- **Frills:** Most ISP Web-hosting packages are pretty basic. Any e-business looking for things like one-button file transfer or visitor statistics will probably want to try a Web-hosting company.
- **Technical support:** Varies among all online companies (and should be carefully researched), however most dedicated Web-hosting companies are better equipped to solve Web page problems than ISPs.

11.3.3 What to Expect from an ISP

E-businesses that have carefully evaluated their options and decided on an ISP should also consider how the process of setting up a Web site varies among ISPs. Here are some general features to look for in an ISP:

- **Password and username:** An ISP should require users to type in a username and password to access their Web sites. Although a password is unnecessary to view most Web sites through a browser, a password should be required for making changes. Otherwise, anyone can enter a Web site and tamper with files.

- **FTP software:** File transfer protocol (FTP) is the simplest and easiest-to-use software to transfer large files from one location to another over the Internet—such us uploading Web page files to a Web host. Many ISPs will make FTP software readily available to customers. Three popular FTP programs are Fetch (for Macintosh), WS-FTP (for Windows), and Cute FTP.
- **URL:** Many ISPs are not very accommodating when it comes to domain names. Usually, when a Web site is set up using an ISP, the owner is assigned a directory on a Web server, and the convention for naming this directory is *~username*. The *~username* designation goes at the end of the URL for the Web site's home page. However, sometimes it is possible to register a shorter URL with a domain name registrar. That domain name can then be "pointed" to the ISP server so that it can serve as an "alias" for the site.
- **Web page editor:** This is not an essential feature for an ISP to provide, because it is easy to download and install an external program, but it may be a valuable tool for small e-businesses working with a tight budget.

After a user has software tools and a user directory on an ISP's Web server, it is time to put a Web site together. To create or revise content for a Web site, simply open the page in a Web page editor, make changes, save the changes, and then transfer the files to the ISP's directory with an FTP program. Finally, review the changes in the browser.

SELF-CHECK

1. List the types of Internet connections an e-business owner must consider before selecting an ISP. What attributes of an Internet connection should be considered?
2. Why are ISPs limiting in their ability to host Web sites when considering domain names? Bandwidth?
3. Why is it desirable to have an ISP protect Web page accounts with a username and password?

Apply Your Knowledge Explain the difference between using a dedicated Web-hosting service and an ISP for hosting a Web page. What are the advantages of each option, and for what type of e-business is each best suited?

11.4 SELECTING A WEB HOST

Most e-businesses choose to house their Web site on a dedicated Web-hosting server, as opposed to using an Internet service provider. Section 11.3 compares and contrasts the two options and points out the weaknesses of the ISP option. Anything other than a small e-commerce site will probably not be adequately served by an ISP.

Once committed to the dedicated Web-host option, an e-business faces the often-daunting task of selecting a provider. Web hosting is a competitive industry with many firms from which to choose. The following sections discuss the issues that must be considered when selecting and initiating service with a Web-hosting service. With some careful research, choosing a provider that offers the best mix of desired features and price can be a fairly easy decision.

11.4.1 High-Performance Web-Host Features

Dedicated Web-hosting services cater to all types of online businesses, but the best ones offer varying service levels that can evolve with a new business. For that reason, it is important to consider how a Web host serves high-performance sites, not just basic ones. Look for superior hosting power—which translates into fast loading speeds, video, and sounds playing without interruption. Accordingly, consider the features described in the following sections when evaluating hosting options:

Disk Space

The size of Web site files dictates how much disk space, or storage, is needed. Sites using Flash, or containing numerous pictures or graphics, need more storage space. Disk space of 500MB is sometimes enough for a basic site, and many low-end hosting packages offer 1GB of space, but most sites will require anywhere from 2 to 50GB of storage. Look for a host and plan that remains cost effective from the low to the high end of these extremes.

Bandwidth

Bandwidth: The measurement of how much data, or information, a server or communication line can send and receive at any given moment.

Bandwidth is the measurement of how much data, or information, a server can send and receive at any given moment. The greater the bandwidth of a host's server, the more traffic (visitors) a site can support at one time. Limited bandwidth can slow page loading when visitor counts rise. Considering that bandwidth is one of the main reasons for not using an ISP, make sure that bandwidth limitations will never be an issue with the dedicated Web host.

Backup Systems

When purchasing a hosting plan, ask what type of precautions a provider has in place to prevent its server from going down. The problem is not always a matter of equipment failure; power outages, maintenance checks, and other manmade or environmental conditions can take a server and its stored Web sites out of commission. Make sure that the host has dual systems (redundancy) in place that allows information to remain accessible from a secondary source, even if the primary server goes down. Web-hosting plans should include frequent—at least daily—backups of the Web site (ideally, to an alternate location) to preserve data in the event of a catastrophic failure.

Technical Support

Inevitably, every e-business will need a little help. Although it is not easy to determine the quality of a host's support until using it, it is possible to compare some basic features. Is support offered 24 hours a day and seven days a week? If not, what are the hours of the host's customer service center? Are both online support and phone support available? (If online support is offered, make sure that it offers access to answers in real time, as opposed to waiting 24 to 48 hours for a response to email.) Always ask whether there are extra charges for live tech support and whether the charge is based on use by the minute, hour, or month.

Data Transfers

Every time someone views information from a site (including text, images, and video), data is transferred. Think of it as traffic (or data) leaving the site. Roughly 1GB of data transfer is the same as 40,000 to 50,000 page views. Hosting plans generally allow for a specified amount of transfers per month, and then charge additional fees when the limit is consistently exceeded.

Database Access

If a Web site incorporates a database (for inventory management, for example), the server must allow for it. Typically, this means ensuring that MySQL or Standard Query Language (SQL) is available, which means that the server is set up to use SQL to access and transfer information from the database. SQL is often an extra-charge feature.

E-commerce Enabled

Confirm that the hosting plan supports e-commerce software, such as a shopping cart program. Many companies bundle hosting with a specific e-commerce solution, and charge extra for using a third-party shopping cart.

In addition, e-businesses need an SSL (Secure Socket Layer) certificate, which ensures that data can be securely transmitted through the Web site when customers make purchases. Check to see whether a hosting plan offers a shared SSL certificate—or if an individual SSL must be purchased by each Web site.

Multimedia/CGI Scripts

One big advantage of dedicated Web-hosting services is their ability to serve complex and memory-intensive content, such as RealAudio sound files or RealVideo video clips. Web hosts also allow processing of Web page forms included by executing computer programs called CGI scripts. These programs receive the data that someone sends (such as a customer services request or an order form) and present the data in readable form, such as a text file, email message, or database entry.

Customer Analysis

To understand customers and their habits while visiting a site, it is advantageous to have Web analysis software available from the host. If this feature is not included with the plan, ask whether there are any restrictions or extra charges for using third-party Web analysis software.

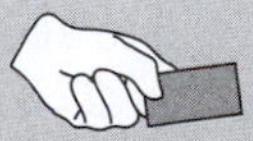

CAREER CONNECTION

Armed with the services of online support companies, a busy mom brings her creative approach to children's photography to the Internet.

When Kristin Chalmers left Los Angeles to move to the Boston area, she knew it was a good move for her family. She wasn't, however, so sure the move would be good for her business. A former modern dancer, Chalmers had established herself as a successful photographer in Los Angeles, creating stunning images for album covers and magazines. Once in Boston, Chalmers began photographing her friends' children as gifts. Her documentary-style approach to photography quickly earned her a following.

The results of her work can be found on her Web site (www.kristinchalmersphoto.com), a stylish presentation of her individual and family portraits. The site itself got off to a rocky start when Chalmers' Web designer "disappeared." Chalmers did some research and found out about Site Welder (sitewelder.com), a service that provides photographers, artists, and other creative professionals with a way to create and maintain Web sites.

These days Chalmers can finish a shoot, return to her studio, and upload the images to her Web site, which features LifePics, an online service that professional photographers can use to

(Continued)

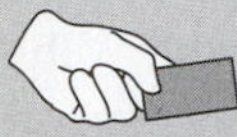

CAREER CONNECTION (Continued)

accept orders from consumers via the Internet. "Because Boston is such an international hub, many of my clients have family all over the world," says Chalmers. "Using the digital ordering service lets those families look at and order whatever prints they want."

Chalmers, who focuses much of her energy on her growing family, is happy with the amount of photography she's doing. At this point, most of Chalmers' business comes through word of mouth and the Internet, and she doesn't see a need to pay for advertising. Instead, she encourages her satisfied customers to post reviews on local parent message boards and Web sites, which have been a great source of new customers.

Tips from the Professional

- Don't spend money on advertising if you don't need to.
- Keep the size of your business compatible with your life.

11.4.2 Plans and Contracts

Once an appropriate Web host has been identified, another decision must be made: Which plan is the right one? Choosing a plan from a list of categories makes it easy to choose one that has the desired elements and falls within budgetary guidelines.

Basic hosting packages offer bare-bones necessities—enough to keep a simple site with minimal images operating. With basic service, the decision is made strictly on price. E-businesses in this category may be best served by a hosting option with an Internet service provider (see Section 11.3).

The majority of e-business startups must make a choice among various mid-level plans, which usually leave the most room for uncertainty. These hosting options vary the most by both price and available features. To overcome indecision, make a list that prioritizes which items are needed most, then try to select a plan acceptable to the budget that offers these high-priority features.

An important factor in choosing a host is the nature of the contractual obligations. Long-term contracts are a distant memory when it comes to hosting a Web site. If a host requires a long-term contract, consider other options first. Find another host that requires no more than a monthly commitment.

In addition to the monthly charges, an account often requires a small setup fee, along with the first few months of service in advance, none of which is refundable. Some companies may require 30 days' notice before terminating service. More often than not, monthly fees are paid *in advance* of using the service, so plan ahead if considering switching providers.

Remember, even agreeing to a short-term (monthly) arrangement means that a contract is still in place. Although it might not bind an e-business to a block of payments over a long period, it specifies the terms of the relationship with the host. Always carefully read the fine print of any contract, terms of agreement, or other legally binding document. Some contracts limit what can and cannot be done on a Web site hosted by the company, and that may include offering certain products or services for sale.

11.4.3 Alternative Host Server Options

One decision that many e-businesses eventually must make is whether to skip a hosting plan and instead rent a dedicated server for their Web site. In that case, the partnership with a particular Web host will require a long-term commitment and signing a contract—or two. Within this category of Web hosting, several different types of server options are available. The following sections explain some of the different server setups that may be available.

Shared server: One server (computer) that is shared to store the pages of many different Web sites owned by different companies.

Shared Server

The hosting plans explained elsewhere in this chapter are examples of using a shared server. In essence, an e-business uses the same computer (server) along with many other Web sites. Although that arrangement translates into lower costs, shared servers offer less flexibility in the types of applications that can be run because the server is configured with the same settings and applications to all who use it.

Dedicated server: A server dedicated entirely to one e-business, which purchases, houses, and maintains the equipment and its functions.

Dedicated Server

Gaining complete control over the type of server and the programs installed requires a dedicated server. As its name implies, the bandwidth, memory, and storage space are dedicated entirely to one e-business, which purchases, houses, and maintains the server, usually in its offices. A dedicated server is a more expensive option and often a necessity for running special programs or maintaining multiple sites or extremely high-traffic sites. The downside of using a dedicated server (in addition to the expense) is that the e-business is responsible for installing software, handling regular maintenance, and fixing any unexpected problems or system failures—an arrangement recommended only for experienced Webmasters or computer technicians.

Co-location server: A server owned by a company but housed in space owned by another firm, which installs the server and ensures controlled environmental conditions and consistent access to the Internet.

Co-location Server

With this option, an e-business purchases the hardware (the server) and leases space (called rack space) for it with a host company. The host company then installs the server and ensures controlled environmental conditions and consistent access to the Internet. Beyond these basic management functions, the owner is still responsible for all other aspects of maintaining the server—meaning this option also requires advanced skills.

Managed server: A server relationship in which a server is leased from a hosting company that takes care of most server management functions.

Managed Server

Sometimes referred to as a virtual server, a managed server is a compromise to a dedicated server. Unlike co-location, an e-business leases the equipment, and the hosting company takes care of most server functions, including installing software and updates, handling security and maintenance, and acting as a troubleshooter for problems.

Virtual dedicated server: A server used by multiple clients that provides increased control by partitioning the server into storage and access units dedicated to just one client.

Virtual Dedicated Server

A virtually dedicated server is one with limited maintenance but increased flexibility. As with shared hosting, others also use the server, but access is limited to a small number of customers. This provides dedicated space and increased control because the host uses partitions on the computer to separate it into several virtual dedicated servers. Although the Web site is on a shared server, it has been configured to appear as a stand-alone, dedicated server with no other users.

As with hosting, the price and the exact services offered with each server package vary. And, because you're usually required to sign a long-term lease agreement, make sure that you understand what the price covers and what the responsibilities are for both you and the host company. Also, make sure that cancellation terms are clearly spelled out so that you can get out of the agreement if you're unhappy with the provider.

IN THE REAL WORLD

Taking Advantage of Web Resources

Idealist.org is an online international directory that lists more than 126,000 member profiles and 70,700 organizations, helping to connect people with the right skills to job and volunteer opportunities at progressive organizations. Originally designed as an "idea list" for people looking to get involved in their communities, Idealist.org streamlined the distribution of information on the site, adding a listserv so individuals could sign up to be notified of the latest listings. Today, Idealist.org shares with its online visitors many of the latest Web site resources available—personalized email alerts, a blog, podcasts, and message boards, to name a few. Using the site, visitors can make donations, post an organization or opportunity, and browse resource centers. Idealist.org also encourages bloggers and Webmasters to post customized sets of Idealist listings on their own blog or site, add free Idealist logos and banners to a site, and add a customizable search box that another site's users can use to search the Idealist database.

SELF-CHECK

1. What is bandwidth and why is it such an important consideration when selecting a Web host?
2. What type of backup systems should a quality Web host offer?
3. What are the important details to consider before signing a contract for Web hosting?
4. What is the difference between a shared server and a dedicated server?
5. What is the difference between a co-location server and a managed server?

Apply Your Knowledge You are searching for a dedicated Web-hosting company. List five features that will weigh heavily in the decision, and explain what your minimum expectations are for each feature.

SUMMARY

Section 11.1

- E-business owners should not shop for personal computers strictly based on price. They should select a system with the power to effectively run the software packages they will use the most, plus provide some room for future expansion. Notebooks cost slightly more than desktops, but their convenience factor makes them a serious consideration for many firms.
- When evaluating equipment needs, e-businesses should consider the functions that must be fulfilled daily—for example, printing, faxing, and scanning—and machines that can perform multiple tasks.
- The two primary options for connecting to the Internet are dial-up and broadband. Dial-up service is too slow to adequately support most e-businesses. Broadband services are much faster and include both DSL service (provided through phone lines) and cable Internet.

Section 11.2

- Web page editors, Web browsers, and email are among the essential software packages that new e-businesses should acquire. In addition, most firms should install quality software to handle word processing, graphics and image editing, accounting, and other functions.

Section 11.3

- While some Internet connections are automatically matched to an Internet service provider, others are not and will require e-businesses to select an appropriate ISP. The choice often rests on low price, but there are other issues to consider.
- Some e-businesses with small or simple Web sites may find that site hosting offered by an ISP is both affordable and adequate for their needs. Many firms, though, will be frustrated by low access speeds, space limitations, and other issues common with ISPs, and will

be better served by a dedicated Web-hosting company.

Section 11.4

- When selecting an appropriate Web host and service plan, some of the high-performance issues that should be considered include disk space, bandwidth, backup systems, and technical support.
- E-businesses that desire expanded storage space, improved customer access, and more control over their Web sites should explore various alternative server options, including buying and managing a dedicated server or partnering with an outside company on a co-location or managed server.

ASSESS YOUR UNDERSTANDING

UNDERSTAND: WHAT HAVE YOU LEARNED?

Go to **www.wiley.com/college/holden** to assess your knowledge of the basics of equipment, software, and Web hosting for an e-business.

APPLY: WHAT WOULD YOU DO?

1. E-businesses have specific needs when it comes to equipment requirements. Determine the types of office equipment required for the following three small business scenarios
   - Wedding photographer
   - International specialty tea distributor
   - Fishing guide
2. Using the guidelines from Section 11.1.1, discuss how a computer will be used in the above three scenarios; include information on what would be required as far as hardware and software.
3. Again, for the three scenarios, explain why a desktop or notebook computer would be the best option.
4. Which of the popular Web page editors would be best suited to a graphic designer who plans a very complicated and interactive Web site?
5. The owner of a gift-shopping service is planning to launch a Web site but can't decide whether to choose an ISP for Web hosting or use a dedicated Web-hosting site. Explain the advantages of using a dedicated Web-hosting site.
6. You're planning to put up a Web site, but because you're selling custom made items, you will only take orders over the phone, not through your site. Is it still important to choose a Web host with e-commerce capabilities? Why or why not?
7. Explain why an owner would decide to rent a server for an e-business site. Give an example of a situation in which a rented server would be the best option.
8. List the advantages and disadvantages of a dedicated server.

BE AN E-BUSINESS ENTREPRENEUR

Question

Select a service or product to sell online from your home. Write a memo to your business partner that outlines the office equipment, including computers, that would be required to open the business. Estimate a low end and a high end for your budget.

Question

Contact an e-business owner or someone who has a Web site. Inquire about the types of software products they use:

- Which Web page editor?
- Which Web browser?

Are they satisfied with their products? Ask for software tips for someone starting an online business.

Question

Imagine that you are going to launch a Web site that offers behind-the-scenes tours of local museums. Using the Internet, conduct research and choose an Internet service provider that is able to accommodate e-commerce.

KEY TERMS

Bandwidth The measurement of how much data, or information, a server or communication line can send and receive at any given moment.

Broadband A term that refers to any high-speed Internet connection, usually cable or DSL.

Co-location server A server owned by a company but housed in space owned by another firm, which installs the server and ensures controlled environmental conditions and consistent access to the Internet.

Dedicated server A server dedicated entirely to one e-business, which purchases, houses, and maintains the equipment and its functions.

DSL (Digital Subscriber Lines)	A high-speed Internet connection using a normal phone line and a digital modem.
Gigahertz (GHz)	Units of measurement indicating how quickly a computer's central processing unit (CPU) performs functions.
Internet service provider (ISP)	A company that provides customers access to the Internet.
Managed server	A server relationship in which a server is leased from a hosting company that takes care of most server management functions.
Megapixels	The unit of measure for digital photo resolution, which is calculated by multiplying the number of vertical pixels by the number of horizontal pixels.
Random Access Memory (RAM)	Memory that a computer uses to temporarily store information needed to operate programs; expressed in billions of bytes, or gigabytes (GB), or in megabytes (MB).
Shared server	One server (computer) that is shared to store the pages of many different Web sites owned by different companies.
Virtual dedicated server	A server used by multiple clients that provides increased control by partitioning the server into storage and access units dedicated to just one client.
Web browser	Software that allows users to view and navigate the World Wide Web.
Web-hosting service	A company that stores Web site files on a specialized computer (called a server) and makes the files available on the Internet.
Web page editor	A program that allows creating and editing the HTML content that makes up a Web site.

REFERENCES

1. Rich Sloan, "Journey from office to home spurs MSI's success," startupnation.com, www.startupnation.com/articles/8992/1/home-based-100-best-financial.htm.
2. Michelle Anton and Michelle Price, "Dorm Was Incubator For Money-Making Side Biz," Entrepreneur.com, http://weekend.entrepreneur.com/category/starting-a-business/.

CHAPTER

12 SUCCESSFUL WEB SITE DESIGN

Planning, Designing, and Launching an Effective E-Business Site

Do You Already Know?

- How to select and register domain names
- The appropriate steps for planning a new Web site
- How to work with a professional Web site designer
- The tests to make before launching a Web site

For additional questions to assess your current knowledge on designing Web sites for e-businesses, go to **www.wiley.com/college/holden.**

What You Will Find Out	What You Will Be Able To Do
12.1 How to choose an effective domain name and register it	Select a domain name and register it; or develop an alternative plan if the first choice is taken
12.2 How to map a site and use effective principles in designing one	Map and design a Web site
12.3 How to select and successfully work with a professional Web site designer	Select a Web site designer; take steps to work effectively with that designer
12.4 Which types of testing must be completed prior to launching a Web site	Test a Web site for browser, monitor resolution, and platform compatibility; conduct a trial run

INTRODUCTION

Web page design is an important topic to many would-be online entrepreneurs—and with good reason. A poorly designed site is almost guaranteed to scare off customers and depress sales, no matter how effective marketing efforts are in generating traffic to the site. Unfortunately, too many e-business owners attack the topic of design from the wrong angle, focusing on aesthetic issues instead of the details that really make a site effective. What a site looks like is important, but how it functions is *more* important. This chapter addresses Web site design with an emphasis on the often-overlooked details, starting in the first section with an important topic: domain names. Choosing and registering an effective domain name is critical in launching a new business, but what happens when that dream name is unavailable? This first section offers several ideas for managing this e-commerce predicament. The second section focuses on design, emphasizing the planning process as the key to creating effective Web sites. The colors, fonts, and graphics employed by a Web site are vital, but so are effective navigational tools and fast-loading pages—that greatly enhance a customer's experience. Some e-business owners design their own Web sites, but many choose to employ the expertise of a professional designer. The third section discusses this topic, including tips for selecting designers, evaluating quotes, and effectively managing relationships with designers. The fourth section reviews the last steps prior to launching a Web site, including conducting compatibility testing so that a site is usable by visitors using a variety of browsers on different computer platforms.

12.1 CHOOSING AND REGISTERING DOMAIN NAMES

In the offline world, the mantra of success for business is "location, location, location." It's not much different for online businesses: Rather than use a numerical address on a building, though, e-businesses use a virtual address or domain name. Usually an online address includes a company's name or initials or some other derivation. A traditional business address is listed in the Yellow Pages, while an online address is listed with search engines.

Even before they start building a Web site, online entrepreneurs need to find a great location for that site. That is why selecting and registering the best possible domain name is such an important piece of an overall strategy. The name selected can influence how easily customers can find a Web site or influence whether they choose to visit at all. The sections that follow describe the process of choosing and registering a domain name and even offer advice on what to do if that perfect name has been taken by someone else.

Uniform Resource Locator (URL): The unique address for each page on a Web site or document posted online.

Domain name: The part of the URL that specifically identifies the name of a Web site.

12.1.1 Decoding URLs

A **Uniform Resource Locator (URL)** represents the unique address for each page on a Web site or document posted online. A Web site may be made of several Web pages, each with its own, unique URL. Before creating Web pages, the first order of business is to select a **domain name,** or the part of the URL that specifically identifies the name of the Web site. A URL can consist of several different pieces, each of which refers to a specific page on a Web site (see Figure 12-1).

Figure 12-1

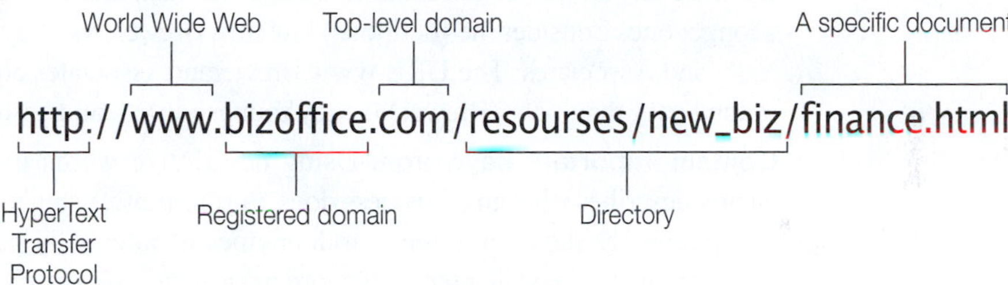

The parts of a typical URL.

Here's how to decode a URL:

- **HyperText Transfer Protocol:** HyperText Transfer Protocol helps direct visitors to a named server.
- **World Wide Web:** Indicates that the user is on the Internet.
- **Domain name:** An e-business's registered domain name always appears as part of the URL.
- **Top-level domains:** These can include .com, .net, .org, and .biz.
- **Directories:** This part of the URL shows up as visitors go deeper into the site.
- **Documents:** At the end; identifies any documents that appear on a page.

12.1.2 Selecting the Right Domain Name

There are two common but opposing approaches for selecting a domain name:

1. **Match (as closely as possible) the domain name to the company's name.** A common approach for an existing business, which is a simple, straightforward, and often quite effective strategy.
2. **Choose a domain that clearly indicates the type of business or the customers being targeted.** A common strategy when the success of an online company hinges on the domain name itself. In this case, the legal company is often irrelevant.

No matter what approach is taken, consider the following list of common denominators in determining the best possible domain. A good domain name should:

- **Be easy to spell.** Hard-to-spell words will make it difficult for some customers to find the Web site. For example, www.BriansBodaciousRibs.com seems harmless enough, but "bodacious" is tough to spell. Better alternatives would be www.briansribs.com or www.goodribs.com.
- **Be simple to remember.** A domain name does not have to be catchy or trendy to work. Simplicity goes a long way in a crowded, overhyped world.
- **Be relatively short.** A shorter name is easier for customers to remember than a longer one. Consider the (fictitious) law firm Brewer, Mackey, Youngstein, Yale, and Associates. The URL www.BrewerandAssociates.com would be much better than www.BrewerMackeyYoungsteinYaleandAssociates.com.
- **Contain important keywords.** Using descriptive words in the domain clearly describes what an e-business does. Furthermore, using relevant words that frequently show up in the search engines is potentially beneficial to a site's rankings. (See Chapter 9 for more information on search engines.)
- **Be alphabetically strategic.** Domain names that begin with a number or start with a letter near the front of the alphabet are more likely to secure a spot at the top of directories and other reference lists. That said, relevancy still counts, so avoid choosing random letters or numbers simply to get to the top of lists.

IN THE REAL WORLD

Daughter Knows Best

University Parent (UP) is the brainchild of Sarah Schupp, 25, named one of America's Best Young Entrepreneurs in 2007 by *Business Week*. The inspiration for UP came out of a time when Schupp's parents came to visit her in Boulder, where she was a student at the University of Colorado. Schupp was unimpressed with the information available to her to find the best places for her parents to stay, eat, and shop. She approached school adminstrators with her proposal to create a guide for visiting parents—the beginning of University Parent. Today, UP produces free, downloadable guides for parents visiting their kids at colleges across the United States. University Parent's site, using the clear choice of domain name www.universityparent.com, is well crafted and simple to use. Schupp, who earns revenue from the advertising placed in the guides, expects to produce 100 guides in 2008.[1]

- **Be intuitive to customers.** Domain names should provide a sense of what products or services a business is selling. For highly targeted or specialized markets, an edgy or more creative name can win customers. For example, a bookseller specializing in romance novels might want to try www.romancingthepages.com or www.steamyreads.com.

12.1.3 Registering a Domain Name

Domain registrar: An organization that takes care of all the paperwork required to register and to activate a new domain name for an e-business.

Once a domain name has been selected, it is time to make it official. Register the name with a **domain registrar.** The registrar takes care of all the paperwork required to activate the new domain name, which includes submitting contact information, specifying the length of time of the registration, and getting a domain listed in the official Internet list of domains maintained by ICANN (Internet Corporation for Assigned Names and Numbers) at www.icann.org.

A number of options are available for registering domains. Many Web-hosting services and ISPs offer registration services along with hosting options, and a variety of third-party affiliate companies act as registrars. The prices vary considerably among online registrars—for example, from $8.95 to $35 per year, but the services provided increase with the prices. Higher fees deliver special services such as data backup or private registration, an option that helps keep company information secret.

Working with one of the online registrars is a fairly simple process, basically a matter of completing forms. The service will search for the availability of the desired domain and suggest available alternatives if the first choice is taken.

12.1.4 What if the Domain You Want Is Taken?

When initially searching for a domain name, the registrar may reply that the first choice is not available. Underneath that notification is typically a box containing a list of suggested alternative domains that are available. Often, the automated system returns a few alternatives that will work just fine. If a good match is not on the suggested list, then what?

Starting from scratch and brainstorming a new domain name is not the only course of action. Furthermore, some e-business owners want a specific domain name and feel that no substitute will work. In that case, there are several strategies for going after that dream domain name, even when it is owned by someone else.

Put the Name on Back Order

Think of this strategy as the official waiting list of domain names. A registrar provides notification when the domain expires and becomes available.

Each registrar manages the process differently. Some charge a small, up-front fee, and others charge a larger commission when the domain is acquired. Some registrars use an auction to sell a domain to the highest bidder when more than one person has indicated interest.

Make an Offer through a Registrar

Instead of waiting for a domain to expire (and maybe be renewed), e-businesses can attempt to purchase domains from their owners. Several registrars have a certified offer option in which an e-business sets a price to buy a domain name, and the registrar presents the offer to the existing owner, which is a great way to find out quickly whether an owner is willing to give up a domain name. Furthermore, the buyer's name and personal information are kept private. If the offer is accepted, the purchase is made via the registrar using a credit card. Certified-offer services often give the seller a chance to respond with a minimum asking price even if they refuse the first offer. The downside of the offer scenario is that a minimum asking price of $100 is not uncommon. The registrar also charges a fee for using the service, regardless of whether an offer is accepted.

Contact the Owner Directly

Contacting the domain owner directly is another option, which removes anonymity, but avoids service fees. Direct contact provides the opportunity for a more aggressive negotiation and may reveal an owner with little interest in the domain and thus willingness to part with it for minimal cost.

If a domain name owner has chosen a private registration, which keeps contact information confidential, the owner may be difficult to locate or contact. If the Web site for the domain name is active, search the pages for contact information. Although an email address works, a phone number is preferable.

Finding the owner of a domain name is easy using the WHOIS feature offered by registrars. The option to use WHOIS is typically provided automatically if a domain search shows that a name is already taken.

12.1.5 Creative Approaches to Domain Names

Approximately 55 million domain names are actively registered, according to WHOIS Source statistics, and more than 300,000 new domains are registered every day. No wonder people are tempted to claim that "all the good ones" are indeed taken (or are being held hostage for a huge ransom). Not true! Plenty of fantastic domain names are available. In fact, the continued popularity of the Internet has prompted many acceptable and creative alternatives for domain registration.

Table 12-1 Extensions Used in Domain Registration

Extension	*Use or Country Represented*	*Generally Used For*
.com	Commercial	General Business
.net	Network	Internet Business
.org	Organization	Nonprofit and Trade association
.info	Information	Resource
.biz	Business	Small Business
.tv	Television	Entertainment, media
.name	Personal use	
.jobs	Business	Employment-related sites
.travel	Business	Travel-industry use
.ws	Former country code	Web
.bz	Former country code	Business
.us	United States	
.vg	British Virgin Islands	
.co.uk	United Kingdom	Commercial
.org.uk	United Kingdom	Organization
.me.uk	United Kingdom	Personal
.de	Germany	
.jp	Japan	
.be	Belgium	
.at	Austria	

Among the easiest ways to find a good domain is to use an alternative extension. The old favorites—.com, .net, and .org—remain the most recognizable, but more than a dozen extensions are now in use, and using these alternatives is no longer considered a stigma. Table 12-1 lists several extensions that can be considered for use.

Acquiring a domain-worthy domain name may also involve using creativity. Most general names (applying to very wide or popular categories) got scooped up during the first Internet craze of the 1990s. All the gems—Business.com, Politics.com, SportsFan.net—are long gone, which should not stop an e-business from getting started. Keep in mind that the Internet is still in its infancy, and there are plenty of domain names that are equally effective as those first category-busters. There are four creative ways to get an outstanding domain.

Make the Domain Name Very Specific

One recent Web trend is that of niche (or specific) sites, and the same trend applies to domain names. Creating a more specific and telling name, rather than one that is very broad, serves well in the search-engine rankings and with customers. For example, www.redsoxfans.com is very specific about its subject and audience.

Make the Domain Name Creatively Telling

Ever hear that saying about thinking outside the box? Even though it is a cliché, it holds true with domain names. Rather than continuously circle around the same type of name, think about other ways that products and services are viewed by target audiences. Make a list of terms and phrases that people use when they talk about these items. Be specific, but with a more creative tone. For example, a site selling food and toys for cats may do extremely well using a domain name like mouseloversonly.com or thescratchingpost.com.

Make the Domain Name Perfectly Meaningless

Any regular Internet user can quickly think of a Web site with an outrageously different but perfectly applicable name—how about Google or Yahoo!? Web sites with extremely odd, fun, or funky domain names can grow a following just like any other site. Fun or funky domain names are for businesses with customers who may appreciate a less conservative approach.

Use Add-Ins

A domain name using common words will make finding an available exact match very difficult. Not to worry: Just mix it up a bit. Try abbreviating your words or using a couple of initials rather than spelling out the whole thing. Or break it up with a hyphen or two (Pearl-Earrings-For-You.com, for example). Another idea is to add "inc" or "corp" to the end of a company name (for incorporated companies only) or add another word that indicates the industry—for example, SmithJewelersInc.com or SmithPearlsandDiamonds.com. Another tip is to include words such as official, favorite, original, or popular—FavoritePearlEarrings.com, for example.

Remember, acquiring the "perfect" domain name will not ensure a successful e-business; nor will lacking the perfect name prevent success. In fact, it is more important to have a well-designed Web site that helps customers easily conduct business—which is the focus of the remaining sections in this chapter.

CAREER CONNECTION

Two friends with a clever idea launch a successful Web site—all from the comfort of their children's playrooms.

It had been over a decade since Meredith Kole and Erica Peale's college days at Syracuse University, but the two still hoped to combine Kole's graphic design skills and Peale's marketing savvy into a business someday. That day came four children (two each) later, when Kole hit on an idea that stuck—a simple, inexpensive way to attach cards to gifts and gift bags, especially for those countless birthday parties their children were always being invited to. The idea was CardStix, self-adhesive greeting cards. At a third of the price of a typical card, CardStix would save other busy moms time and money. To make it even better, this was a business Kole and Peale could manage at home without sacrificing precious time with their families.

Though the partners were in different states—Kole in New Jersey and Peale in Virginia—the two decided to go for it, hiring a Web designer and a publicist and launching the business in November 2006. Less than a year later, CardStix for babies, kids, tweens, weddings, holidays, wine bottles, and more were found in 200 stores nationwide. "In the beginning it was frustrating because people seemed scared of a new idea," says Kole, "but now they get it." The products have been featured in *USA Today, Woman's World Weekly,* and *Modern Bride.*

When it came to the Web site, the pair faced an unfortunate obstacle: The obvious choice for a domain name—cardstix.com—was already taken by a company that sells tickets to the St. Louis Cardinals' baseball games. Although Kole and Peale offered to buy the name from the ticket company, they weren't selling. The partners ultimately settled on cardstixcollection.com. "We were upset at first, but it hasn't held us back at all," says Kole.

As far as the site's design, Kole and Peale had a goal in mind. "We wanted customers to understand what CardStix were the minute they saw the image on the site," says Kole. Being a startup, the partners employed the services of a freelance Web designer, rather than a big design company. Kole used her design skills to craft the look of the site, but the freelancer was the programmer. "We wanted the kind of Web site we could get for $15,000, but as a startup we were limited as far as what we could afford," says Kole, who has since learned a lot about Web sites, including which fonts works best with search engines. "If I ever had to do a Web site again, I wouldn't think about paying the $15,000," she says.

Tips from the Professionals

- Make your business a part of your life.
- Be flexible with your site design—go with what works best, not necessarily with what you think looks best.
- Maintain a personal touch.

SELF-CHECK

1. What are five common denominators for effective domain names?
2. What does a domain registrar do?
3. Offer four courses of action that an e-business may take if the first choice for a domain name is already owned by somebody else.

Apply Your Knowledge An e-business owner named John Smith has started a new e-business called John Smith Office Supplies Inc. Brainstorm at least ten unique domain names for this firm, using a variety of strategies for creating a distinctive and effective label for the company.

12.2 PLANNING AND DESIGNING AN EFFECTIVE WEB SITE

In the early days of the Internet, simply having a Web site was a way to differentiate a business from its competition. As interest in the Web developed and grew, companies of all shapes and sizes focused their efforts on capturing people's attention with Web sites. Because of growth in online competition, planning a site and building a distinctive design became more and more important. After all, a great site encourages current customer loyalty and promotes an e-business's presence to the new shoppers who come online every day.

The same basic principles of Web site design apply as much now as they did when the Web began in the mid-1990s. Technologies used on the Web might come and go, but including the latest and greatest technology on a site is not always necessary. Customers are drawn to sites that are simple, focused, easy to use, well organized, and useful. Everything else is just sound and fury.

This section explains how to create a Web site that serves both a business and its customers. The process starts with defining exactly what the site should be, then turns to implementing the ideas developed by using effective design principles and keeping customer needs in mind.

12.2.1 Mapping a Successful Site

When people build a new house, they don't just hire a contractor, bring over the concrete and tools, and say "Go for it." Before construction even begins, they craft a carefully detailed plan that they review, edit, and approve. Web sites should be treated the same way. The best sites are not dreamed up by eccentric designers and thrown together quickly. Good sites require a clear road map from the people who run the business to ensure that the focus of the firm is never lost.

Start the Web site planning process by making a list of all the functions that will be provided on the site. Owners tempted to believe that their site has just one function—to sell things—can identify subfunctions by answering these questions:

- **What kinds of products will be sold?** The number and organization of pages on a site depends on the makeup and complexity of the products or services. For example, there should be at least one page for each category of product.
- **How many distinct categories of products will there be?** There should be a separate page for each product category. Consider splitting up categories like consumer electronics and computer products, for example.
- **Will customers be able to create an account?** If so, a page is needed where customers can log in, update their personal information, view their orders, and enter payment information.
- **Will customers be provided with additional content?** Some Web sites make money by offering a subscription for their customers to read premium content such as special articles, interviews, or video, audio, or photo excerpts.
- **How will customers pay for their orders?** Sites need to be able to accept credit card orders as well as other alternative payment options.
- **Will there be instructions for using the Web site?** There should be a page for Frequently Asked Questions (FAQ) to help their customers use the site properly.

Site map:
A diagram showing the pages needed by a Web page to accomplish its desired functions, as well as the relationship of those pages to one another.

After developing a list of site functions, the next step is to draw a **site map**—a diagram showing the Web pages needed in order to accomplish those functions and the relationship of those pages to one another. At this point, it is not important to think about how the Web site or the individual pages will look; just identify the different pages that need to exist. Assign each page to a box on the map, and check off the function that the page will manage. The results will be a map of the site that looks like a flowchart (see Figure 12-2).

At the top of the map is the home page, which is the launch pad to the rest of the Web site. The page answers all the basic questions that customers have about the business, just like the friendly receptionist in the lobby of a 50-story building. Whether the visit is the first—or the 50th—for customers, the home page must answer their questions in a clear, concise, and organized way or be able to point them in the right direction quickly.

Build a Web page that holds a text version of this map for viewing by customers. Just like a road atlas helps drivers follow their route, the site map helps online customers find anything available on the site without taking a wrong turn—or, in this case, a wrong click.

Below the home page are the main category pages. Although the first draft might look like the one in Figure 12-2, the beauty of a map is that the

Figure 12-2

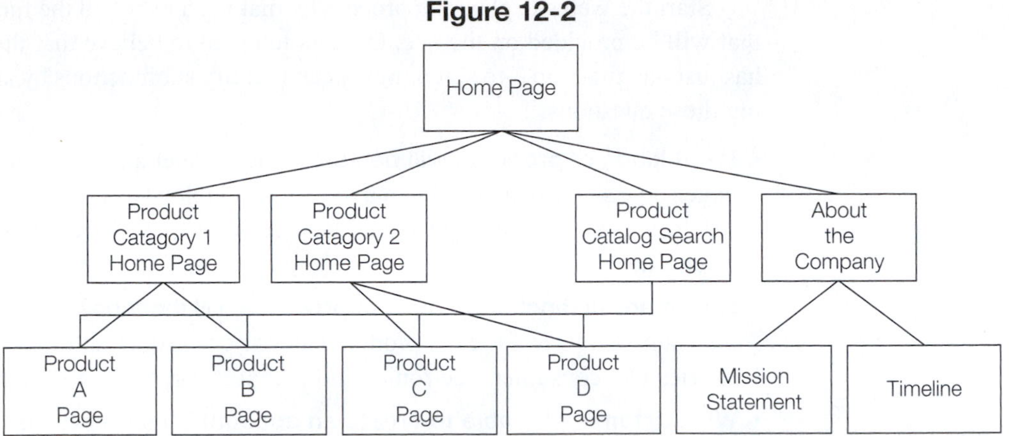

The home page on a Web site leads into all the categories.

site plan can expand and grow from the basic model. As the design gets more complex, it is simple to add more levels to the Web site map. When building a site map this way, it is easy to visualize how the entire site operates, because it captures how pages support each other.

12.2.2 Basic Design Principles

First impressions are lasting ones, or so the old saying implies. When visitors first visit a Web site, they decide what they think about it within the first few seconds. Often a favorable impression is based entirely on the design elements encountered. From classic to vintage or from plain-Jane to modern, establishing the appropriate look sets the tone for an entire site. When thinking about site design, consider these elements that contribute to a timeless look. Don't forget to include the essential parts of an e-commerce Web site, as outlined in Figure 12-3.

Figure 12-3

Most e-commerce Web sites have a basic list of pages that they provide to their customers. As you're designing your own site, take a look at the functions most sites provide and decide which ones are right for your business:

- ✓ Home page
- ✓ Catalog page
- ✓ Customer account page
- ✓ Order information page
- ✓ Frequently Asked Questions page
- ✓ Content pages
- ✓ Map and direction page (if you have a retail site)
- ✓ Checkout page
- ✓ Payment processing page (possibly on someone else's site)
- ✓ About Us or Company History page (describes mission, purpose, or employees, for example)

Site-builder checklist.

Structure

The foundation of a site's design is its structure, or its layout. Determining the layout of a site requires making decisions about these elements:

- **Number of pages:** Consider the depth of the site (the number of pages that are necessary).
- **Placement of the navigational toolbar** (the series of buttons or links that visitors use to visit different areas of your site): Referred to as a toolbar, navigation bar, or menu bar, it is commonly placed along the left side of the site, along the top, or in both places.
- **Buttons, tabs, and links:** Buttons in the navigation bar come in unlimited designs, shapes, and colors (depending on the software you use). Another option is to use text, rather than a button, as a link. It might be desirable to repeat a navigational bar in the form of tabs at the top of the page or even use links at the bottom of the page.

Color

The color scheme selected is an especially influential design element. Will the target audience prefer bold and bright or soft and understated? Another consideration is how to incorporate those colors (or lack thereof) into the site. Color can be used as a background for an entire site, to highlight sections of text, or to separate segments within a site by using borders or blocks of color.

The psychology of color choice is thought to influence everything from customers' moods to their buying behavior.

FOR EXAMPLE

For more information on how color can affect customers, check out the "Color Think Tank" on the Pantone (a leading color company) Web site: www.pantone.com.

Font

The type and size of font used throughout a site makes a strong statement. There are thousands of font styles to select from, and each sends its own message to customers. Additionally, the text size used contributes to not only the look of the site, but also its readability. For example, text that is too small may not be easy to read. Table 12-2 lists sample fonts and explains what the styles say to customers.

Images

The use of photos and graphics (animated or otherwise) can complement a site, if they are used correctly. Images help draw readers' eyes to specific areas of a site and can help illustrate information and ideas. When selling

Table 12-2 Common Fonts for Web Sites

Font	*Message It Sends*
Arial	I am common and nondescript.
Comic Sans	I'm choosing whimsy over seriousness.
Courier New	I'm old-fashioned, from the era of newsroom typewriters.
Georgia	I'm classic and professional and layered with style.
Times New Roman	I'm quite traditional.
Trebuchet	I'm professional yet relaxed (similar to casual Friday in a workplace).
Verdana	I emit a friendly, modern vibe.

products, high-quality images are a necessity. When designing the site, think about how many images will be used, what size they need to be, and where they should be placed for the best effect.

Media

As the Internet matures, more Web sites are incorporating video and sound clips. For some sites, this capability becomes an intricate design element. For others, whether to use some form of media becomes a function issue (do customers even have the ability to view video and sound clips?). If that is the case, evaluate whether customers will view this media as adding to or detracting from a site's usability.

12.2.3 Critical Design Decisions

A number of decisions to make when developing the design—the look and feel—of a Web site should be controlled in large part by the nature of the e-business and the products or services offered for sale. Generally, one or more of these characteristics dictate a site's look:

- **Industry or line of business:** Conservative industries, such as accounting or financial services, will probably want to select subdued colors with a simple layout. Alternatively, if a potential customer is searching for a graphic designer, the customer might expect to see a bright, funky design with lots of colorful images.

- **Products or services offered:** Selling products or services that have a serious message (such as medical equipment) begs for a low-key design approach. Plus, the information provided may require many layers of pages. On the other hand, products that are fun or made for recreational purposes might sell better if the site is light and whimsical and filled with product images rather than product data.
- **An existing brand:** A site's style or look might be predetermined by a company's physical store or product base. The site's image must be consistent with an established brand. Pull design elements for the Web site from marketing materials, or from the existing bricks-and-mortar location.
- **Customers' demographics and psychographics:** Age, gender, education, and geographic location of customers are among the factors that should be considered to create the appropriate feel for a site.

An essential consideration in designing a Web site is to create a timeless look. A common pet peeve among customers is a site that is outdated and stuck in the 1990s. An outdated Web site gives the image the company does not care about its business or its customers. To create a Web site that is considered timeless, keep these three suggestions in mind:

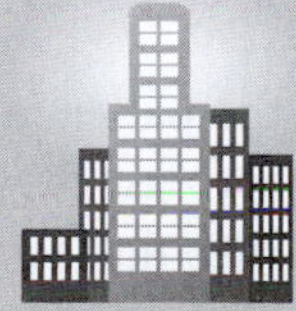

IN THE REAL WORLD

Avoiding Design Mistakes

Laura Wheeler knows a thing or two about bad Web sites, and she's happy to share her thoughts on her site Bad Website Ideas (www.badwebsiteideas.com). Wheeler, a Web designer and home business shoestring startup expert, covers design problems such as Bad Backgrounds, Useless Pages, Excess Ads, Flashing Text, even Purely Ugly. Though the site does not show examples of existing bad sites, Wheeler's goal is to teach others "how to avoid the really bad website mistakes."

1. **Keep it simple.** Keeping design elements simple and using only one or two trendy features increases the design life span of a site. A prime example is Google. Its overall site design is clean and basic, which lends itself to its original purpose as a search engine.
2. **Keep the information updated and relevant.** This advice includes keeping everything from text and photos to hypertext links and copyright dates update. Keeping the substance of a site current offers value.
3. **Avoid images or graphics that visually date the site.** Avoid using photos of current events that can quickly date a site. Similarly, photos of people can be telltale signs of an outdated site because of clothing and hair.

12.2.4 Checklist for Customer-Friendly Web Sites

When designing a Web site, keep the customer experience first and foremost. E-commerce sites exist to deliver products or services to customers. Good sites accomplish that task in such a way that customers want to return to purchase again. Bad sites send customers looking for an alternative. Thus it is essential to build in customer-friendly functionality.

In planning and designing a site, consider the subject of customer-friendly functions at three levels. At the first level are basic functions. Customers always expect this lowest, or base, level of functionality. Basic functions include these features:

- **Quick-loading pages:** Customers do not have the patience to wait for pages to load. E-commerce sites are even expected to ease the problem for customers using slow dial-up connections. Web sites that fail to account for varying speeds of Internet access in Web design will lose sales—it is that simple.
- **Easy navigation:** When customers go from page to page, the navigation tools should allow customers to readily find and identify navigational buttons and links, immediately return to the home page; return to the last-visited page by clicking a link, and see pages and sections visited on the site through a link history.
- **Working links:** All internal and external links should be valid and working. Customers do not want to click a link and find a message saying "Page Not Found." Broken links that go nowhere also diminish the credibility of a site and indicate that it is not regularly updated or maintained.
- **Viewable images:** All images—especially product images—must load correctly and quickly. Avoid using grainy pictures or tiny images that are difficult for customers to see.

At the second level of site functionality are interactive functions, which actively engage customers. Although an interactive function is unnecessary to place an order, interactivity can increase value and sales. Samples of interactive functions include:

- **Site search:** Give customers a tool that allows them to quickly search for information within the site.
- **Downloadable documents:** Consider offering visitors the option to download information—PDF documents of articles, research papers, product reviews, and owner's manuals.
- **Discussion boards and blogs:** Message boards, bulletin boards, discussion boards, chat rooms, and blogs are options that allow visitors to interact with an e-business and with one another. Many people consider discussion boards a free form of tech support.

The third level is reserved for tools and features that offer customers an enhanced experience on a site. Items of enhanced functionality often include:

- **Online demonstrations and tutorials:** Depending on the complexity of the products or services, online demos and Web-based tutorials can be useful.
- **Live or 24/7 customer support:** The Internet never sleeps, and neither do some customers, who may need questions asked in the middle of the night before making a purchase.
- **Second-language viewing options:** Not all customers speak fluent English. Savvy Web site owners offer customers the option to view sites in other languages. (Spanish is the most popular alternative in the United States.)
- **New media:** Video and sound clips serve a purpose, and these options have increasingly become standard. Try adding podcasts or Web conferences (conference calls over the Internet that allow for participant interaction).

IN THE REAL WORLD

The Story Behind the Site

Diane Gracely's dream was to have a home business run by family. A new interest in golf led the 43 year old to that dream when she noticed something missing from the world of golf accessories—classic knit golf club covers, the kind from the early days with the pom poms. With the encouragement of her family and a friend who owned a yarn store, Gracely began Kewl Tubes (as in "cool") in February 2006 and now designs and sells custom tube-style club covers to customers worldwide. Gracely knits the designs from her home in Reading, Pennsylvania; her mother-in-law assists with orders; and her husband is her partner. The designs have been purchased by pro and amateur golfers, pro shops, retail stores, golf tournaments, college golf teams, and more. Gracely's Web site, www.kewltubes.com, is a simple, no-frills site that allows customers to view color options, check out design samples, and place orders. Those customers who read Gracely's "About Us" page may be surprised to learn that Gracely's dream has a story behind it. At 15, Gracely was diagnosed with Charcot-Marie-Tooth disease, a degenerative neurological disorder that greatly affected her mobility and led to years of foot reconstruction surgeries. Though the surgeries have brought her relief, she still experiences some problems—making the success of her home-based business even more important. Gracely's site was named as one of StartupNation's top 100 home-based businesses of 2007.

SELF-CHECK

1. In what way is page structure an important component of design? How about color?
2. What four critical factors control the direction of Web page design?
3. What is the basic level of functions that should be incorporated into every e-commerce site design?

Apply Your Knowledge Draw a simple site map for a Web site selling designer hats, belts, and shoes. Include the basic functions that will make the site useful to customers.

12.3 WORKING WITH A PROFESSIONAL WEB DESIGNER

Effective entrepreneurs get ahead by understanding their strengths and weaknesses: They focus on their strengths and get others to manage functions that are their weaknesses. Many people who want to operate their own online business are not necessarily designers, and nothing is wrong with that. Instead, many e-business owners hire a professional designer to create their Web site. The right interactions and communications with a professional designer can fuel a great site, and can even improve an overall business model so that increased orders and higher visibility help recover the time and money spent on the professional expertise.

Some people consult with professional designers to create their sites and then obtain the tools necessary to maintain their sites without any additional help. Other business owners contract with professionals to create and maintain their sites. Both approaches have advantages and disadvantages, and deciding on an appropriate level of outside help is an important part of designing and operating a Web site.

12.3.1 Choosing the Right Designer

Half the battle of finding a Web site designer is deciding to hire one in the first place. The other half of the battle involves knowing where to look and talking to potential candidates. Finding the right designer is similar to finding other specialists needed to solve specific problems. Consider these methods for finding a qualified professional Web designer:

- **Listen to word-of-mouth advice.** Talk to friends, business associates, or anyone else with a Web site. Find out which Web site designers they have used, and solicit their opinions regarding these professionals.
- **See the work designers have done.** Visit Web sites that are enjoyable to use. Most of the time, a small link or reference at the bottom of the home page mentions whether a professional designer created the site. Follow the link back to the designer's site for more information.
- **Evaluate designers' portfolios.** Use search engines, read relevant magazines, or look around to find a few companies. Then evaluate the samples or references they provide. See whether their work for other people is good enough or fits the style desired.

Consider two primary options when shopping for a design professional: working with a design firm or hiring an individual freelance designer.

Using a Web Design Firm

From the early days of the Internet, Web design companies have focused on providing quality work for their clients. Going to a design firm provides specific benefits for completing a project:

- **Reliability:** If a designer is having a bad day, week, month, or even year, a design firm can shift the workload away from that person and get backup or additional resources to cover the job. Design firms typically have contacts with freelance designers who come into the firm when needed to help tackle a big problem.
- **Coordination:** If several designers are working on a project, a design firm can coordinate the work and provide a single point of contact who communicates ideas and tasks to the design team.
- **Experience:** Design firms have a portfolio of past projects and experience that lends itself to a project. The firm can bring their know-how and expertise without having to navigate a large learning curve.

Using a Freelancer

Instead of using a firm for Web design, another option is to choose one of the many talented individuals who work on a freelance basis and take on specific clients and projects that fit into their schedules. Some are part-timers, some do it as a full-time career. Some are very good, but others might lack desirable skills. Though it can be risky, choosing a freelance designer over a design firm comes with its own set of benefits:

- **Costs less to hire:** When hiring a design firm, part of the cost goes toward maintaining the overhead costs of the company. A freelance designer typically charges less per hour or per project than the average design firm.
- **Works more nimbly:** A design firm may require decisions and work to be done in various committees, with approval required at all stages by the firm's managers. The design firm system can slow the progress of a Web site's development, and if speed is a top concern, a freelance designer may produce results more quickly.
- **Provides a unique style:** Although designing a Web site is definitely a mixture of art and science, the creativity may not come from a firm that has developed policies and procedures for designing clients' Web sites. An individual freelance designer can bring their own creative style to a project, which may result in a truly unique Web site.

12.3.2 Web Design Pricing Issues

When choosing a Web site designer, comparing quoted prices is an important aspect of the decision-making process. However, consider factors that can skew the math and thereby make comparisons invalid. A price for designing a Web site is normally determined in one of two ways:

Flat-fee pricing: One price covers complete Web site development.

Per-hour pricing: Web site development time is billed at an hourly rate, often with no upper limit for billing.

1. **Flat-fee pricing:** One price covers the complete site development.
2. **Per-hour pricing:** Development time is billed at an hourly rate, with no upper limit for billing.

Flat-fee and per-hour pricing are different approaches to determining price, and on the surface, both options appear to have advantages. For example, the flat-fee option implies that the cost will never exceed the quote—but that is not always the case. If a designer or firm quotes a flat fee for a project, ask for a specific list of what is provided and what is excluded for that fee. Some quotes exclude "extras" that are an important part of the design and launch process. Also, ask about what happens if someone has to spend overtime hours to complete the project. One benefit of having a flat fee is not worrying about the number of hours invested in building a site. But some design professionals specify a maximum number of hours for the flat fee offered. Extra hours require the client paying more. The lesson is to require the offer in writing, read the contract carefully, and ask questions before signing.

When requesting a quote on the basis of per-hour pricing, always ask for time estimates on the various pieces of the project, function by function. A comprehensive quote with a detailed breakdown ensures that the designer has factored in all the tasks expected by the client, plus exposes any unrealistic time estimates. Detailed, itemized quotes are also much easier to compare and to determine which designer is actually providing the lowest price—or the highest level of service—for their time.

Another strategy for effectively working with a per-hour designer is to ask for limits to be put into place. Without limits, a designer can easily quote a specific number of hours and then exceed that number at their discretion. Establishing limits for specific parts of the project is important, especially for less-complicated pages. The designer should also be required to obtain approval to exceed the time quoted and provide an explanation of why the extra time is needed.

Regardless of how a designer or firm charges for their services, establish before you begin who pays if a bug or error in the work is discovered in the future. Web designers may offer a lower quote in return for excluding the cost of corrections or changes after the project is complete. Wise business owners avoid such offers. Request written assurances that the designer will spend the time necessary to correct any problems and specify that full payment will be withheld until the Web site is designed, launched, and functioning to your satisfaction.

12.3.3 Managing the Web Designer Relationship

When hiring a Web site design professional, the expectation is that an e-business owner does not need to know how to use HTML or have any design skills. That is why a professional is being hired. However, the design professional will have expectations about how e-business owners participate in the project, how business operations are reflected in the site, and who owns the rights to the resulting site and its content. E-business owners must clearly understand their role in the process so that the owner can contribute to a successful site.

After a design firm or freelance designer has been selected, every e-business should complete the following seven steps to ensure a successful relationship with the designer and to proceed efficiently with the design process.

Outline the Business and Its Practices

Web site designers are not necessarily businesspeople. Designers cannot be expected to understand the intricacies of every e-business. Before design begins, e-business owners need to explain how their site should operate and why "the owner wants the site to operate in that manner." Specify any rules for selling goods and services. For example, if a minimum order amount or specific product combinations are excluded, business rules relating to the order requirements must be a part of the Web site plan.

Prepare Site Specifications Upfront

Before meeting with a designer, the e-business owner should have a clear idea of site structure. Prepare a written map of the site (as discussed in Section 12.2.1) and provide notes on the various Web pages that are essential to the site. Feel free to brainstorm with the Web designer about the site, but the process will be much more efficient with an initial road map already in place.

Establish Firm Milestones

During the initial meeting with the Web designer, establish rough dates for checking on progress, plus firm dates for important milestones—end dates for specific portions of the site. Although some Web designers would like to avoid specifying dates, maintaining firm-specific dates is required to manage a professional relationship. E-business owners need to see steady progress on their site and have the ability to make necessary changes before everything is completed.

Have All Relevant Content Prepared

Make sure that the content for the site is available in electronic format. The content consists of not only the names and descriptions of products, but also any product databases, pictures, pricing information, company logo (unless the designer is creating the logo), mission statement, contact information, and other data. If necessary, hire a typist to create electronic text or Word document files containing the pertinent information.

Make Computer Systems Available

Web site designers need to have access to an e-business's computer systems while building a site; this is especially true for more complex sites that operate on a Web server and communicate with programs such as a database, a supplier's inventory system, or a third-party payment solution. The quicker that access is provided, and the more documentation that is made available about the interlocking programs, the quicker the designer can turn around a correctly built Web site.

Be Readily Available to Assist the Designer

Make sure that the owner or key decision maker is available to answer questions and to provide information to the Web site designer. Avoid leaving a designer waiting to get necessary information or answers to questions. No matter how much detail is provided in the beginning, questions will be asked. E-business owners should be accessible at all times during the design process, or call in and check email regularly.

Clarifying Who Owns What

An important and often overlooked aspect of the design process is establishing ownership of the work after it is complete. Many e-business owners assume that paying a professional to do the work automatically creates a work-for-hire agreement giving the owner full rights to the resulting site and its content. That is not always true. In fact, the ownership and the work-for-hire relationship should be specifically detailed in the contract before design begins. Be certain that items such as photos, graphical images, and functions do not carry any unexpected licenses or require extra payment.

After the site design is complete, ask the designer for a copy of the Web site, either available online as a backup copy or on a CD or DVD to ensure that the e-business owner has a full copy available to keep the Web site operating if the Web server crashes or the relationship with the Web designer is dissolved.

IN THE REAL WORLD

A Site Designed for a Cause

In some cases, a successful Web site design can do more than just make a profit—it can save lives. Nothing But Nets is a grassroots campaign to save lives by preventing malaria, a leading killer of children in Africa. The campaign was the result of an article written by Rick Reilly in *Sports Illustrated*. Reilly challenged each reader to donate $10 for the purchase of anti-malaria bed nets. The response was incredible—more than $1 million—and has continued through the campaign's site, NothingButNets.net, which was a 2007 Webby award winner. The site, offers resources on malaria, downloadable toolkits to help raise awareness and organize fundraising events, and the ability to create or join a fundraising team. With its hip design and user-friendly approach, NothingButNet.net makes it seem easy for one person to make a difference; the site features a "Net-O-Meter" with a running tally of each net that's been purchased as well as NothingButNet merchandise for purchase.

SELF-CHECK

1. What are the advantages of using a Web design firm? Of using an individual freelance designer?
2. Explain the difference between flat-fee and per-hour pricing and the issues related to each option.
3. Why are milestones important in managing a Web site design project?

Apply Your Knowledge You are an e-business owner with no Web design experience trying to decide whether to create a site yourself or hire an outside designer. Identify five critical issues in making the decision. Explain the advantages or disadvantages of creating the site yourself or hiring a designer. Choose an option and explain why you made the choice.

12.4 LAUNCHING A NEW WEB SITE

Launching and *uploading* are both terms used to represent when a site is made available to the public over the Internet. Before uploading a site to the Internet, though, the site should be fully functional. Site design and content should be complete, navigation tools should work properly, and all parts of the site—even the smallest parts and pieces—must be in place and working.

What if an e-business is working in a competitive market and getting online fast seems to be more important than getting all a site's bug worked out? Launching an incomplete site is a bad idea and only diminishes a business's credibility. Remember, first impressions are the most important. By ensuring that the site is fully functional and working properly, the e-business will be able to compete effectively the first day.

The sections that follow will review some of the critical aspects to consider when publishing a site to the Internet. Some of the tasks are tedious, but the time investment in the beginning will help ensure e-business success in the long run.

12.4.1 Things to Know Before Launching

E-businesses working with an experienced professional Web designer will probably encounter fewer problems than entrepreneurs that work alone, but all first-time e-business owners will need to keep perspective when launching a new site. Things rarely go perfectly from the beginning, which is why a carefully planned testing and evaluation phase is so important. Patience is also important; e-business owners should keep the following truisms in mind in preparing for launch:

- **Some functions are limited until after the launch.** A few features may fully function only after a site is live. For instance, forms can frequently be activated only after the site is launched.
- **Little details count.** Bring out the magnifying glass when reviewing a site for mistakes before launching. Check for misspellings, broken links, and other problem points. One seemingly minor error can undermine the entire function of an e-commerce site.
- **Automated Web builders are different from designers.** Sites created by a professional designer, or by using a Web authoring program, launch immediately because all the completed files are uploaded to the server at one time. Automated Web builders or template programs, often require publishing a site page by page to the Internet. Use special care with automated Web builders: Correcting problems to buttons or to the site's menu bar may be difficult after the site is published.

- **Third-party data takes time.** Newsfeeds, syndicated content, or other data from third parties may not be instantly available when the site launches. A delay of several hours, or even a full day, may occur before the site is entered into a customer database and the content is delivered.
- **Rankings are not immediate (or guaranteed).** After a site is launched, time is required for a search engine to scan and rank a site. Initially, only people who are purposefully looking for a site by typing the exact URL or company name in a search will find it, but this is no cause for immediate concern.
- **Sites look different to different people.** The code or language used to design a site appears differently when it's viewed with various browsers. That is why it is so important to test content with every browser available and minimize the differences so that the site looks its best in any browser. Section 12.4.2 offers advice on compatibility testing strategies.

12.4.2 Compatibility Testing

Many people consider compatibility testing the fun part of launching a site, but it is also an essential part of the process. Any slight variation between the code and the way each browser interprets the code makes a noticeable difference on the user's screen. Minor differences may appear across platforms (Mac versus PC) and between varying screen resolutions on different monitors.

Browser Compatibility

Compatibility: How effectively a Web site functions with a particular Web browser, monitor resolution, or computer platform.

Compatibility refers to how effectively a Web site functions with a particular Web browser (or monitor resolution or computer platform). The best way to check for browser discrepancies is to install every possible browser (or at least the mainstream ones) and run a trial version of the Web site in each one. Because browsers can be downloaded for free, the only cost is time, and it is an outstanding investment. When reviewing the site in each browser, look for glaring inconsistencies that make information difficult to read, prevent images from loading, or omit information. Completely eliminating problems may be impossible, but minor formatting changes can minimize problems without undermining design. The rule of thumb is to optimize Web site appearance for major browsers, while working to achieve decent functionality on lesser browsers.

Resolution: The number of pixels that make up an image on the computer screen, usually expressed as a horizontal by vertical measurement.

Screen Resolution

It is a good idea to test how a site looks in different monitor resolution settings. **Resolution** refers to the number of pixels that make up an image on the computer screen. Standard resolution settings are 640 × 480, 600 × 400, and 1024 × 768. Within each resolution is a designated amount of viewable space, which can affect how a Web site looks on a computer. Computer users can choose which resolution to use on their computers. Take a look at what the site looks like in a variety of resolutions on different browsers. Some changes may be necessary to make the site easily viewable in some resolutions. Recommend resolution settings (for example, on an FAQ page) for optimal viewing of the site.

Testing on Different Platforms

Another major element in testing a site before launching is to evaluate the site's performance on different operating systems. Windows is still the dominant operating system, but Macintosh OS X and Linux are quietly taking a larger portion of market share. The reality is that Web sites designed on one operating system do not always look or function the same on another platform (and that includes different versions of Windows or Mac OS X). Ideally, e-business owners should maintain multiple platforms in their facility (at least Windows and Mac) to continually monitor their sites. Another option is to use a site that offers the service remotely (over the Internet) for free or for a minimal fee. For example, BrowserCam.com (www.browsercam.com) uses screen captures to provide views of a site on any operating system and in any browser.

12.4.3 Trial Run and Launch

When a major company releases a software program, the company often begins with limited distribution in a **beta version.** "Beta" means that the work is in test mode and is subject to change. A beta test is also a good strategy for small e-businesses to employ—showing a beta version of its Web site to a limited group of users in a trial run. The users can ideally include friends, family, and a few prospective customers who are willing to provide honest feedback. Upload the site and run a live trial version of it for a day or two. Everyone has an opportunity to visit the site several times before closing the site for final changes.

Beta version: Software or a Web site in a test mode and subject to change.

Beta users should be on the lookout for common errors—features or links that fail to work or graphics that load improperly—and the beta users should review the general appearance and overall ease of use of the site. Is the site intuitive to visitors? Do the names of the page links and buttons make sense? Take the beta tester's feedback and make the appropriate changes, and get ready for the real launch. Check the list in Figure 12-4 to make sure you're ready for the real launch.

Consider when a site is launched, particularly when using an outside Web site designer. Request that the site be launched early in the week. That way, if a problem surfaces, there is ample time—the entire workweek—to repair the site. Launching a site created by an outside designer on Friday

Figure 12-4

Are you ready to take your Web site live? Before you push that last button to make your site a reality, be sure that you check off each box (as it applies to you) on this list:

- ❑ My site map (or the layout and structure of all my Web pages) is complete.
- ❑ The site map matches my Web pages—exactly.
- ❑ Each Web site page is displayed and is fully accessible.
- ❑ Every link throughout the site works properly and takes me to the appropriate page.
- ❑ All graphics and photos are loaded quickly and completely, and the images are crisp and clean.
- ❑ My content is free of misspellings and grammatical errors.
- ❑ Pricing information and product or service descriptions are correct.
- ❑ Pages with online forms or registration information function when I press the Submit button, and the information is sent (in the specified format) to the designated point of contact.
- ❑ Text boxes or drop-down boxes on forms and other pages work correctly.
- ❑ Buttons for top-level menus work. (Ensure that these buttons, like the one that returns users to your home page, function properly on each and every single page.)
- ❑ Special commands that are spelled out with coding language (HTML or PHP, for example) show up properly when the site loads.
- ❑ My credit card processor or other payment service option is in place and working.
- ❑ All e-commerce–related functions, such as my shopping cart, operate correctly.
- ❑ Any membership icons/logos (such as member of Better Business Bureau and/or Chamber of Commerce emblems) are included.
- ❑ I tested the site for browser compatibility and screen resolution.
- ❑ The site was tested using a dial-up connection and a broadband connection.
- ❑ Contact information using my email address or phone number is clearly displayed and easy to find.
- ❑ The copyright symbol and current year are prominently placed at the bottom of every page.

Your site-launch checklist

afternoon is a formula for frustration; few things are more frustrating than having to endure an entire weekend with a nonfunctioning site.

Even companies that design their own sites should be cautious about their launch schedule. Avoid getting greedy; choose a period when business is likely to be slow. The slower period actually gives a company an extended period for a trial run—and more opportunities to correct errors. Instead of launching on busy holiday weekends, launch a site in advance, then use strategic marketing to direct users to the site once the site has proven itself able to manage heavy traffic.

Remember, nothing has to be forever on the Web. If a mistake is discovered after a Web site is launched, do not panic. Corrections can often be easily and instantaneously made—that is one of the beautiful things about doing business on the Internet.

IN THE REAL WORLD

Going Online with Action Sports

NossaTV, an action sports video service, tested the beta version of its site (www.NossaTv.com) in 2007 in anticipation of its full launch in spring 2008. The site, which offers enthusiasts a way to view free, full-length films of skateboarding, surfing, etc., from independent filmmakers, is supported by advertisers looking to reach this niche market of action sports consumers. Using a feedback option on the beta version, NossaTV's creators encouraged users to have a say in how the site works and what it looks like. In late 2007, the NossaTV.com player only ran on Windows XP; however, the site offered visitors a way to sign up and be notified when the Mac-compatible version was online.

SELF-CHECK

1. When testing a Web site prior to launch (when it is not live) is it reasonable to expect all functions to work? Explain why or why not.
2. What are the three primary types of compatibility testing that should be conducted before going live?
3. What is beta testing and how can it be used prior to launching a Web site?

Apply Your Knowledge Download three different Web browsers available for your computer. Select a little-known e-commerce site and tour the site using the different browsers. Make note of any differences. What changes would you make, if any, to improve performance/appearance?

SUMMARY

Section 12.1

- Two common strategies for selecting domain names are to match the company name as closely as possible or choose a name that clearly indicates the nature of the business. Effective domain names are short, are easy to spell and remember, contain important keywords, are intuitive, and are alphabetically strategic.
- Domain names must be registered with a domain registrar to verify their availability and assign exclusive use to a given business. If a desired name is unavailable, there are a variety of options, including selecting a similar alternative, putting the name on back order, or making an offer to purchase from the existing owner, either directly or through a registrar.

Section 12.2

- The first step in effective Web site design is listing all the functions that need to be accomplished by the site, and then drawing a map that illustrates the pages needed to complete those functions and how they relate to each other.
- Positive customer impressions are made by using basic principles of good design, paying special attention to page structure, color, fonts, images, and use of new media.
- Web site design should be determined by factors such as the nature of the e-business, the products sold, and the demographics of the target customers. Web sites should strive for simplicity and timelessness so that the site is easy to use and does not become outdated quickly.

Section 12.3

- When working with an outside designer, e-businesses typically choose between working with a design firm or an individual freelance designer. The cost of Web site design is usually quoted on a flat-fee or hourly basis.
- Working effectively with an outside designer demands considerable advance work, including preparing a site plan, establishing milestones, having all content prepared, and clarifying ownership of the material created. E-business owners should be prepared to be readily available to answer questions and provide data to avoid delaying the process.

Section 12.4

- Prior to launching, all new Web sites should be tested for compatibility with a variety of browsers, monitor resolutions, and computer platforms. Wise business owners go through beta testing with a limited number of users to identify and correct problems prior to a full launch.

ASSESS YOUR UNDERSTANDING

UNDERSTAND: WHAT HAVE YOU LEARNED?

Go to **www.wiley.com/college/holden** to assess your knowledge of the basics of designing a Web site for an e-business.

APPLY: WHAT WOULD YOU DO?

1. Decode the following three URLs, identifying each element of the addresses:
   - http://shopping.discovery.com/category-1_SHOPBYSHOW/3_SHOW_SER_DIRTYJOBS-27993.html
   - http://www.chickchocolates.com/findstore.asp
   - http://custom-hats.lids.com/faq.html
2. Evaluate the following domain names using the criteria outlined in Section 12.1.2:
   - insanechicken.com
   - findyourfate.com
   - evitamins.com
3. You've been making it for your friends and family for years, and you've finally decided to sell your peanut brittle on the Internet. The domain name peanutbrittle.com is taken; come up with two alternative names.
4. For the same peanut brittle business, draft an effective site map for the Web site.
5. Discuss your first impression of www.flickr.com, an online photo management site. Base your impression on the site's structure, as well as the site's use of color, font, images, and media.
6. You're about to sign a contract with a Web designer to design your business site. Draft a memo outlining the seven steps to ensuring a successful working relationship.
7. Explain the difference between an automated Web builder and a designer.

8. You and your business partner are hoping to launch your Web site sometime in the next week. Create a checklist of ten things that should be done before the business goes online.
9. Give an example of a situation in which launching a beta version makes good business sense.

BE AN E-BUSINESS ENTREPRENEUR

Making a Name for Your Business

A Web site domain name can mean the success or failure of an e-business. Based on a hobby or interest, come up with a Web site idea and an effective domain name. Complete the following:

- Write your first choice for a domain name.
- Determine if the name is already being used.
- If necessary, come up with a viable alternate name.
- Evaluate the name you choose using the criteria from Section 12.1.2.

Customer-Friendly or Not?

Good Web sites provide the kind of experience that makes customers want to come back. Find two competing Web sites (Shoes.com and Zappos.com, for example) and rate the two using the following guidelines:

- Does it have quick-loading pages?
- Is it easy to navigate?
- Do the links work?
- Are images available?
- Is there a site search option?

Serving Up Customer Satisfaction

In today's competitve market, a site's design needs to capture the attention of an increasingly tech-savvy market. Customers are looking for tools and features that offer an enhanced experience:

- Online demonstrations and tutorials
- Live or 24/7 customer support
- Second language versions
- New media

Judge your favorite retail Web site based on those tools and features. What is missing? What is effective?

KEY TERMS

Beta version	Software or a Web site in a test mode and subject to change.
Compatibility	How effectively a Web site functions with a particular Web browser, monitor resolution, or computer platform.
Domain name	The part of the URL that specifically identifies the name of a Web site.
Domain registrar	An organization that takes care of all the paperwork required to register and to activate a new domain name for an e-business.
Flat-fee pricing	One price covers complete Web site development.
Per-hour pricing	Web site development time is billed at an hourly rate, often with no upper limit for billing.
Resolution	The number of pixels that make up an image on the computer screen, usually expressed as a horizontal by vertical measurement.
Site map	A diagram showing the pages needed by a Web page to accomplish its desired functions, as well as the relationship of those pages to one another.
Uniform Resource Locator (URL)	The unique address for each page on a Web site or document posted online.

REFERENCES

1. Nick Leiber, "America's Best Young Entrepreneurs," BusinessWeek.com, www.businessweek.com/smallbiz/content/oct2007/sb20071019_394343_page_2.htm.

CHAPTER

13 TRACKING AND ANALYZING CUSTOMER DATA

Gather the Information Necessary for Measuring Web Site Performance

Do You Already Know?

- What log files are
- How traffic-analysis software works
- How to use cookies to track visitor information
- How to use benchmarks to identify problem areas

For additional questions to assess your current knowledge on tracking and analyzing customer data for e-businesses, go to **www.wiley.com/ college/holden.**

What You Will Find Out	What You Will Be Able To Do
13.1 Which data to track and how to interpret the various customer visit logs created by Web servers	Interpret log files, referrer files, error logs, abandoned shopping cart logs, and entry and exit logs
13.2 How traffic-analysis software works and which packages are right for various types of e-businesses	Select and use traffic-analysis software that is appropriate for your e-business
13.3 The various methods for purposefully collecting customer information	Use cookies, keywords appended to links, customer path analysis, and log-in forms to gather customer information
13.4 How to use benchmarks to identify trends and the need for changes; how to correctly implement and follow up on changes to a Web site	Identify when and where changes are appropriate; effectively implement changes; follow up after changes

INTRODUCTION

Every retail business needs to do a thorough job of tracking their customer traffic to determine what is working and what is not. This tracking needs to include more than just keeping an eye on sales numbers—it is just as important to determine in which parts of the stores customers are spending most of their time, which products they are browsing, and—just as importantly—which departments and products they are avoiding. Tracking customer traffic for e-businesses is a challenge because online stores are not nearly as transparent as physical retail stores. Yes, customers are "visiting," but it takes special tools and techniques to follow their activities. The chapter's first section provides an introduction to tracking and analyzing customer activities in online stores, starting with a discussion of which data to track and which to ignore. Also included is a helpful primer on interpreting the various customer logs that are generated by Web servers. Customers generate a mountain of data when visiting a Web site. The second section reviews the various types of software available to make the job of compiling and analyzing the data much simpler. Web servers passively collect a lot of useful information; however, customer data collection may need to be more aggressive on occasion. That is the focus of the third section, which discusses how to use cookies, customer sign-in forms, and other techniques. The chapter's fourth section includes an explanation of how to use gathered data to decide if changes are needed, how to effectively implement those changes, and how to follow up to make sure that the changes accomplished their intended result.

13.1 ASSESSING WEB SITE TRAFFIC

After building and launching a Web site, the first question that every e-business owner should ask is "How can I improve this site?" The initial version of a Web site is rarely the current version. Once a site is created and launched, it is important to watch how users interact with the site, to make changes to improve their experience, to watch how users react to changes, and to continually make changes to keep the site updated. The process is ongoing as an e-business evolves, defines itself, and works to meet the changing needs of its customers.

Analyzing Web site data can reveal a lot about an e-business that other metrics (measurements)—such as sales volume and average order amount—cannot. By tracking the appropriate data, the e-business owner gathers useful pieces of information: which pages on a site are the most and least popular, how many people start a visit on the home page, and the average number of pages a user sees before leaving. Owners also find out where users come are on arrival at the site and also determine the location where the user leaves the site.

The chapter examines a broad field of Web site analysis, from traffic monitoring to gathering customer feedback to deciding when to make changes. Direction is provided for analyzing the massive amount of raw data available for a typical site and turning the data into useful statistics that can change an e-business. The text points out which pieces of information are more important than others, and explains how to focus analysis of information to study individual user behavior. Data analysis is not simply shuffling numbers and generating tables, but is part of a program to make useful updates to a Web site and study the immediate and lasting effects of these changes.

The best changes that come from Web site analysis are gradual, or evolutionary, changes. Look at how sites like Amazon and MSN handle changes. The interfaces of these two sites do not radically change every week, although subtle changes are always being introduced in response to customer comments and to enhance the shopping experience.

13.1.1 Tracking the Trends in Web Site Traffic

An interesting exercise that every e-business owner should try before beginning Web site traffic analysis is to sit at an outdoor café on a busy street and watch *automobile* traffic drive past. A series of patterns should soon emerge. Estimate the number of cars that drive past; determine the most popular makes, models, and colors; gauge the average speed; and ascertain whether the cars are driving past in groups or as a continuous stream.

Intuitively, the exercise is not all that different from monitoring Web site traffic. Even if the e-business owner cannot physically see customers zipping in and out of the site, tools are available that e-business owners can use to gain a basic understanding of the traffic patterns produced by their Web site visitors. To reveal the trends that are occurring, e-business owners will need to gather some very basic information:

- The total number of visitors coming to the Web site
- The number of unique visitors coming to the site
- Which Web sites are referring visitors
- Which Web pages on the site are the most frequently viewed and the least frequently viewed
- The number of Web pages that the average visitor sees in one visit

Simple methods for tracking the usage are available without researching Web site files and logs, although the methods mainly involve direct customer interaction. For example, an e-business owner can contact a research group to find sample visitors and do usability testing, where the research group introduces a visitor to a Web site, and asks the visitor to interact with the site. Then the visitor's activities are studied to see whether the visitor can intuitively navigate around the Web site, place an order, and perform basic functions. Based on the user interactions, the research group makes recommendations regarding changes to the Web site to make it more user-friendly.

E-businesses can also solicit customer feedback through surveys, follow-up phone calls, or email response forms. Many Web sites gather feedback by contacting past customers and then getting their opinions about a variety of issues. The method is useful but it can be time-consuming, expensive, and slow to deliver results.

Ultimately, the best resource for learning about e-business customers is the large amount of data collected by Web servers regarding Web site visitors. The sections that follow provide an introduction to this topic.

13.1.2 The Basics of Analyzing Traffic Data

Every time a Web server receives a request from a visitor and displays a Web page for that visitor, it creates an entry for the request in a log file on the Web server. The **log file** records all the activity a Web site experiences—the requests it receives and the information sent out to different visitors. Sometimes, log files are called access log files and other times the Web server breaks the log file into different files; for example, an error log, request log, and referrer log.

Log file:
A list of entries of the different requests received by a Web server and the file or information that it has sent back to the user requesting it.

A log file reveals useful information about a Web site:

- The popularity of various pages within the site
- The usability of the site
- The types of visitors that come to a site
- The ability of a site to present its Web pages effectively

A Web site measures a **hit** whenever a piece of that site—whether it is a Web page, graphics file, or other object—is sent over the Internet to someone's Web browser. A statement such as, "That Web site received a million hits last month," means that a Web site handled a million different requests for everything from text to images to audio tracks. Although some people equate hits with visitors, that is incorrect. A single Web page may contain nine different graphics and thus generate ten hits every time it is accessed. Why? When a visitor wants to view the Web page, the Web server sends out the HTML code of the page as the first request, and then the server sends nine separate graphics files, one by one, and records each of those transmissions as a separate hit.

Hit:
A statistic recorded whenever a piece of a Web site—for example, a page file or graphics file—is sent over the Internet to someone's Web browser.

The process explains the reason that measuring hits is not as important as other metrics. Although measuring hits provides a good baseline for understanding the level of demand, a hit rarely translates into success when wooing advertisers, asking banks for financing, or planning a marketing campaign.

Page view:
A statistic recorded when a Web site visitor views a particular page.

Instead of hits, a page view is actually a better measurement for Web traffic. A **page view** is exactly what it sounds like—one is recorded when a Web site visitor views a particular page. The number, which is independent of the number of elements that might be present on a Web page, usually correlates to the number of visits to a particular page, especially a home page.

IP (Internet Protocol) address:
A series of four sets of numbers, in a range from 0 to 256, that defines a computer's location on the Internet.

Because most Web sites have multiple pages, e-businesses need to determine the number of visits, or unique visitors, that the site receives. One way to accomplish viewer tracking is to view log files (which are discussed in more detail in Section 13.1.3) for information identifying visitors. The most commonly referred to identifier is an **IP address.** An IP—or Internet Protocol—address, is a series of four sets of numbers, in a range from 0 to 256, that defines a computer's location on the Internet. An example of an IP address is 207.171.166.102 (which belongs to Amazon). Each IP address is unique to one computer at a time. Many users are assigned an IP address dynamically, which means that the user is assigned a unique set of numbers the moment the user signs on to the Internet, and the user loses the right to those numbers when the user logs off. Users of cable modems and of university computers have the same IP address, or static IP address, all the time.

By sampling IP addresses encountered on the log files over a given period, then counting the number of pages each of the visitors viewed, an e-business owner can calculate a rough estimate of the average number of pages viewed per user.

The method will provide helpful data, but most e-business owners—not to mention their investors and potential advertisers—will want a more precise system for measuring unique visitors. The best way to accomplish retrieval of precise data is to implement a system utilizing cookies, which is explained in Section 13.3.1.

13.1.3 Interpreting Log Files

The log file resides on the hard drive of a Web site's server. Depending on the operating system used by the server, a regular text editor can often be used to open and view the log file. The log file is the list of the requests that the Web server has processed. A typical request entry looks like this:

```
208.215.179.139 - - [06/May/2006:06:01:16 -0400] "GET /index.html
HTTP/1.1" 200 32768 "http://search.yahoo.com/search?p=ecommerce+
products" "Mozilla/4.0 (compatible; MSIE 5.0; Windows 98; DigExt)"
```

The number "208.215.179.139" corresponds to the IP address of the computer from which the request was made. When there are multiple lines with the same URL, it means that either one person is requesting different files or multiple people are using the same computer.

The next string of characters, "[06/May/2006:06:01:16 -0400]," is the exact date and time of the request. The "-0400" at the end refers to the offset from Greenwich Mean Time. In this case, the time is marked as the U.S. Pacific time zone.

The segment of the entry ""GET/index.html HTTP/1.1"" refers to the item being requested and the method used to transfer that file from the Web server. The segment may be Web pages (.html or .htm), graphics files (.gif or .jpg), or other content, such as JavaScript programs (.js), audio files (.mp3 or .wav), or video files (.mov). Most files are transferred by HTTP, although occasionally large files are sent by FTP (File Transfer Protocol).

The number "200" is the result code for the request, or the initial response that the Web server sent to the visitor when the request arrived. The "200" means that the request was successfully processed. If the file was not found, the result code for the request would return "404." Numerous entries with the result code "404" are a signal to check all Web links to ensure that visitors are not referred to a dead link—a file that no longer exists.

The number "32768" is the size, in bytes, of the file that was sent back. The number will typically be very large for Web pages with lots of graphics, audio, or video files.

The ""http://search.yahoo.com/search?..."" part of the log is the referrer URL, or the URL from which the request originated. In this example, the visitor was searching Yahoo! and clicked a result link to access the Web site. The search terms used were "ecommerce" and "products." See Section 13.1.4 for more information on referral links.

The text ""Mozilla/4.0 (compatible; MSIE 5.0; Windows 98; DigExt)"" designates the name and operating system of the Web browser program the visitor is using to make the request. Generally, the browser will be Mozilla, which is MSIE 5.0, or Microsoft Internet Explorer 5.0, running on Windows 98, or a search-engine robot, like Googlebot.

Log files contain a tremendous amount of information about visitors, as seen in the sample. While manually searching the listings, trends will become apparent, such as which Web pages show up most often or which IP addresses appear week after week. When log files contain thousands of lines, manual scanning is limited. Section 13.2 discusses traffic-analysis software that can quickly read these log files and break down the information into easy-to-read statistics.

13.1.4 Referrer Files

Referrer file: A specialized log file that displays the sources of all Web page requests, usually other Web sites.

Often, the server maintains a separate log file, called a **referrer file,** which contains the sources of all Web page requests. The sources displayed are mostly other Web sites connected by links or search-engine links where the visitor typed certain keywords and found the final site as one of the results.

For example, consider the following referrer entry:

http://www.somewebsite.com/links.html- /

The sample explains that a specific Web page (links.html) on a certain Web site (www.somewebsite.com) is offering a link to the Web site visited; that was the page the visitor was viewing when the link was clicked.

Another sample referrer entry is:

http://search.yahoo.com/search?p=ecommerce+products

The sample reveals that the visitor came from the Yahoo! search engine. The link also shows the keywords ("ecommerce" and "products") that the visitor typed at Yahoo! The information alone can be invaluable when planning Web marketing campaigns. Specific keywords or phrases that repeat in referrer files are powerful terms that successfully attract people to a site.

When running a Web marketing campaign, an important step is to distinguish search-result referrals from sponsored-ad referrals. If a keyword is included at the end of the link provided for a sponsored ad, the keyword will appear correctly in the referrer file. For example, when linking to a home page and creating a Google AdWords campaign, adding the link "http://www.yourwebsite.com?google" will help interpret the results.

The referrer files may also reveal links that come from within the Web site, like this one:

http://www.yourwebsite.com/page1.html" - /page2.html

This line indicates that the user is on Page 1 of the Web site and is clicking to move on to Page 2.

Other entries may appear as:

"-"

Typically, the entry means that the user typed the URL directly into the Web browser or has the Web site set up as a bookmark in their browser so that they can go directly and quickly to the site. The entry is a good thing to see because it indicates that people are being drawn naturally to the Web site without having to find it from another Web site.

13.1.5 Other Useful Logs

Other types of log files that are worth reviewing on a regular basis reveal important information about a Web site and its visitors, including problems that may be interfering with sales completions.

Error log:
A file generated by a Web server that tracks errors that occur while visitors are using a Web site.

Error logs

Error logs are files that track errors occurring while visitors use a Web site. Different Web servers keep different fields of information, but date and time, client IP, and an identifying field are usually present. No matter what the format, the most important information is contained in the last field on each line, which explains the reason for the error. Be on alert for three types of common errors:

- **Send aborted:** A visitor has stopped the transfer of the file from the Web server to the computer. The situation occurs mainly when large graphics files (or other media files) are taking too long to load on a visitor's machine, and the visitor stops the process and moves to another page. If the message appears repeatedly, condense the files to optimize Web pages for faster loading.
- **File does not exist:** A user is linking to or searching for a specific file on the Web server using a Web address that is no longer valid. Perhaps a search engine is referencing a page that is no longer on the Web site or an advertised Web link is misspelled. When seeing the message, place a new item in the location or create a catchall link that sends incorrect references to the home page or special error page.
- **File stopped transferring:** If no mention is made of the client stopping the transfer, a faulty connection may be between the Web server and the visitor. Although a transfer stoppage occasionally happens, if it happens repeatedly, the Web server's Internet connection is not as reliable as it needs to be. Consider changing Internet service providers.

Abandoned Shopping Cart Logs

Typically, an e-commerce shopping cart creates a text file that contains a customer order. As the customer makes changes to that order, the shopping cart program adds to, or deletes from, the file. When the customer checks out and pays for the order, the shopping cart converts the file and deletes it from memory.

Numerous studies indicate that Web site visitors abandon their shopping carts as much as 90 percent of the time. **Abandoned shopping cart logs** are files created by the server as a record of uncompleted transactions. By looking at the shopping cart files that do not result in orders, the e-business owner can estimate how many people start the process but fail to finish. Comparing the number of abandoned shopping cart logs to the number of orders received allows calculation of the percentage of potential customers that complete an order.

Abandoned shopping cart log: A file created by a Web server as a record of transactions that are started but not completed.

Shopping cart logs can also reveal which products are most popular by counting which products are added to the carts. If someone took the time to physically add a product to the shopping cart, intent and demand for the item is indicated. The information can be used to help guide future product orders. Of course, if a popular product is also overly represented in abandoned shopping carts, it also may reveal a problem that is preventing customers from closing the sale. Though the log cannot explain why the customer changed their mind (maybe they discovered an unexpectedly high shipping cost or the need to purchase a companion product), the e-business owners have noticed that change may be needed.

Entry- or Exit-Page Logs

Entry-page log: A file generated by a Web server that serves as a record of where visitors entered a Web site.

Entry- or exit-page logs are usually derivative files of the log file. **Entry-page logs** are a record of where visitors entered a Web site, which shows the areas that attract people to a Web site. Maybe a seemingly unimportant product page shows up repeatedly in this file, which may suggest that people are interested in the product or the page and that similar products or pages could be used to attract more people. Alternatively, entry-page logs without targeted "landing pages" created specifically to attract users to the site mean that these pages are not working correctly and changes need to be made.

Exit-page log: A file generated by a Web server that shows the point in a customer's path where the customer left a Web site.

Exit-page logs are files that show the point in a customer's path where the customer gives up and goes somewhere else. Sometimes, the exit page log points to the final order-confirmation screen, which is the ultimate good news that every e-business owner wants to see. Most times, however, the e-business owner sees visitors exiting from another page, which should encourage investigation into why the customer left at that point in the online shopping trip. Perhaps the exit page gives a negative impression of the Web site. Perhaps customers are being encouraged to check out another Web site and are following that link instead of staying around to make a purchase. Or, a page on the site may contain invalid, outdated, or useless information and links. The log is an essential tool for identifying the problems in a Web site so they can be corrected.

SELF-CHECK

1. What is the difference between a hit and a page view? Why is a page view a more valuable measurement?
2. What is a log file? What different kinds of useful information does it contain?
3. What are some other types of log files compiled by Web servers and what is the value of each for Web traffic analysis?

Apply Your Knowledge Try the exercise suggested in Section 13.1.1. Set up at a busy intersection and watch traffic for a short period of time (15 to 30 minutes). Record data in at least four categories, for example number of cars on each street, color of cars, speed (fast or slow), and time spent stopped. Summarize the data in tables and comment on trends observed.

13.2 TRAFFIC ANALYSIS WITH SOFTWARE

The Web site traffic data compiled in the various log files reveals much information about the typical e-business. To give the numbers perspective so that owners can make higher-level decisions, the traffic data must be matched with other indicators of activity on the Web site, including:

- Number of orders
- Average order size
- Number of registered customers
- Total sales volume
- Average number of products per order
- Most common search terms

The reason to compare the numbers is to provide data reflecting how much Web site traffic is influencing sales. Suppose that traffic-analysis data shows that a Web site has 1,000 unique visitors one month and sales data reveals 250 orders from 200 unique customers that month. The e-business owner should be considering why only 20 percent of the visitors made purchases. What changes could be made to the Web site to increase the conversion rate? What can be done through marketing that will double the number of unique visitors each month? In theory, making these changes would deliver a similar increase in orders and unique customers. In both instances, the data will lead the way to action plans for change, which should increase revenues.

For the busy e-business owner, the best solution for gathering the information necessary to make changes is to use traffic-analysis software. The sections that follow explain what traffic-analysis software does, and offer ideas for various levels of software that may be appealing to different types of e-businesses.

13.2.1 How Traffic-Analysis Software Works

After a Web site is launched, the log file begins to generate massive amounts of data as it records every interaction between visitors and the Web server. As the number of visitors grows, so does the number of lines in the log file. As Section 13.1 showed, the data generated in log files can be valuable, but can also be extremely time-consuming to analyze. While the owner of a small Web site may be able to obtain the needed information by manually scanning the files, most growing e-businesses will need software to obtain the information. Smart owners utilize software tools that are available for analyzing the traffic data.

Traffic analysis software analyzes the log files generated by the Web server to build a summary of Web site traffic criteria. The software programs perform a variety of basic tasks that perform the following basic functions:

- Analyze each log file entry.
- Group together similar entries.
- Factor out known entries, like search-engine bot programs.
- Calculate totals and averages.

E-business owners can choose from different versions of software with three levels of analysis: basic, advanced, and enterprise (big business). As more functions are added to each higher level of software, the price also increases.

IN THE REAL WORLD

An Education in Data

Launched in September 2000, the Family Education Network is an online network of learning and information resources for parents, teachers, and students. To analyze its customer data, the company used a log file-based Web analytics program that required a good deal of effort from the information technology staff in order to keep the software running. To make matters worse, the program experienced crashes involving the loss of as much as a week's data, making it an unreliable source of data. "Because of the data problems, the marketing staff had very little confidence in it," says Kevin Young, the Family Education Network's marketing director. As a result, the marketing staff hesitated to use the analytics to make its marketing decisions. The company made the decision to switch to WebTrends, a Web analytics company. "We haven't lost a row of data since we switched over to the hosted service," says Young. With the improved source of information, Family Education Network has been able to better measure the effectiveness of the company's newsletters, which drive customers to the company's various sites. Based on this information, the company cancelled 12 of its 25 newsletters, focusing its energy on improving the performance of the remaining 13. Those newsletters now generate twice the number of visits as the original 25—and each visitor is viewing 50 percent more pages; at the same time, the cost of producing the newsletters has dropped by about 50 percent.[1]

13.2.2 Basic Traffic-Analysis Software

Basic traffic-analysis software is a tool for creating summaries of traffic information for a given period of time. Some tools, such as Urchin, provide text output. Other packages—for example, Webalizer, WebTrends, or FastStats—present data in both columnar and graphical format for easy viewing.

Statistics that every program should produce or estimate are:

- Total number of visitors and unique visitors
- Average number of daily visitors
- Total and average number of page views
- Total and average number of hits
- Average length of a visit (in minutes or number of page views)

Although various packages may also be capable of generating additional results, these categories are typically calculated with basic analysis software. For example, a free traffic analysis package that creates a text summary and has been given a request for creating a summary for April 2006 traffic data may produce something like this:

```
Period: Sat-1-Apr-2006 12:00 to Sun-30-Apr-2006 23:59 (30 days).
Total successful requests: 2,221
Average successful requests per day: 74
Total successful requests for pages: 948
Total failed requests: 75
Total redirected requests: 349
Number of distinct files requested: 42
Number of distinct hosts served: 618
Number of new hosts served in last 7 days: 72
Total data transferred: 25,349 kbytes
Average data transferred per day: 844,967 bytes
```

The data reveals important numbers for estimating future demand. By viewing the total number of requests and the average amount of data being transferred, an e-business owner can see the bandwidth required for the Web site. The summary also shows how many different Web pages are being viewed on the site. In the example, 42 different Web pages were requested. If the analysis shows that the Web site has only 50 total pages, it would mean that customers are using a large portion of the site. If the site has 300 total pages, it may be time to see which pages are being used and which pages are not, and to drop pages that do not receive many visits or change the pages to resemble the pages that attract visitors.

Within the realm of "basic" traffic analysis software, more powerful programs are available that provide enhanced displays of the data summaries.

One example is Webalizer, which presents data as bar graphs and summary tables. The visually oriented presentation is more appealing to many e-business owners. With a quick glance, the e-business owner can view a detailed picture of the Web site's usage statistics, analyzed by month and arranged by different criteria.

13.2.3 Advanced Software Solutions

Most e-business owners will want to see more advanced information about how their Web site operates so that they can make targeted changes and updates to improve performance. Now is the time to review advance traffic-analysis software. Powerful software tools in the category include WebTrends (www.webtrends.com), Mach5 FastStats (www.mach5.com), and Netanalysis (www.digital-detective.co.uk). Advanced traffic-analysis software not only completes the basic functions, but also provides more defined criteria, including:

- A detailed analysis of page views
- The most common referral links used by visitors
- The pages from which users are most often exiting the site
- The number or percentage of return visitors
- The most popular Web browsers used by visitors
- The most popular search engines that deliver traffic
- The amount of nonhuman traffic (like search-engine programs)
- The busiest and slowest parts of the day for Web traffic

The tools generally include predefined reports that help explain visitors' and customers' sophisticated interaction with a Web site. For example, WebTrends can provide a series of dashboard reports in the form of graphs. Dates are easily modified, and the graphs are updated automatically, which is an easy method to compare traffic levels for different weeks, months, or even seasons.

Working with the software packages is very straightforward. Log files either need to be uploaded to the software, or permission must be granted to allow the programs to read the log files automatically. Often the programs must be loaded directly on the Web server to work properly.

Enterprise/Big Business

As an e-business grows, moving up to an enterprise-level (big business) solution may be in order. Enterprise-level solutions include:

- WebTrends Enterprise: www.webtrends.com
- Urchin: www.google.com/analytics
- Mediahouse LiveStats: http://media3.net/livestats.htm

With each of the solutions, the service must be installed on the Web host server. The key to using these programs is being able to write queries to the database, which means that an e-business must develop its own specific requests for summary data. Enterprise software has few limitations for analyzing Web site traffic data. The disadvantage of enterprise solutions is that some programs require knowledge of a specific computer language, like SQL, to create reports. Because relatively few e-business owners are also expert computer programmers, this level of solution is generally reserved for companies large enough to have in-house information technology departments, or the resources to hire contractors providing this capability.

SELF-CHECK

1. How does Web analysis software work? What are three common types of data analyses the packages perform?
2. What extra features do advanced analysis software packages offer?

Apply Your Knowledge Complete an online search for three different traffic-analysis software programs. Summarize the primary features of each program. Recommend the one you believe is best for a new one-person e-business. Explain your choice.

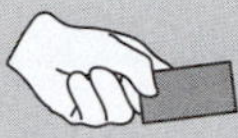

CAREER CONNECTION

Using Web analysis tools, a radio station finds ways to improve the listener experience.

Even with an audience of more than one million weekly, executives at the country's most listened-to public radio station knew that there was room for improvement. Based in New York City, WNYC had a track record of incorporating new technologies such as Web streaming into its site (www.WNYC.org). When Bill Swersey, the station's director of digital media, began investigating Web analytics in 2006, his goal for the station was to learn more about how visitors use the site so that producers could make more informed decisions about what content to produce for the Web.

After investigating the options, WNYC deployed Google Analytics, which has helped Web and show producers assess what's really capturing the attention of visitors. "How do we go about creating a really effective site that expands our reach and serves our listeners?" asks Swersey. "This is something that Web analytics can help us address."

In redesigning portions of WNYC's Web site, Swersey and his team were able to identify critical areas that needed improvement or change—labor-intensive slide shows that were rarely viewed, for example. "Google Analytics represents a sea of change," says Julie Burstein, executive director of Studio 360, one of WNYC's programs. "If we mention something on the air, by the end of the day, we can see how people are responding."

For Swersey, analytics are paying off by enabling producers to understand their audiences' core interests. "Producers are no longer working in the dark, creating what might be great content but that doesn't connect with their audience," he says. "They now have sheer numbers letting them know what's most interesting and most useful to visitors. It's very empowering."[2]

Tips from the Professional

- Embrace technological change.
- Research the resources available.

13.3 COLLECTING CUSTOMER INFORMATION

E-business owners must understand that although a Web server automatically collects valuable data in the log files, the server does not collect all information needed to make informed management decisions. This section explains using a Web site to intentionally collect more specific information without forcing customers to reveal Social Security numbers.

13.3.1 What Are Cookies?

Cookie: A file created by a Web server and placed on a Web site visitor's computer to keep track of the visitor's activity and interaction with the Web server.

Any Web server can create and place a standard file on a visitor's computer, a standard file to keep track of that visitor's activity and interaction with the Web server. That file is known as a **cookie**—because the file leaves "crumbs" of information that the Web server can access when the user visits that Web site. A cookie is a Web site owner's friend in many respects because a cookie can show what an individual user is doing on the site. Using cookies enables tracking individual behavior and calculating a unique visitor's session length more precisely than by using log files. Furthermore, using and tracking cookies gives e-business owners the power to focus on one user for a specific time period—from a few days to a few months—to see what the visitor does on every visit. Cookies reveal which Web pages the unique visitor views, as well as in which order the pages are viewed. The data can be correlated to the user's ordering information and sign-up activity.

Cookies are especially valuable to help focus the traffic analysis from a site-specific level to a customer level. Adding cookies to server log files provides the ability to precisely gauge the efficiency of marketing campaigns. Instead of relying solely on advertiser reports, an e-business owner is able to determine the effectiveness of the ad campaigns.

Using cookies starts with a simple request to the Web host to enable the cookie on the Web server. After that, the provider must be told which basic fields to use and capture in the cookies. Possible information to capture includes:

- The visitor's IP address
- The visitor's username or account name
- The date and time of the visits

After enabling cookies on a Web server, the final step is to ensure that traffic-analysis software can access the cookies on the Web server. The software can incorporate the cookie information into reports and update figures accordingly.

Cookies are not a perfect way to gather information. Customers can refuse to have cookies stored on their computers, or customers may use public computers, so the cookies will not be consistent. Even if it is not possible to obtain a 100 percent view of Web site traffic, using cookies is still more precise than simply analyzing log files.

IN THE REAL WORLD

Cooking Up a Cookie Policy

AllThingsD.com—a Web site devoted to technology, the Internet, and media—takes an unusual approach to cookies. Rather than burying its cookie information deep inside the site's privacy policy, AllThingsD tells the customer right away how it feels about cookies: "Some of the advertisers and Web analytics firms used on this site may place 'tracking cookies' on your computer. We are telling you about them right upfront." The site goes on to offer links to pages where customers can opt out of the cookies set by the site's ad-placement contractor and analytics contractor. AllThingsD goes even further, giving links to programs that can clean out all tracking cookies from all Web sites. The site explains that like most other Web sites, it may place cookies on your computer (in addition to any placed by advertisers). But these cookies do not tell the site what customers do or where they go online; instead, they do things like save registration information.

13.3.2 Adding Information to Links

When viewing log files, "referral URLs appear as keywords in the string and are instantly recognizable. (Refer to Section 13.1.3 for more information on interpreting log files.) Often keywords are search terms used by visitors when using search engines. At other times, however, the specific terms were created for the purpose of communicating information.

An easy, effective analytical technique is to add keywords to a URL to track the success of a marketing campaign. Add the keywords after the name of the HTML file by inserting a question mark (?) followed by the keywords, like this:

```
<a href="http://www.yourwebsite.com/index.html?GoogleAd1">
```

When someone uses the targeted URL, traffic-analysis software can calculate the number of times the keyword (GoogleAd1, in this example) was sent in the URL as a percentage of the total number of requests for the URL.

Keywords offer additional analytical utility. By continuing to include the keyword in URLs (Web pages) that customers encounter throughout the ordering process, traffic-analysis software can determine the conversion rate of browsers to buyers. Analysis is accomplished by calculating how many buyers used a keyword as a percentage of the total number of the browsers that visited the Web site.

13.3.3 Analyzing Customer Paths

Online customers follow a path of specific Web pages that take the customers from start to finish on a site. Although individual customers may check out different parts of a Web site along the way, the customers need to visit a minimum number of Web pages in order to be differentiated from a browsing customer and a paying customer. The minimum number of pages is called the **critical path** of a Web site.

Critical path: The minimum number of pages through which a Web site visitor must navigate to go from being a browsing customer to becoming a paying customer.

Suppose that a Web site targets different levels of customers and has a special section for small-business customers. The critical path may look like this:

Home page□Small-business home page□Small-business catalog page□Order-review page□Order checkout page

When a critical path for customers has been identified, the knowledge can be combined with the results of traffic analysis to determine when and where customers are abandoning the order process. The knowledge provides e-business owners with an easy method to identify the weak points in the purchasing process, and to make changes that improve the buying experience for users. The results of such an analysis and the improvement process should be an increased number of completed orders and a decreased number of abandoned shopping carts.

Suppose that an e-business owner is studying the order checkout path on their Web site. The following are three ways to integrate research:

1. If the report of the most common exit pages shows the order-review page as a common exit page, the order-review process may be confusing to users.
2. If the referrer file indicates that a number of people are viewing the Frequently Asked Questions (FAQ) page or privacy policy page from the order-review page, customers most likely need or want more information before checking out. When customers go out of the critical path, a percentage of customers never return to the review or checkout phase. Therefore, the desired content could be integrated into the order-review page to reduce the number of people who exit before completing the review page.
3. An order-checkout page that involves multiple steps and shows people linking back and forth to the same pages could indicate that customers are caught in a loop and cannot exit the loop to finish the orders. To convince customers to move forward to purchase, clearly labeled steps to purchase may need to be provided on one page.

Besides keeping customers from abandoning the order process, the other reason for studying customer paths is to assist with a Web site redesign. Customers eventually make their own path through a Web site, despite any warnings or guidelines posted. E-businesses can either try to steer the customers where the business wants customers to go, or study customer paths and incorporate that information into the site design so that the most common paths are recognized and supported by the site links and structure. Just as a river cuts its own path through the countryside, customers will naturally cut a path through a Web site. E-business owners should always support the customers' paths and optimize their site around those paths to avoid losing customers, rather than fight it and risk losing those customers.

IN THE REAL WORLD

Transparent Analytics

Amazon.com has set high standards for how well it tracks customer information as well as for how it finely tunes its product recommendations and site content based on that data. By tracking the products a customer views and/or purchases, Amazon creates recommendations of similar items. If a customer buys a children's book about the artist Georgia O'Keefe, for example, a recommendation to buy a children's book about Henri Matisse might come up. Amazon even goes as far as exposing its analytics data on actual buys, with the feature "What Do Customers Ultimately Buy After Viewing Items Like This?" A customer looking at a Canon A630 digital camera would be offered the following four bullets:

- 56% buy the item featured on this page: Canon PowerShot A630 8MP Digital Camera with 4× Optical Zoom (271) $349.00
- 17% buy Canon PowerShot A570IS 7.1MP Digital Camera with 4 × Optical Image Stabilized Zoom (146) $154.74
- 14% buy Canon PowerShot A560 7.1MP Digital Camera with 4 × Optical Zoom (102) $134.94
- 7% buy Canon PowerShot A720IS 8MP Digital Camera with 6 × Optical Image Stabilized Zoom (27) $194.99

By showing these percentages, Amazon demonstrates yet another way an e-business can use analytics to improve a shopping experience.

13.3.4 Asking Customers for More Data

Anyone who walks into a modern retail store to make a purchase quickly realizes that the store wants to know about its customers. The clerk asks for Zip code and address, even when customers are paying cash. Other stores use customer loyalty cards in exchange for a modest discount on some products. The stores use these strategies to understand their customers and how the customers shop. Although the process can be annoying, most people accommodate the request. With the information gathered, the store can accurately predict, for example, which customers from which Zip codes will buy certain brands in specified quantities at different times of the year—and adjust the product mix on the shelves accordingly.

Gathering customer information is a delicate, but ultimately profitable, venture because analyzing that information provides a keen focus on how customers interact with a business. As e-businesses understand their individual customers better, the e-business can move the focus of the data analysis from the overall Web site statistics to customer statistics. In the customer level of analysis, the common factor is not the entire Web site, but rather the *average* customer and what the customer does on a visit to the Web site.

Existing customers have already provided information about themselves, including their names, mailing addresses, credit card data, and their product preferences (from purchase history). In the future, information gathering should move beyond waiting for customers to purchase before asking for information about the customer. Consider signing up users on arrival at a Web site or when the customer wants to learn more or do more on the site. Then tie the information into both the traffic and ordering statistics to obtain a true customer-focused look at Web site activity.

When a customer must log in to a Web site to utilize it, it is possible to track every movement and tie those movements to a specific user ID number. Typically, users need an incentive to reveal personal information and complete a sign-up process. Some Web sites offer members exclusive, premium content that casual browsing customers cannot access. Other sites require accounts to be created before products can be added to the shopping carts.

When using a sign-up process, Web sites should be prepared to lose a certain percentage of browsers who could have become buyers. If a big drop-off in activity occurs after instituting a sign-up process, consider using a "guest account" system that gathers minimal information. Guests can shop and use most features, and convert to a permanent account to make a purchase.

Most Web sites ask for basic information whenever someone signs up for an account: user's name, street address, phone number, and email address. However, the basic fields do not reveal much information about customers. Gathering more information about customers can be accomplished by asking questions in the following categories:

FOR EXAMPLE

See Figure 13-1 for an example from Bluefly.com of a log-in feature used to collect customer information.

- Demographic information: Gender, ethnicity, age, marital status, or number of kids

Figure 13-1

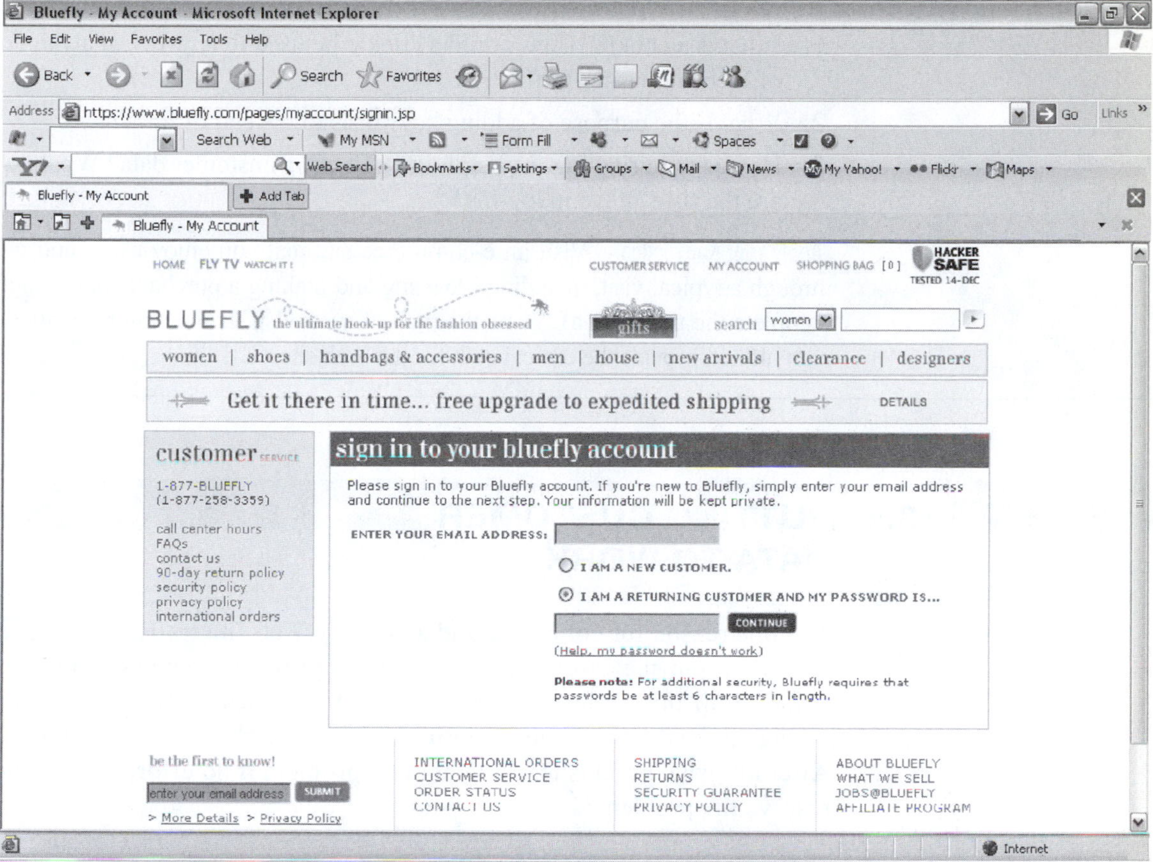

A sample of a log-in feature used to collect customer information.

- Psychographic information: Likes, dislikes, brand recognition, or purchase reasons
- Lifestyle information: Income, housing status, or types of cars
- Interests and preferences: Favorite subjects, products, or people

Gathering this information can be a burden on customers (or even scare them off), so include the option “Prefer not to answer” in each category and be certain to include a way for the data gathered to benefit the customers. For example, provide products or information that will appeal to demographic groups visiting the Web site. Or make changes to the Web site design to enhance the user experience: If the data gathered suggests a high percentage of older users, a wise change would be to increase the font size for easier reading.

SELF-CHECK

1. What is a cookie? How would a cookie be used to improve analysis of Web site visitor traffic?
2. What is the purpose of adding keywords to the end of links?
3. How is requiring log-ins helpful in gathering customer data? What are the risks of using log-ins?

Apply Your Knowledge Visit an e-commerce site that you enjoy using and go through a typical visit, including browsing and making a purchase (but do not complete the transaction). Write the path of your visit. Is the path the critical path? If not, provide the critical path for the Web site.

13.4 PUTTING CUSTOMER DATA TO WORK

The one reason for collecting and analyzing Web site traffic and usage data is to put the information to work improving business. The true value of all this collecting and analyzing becomes evident only after acting on the data and implementing appropriate changes to a Web site. After all, what good is learning about a problem if no effort is made to resolve the problem?

13.4.1 Using Benchmarks to Assess Change

Benchmark: A statistical point of reference for comparing future results.

After implementing data collecting systems, e-businesses need to monitor the activity long enough to establish a **benchmark**—a point of reference against which future results can be compared—for all critical statistics. For Web sites, the beginning benchmarks together describe an average visitor's behavior. With an understanding of average behavior, an e-business owner can discern long-term trends in visitor statistics, and determine a cause-and-effect relationship between purposeful changes, such as a new marketing program or a change in Web site design. If traffic suddenly experiences a big increase or suffers a huge drop, and no purposeful changes have been made, determine the reason for the statistical change and take action. Perhaps a new competitor has emerged, or the Web host has had an unusual number of service outages. Change to correct the new business or operating environment may be needed.

To fully investigate an unexpected deviation from the benchmark, create a variety of reports that provide detailed information from near the time of the change in data. If the number of orders decreases *and* the number of error-log entries about pages not delivered correctly increases, then the Web server or Internet service provider is experiencing outages. If the Web site suddenly is mentioned as part of a big news article, a spike in visitors to the site may occur, as well as an increase in orders placed.

Other problems are less obvious to identify. Diagnosing situations involves viewing Web page activity and seeing what statistics have been affected by the change in activity. While reviewing the Web site, consider any changes that have been made to the Web pages—big or small—and determine whether the dates of those changes are the same as the change in usage. A simple change can disrupt an otherwise stable process and cause unexpected problems. Being watchful of trends relative to benchmarks can make it easier to identify problems before they get out of hand.

13.4.2 Identifying Potential Areas for Improvement

Sometimes a Web site's problems are not so obvious, and that is where traffic data collection and analysis becomes important. Section 13.4.1 explains that once customer behavior benchmarks have been established, it becomes easy to follow trends. With careful analysis over time, a diligent e-business owner can predict expected trends. Deviations from predicted trends indicate that adjustments should be made to improve the predictability.

Watching traffic trends should involve more than just looking at unique visitor statistics. Other valuable data includes:

- The Web pages users gravitate to
- The Web pages users avoid
- The Web pages viewed most often
- The Web pages viewed least often

Find out also whether common factors can help predict what makes a page on the site popular or unpopular.

Sometimes, the problem is a factor that the data can only partially identify. Suppose that an e-business owner reviewing the traffic report discovers that most customers check out their Web site every morning. In addition to the traffic data, the owner also knows that their product catalog gets updated only at the end of the business day, after hearing from suppliers. Timing is the key to put the two pieces of information together when a site receives heavy traffic before the daily catalog update. Visitors may move on if the customers begin to see the site as unresponsive. The challenge for the owner is to determine a way to update inventory in the mornings.

Every Web site owner should regularly play the role of a customer. The owner should start at the home page, navigate through the site, view products, and try to place an order. Instead of navigating in a way that feels comfortable, the owner should use traffic reports and usage data to show how to proceed. If any page encountered seems frustrating to use, review the exit-page logs. Often the review will confirm that customers have the same reaction, and that the page is in need of an overhaul.

Traffic data is valuable, but never overlook the importance of direct customer feedback as a prompt for Web site improvements. Encourage regular dialogue with and between customers, use follow-up surveys, and always stay in contact with the customer base. Customers are usually candid about what on the site works well and what has to be changed. After customers identify a concern, research the data to confirm the problem area and to choose a course of action.

13.4.3 Making Effective Changes

Every e-business owner will face a time that traffic data analyses (or maybe customer complaints) expose an area on the Web site that must be improved. Avoid quick fixes, which often result in other issues.

Before repairing a problem, carefully look at all factors that may be influencing the poor performance. Often one problem is actually the result of interactions between several different factors. When making a change, a good rule of thumb is to implement the lowest-impact fix possible that still corrects the problem. Another strategy is to identify another area of the Web site that performs well, and try to make changes that mimic the successful part. Sometimes it is helpful to look at similar Web sites (even those of competitors) to see whether they manage a problematic process in a different way. Finally, asking customers for a solution can be helpful—the customers may already have a solution in mind.

When a workable solution to the problem has been developed and the time to update arrives, follow these steps:

1. **Acquire a beginning set of benchmark statistics before implementing the change.** Having a set of data specifying how the Web site operated before the change is essential to use for later comparison.
2. **Announce the maintenance, then make the change.** Many Web sites post notices to customers about maintenance periods, explaining that the site will be unavailable for a few hours while new updates are posted. Typically, the updates take place during the night for U.S. customers so that the updates have the least effect on traffic. Use the maintenance period to send new versions of the Web pages to the Web server.
3. **Gather traffic statistics after the change is posted to the Web site.** Watch the usage data after the new version is available, and

determine whether traffic increased, as predicted, or decreased. Notice also whether other parts of the Web site were affected and whether orders increased. Start gathering daily statistics the first day the change goes into effect.

13.4.4 Following Up

In a perfect world, a Web site update would correct all problems, traffic would increase, and higher revenues would naturally follow. As amazing as the Internet is, it is far from perfect. The reality is that any change to a Web site—even a relatively minor one—can affect all other processes on the site. Therefore, it is essential to conduct a careful follow up to any changes to ensure that there has been no disruption to other site functions. Studying customer reaction is also important to ensure that the changes recap as many benefits as possible.

Although the techniques discussed in this chapter provide insight into customer behavior, traffic analysis is not a method of mind reading that can predict activities with 100 percent accuracy. That is why e-business owners must stay attentive and flexible and determine whether updates actually provide value after they are implemented. In fact, sometimes, rolling back the change is a necessity—to remove the update or to go back to the old process.

In the end, customers are the ultimate guide to managing a Web site. Perhaps reinforcing one change with a more systematic update of the entire Web site process is necessary. Perhaps the changes can come about only when customers make changes to their Internet usage. For example, if many customers still use dial-up modems to access the Internet, it may not be practical to update a site with video and audio content until enough customers adopt a broadband Internet connection. By diligently monitoring and analyzing traffic data, the e-business owner will know when to make the changes.

SELF-CHECK

1. What is a benchmark? How would a benchmark be used to help determine whether a change is needed on a Web site?
2. Should Web site changes be made at any particular time of the day or week? Explain.
3. Why is it important to follow up after making changes to a Web site?

Apply Your Knowledge Traffic data analysis has indicated that a change is necessary to your Web site's shopping cart system. Write an action plan for this change, focusing on how the change will be announced to customers and how the change will be implemented. What steps will be taken afterward?

SUMMARY

Section 13.1

- Tracking Web site traffic through direct customer interaction is possible (for example, by surveying them), but it is usually more effective to analyze the visitor data gathered by a Web server.
- The log files gathered by a server contain a wealth of information about customer visits to a Web site, including their IP address, the time of the visit, and where the customer came from.
- Specialized log files are often compiled separately and contain their own useful information. Referrer files pinpoint the source of Web file requests. Error logs compile user problems during visits. Abandoned shopping cart logs are captured for transactions started and not completed. Entry and exit logs show where visitors enter and leave a site.

Section 13.2

- Traffic-analysis software greatly simplifies the job of analyzing log file data, which is often far too large to be managed manually. There are three levels of software—basic, advanced, and enterprise—which offer increasingly powerful analytical tools.

Section 13.3

- In addition to analyzing traffic data recorded passively by Web servers, many e-businesses will want to take a more active approach to collecting customer data to obtain more reliable information about usage trends.
- Cookies are files created by servers and placed on a visitor's computer that make it easier to track their movement through a Web site. Other methods for collecting data include adding keywords to Web links, following customer paths, and using log-in surveys.

Section 13.4

- Once data collection begins, e-business owners need to establish benchmarks for various measurements, then watch for statistical trends varying from those benchmarks. The unusual trends are often a signal that Web site changes are in order.
- Change should be made only after careful analysis to identify the source of the problem and should make the smallest possible impact on the overall site. After implementing a change, a comprehensive follow-up monitoring program should be launched to ensure that the change achieved its desired results without causing other problems.

ASSESS YOUR UNDERSTANDING

UNDERSTAND: WHAT HAVE YOU LEARNED?

Go to **www.wiley.com/college/holden** to assess your knowledge of the basics of tracking and analyzing customer data for an e-business.

APPLY: WHAT WOULD YOU DO?

1. List three traditional data tracking methods available to an e-business owner who does not want to analyze Web site file and logs. Give three examples of information to be gathered.
2. Identify the types of information contained in the following Web site log file:

   adsl-36-172-142.ilm.bellsouth.net - - [21/November/2007:13:42:07 -0700]

   "GET /about.htm HTTP/1.1" 200 3741

   "http://www.e-angelica.com"

   "Mozilla/4.0 (compatible; MSIE 5.0; Windows 98)"
3. Explain what information an e-business owner can glean from an abandoned shopping-cart file. How is this useful?
4. You've recently launched a redesigned Web site for your comic book e-business. What level of software program would you need to use in order to determine how many of your customers are repeat visitors?
5. Though many customers dislike the use of cookies, many Web site owners continue to utilize them. Explain how the information gathered by a cookie can benefit an e-business.
6. As the owner of an online surfing gear business, you periodically study the customer paths on your site. This week you've noticed a high percentage of customers abandoning their orders at checkout. Outline the possible reasons as well as how you would correct the problem.
7. You sell specialty food items from India and have decided to add a log-in feature to your Web site. Compose five questions that will provide you with useful information about your customers.
8. Traffic analysis of your Web site has revealed a problem with the check-out feature; namely, if a customer chooses to continue shopping after adding an item to a shopping cart, the item is lost. Outline the steps you would take to correct the problem without disrupting business.

BE AN E-BUSINESS ENTREPRENEUR

Utilizing Log Files

E-business owners can use tools to better understand the traffic patterns produced by Web site visitors. Part of the process is revealing any trends that are occurring. As the owner of a Web site that sells music downloads, explain the usefulness of five types of log files in gathering customer information.

Traffic-Analysis Technology

The same business could benefit from one of the traffic-analysis programs discussed in Section 13.2. Using the Internet to conduct your research, determine which program would be best suited to the needs of the business. Explain your decision.

Collecting Customer Data

By gathering customer information, an e-business can better understand its individual customers. Choose an existing Web site and compose a log-in page for new customers. Discuss how such a feature could discourage or encourage purchases.

KEY TERMS

Abandoned shopping cart log A file created by a Web server as a record of transactions that are started but not completed.

Benchmark A statistical point of reference for comparing future results.

Cookie A file created by a Web server and placed on a Web site visitor's computer to keep track of the visitor's activity and interaction with the Web server.

Critical path The minimum number of pages through which a Web site visitor must navigate to go from being a browsing customer to becoming a paying customer.

Entry-page log A file generated by a Web server that serves as a record of where visitors entered a Web site.

Error log	A file generated by a Web server that tracks errors that occur while visitors are using a Web site.
Exit-page log	A file generated by a Web server that shows the point in a customer's path where the customer left a Web site.
Hit	A statistic recorded whenever a piece of a Web site—for example, a page file or graphics file—is sent over the Internet to someone's Web browser.
IP (Internet Protocol) address	A series of four sets of numbers, in a range from 0 to 256, that defines a computer's location on the Internet.
Log file	A list of entries of the different requests received by a Web server and the file or information that it has sent back to the user requesting it.
Page view	A statistic recorded when a Web site visitor views a particular page.
Referrer file	A specialized log file that displays the sources of all Web page requests, usually other Web sites.

REFERENCES

1. "Education Site Boosts Newsletter Visit Rate 100% While Reducing Cost 50%," WebTrends.com, www.webtrends.com/upload/cs_familyeducation.pdf.
2. "WNYC leverages Google Analytics to create compelling online content for its award-winning radio programs," Google.com, www.google.com/analytics/case_study_wnyc.html.

CHAPTER

14 E-BUSINESS SECURITY

Keeping You and Your Customers Safe in the Online World

Do You Already Know?

- How to keep a Web site safe for online shopping
- What a denial-of-service attack is and how to prevent one
- How to create an e-business security plan
- How to protect and back up critical data

For additional questions to assess your current knowledge on security for e-businesses, go to **www.wiley.com/college/holden.**

What You Will Find Out	What You Will Be Able To Do
14.1 How to deal with consumer fraud and create a safe environment for online customers	Avoid consumer fraud and minimize charge-backs; keep Web sites and customer data secure
14.2 The major security threats facing e-businesses—denial-of-service attacks, hackers, malware, and more	Protect a Web site from denial-of-service attacks, hackers, viruses and malware, domain theft, and email scams
14.3 The value of security planning and the necessary steps for creating a security plan	Create and implement an effective security plan
14.4 How to protect and back up critical customer data	Protect customer data; implement effective backup systems; successfully employ firewalls

INTRODUCTION

Even though online shopping has become largely accepted by most segments of the public, many people are wary of the security of the Internet—and with good reason. The explosive growth of the Internet has attracted countless thieves and opportunists seeking to take advantage of weaknesses in the retail realm. Stolen customer data is extremely valuable to thieves—and very costly to e-businesses that fail to protect their shoppers' personal information. This chapter reviews the many online security risks faced by e-businesses, but also provides sound advice for minimizing these risks. This chapter's first section introduces the topic and provides a basic guide to safe online business practices by discussing credit card fraud, securing customer data, writing effective security and privacy policies, securing online transactions, and obtaining and displaying seals of approval. The second section reviews in detail the many techniques used by Internet thieves to steal data, and how businesses can protect themselves against each type of security breach. Among the topics covered are denial-of-service attacks, hackers, viruses and malware, domain theft, and email scams. Prevention is the best remedy for Internet thieves. The third section explains how to prepare and implement an effective security plan. The fourth section concludes with an important explanation of advanced topics in e-business security—specifically strategies for protecting and backing up customer data, and effectively using firewalls to protect against unwanted intrusion.

14.1 E-COMMERCE RISKS AND SECURITY

Internet-related fraud accounted for more than half (53 percent) of all complaints reported to the Federal Trade Commission in 2004. The list of complaints translated to more than $265 million in losses. Yet that number was just a small portion of the total dollars that e-commerce suffered that year. The final tally for the year reportedly totaled $2.6 billion. Who paid the price? Both consumers and e-commerce merchants are vulnerable to becoming victims of cybercrime. The burden is on e-business owners to provide a safe, secure shopping environment for their customers.

14.1.1 Consumer Fraud and Charge-Backs

E-business owners are responsible for protecting the customers. With identity theft and fraud continuing to rise at alarming rates, credit card companies and regulatory agencies are burdening e-commerce merchants with the bill (including shipping fees and the costs of the goods). E-business owners can prevent their customers from being victims of identify theft and fraud by being vigilant about credit card payments accepted and by keeping customers' information as private as possible.

Charge-back: When customers using credit cards and other online forms of payments request that charges be removed.

Most often fraud occurs in the form of **charge-backs,** which are when customers using credit cards and other online forms of payments (that access credit cards and bank accounts) request that charges be removed. The Fair Credit Billing Act (FCBA) allows consumers to dispute purchases for two reasons:

1. The card is stolen or otherwise used without the legal cardholder's permission.
2. The customer does not believe the merchant fulfilled their obligation in delivering the product. Usually the product never arrived or the customer received something different than expected.

Unfortunately, charge-backs occur often and are difficult for an online business to prove a customer wrong. Online purchases lack the same ability to authenticate or verify a cardholder's identification as in a bricks-and-mortar environment. Fortunately, tools are available to minimize the risk of excessive charge-backs. To avoid charge-backs, use the following basic security strategies:

- **Verify the cardholder's address.** Credit card merchants offer an address verification service (AVS) that compares the billing address a customer provides with the cardholder's name. The merchant is notified immediately if the billing address and name do not match the information associated with the account.
- **Obtain the card verification value.** When completing an order from a customer, ask for the card verification value (CVV2). Because the set of numbers appears only on the customer's credit card, the customer must have physical access to the card to obtain the numbers.
- **Process only approved transactions.** If a card is declined for any reason, do not process it. Avoid believing that the message is a mistake and trying to process the order anyway.
- **Scrutinize email addresses.** Always ask for a customer's email address at the time of purchase. If the address appears suspicious, call the customer to verify the order.
- **Be wary of excessive orders.** Buyers using stolen or compromised credit cards often place extremely large orders or purchase several units of the same item. Call the number on the billing address to verify unusual orders.
- **Maintain good records.** Keep copies of online order transactions, verification emails, and records of any other communication with customers.
- **Maintain good communication.** Notify the customer immediately when shipping is delayed, or if a product is out of stock. Do not process any charges until a product ships.

Any charge-back can be disputed by contacting a credit card vendor directly. Before calling, be prepared to show compliance with verifying the card's authenticity at the time of purchase. Be patient: It may take several months to settle a claim.

14.1.2 How Secure Is Your Customer Information?

In fulfilling the security obligation to customers, e-business owners should manage the private information with the utmost care. Specifically, customers want to know how sensitive data, including credit card numbers, Social Security numbers, birthdates, and phone numbers, are used and protected.

Every Web site (usually in a privacy or security policy) should explain how and why it collects and saves customer information. The following includes questions that e-business customers will want answered:

- Does the e-business see customers' credit card numbers before they are processed?
- Are credit cards processed in real time, which means that the e-business may have access to only the last four digits of an account?
- Are the charges processed manually, which means that the e-business will see and have access to the full account number?
- How many people have access to the information?
- Are customer files recorded only as electronic files, or printed for filing and storage?
- What precautions are taken to keep data secure? Are paper files locked away? Is a firewall or other security layer enabled to protect electronic files?
- Are the computers password protected? How are these passwords maintained and secured?
- Who has access to the computers?

The Federal Trade Commission and other agencies offer information to help businesses comply with e-commerce policies. Visit the FTC Web site, www.ftc.gov.

14.1.3 Security and Privacy Policies

When defining security concerns, online merchants have two goals: (1) Do everything possible to make the site secure and safe; and (2) promote buyer confidence by notifying visitors that all the necessary precautions have been taken to keep online shopping experiences safe. Furthermore, regulatory agencies may want confirmation that an e-business is upholding its customers' best interests.

To maintain security, develop and write clear policies to manage security issues and publish the policies on easy-to find pages on the Web site. Security and privacy policies are both essential parts of every e-commerce site.

Security Policy

Online merchants are not expected to reveal the type of antivirus software used, but a security policy should explain what protection is in place when customer orders are being processed. Furthermore, visitors should be educated about how information is collected, stored, and protected.

PATHWAY TO... WRITING AN ONLINE SECURITY POLICY

When drafting an online security policy for your e-business, be sure to address these points:

- Assure your customers that it's important for you to protect their personal information.
- Explain the ways in which you protect their personal information (using SSL encryption technology, for example).
- Invite customers to make a purchase by phone, rather than online, if they feel more comfortable. Be sure to provide a toll-free number.
- Also invite customers to alert your business if they suspect fraud, misuse, or unauthorized access to their personal information as a result of using your Web site.
- Finally, explain that under the Fair Credit Billing Act, all major credit card companies protect cardholders against fraud, subject to a $50.00 deductible.

Privacy Policy

The privacy type of policy was once best known for notifying customers whether their email addresses were shared with or sold to third parties.

Privacy policies are now much more inclusive: Privacy policies include details on what information is collected and why; how customers can update, change, or delete stored information; and how the customers can notify a business if the customer believes that their information has been breeched. When developing a privacy policy, consider the three categories of concern:

1. **Personally identifiable:** Information that connects a customer to a Web site
2. **Sensitive:** Information that is private to customers, such as transaction histories or email addresses
3. **Legally protected:** Information that is protected by the law, including credit card numbers, financial accounts, medical records, and even education-related details

FOR EXAMPLE

See Figure 14-1 for an excerpt from the privacy policy of craigslist.

Well-written policies have other side benefits: They encourage wary customers to order (knowing that the e-business has made certain promises in writing), and they minimize customer service communication by answering frequently asked questions.

Figure 14-1

Privacy Policy terms of use | feedback forum

craigslist has established this privacy policy to explain to you how your information is protected, collected and used, which may be updated by craigslist from time to time. craigslist will provide notice of materially significant changes to this privacy policy by posting notice on the craigslist site.

1. **Protecting your privacy**
   - We don't run banner ads, pop ups, pop unders, or any other kind of commercial ads.
   - We don't share your information with third parties for marketing purposes.
   - We don't engage in cross-marketing or link-referral programs with other sites.
   - We don't employ tracking devices for marketing purposes ("cookies", "web beacons," single-pixel gifs).
   - We don't send you unsolicited communications for marketing purposes.
   - We offer email anonymization & relay, to reduce 3rd party harvesting & spam.
   - Account information is password-protected. Keep your password safe.
   - Forums use basic webserver authentication. Close your browser to log out.
   - craigslist does not knowingly collect any information from persons under the age of 13. If craigslist learns that a posting is by a person under the age of 13, craigslist will remove that post.
   - craigslist, or people who post on craigslist, may provide links to third party websites, which may have different privacy practices. We are not responsible for, nor have any control over, the privacy policies of those third party websites, and encourage all users to read the privacy policies of each and every website visited.

An excerpt from the privacy policy of craigslist.

IN THE REAL WORLD

Outlining E-Business Security Measures

Aboriginal Art Online, an Australian company that opened in 2000, offers paintings and prints by Aboriginal artists. From the company's site (www.aboriginalartonline.com), customers can view and purchase art and books as well as read articles on Aboriginal art and culture. The site offers a comprehensive policy that outlines the measures taken by Aboriginal Art Online to ensure the quality and security of its e-business. Among those measures, the company processes credit card numbers in an encrypted form over a secure link, and the data is not stored permanently. The site goes on to provide details as to which e-commerce service provider and bank are utilized. The company also explains what signs customers can look for to be sure that online transactions with the site are secure, including a closed padlock icon on the browser window.

14.1.4 Keeping Web Sites Secure

Despite e-business efforts to publish and follow security and privacy policies, buyers are still uncertain about online security and privacy. A Forrester Research report shows that 61 percent of people are hesitant to reveal personal information or credit card numbers to Web sites. Because more than half of potential customers are seeking a reason *not* to make online purchases provides e-businesses a strong incentive to make their site secure. One of the easiest ways to secure a site is by using **Secure Socket Layer (SSL)** certificates.

Secure Socket Layer (SSL) encryption: A method of communication for scrambling information as it travels across the Internet; only an authorized sender or receiver can view it.

SSL is a protocol, or method of communication, for scrambling information as it travels across the Internet. The data is encoded so that only the authorized sender and receiver can view it. Displaying an SSL certificate on a Web site shows customers that confidential information is protected when sent over the Internet to be processed.

Using SSL is a matter of licensing the right to use the protocol through an approved vendor and installing the license on a server. Certificates can be obtained directly from a private company, such as VeriSign, or Web-hosting or domain registration companies. The companies can be resellers or certified partners for organizations such as VeriSign and Web Trust. Prices range from as low as \$29.95 to more than \$200 annually. The difference in price depends on the type of certificate chosen and the level of validation attached to it.

E-businesses using an e-commerce–enabled server that is shared by others, or those signing up for a storefront, may not need to purchase an individual SSL certificate. Some hosting companies provide encryption service to all customers through a single server.

14.1.5 Displaying Seals of Approval

Seal of approval: A certification provided by a third-party organization that has examined a Web site and confirmed that the site meets minimum security requirements in a given area.

Online shoppers search for signs that the business is legitimate—particularly if the shopper is familiar with the business. Offline, people look for a valid business license hanging behind the counter or a local chamber of commerce sign.

The online equivalent to the local chamber of commerce sign is a **seal of approval** from third-party organizations that examine Web sites and confirm that the site has met minimum security requirements in a given area. Customers feel safer shopping online with an e-business that posts a seal of approval on the site. Table 14-1 lists organizations that provide seals.

Table 14-1 Organizations Providing Reliability and Privacy Seals

Organization	*Seal Type*	*Reliability*	*Fees*
BBBOnline www.bbbonline.org	Reliability or Privacy	BBB member; in business 1 year; pass privacy profile	Membership fee; licensing fee based on size of company and annual sales ($200 if under $1 million)
TRUSTe www.truste.org	Web Privacy	Pass site audit	Based on annual sales ($559 if under $500,000)
Guardian eCommerce www.guardianecommerce.net	Site Approval and/or Privacy	SSL certificate	$34.99 annual fee
PrivacySecure www.privacysecure.com	Privacy	In business 1 year; pass credit check	Monthly fee, based on number of employees ($12.50/mo for 1–3 employees)

Although the seals are not required, they definitely boost buyer confidence. Several types of seals for which e-businesses can apply include:

- **Reliability:** Posting the seal confirms that a site's sponsoring companies have verified information about the business. The seal also confirms that the business agrees to abide by certain online advertising and operating standards and dispute-resolution guidelines. Often part of the qualifying process for the seal requires being in business for a specified period of time (usually a one-year minimum).

- **Privacy:** E-businesses are eligible to display a privacy seal on the site if the site meets guidelines, which include creating and posting a privacy policy and adhering to the policies, along with other industry standard recommendations. The organization issuing the seal is likely to conduct a security and privacy assessment on a site before providing the seal.
- **Children's privacy:** The Children's Online Privacy Protection Act (COPPA) provides a seal of its own. Sites requesting the seal must prove that the site will not collect any personal information from a child without first obtaining permission from a parent.

Application and licensing fees can range from slightly less than a hundred dollars to several hundred dollars for each seal. Licensing fees may be a difficult investment for a startup business, but the step should be seriously considered as a business grows and reaches out to new customers.

SELF-CHECK

1. What are the legitimate reasons for which customers can request a charge-back? List three ways to minimize credit card fraud.
2. List four types of information customers will want to know about how data is managed.
3. Explain three categories of concern to be considered when developing a privacy policy.
4. What is an SSL certificate and how does it work?
5. How does an e-business receive a seal of approval? Why are seals of approval important?

Apply Your Knowledge Visit several popular e-commerce sites and review privacy policies. Summarize five topics that are covered in the security policies you reviewed.

14.2 INTERNET SECURITY THREATS

E-businesses that have not received an online security threat should consider themselves lucky. Recent studies show that companies suffer from at least one security incident a year from viruses, worms, spyware, and other malicious efforts. When suffering from an Internet-related attack, large companies are reportedly losing an average of $2 million in revenues per attack.

Security threats are the reason that e-business owners need to minimize the opportunity for any type of security interference that threatens success. Before determining how to create a defense plan against security threats, first learn what to expect. This section reviews the most common security threats that could attack unwary e-businesses.

14.2.1 Denial-of-Service Attacks

Denial-of-service (DoS) attack: Any incident of an Internet thief preventing an e-business or its customers from accessing Web sites and other online information or applications

Any incident of an Internet thief preventing an e-business or its customers from accessing Web sites and other online information or applications is called a **denial-of-service (DoS) attack.** Most DoS attacks have gone after major sites (including Yahoo!, Microsoft, and Amazon), but it is naive to believe that small e-commerce sites cannot be impacted by such a malicious action. DoS attacks can be directed against online payment providers, online banks, and Web site hosts, meaning that any e-businesses dependent on providers may be offline for several hours or more.

Small or mid-sized businesses are more likely to experience a DoS attack than large ones because these are most vulnerable. Online security is often at the bottom of the list of concerns for smaller e-commerce sites, which lack sophisticated security tools. Intruders surf the Internet every day seeking sites with security holes. DoS attack-launching tools are now inexpensive and available for would-be attackers. An intruder can divert legitimate traffic away from a site and drive it to other sites. The attacker gets paid every time customers visit a rogue site, whether the customer intended to go to the site or not.

Fending off a DoS episode is not easy. When an e-business is under attack, the choice of responses becomes limited. To reduce the chances of an attack and to minimize the damage, an e-business should take the following important steps:

- **Quiz the Web host.** When selecting a hosting company, understand what security measures the Web host has in place. Ask how the host works with clients that experienced a DoS attack, and whether security experts are part of the Web host's support staff.
- **Update the basics.** Individual users and their computers also create security holes. The best defense is to continually update antivirus and spyware programs as well as download the most recent patches (or fixes) for computer systems and browsers.
- **Increase capacity.** Having more server capacity to manage traffic can be helpful during a DoS attack. Because a DoS attack attempts to increase the demand on a site to a level that prevents access, the additional capacity may diminish the damage of smaller attacks.
- **Report attacks.** If a site receives a DoS attack, report it to the FBI. Attackers often use Yahoo! and other free email services; the FBI may be able to

trace the accounts. The FBI has created a special division, the Internet Crime Complaint Center, to address these concerns (www.ic3.gov).

- **Block traffic.** Work with Web host companies to block traffic coming from suspicious or malicious IP addresses. Blocking traffic will increase the risk of blocking legitimate users; however, safety for legitimate users is first.
- **Be aware.** As DoS attacks increase in frequency and type, stay current on security issues. The best defense against attacks is being aware and knowledgeable of current threats and recommended preventive measures.

14.2.2 Hackers

Hacker:
A person that intrudes upon or gains access to a company's information systems without official permission.

Behind every DoS attack or any other harmful Internet-related threat is usually a single person or group of people responsible for starting the malicious activity. Discovering the identity of electronic thieves—often called hackers—is not easy. In general, a **hacker** is anyone not authorized nor given permission to intrude upon or gain access to a company's information systems.

The challenge of trying to break through a security system of a high-profile business or government site and bragging of successful attempts is the motivation for one type hacker. Other hackers are excited by the possibility of making money from a Web site. Among the most popular methods of hacking for pay are:

- **Stealing keystrokes.** Even inexperienced hackers can monitor and record the keystrokes on a computer by using a program called a keystroke logger tool that send the collected information back to the hacker. Capturing the data provides easy access to a computer system.
- **Stealing sales.** Hackers divert traffic to a rogue site (which may even appear the same as the original site) where customers spend money, believing the site is legitimate.
- **Stealing data.** By obtaining passwords to secure data, hackers can build a lucrative business. With passwords, hackers gain access to pertinent information, such as bank accounts, birth dates, and Social Security numbers.
- **Stealing credit card numbers.** Hackers enjoy obtaining customers' stored credit card numbers. The numbers can easily be resold for cash before anyone realizes the accounts have been compromised.

E-business data is valuable to an Internet thief. Sites that fall prey to this type of hacker are vulnerable because the site is an easy target. Consider a breach in terms of a home's security: Locks and alarms do not always stop a thief, but rather deter the thief. Given the choice, most bad guys are going to break into places that are easiest to access without being noticed. The same is true for Web sites.

If a hacker sees that a Web site's security is sloppy, the hacker will take advantage of the situation. Computer programs are available that allow hackers to scan the Internet seeking vulnerable sites.

Implementing firewalls and antivirus software certainly helps deter hackers, but e-businesses can take additional measures to ensure the Web sites are hacker-proof:

- **Use uncommon passwords.** Instead of choosing easy-to-remember passwords (such as birthdays), use a nonsensical or complex mixture of words and numbers. Create a different password for each application or program accessed. For added security, use a password generator, software that creates random passwords.
- **Change passwords frequently.** Merely creating good passwords is not enough—the passwords must be created repeatedly. Generate new passwords every nine months for frequently used applications. Change other passwords for low security-risk applications or Web sites on an annual basis.

IN THE REAL WORLD

Hackers Take on New Targets

As social networking sites such as MySpace and Facebook have become more prevalent, Internet users have grown comfortable with displaying more of their personal information. This trend has not gone unnoticed by computer hackers, who are finding increasingly sophisticated ways of gaining access to that information—and going undetected by traditional security programs. In November 2007, it was revealed that hackers had infiltrated News Corp.'s MySpace page, including the home page of singer Alicia Keys. Hackers had linked the page to a site in China that tried to dupe users into downloading PC-destructive software. "We're going to see a lot more of this in the consumer space," says John Pescatore, an Internet security analyst for leading information technology research and advisory company Gartner, Inc. Due to an increase in email-borne viruses, most PC users have learned to be wary of suspicious attachments or links, but it may be more difficult to detect these risky emails when hackers are exploiting the users' own lists of friends and business contacts from social networks. "We've definitely seen the bad guys use malware to go after friends' lists on MySpace and Facebook," says Pescatore. "They're exploiting trust." [1]

- **Keep data hidden.** Hackers can originate close to home. Whether working from home or in an office surrounded by employees, develop the habit of protecting personal information. Never leave account numbers, passwords, and other pertinent data in the open.
- **Shut down computers.** E-business owners, as well as home-based businesses, should limit the possibility of unwelcome access by shutting off computers at the end of the day. Since bandwidth is shared on cable modems, computers connected to the Internet with cable modems have increased vulnerability to threats.
- **Update computer systems automatically.** Configure computers for automatic updates to operating systems to maintain security.

14.2.3 Viruses and Malware

According to the McAfee security firm, more than 100,000 active viruses are currently threatening computers. Named because of the germlike nature of an illness that rapidly spreads, viruses were originally a nuisance more than anything else. A **virus** is a program or programming code that spreads from computer to computer, usually through email attachments. The attachments can be a Word document, photos, games, or any other type of application that plays host to the virus. By opening the attachment, the user unknowingly unleashes the virus onto the computer. Viruses are almost impossible to detect without using antivirus software. Viruses can be prevented by installing—and regularly updating—an antivirus software program.

Virus:
A program or piece of programming code that spreads from computer to computer, usually through email attachments.

The ability to hide a virus, combined with the ease of distribution, means the attacks are an increasing threat to the health of individual computers and online businesses. Computer experts now refer to viruses as **malware,** which is shorthand for "malicious software." There are additional types of malware, viruses, and annoyances of which every e-business owner should be aware.

Malware:
Shorthand for "malicious software"; another term for a computer virus.

Worms

Unlike most viruses, a worm does not need a computer user's help to spread. A **worm** is a type of virus that replicates itself and then spreads to other computers through a shared network. One worm that garnered quite a bit of attention was rbot.cbq, a derivative of the Zotob worm. The worm hit big media companies like CNN and the *New York Times* by taking advantage of a flaw in Windows 2000.

Worm:
A type of virus that replicates itself and spreads to other computers through a shared network.

Trojan Horse

A computer **Trojan Horse** uses the same type of subterfuge that the Greek Trojan horse did. Delivered in a seemingly harmless package (usually via email), the Trojan Horse sneaks onto computer systems. Then, without the

Trojan Horse:
Malware delivered in a seemingly harmless package (usually via email) that sneaks onto a computer, opens, and performs unwanted activity.

user's permission, the Trojan Horse opens and performs unwanted activity, such as shutting down the computer. Unlike some other threats, a Trojan Horse does not replicate itself.

Adware

Adware: Software with integrated advertising functions bundled with a software package.

Adware is software with integrated advertising functions or bundled with a software package. The phenomenon began as annoying pop-up windows that disrupted computers with unwanted ads. Adware is now big business, and money is made every time the software displays ads for unwitting users to view.

Spyware

Spyware: A type of malicious software that plants itself deep into a computer system, posing as a legitimate program.

Much like adware, **spyware** is a type of malicious software that plants itself deep into a computer system, posing as a legitimate program. Spyware wants to stay around as long as possible to collect information about the user. Spyware can redirect users to specific Web sites, or can track and record personal information to send back to the spyware's originator.

14.2.4 Keeping Domain Names Safe

Ever since the Internet gained in popularity, devious, creative minds have found ways to cause problems. Besides highly publicized threats such as viruses and DoS attacks, another lesser-known cybercrime can be especially serious for e-businesses: disrupting or stealing domains.

Domain slamming: Whenever a Web site owner is tricked into moving a registered domain from one registrar to another.

One frequently encountered problem is called **domain slamming.** The phenomenon occurs whenever a Web site owner is tricked into moving a registered domain from one registrar to another. For example, the owner receives an email to renew the domain—but the message is from a competing registrar. Although domain slamming may be more detrimental to the original domain registrar, domain slamming is still costly and is often risky for e-businesses. When a thief takes possession of a domain, which can occur during registration of a domain name, the domain may be lost forever. Whether a domain is hijacked for a day or an eternity, common problems that occur when an e-business's name is stolen include:

- **Reselling:** A hijacked domain name can be resold to an unsuspecting third party. Popular names can sell for millions of dollars, making domain hijacking lucrative.
- **Lost sales:** Losing an active e-commerce site means lost sales. In addition, companies can accumulate enormous legal expenses in recovering domain names.

- **Damaged reputation:** Even if a hijacked domain is recovered, customers may not be convinced that it is safe to shop again. Stolen domains may also be used to redirect visitors to sites that download adware or spyware onto computers, which continues to erode customer attitudes.

If a hacker can obtain enough personal information about an account, the hacker can transfer a registered domain into the hacker's name and take ownership in a matter of hours. Most information needed to achieve the process can be found simply by viewing the public records of the WHOIS directory.

To prevent having personal or business information readily available for public viewing, choose to make contact information private. The WHOIS directory will then show a third-party vendor—a proxy—as the point of contact. Reputable domain registrars offer the private registration service for a small annual fee, starting at under $10 per year.

Sadly, domain stealing is becoming more common. Domain registrars and the Internet Corporation for Assigned Names and Numbers (ICANN) continue to implement policies that prevent or limit the damage. No policy is foolproof, so use the following tips to minimize the risk of domain hijacking:

- **Lock down:** Registrars offer the simple, free service of locking down a URL, which restricts others from making changes to an account. Request lock down when registering a domain, or change the lock-down status by using account management tools on existing accounts.
- **24/7 support:** Use domain registrars that offer 24-hour support, which is important so that if a domain hijacking is discovered, the investigative and recovery process can begin immediately.
- **Standard notification:** Choose domain registration services that state standard methods of contacting the owners for changes or that will agree to contact the owners via multiple methods (such as by both phone and email).
- **Review status:** Frequently check the WHOIS directory to see who is listed as the owner of the domain, and to confirm that the contact information is current and correct.

14.2.5 Email Scams

Two common email scams are phishing (fishing) and pharming (farming). Both methods use unscrupulous means to get personal information or private account information.

Phishing:
An email scam that poses as a legitimate source asking for personal information; instead the data is stolen.

Phishing

Phishing is a scam that begins with the receipt of an email that appears to be from a legitimate source, such as PayPal or a credit card company.

The email requests immediately updating account information which has been compromised or needs to be verified for other reasons. When the link (included in the email notice) is clicked, the link takes the user to a bogus site that captures personal information as the account is "updated."

Legitimate companies are alerting users to potential phishing scams and making it easier to identify emails that do not originate with the company. Generally, though, e-businesses should be aware of the following:

- **Account verification:** Most legitimate emails from a member-based company or financial institution now include the last three or four digits of the actual account number. If the email does not have any highly personalized or account-specific information, the email could be a fake.
- **Contact information:** Check whether the contact information at the bottom of an email matches the source that supposedly sent it. Email contact information should originate from the company's primary URL, such as support@paypal.com—not support@paypalsecurity.com.
- **Collecting data:** A legitimate request should not ask users to submit, update, or verify private and confidential information by completing an email-based form or by replying to that email.
- **Notice of urgency:** Most phishing scams insist on an immediate reply. Bogus emails scare users into believing their information is being compromised—right now.
- **Contact customer support:** If an email appears legitimate but the information is uncertain, play it safe and call the toll-free customer service number listed on the legitimate company's Web site.

IN THE REAL WORLD

Phishing Police

The Anti-Phishing Working Group (APWG) is a global association focused on eliminating fraud and identity theft resulting from phishing, pharming, and email spoofing of all types. The APWG's more than 2,700 members include VISA, Microsoft, and Yahoo!, as well as eight of the top ten U.S. banks and four of the top five U.S. Internet service providers. The site offers educational materials as well as ways to report phishing emails and pharming sites. The site includes a Phishing and Crimeware map that illustrates where such criminal Web sites are hosted on the Internet.

Pharming

Pharming:
A scam (often delivered as an email virus) that reroutes Internet users away from a site the user intended to visit to a bogus lookalike site that steals personal data.

Pharming scams reroute Internet users away from a site the users intended to visit to a bogus lookalike site. When the user logs in, providing passwords and personal information, the data is captured, or "pharmed" out, and used for malicious purposes.

There are two ways to fall victim to a pharming scam:

1. A virus, delivered by email, compromises a computer's information. The virus can enable the computer to redirect users to a bogus site when they type a URL into their browser.
2. A hacker uses DNS (Domain Name System) poisoning, which alters the string of numbers in the DNS, causing the real URL to be redirected to a fake domain. Pharming that uses DNS poisoning is more destructive because it affects more users and is costly to the owners of sites that have been poisoned.

Because no standard method exists to confirm that a site is legitimate, it can be difficult to avoid becoming a victim. An individual user's best protection against pharming attacks is to maintain firewalls, antivirus software, and browsers by installing patches and updates on a routine weekly or daily basis.

Protecting a Web site from becoming a victim of DNS poisoning is much more difficult. In fact, there is no sure way to keep it from happening. The best defense is to confirm that the Web host servers are using the latest updates of DNS software and that all patches are installed.

IN THE REAL WORLD

Security at PayPal

PayPal, which began largely as a popular way to pay for goods on eBay, is now a global leader in online payments, with more than 153 million accounts. Like other companies, PayPal has been attacked by email scammers attempting to steal valuable credit card details from unsuspecting customers. PayPal has worked hard to defend itself and its customers, launching its Security Center on its Web site (https://www.paypal.com/us/cgi-bin/webscr?cmd=_security-center-outside), where customers can access fraud-fighting tips, tools, and technology.

SELF-CHECK

1. What is a hacker and what do hackers steal or attempt to steal? List five ways to prevent hacker intrusion of a computer system.
2. What is a security threat? Explain the following: worm, Trojan Horse, adware, spyware, pharming, and virus.
3. What is domain slamming? List three tips for preventing domain theft.
4. What is phishing? How can phishing be prevented?

Apply Your Knowledge Denial-of-service (DoS) attacks can be damaging to a small e-business. Develop and write a brief plan for defending against DoS attacks, including five different strategies to be implemented.

14.3 SECURITY PLANNING

To protect an e-business from an unwanted computer invasion or an IT catastrophe, develop a plan. The plan should be written to provide management and employees a written course of action in the event of a security crisis. Implement the plan by investing in an online security system (one or more) and hire professionals to ensure proper preparation.

Where does an e-business start? Begin with the four major components for building an effective security plan:

1. Writing policies and procedures
2. Inventory and skills assessment
3. Risk analysis
4. Action plan and budgeting

The following sections offer guidance to develop details in each component to ensure a successful security plan.

14.3.1 Policies and Procedures

Small online businesses may be skeptical of the need to write formal policies; however, formal policies are essential tools for success. The purpose of a security plan is to protect both an e-business and its customers. By establishing and implementing written security policies, an e-business can reduce flaws in their security plan and minimize the risk of internal and external security breaches.

Security plans for large companies are elaborate, but small firms can manage with a basic plan. A baseline rule for establishing security policies is as follows: The magnitude of the policy the should fit the breadth of the organization and the depth of the risk factor that needs to be protected. For example, IBM may require several hundred policies, whereas a small e-commerce site might need only five policies.

Follow these steps to create security policies (as many as needed):

1. **Write the overall goals or objectives for the security policy.** The ultimate goal is to protect the e-business. Try dividing the overall goal into mini-goals and focus on each one. For example, focus on outside threats and establishing guidelines for employees.
2. **Create a list of areas within the organization that require protection.** After each item, note which items should be implemented in a formal policy. Use the checklist in Table 14-2 as a guide to the areas open to possible security risks.

Table 14-2 Security Coverage Checklist

Security Risk	*Currently Secured?*	*Requires Formal Policy?*
Desktop computer(s)	❑Yes ❑No	❑Yes ❑No
Laptop computer(s)	❑Yes ❑No	❑Yes ❑No
Employee computers (home/work)	❑Yes ❑No	❑Yes ❑No
BlackBerry/PDAs/handhelds	❑Yes ❑No	❑Yes ❑No
Server	❑Yes ❑No	❑Yes ❑No
Wireless network	❑Yes ❑No	❑Yes ❑No
Firewall	❑Yes ❑No	❑Yes ❑No
Cable modem/Internet connection	❑Yes ❑No	❑Yes ❑No
Software	❑Yes ❑No	❑Yes ❑No
Bank/financial information	❑Yes ❑No	❑Yes ❑No
Credit card numbers	❑Yes ❑No	❑Yes ❑No
Customer data	❑Yes ❑No	❑Yes ❑No
Email	❑Yes ❑No	❑Yes ❑No
Passwords	❑Yes ❑No	❑Yes ❑No
Database	❑Yes ❑No	❑Yes ❑No
Web-based applications	❑Yes ❑No	❑Yes ❑No
Inventory	❑Yes ❑No	❑Yes ❑No
Actual products	❑Yes ❑No	❑Yes ❑No
Back-end system	❑Yes ❑No	❑Yes ❑No
Offices/other facilities	❑Yes ❑No	❑Yes ❑No
Other physical property/facilities	❑Yes ❑No	❑Yes ❑No
Files/other miscellaneous	❑Yes ❑No	❑Yes ❑No
Intellectual property	❑Yes ❑No	❑Yes ❑No

3. **Determine the scope, or number, of policies that are legitimately warranted for the size and needs of the organization.** Refer to the checklist in Table 14-2 to combine several components into a single policy. Other areas may produce larger or more frequent risks and require a stand-alone policy.

4. **Starting with the first policy, write its purpose and provide an overview of the importance to the organization.**
5. **Detail the scope of the policy.** Name which employees or level of employees to which the policy applies. List by name which locations, systems, and data are affected by the policy.
6. **Write the operational guidelines of the policy—facts relating to actions and behaviors permitted and not permitted.**
7. **Add a paragraph about how to implement the policy.** Provide information of how to notify employees of the policy as well as what the penalties are if the rules are not enforced.
8. **Document the date the policy was created.** Each time the policy is updated, add the revision date.

14.3.2 Inventory and Skills Assessments

Create a catalog, or inventory, of the e-business's equipment, as well as the information that will be protected. Table 14-3 provides a sample inventory assessment guide.

Table 14-3 Equipment Inventory Assessment Guide

	Description or Serial Number	*Registration*	*Username*	*Travels Offsite? Y or N*	*Security Risk High/Low*	*Other Information*
Hardware						
Software						
Peripheral components						
Servers						
Web apps						
Documents						

When filling in the guide, the final inventory list should capture the following information:

- **Hardware:** Record a complete list of laptops and desktops, including supplemental information, such as their serial numbers as well as who uses each machine. Also list any warranty information about each machine. Denote which systems have DVD and CD-RW (writable CD) components. For laptops, note whether the equipment is taken offsite.
- **Software:** Include details such as user registration information, licensing restrictions (single or multiple user), and registration numbers. List software installed on each computer.

- **Peripheral components:** The list may include data drives, printers, scanners, PDAs and other handheld devices, portable memory storage devices, extra monitors or keyboards, and networking equipment.
- **Web-enabled applications:** Detail which computers maintain the primary license for each application. Remember instant-messaging (IM) programs and music- or video-related applications that employees may have installed on PCs. Increasingly, IM and music- or video-related programs are becoming an easy delivery method for viruses, worms, and other malicious activity.
- **Documents:** Include all documents, including critical files, intellectual property, promotional materials, financial data, customer data (contracts and invoices), and current and archived email messages.

After completing the equipment assessment, conduct a skills inventory by composing a list of the security expertise of employees, including certifications and other specialized training. The skills inventory will reveal training needs for staff. A skills assessment will provide tools for determining if outside security consultants should be hired.

14.3.3 Risk Analysis

The risk analysis compiles advanced information about a Web site and helps identify possible security threats. A risk analysis forces e-business owners to evaluate what holds the most potential for harming their online business. The first action is to list all potential threats that could compromise security. Classify the security occurrences, or events, in the following categories:

- **External threats:** Include any risk that originates outside the business, including viruses and worms, malware, malicious intruders (including hackers, former employees, and competitors), and disasters (floods, tornadoes, hurricanes, and fire).
- **Internal threats:** Although not always intentional, these incidents occur from within an e-business's operations include malicious intent (on the part of employees), accidents, user error (accidentally deleted data, dropped monitors, and so on), and system failures.

After identifying all possible threats that could stop an e-business, prioritize each according to the level of risk. Assign a low, medium, or high risk value for each item. Ranking risks requires open-mindedness and honesty in evaluating the security of an e-business. If objectivity is a concern, consider hiring outside help.

If risk analysis reveals an e-business to be at a medium to high risk level for attacks, accidents, or failures, hire a technology consultant to evaluate the business and offer solutions. The costs involved in improving security will pay for themselves in the long run by reducing the odds of lost data, damaged reputation, and putting customer information at risk.

14.3.4 Action Plan and Budgeting

The action plan is the heart of a security-planning document. Based on the information collected in other assessments, inventories, and analyses, strengths and weaknesses in the realm of security should become apparent. Focus on **Points for Improvement** (PfIs; pronounced pif-fies), which are the specific points where a weakness needing correction has been identified.

Points for improvement (PfIs): Specific points in a security plan where a weakness needing correction has been identified.

By concentrating on PfIs, create a step-by-step plan of action to strengthen security. Be specific. Examples of steps to include in a plan of action are:

- Purchase and install external security locks for all laptops.
- Turn on the Automatic Update feature on all desktop computers to activate a fixed schedule for installing all new software updates.
- Purchase a password generator and select a date on the calendar to change passwords once per quarter.
- Create a scheduled backup, specifically for customer data such as order histories.

A thorough action plan has been developed when all PfIs have been acknowledged and the security holes have been sealed. Compare the action steps with the security policies and procedures. The action plan should consider the policies and contribute to each one being effectively implemented.

The final component of a security plan is to build a budget to implement the plan. Identify all purchases required, including a price estimate for each item. Identify which purchases are required and which purchases are supplementary.

Determining the amount to spend depends on a specific e-business's circumstances. Research indicates that the average small business spends less than 10 percent of the entire annual budget on information technology (IT). For calendar year 2006, most companies expected to spend between 8 and 12 percent of the allotted IT funds specifically on security. According to the experts, the final dollar figure was a minimum of $6,000 per employee.

The resources that require cash in an e-business should also be included. For example, budget time for employees to attend an Internet security class. Even if a vendor offers such a training session free of charge, attendance will require a small investment in human resources capital.

The last piece of this plan should include a timeline for change. Assign both a reasonable date for completion and a person who is responsible for each action item. Schedule recurring dates for reviewing the progress of the plan's implementation.

IN THE REAL WORLD

Protecting Site Data

Jeff Fritz, the CEO of Lighthouse1, is not taking any chances when it comes to the security of the Minneapolis company's Web site (www.lighthouse1.com). After all, security is the foundation of what the company does—online health-care administration solutions. The company manages extremely private health data that has to be strongly encrypted and controlled. "Access rights and security protocols are very important—not only from a basic ethics standpoint, but from a regulatory standpoint as well," says Fritz. Although Lighthouse1 undergoes rigorous internal and external security audits that may be above and beyond the protection other companies require, Fritz believes that more companies should take precautions to keep sites safe. "If [entrepreneurs] are delivering products or services over the internet, I recommend that they engage a third party to help them put a security plan in place," Fritz advises. [2]

SELF-CHECK

1. Why do small e-businesses need a security plan? How detailed should the plan be?
2. What categories should be included in a typical business inventory?
3. What is a PfI? How do PfIs make creation and implementation of an effective security plan easy?

Apply Your Knowledge Assume that you are the owner of a small e-business operated out of your basement. You have two part-time employees. Conduct a simulated risk analysis, and list external and internal threats faced by the business.

14.4 ADVANCED TOPICS IN E-BUSINESS SECURITY

The previous sections provide a basic overview of the various risks faced by e-businesses (credit card fraud, hackers, and more) and the various strategies for providing a secure purchasing environment for customers and maintaining a level of protection against a variety of potentially disastrous events. As e-businesses grow, the level of risk increases, and owners will consider a variety of security-related issues. Data protection, in particular, is an important topic. E-businesses gather a tremendous amount of information about their customers—data that can be critical in making important management decisions and maintaining strong relationships with buyers. This data can be priceless; for some e-businesses, the data may be the most valuable component of the enterprises. The data is also attractive to thieves and other wrongdoers who would like to breach a security system for personal profit.

The sections that follow provide an overview of providing additional measures of protection to ensure that valuable data remains protected, no matter what disasters or security breaches befall a growing e-business.

14.4.1 Protecting Critical Data

Fortunately, only a tiny percentage of customers are thieves who try to defraud e-businesses. A bigger challenge is protecting customer data from online thieves and from potential carelessness. One of the following violations could place customer data in the wrong hands—and potentially leave an e-business owner in jeopardy:

- **Online security breach:** A lone successful hacking attempt can leave an online database of records vulnerable. Names, addresses, and credit card numbers—some of the most sought-after information—are easily left at risk.
- **Offline theft:** Someone can break into an office and access customer files filled with personal financial data. Or the thief might be an employee or someone knowingly invited into an office.
- **Sloppy disposal:** All businesses find themselves with extra copies of customer data, and decide to dispose of old files. The manner in which the information is disposed could leave customer records vulnerable.
- **Vendor carelessness:** Any vendor with access to customer data can create a security mishap. For example, there have been recent scandals in which credit card companies and delivery services have mismanaged or lost customer information. The manner in which vendors manage data can also affect a Web site's reputation.

Protect critical data and minimize the risk of theft by implementing the following steps:

Store Data Properly

Two basic methods of storing data are hard copy files and online databases. Be certain both are tightly secured:

1. **Hard copy:** Paperwork and hard copies of backup files that contain sensitive customer information may be stored in fireproof locked

file cabinets or in rooms and storage facilities with locks and limited access.

2. **Online:** Online information should be password protected and behind a protective firewall.

Dump Data Properly

When disposing of hard copy documents, thoroughly shred the files. Professional document disposal services can be hired to come to a location to shred documents. Before disposing of old computers and electronic files, all drives should be erased or overwritten (as opposed to simply deleting individual files). Downloadable programs such as KillDisk (www.killdisk.com) or Eraser (www.heidi.ie/eraser) make the job easier.

Add Layers of Security

Be sure to protect all company information, as well as customer data. Maintaining multiple layers of security processes can become a compliance issue should data be compromised. Include the following items in the security layers (see Figure 14-2):

Figure 14-2

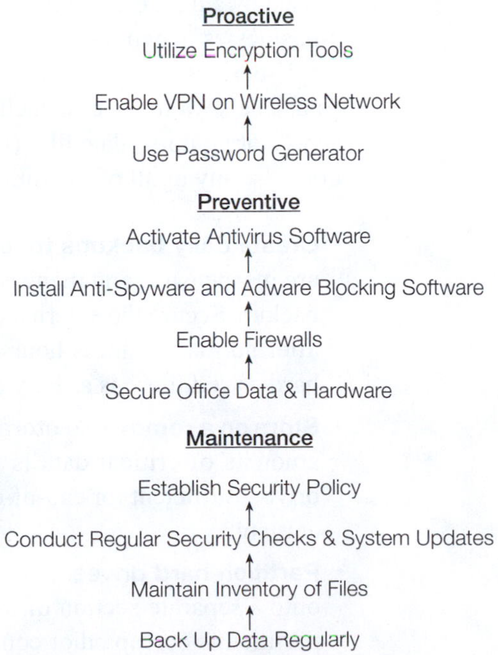

Layers of security.

- **Security policy:** Write an official security policy (see Section 14.1.3).
- **Encryption:** Use encryption tools to code information. The proper password is required to decrypt the information for proper viewing.
- **Antivirus:** Maintain current antivirus software with regular updates.
- **Firewalls:** Maintain active firewalls on your computers and servers.
- **VPN:** Use a VPN (virtual private network) when sending information over a wireless connection.
- **Backups:** Back up data on a regular basis.
- **Offline security:** Lock up data that is stored offline.
- **Inventory:** Keep an inventory of files.

Institute a Notification Policy

Part of taking preventive measures is also planning for the worst. Create an internal policy as a follow up to the privacy policy. The internal policy should describe how a security breach would be managed, including the process for notifying authorities and customers.

14.4.2 BackUp Systems

Consider the information stored on the typical e-business computer and the amount of time spent creating, updating, and maintaining a Web site. Now imagine that all that information disappears in a blink of the eye, whether caused by a hard drive failure, a fire, or even a spilled cup of coffee. Some e-businesses may not survive such a disaster.

E-businesses can avoid disasters by properly backing up and storing the data. The keys to success include using multiple backup methods, and always storing up-to-date files (i.e. daily backups) in a fireproof, offsite location. Use any or all of the following methods:

- **Create daily backups to an external hard drive.** External hard drives are inexpensive, and many easy-to-use programs are available for a daily backup. Secure the external drive in a safe location away from computers after normal business hours. With daily backups, restoring data after a hard drive failure is as easy as clicking a mouse.
- **Store on a removable storage device.** A common way to back up small amounts of critical data is to save it to an external Zip disk or Flash drive—sufficient for end-of-day backup; take the removable device home at night.
- **Partition hard drives.** An easy way to back up files is to move the files onto a separate section of the hard drive created by partitioning. If one partition is corrupted or compromised, accessing the second partition is possible.

- **Burn to a CD or DVD.** CDs or DVDs are options for short-term data storage because they are inexpensive, capacity is almost double the amount of an average Zip drive, and they less physical storage space. Store multiple copies in multiple fireproof locations.
- **Use a tape backup system.** As e-businesses grow, sophisticated backup systems using digital tapes will become a necessity. The systems are expensive, but can store large amounts of data and ensure that no information is ever lost, no matter what system failures occur.
- **Use a remote backup service.** Backup services range from $10 per month to hundreds of dollars per month depending on the desired features and amount of storage space required. An advantage of using a remote or Web-based backup service is that the data is stored offsite.

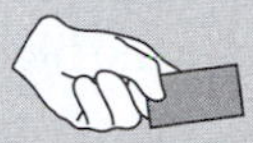

CAREER CONNECTION

An online counseling service offers mental health services to clients, as well as sound technical advice to other counseling practitioners.

Dr. Greg Mulhauser heads CounsellingResource.com, an online counseling service that also offers consulting services to corporate clients and individual practitioners in the mental health professions. The site, which Mulhauser launched in 2002, is a place for visitors to learn about counseling and psychotherapy, look up books and articles, identify particular types of psychological distress, or find information about medications. Because the business is online, Mulhauser takes the practice of data backup very seriously: "At any given time, I am working with anywhere from a handful to more than a dozen individual counseling clients . . . my sudden disappearance due to data loss could have a major impact not just on me and my business, but also on them and their lives."

From the beginning, Mulhauser had specifications in mind for a backup system, including the need for immediate accessibility; his backup would also need to be secure from tampering and safe if the company's physical premises were destroyed. Finally, Mulhauser wanted backups to happen automatically, without his intervention.

Today, Mulhauser's primary backup is maintained on an external hard drive plugged into his main computer. A smaller duplicate set of irreplaceable data is maintained on another machine in another location (another continent, actually). Mulhauser, who offers guidance to other practitioners, eschews the services of expensive remote backup companies, instead utilizing a reliable Web-hosting company that offers a large storage area. "Since most reputable hosts also maintain backups of their clients' files, this means you will have backups of your backups," offers Mulhauser, who also uses DVDs to create backups of some irreplaceable data. To satisfy his need for the backup to happen on its own, his system automatically completes the scheduled backup tasks each night.

(Continued)

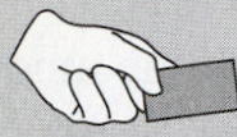

CAREER CONNECTION (Continued)

Tips from the Professional

- Ensure business continuity with backup methods.
- Consider cost-saving alternatives.
- Utililize remote storage options.[3]

14.4.3 Firewalls

Firewall: A software tool that monitors traffic, decides what is safe, and either grants or denies permission to enter a computer.

A firewall is one of the best lines of defense against viruses and intruders. Imagine a firewall as a security guard standing watch at all the doors and windows of a computer. A **firewall** is a software tool that monitors the traffic, decides what is safe, and then grants permission to enter a computer. Or if the firewall detects a possible threat, the firewall shuts the door and blocks the intruder.

Firewalls are important because hackers can be very aggressive. Hackers actively search for networks that are unprotected or have disabled firewalls. To an Internet thief, an unprotected network is the equivalent of having an open invitation to enter a computer and browse all the files. Unprotected networks are vulnerable to installation of harmful programs that infect or shut down computers—or worse yet, gather and send out pertinent information, such as passwords and bank account numbers to the hacker without the user's knowledge.

If a virus manages to breach a computer's front lines of defense, a firewall cannot remove or quarantine infected files. Antivirus software is necessary to remove and quarantine infected files.

Erecting a firewall is simple. Windows operating systems, Vista and XP, as well as other operating systems include built-in firewalls that offer basic protection. Note: Although the Windows XP firewall protects against traffic attempting to come into a computer, it does not provide the same type of protection against information leaving a computer.

For added security, consider doing the following:

- **Enable individual firewalls.** When a computer is part of a local area network (LAN), most routers have a firewall installed. For the best defense, enable a personal firewall on each computer.
- **Add an enhanced firewall.** Install a second dynamic firewall to gain protection from both incoming and outgoing traffic and to provide an additional layer of security. Firewall software combined with antivirus software may be purchased for about $29. One popular business firewall solution is made by Check Point (www.checkpoint.com).

SELF-CHECK

1. List the methods for securing customer data. List five types of security layers that e-businesses can use.
2. Why should data backups be stored offsite?
3. What is a firewall and how does a firewall work?

Apply Your Knowledge You are the owner of a small e-business operating with a single PC. Develop and write a brief plan for backing up data, including three different backup systems and backup schedules for each. Remember to indicate the frequency of backups for each system. Where will you store the backed up information for each system?

SUMMARY

Section 14.1

- Charge-backs are the most common form of credit card fraud experienced by e-businesses. Several effective strategies for minimizing charge-backs and credit card fraud, including verifying the customer's address and getting the card verification value, are available.
- Personal customer information should be managed with the utmost care to prevent theft. Furthermore, customers expect to know how their data will be managed. Customer data is best managed by writing and implementing security and privacy policies.
- Web site transactions can be kept secure by using Security Socket Layer (SSL) encryption to protect data during online transfer.

Section 14.2

- Numerous strategies are used by Internet thieves to steal data. Denial-of-service (DoS) attacks prevent e-businesses or their customers from accessing Web sites. Hackers break into computer systems without permission to steal data. Viruses and malware are malicious programs that are spread from computer to computer causing various types of damage. Domains can be slammed (registrar switching by trickery) or even stolen from the owners by subterfuge. Email scams such as phishing and pharming are used to trick users into revealing private data.

Section 14.3

- The best way to prevent e-business theft and fraud is to develop and implement an effective security plan. The primary steps in creating a plan are writing security policies and procedures; conducting an inventory and skills assessment; conducting a risk assessment; and creating an action plan and security budget.

Section 14.4

- E-businesses should take extra steps to protect customer data, including implementing effective storage and dumping procedures and adding multiple security layers.
- E-businesses should use multiple redundant systems to back up critical data. Options include daily backup to CDs or external hard drives or using a remote backup service.

ASSESS YOUR UNDERSTANDING

UNDERSTAND: WHAT HAVE YOU LEARNED?

Go to **www.wiley.com/college/holden** to assess your knowledge of the basics of security for an e-business.

APPLY: WHAT WOULD YOU DO?

1. Charge-backs can be a difficult byproduct of operating a business online. Draft a checklist of five procedures that would help prevent charge-backs for an online perfume business.
2. A seal of approval is one way to assure customers that an e-business has met minimum security requirements. Give an example of a seal of approval and describe the type of business that would benefit from its display.
3. List five security threats faced by small e-businesses. Discuss how the threats to small businesses differ from those faced by large businesses.
4. Explain how spyware could have a negative impact on an e-business that sells magazine subscriptions. How could that business prevent a spyware incident?
5. Outline the ways in which a computer-repair e-business should protect itself from domain slamming.
6. As the owner of a startup fitness equipment company, you have concerns about the security of your e-business. List in order of priority three steps you should take to prevent a phishing scam from interrupting daily operations. Similarly, what can be done to prevent pharming?
7. Your partner is not convinced that a security plan is necessary for your company; after all, you're selling knit handbags to a fairly exclusive clientele in Los Angeles. Draft a memo to convince her otherwise.
8. For the same business, create a plan of action to strengthen security, keeping your focus on Points for improvement.
9. You've been hired to manage the data protection of a small publicity firm of five employees—three of which are onsite and two of which work from home. How will you back up the firm's work and data?

BE AN E-BUSINESS ENTREPRENEUR

Easing Security Concerns

Customers today look for confirmation that their personal and financial information will be protected during online transactions. Compose a security policy as well as a privacy policy for an online matchmaking business. Identify any concerns that would relate to this type of venture.

Outsourcing Security

As the owner of an executive recruiting firm, you manage a great deal of confidential and personal information. List your top three online security concerns. Which of those issues requires the assistance of outside services? Conduct an Internet search to locate one such service.

Crafting a Security Plan

Using the guidelines presented in Section 14.3, outline a security plan for an existing small e-business such as Pete's Collectibles, an online coin dealer (www.pccoins.com). Consider the following components:

- Writing policies and procedures
- Inventory and skills assessment
- Risk analysis
- Action plan and budgeting

KEY TERMS

Adware Software with integrated advertising functions bundled with a software package.

Charge-back When customers using credit cards and other online forms of payments request that charges be removed.

Denial-of-service (DoS) attack Any incident of an Internet thief preventing an e-business or its customers from accessing Web sites and other online information or applications.

Domain slamming Whenever a Web site owner is tricked into moving a registered domain from one registrar to another.

Firewall A software tool that monitors traffic, decides what is safe, and either grants or denies permission to enter a computer.

Hacker	A person that intrudes upon or gains access to a company's information systems without official permission.
Malware	Shorthand for "malicious software"; another term for a computer virus.
Pharming	A scam (often delivered as an email virus) that reroutes Internet users away from a site the user intended to visit to a bogus lookalike site that steals personal data.
Phishing	An email scam that poses as a legitimate source asking for personal information; instead the data is stolen.
Points for improvement (PfIs)	Specific points in a security plan where a weakness needing correction has been identified.
Seal of approval	A certification provided by a third-party organization that has examined a Web site and confirmed that the site meets minimum security requirements in a given area.
Secure socket layer (SSL) encryption	A method of communication for scrambling information as it travels across the Internet; only an authorized sender or receiver can view it.
Spyware	A type of malicious software that plants itself deep into a computer system, posing as a legitimate program.
Trojan Horse	Malware delivered in a seemingly harmless package (usually via email) that sneaks onto a computer, opens, and performs unwanted activity.
Virus	A program or piece of programming code that spreads from computer to computer, usually through email attachments.
Worm	A type of virus that replicates itself and spreads to other computers through a shared network.

REFERENCES

1. Amanda C. Kooser, "Come on, Defense!: Keep your site secure and your customers happy," Entrepreneur Magazine, September 2007, www.entrepreneur.com/magazine/entrepreneur/2007/september/183030.html.
2. Aaron Ricadela, "Looming Online Security Threats in 2008," Businessweek.com, www.businessweek.com/technology/content/nov2007/tc20071119_234494.htm.
3. Dr. Greg Mulhauser, "One Example of a (Hopefully!) Sound Backup Strategy," CounsellingResources.com, http://counsellingresource.com/practice/security/backup-case-study.html.

GLOSSARY

Abandoned shopping cart log	A file created by a Web server as a record of transactions that are started but not completed.
Accrual basis	An accounting method that reports income when it is earned (rather than received) and expenses when they are incurred (rather than paid).
Adware	Software with integrated advertising functions bundled with a software package.
ALT attribute	A description of a Web page graph stored in the code and read like a <META> tag by search engines.
Angel investor	An individual, often a retired entrepreneur, who is willing to invest money in a startup or young company.
Assets	Everything of value that a business owns.
Autoresponder	Software that sends automatic replies to customer requests for information, or responds after a customer has subscribed to an email publication.
Balance sheet	A financial statement that reports a firm's financial position at the end of a period of time.
Bandwidth	The measurement of how much data, or information, a server or communication line can send and receive at any given moment.
Banner ad	A rectangular advertisement that displays basic information about an e-business and takes the customer to the Web site when they click on the ad.
Barter	Paying for products and services by exchanging other products or services.
Benchmark	A statistical point of reference for comparing future results.
Beta version	Software or a Web site in a test mode and subject to change.
Blog	Short for Web log. An online digital diary or forum where text, photos, and other material can be posted and made available to the public.
Bookkeeper	A person who manages the recordkeeping activities for a small business, including recording receivables and payable, making deposits, managing payroll, and sending out tax forms.
Bootstrapping	Starting a business with minimal financial resources by working hard, doing without, and keeping costs low.

Brand The message that a company portrays in everything it does, from communicating about the business, to acting a specific way, to providing value through products and services.

Broadband A term that refers to any high-speed Internet connection, usually cable or DSL.

Broker An independent sales representative who makes a commission from signing up new merchant account customers.

Browser A computer program that works with the World Wide Web to provide a graphical user interface for the Internet.

Business incubator An organization that supports entrepreneurial development by providing shared resources for businesses at reduced cost.

Business license A document granting an owner the right to do business within a city, county, or state.

Business plan A detailed written document that describes all aspects of a proposed business venture.

C corporation A traditional corporation, with no limits on the numbers of shareholders, or who those shareholders are.

Calendar year An accounting schedule using a 12-month period ending on December 31.

Capital The money that the owners invest in a business.

Cash basis An accounting method that reports income when it is received and expenses when they are incurred.

Cash flow statement A financial statement that shows a firm's net profit after taxes.

Certified Public Accountant (CPA) An accountant that has completed specialized training, has passed exams, is certified, and is well versed in the latest tax laws.

Charge-back The dollar amount of a sale taken out of an e-business bank account when a customer disputes a purchase with their credit card company.

Chat An Internet communication system in which individuals type messages to one another in real time.

Classified ad A simple text-based ad that is organized by category.

Clickthrough Rate (CTR) A banner ad charge determined by the number of viewer clicks that prompt a link to the advertiser's Web site.

Code of conduct A business's written statement of ethical practices or guidelines to which it adheres.

Co-location server A server owned by a company but housed in space owned by another firm, which installs the server and ensures controlled environmental conditions and consistent access to the Internet.

Compatibility How effectively a Web site functions with a particular Web browser, monitor resolution, or computer platform.

Cookie	A file created by a Web server and placed on a Web site visitor's computer to keep track of the visitor's activity and interaction with the Web server.
Copyright	The exclusive legal right to reproduce, sell, or distribute a literary, artistic, or other type of creative work.
Corporation	A form of business that exists independently from its owners, providing for an indefinite life and limiting the liability of its stockholders.
Cost of goods sold	The cost of merchandise sold during a period.
Cost Per Click (CPC)	A banner ad charge system in which the advertiser determines how much is paid for each click on their ad or keyword. Different advertisers wanting to use the same ad space or keywords bid against each other.
Cost Per Thousand (CPM)	A banner ad charge determined by the number of people who visit the Web page on which the advertisement appears.
Critical path	The minimum number of pages through which a Web site visitor must navigate to go from being a browsing customer to becoming a paying customer.
Customer pledge	A written guideline of what customers can expect when doing business with a firm.
Dedicated server	A server dedicated entirely to one e-business, which purchases, houses, and maintains the equipment and its functions.
Demographics	Statistical data used to describe a population or groups within it.
Denial-of-service (DoS) attack	Any incident of an Internet thief preventing an e-business or its customers from accessing Websites and other online information or applications.
Direct competitor	A competitor that is a similar size, caters to the same target market, and offers a similar product mix.
Discount rate	The part of every credit card sale taken by the merchant account provider, typically between 2 and 4 percent.
Domain name	The part of the URL that specifically identifies the name of a Web site.
Domain registrar	An organization that takes care of all the paperwork required to register and to activate a new domain name for an e-business.
Domain slamming	Whenever a Web site owner is tricked into moving a registered domain from one registrar to another.
Drop-shipper	A wholesaler that is paid by an online merchant to ship a product to a customer.
DSL (Digital Subscriber Lines)	A high-speed Internet connection using a normal phone line and a digital modem.
Electronic checking	A payment system that allows a customer to electronically transfer funds from a personal or business bank account into an e-business bank account.

Employer Identification Number (EIN) A nine-digit number that is used to identify a company whenever its owner files official forms and tax returns.

Enrolled agent A federally licensed accounting professional that can prepare taxes, assist in long-term financial planning, and represent a business in the event of an audit.

Entry-page log A file generated by a Web server that serves as a record of where visitors entered a Web site.

Error log A file generated by a Web server that tracks errors that occur while visitors are using a Web site.

Ethics A set of rules or moral principles that together define whether behavior is "right" or "wrong" according to society.

Excise taxes Taxes on the manufacture, sale, and consumption of various consumer goods and services.

Executive summary A brief section at the beginning of a business plan that highlights the major points from each of the other parts of the plan.

Exit-page log A file generated by a Web server that shows the point in a customer's path where the customer left a Web site.

Fad An intense, widespread, and short-lived enthusiasm for a product or activity.

Feasibility study A preliminary study undertaken to determine and document a project's viability. The results of the study are used to make a decision whether to proceed with a project.

Firewall A software tool that monitors traffic, decides what is safe, and either grants or denies permission to enter a computer.

Fiscal year An accounting schedule using a 12-month period closing at the end of any month other than December.

Fixed costs Costs, such as rent, which do not fluctuate. Often called overhead.

Flat-fee pricing One price covers complete Web site development.

Freelance contractors Self-employed workers hired under the terms of a contract to provide a service.

Frequently asked questions (FAQs) A page generally presented in question-and-answer format covering topics of high interest to customers. Each brief answer provides essential information about the business or its products.

Fulfillment The practice of delivering a product to a buyer after payment has been received; also known as filling the order.

Fulfillment house A business that specializes in packing and shipping other business's goods.

Gigahertz (GHz) Units of measurement indicating how quickly a computer's central processing unit (CPU) performs functions.

Grant Monetary award that does not have to be repaid.

Hacker	A person that intrudes upon or gains access to a company's information systems without official permission.
Hit	A statistic recorded whenever a piece of a Web site—for example, a page file or graphics file—is sent over the Internet to someone's Web browser.
Hypertext link	Built-in connection to another related Web page or part of a Web page, which is accessed by the user pointing at and clicking the link.
HyperText Markup Language (HTML)	A computer language used to create World Wide Web pages.
Income	The sales a business makes during a period.
Income statement	A financial statement that summarizes the changes in a firm's financial position over a specified period of time.
Indirect competitor	A competitor that sells some of the same products, but has a broader or different overall focus.
Intellectual property	Property that derives from the creative work of the mind.
Internet	A global network of interlinked computer networks.
Internet mailing list	A group of people with similar interests who discuss their favorite topics via email.
Internet service provider (ISP)	A company that provides customers access to the Internet.
IP (Internet Protocol) address	A series of four sets of numbers, in a range from 0 to 256, that defines a computer's location on the Internet.
Just-in-time (JIT) inventory management	An inventory system in which vendors deliver their products just before a business needs them for shipping out.
Keyword	A specific word that is tied to a particular subject; what is typed into a search engine's "search" box.
Keyword density	The number of keywords on a page multiplied by the number of times each one is used.
Keyword spamming	Hiding paragraphs of keywords by matching the keyword text color with the color of the page background.
Liabilities	All the debts of a business.
Liability	A debt or financial responsibility for which someone is responsible.
Limited liability company (LLC)	A business form that combines the flexibility and tax advantages of a partnership with the formal structure and legal protection provided by a corporation.
Log file	A list of entries of the different requests received by a Web server and the file or information that it has sent back to the user requesting it.
Malware	Shorthand for "malicious software"; another term for a computer virus.

Managed server A server relationship in which a server is leased from a hosting company that takes care of most server management functions.

Marketing The process of promoting and selling products and services.

Market research Gathering information about consumers, their needs, and their preferences.

Megapixels The unit of measure for digital photo resolution, which is calculated by multiplying the number of vertical pixels by the number of horizontal pixels.

<META> tag Computer code, usually invisible to a Web page viewer, that defines the name, purpose, author, and date of a Web page. Search engines read this tag to catalog Web pages more efficiently.

Merchant account A specialized bank account that allows a business to accept credit cards.

Net income The excess income over expenses incurred during a period; also called profit.

Net loss When expenses are greater than income.

Newsgroup A collection of messages posted by individuals to a news server, a dedicated computer maintained by a company, group, or individual for storing the messages.

Newsletter An electronic communications tool, often distributed by email, containing articles and other information promoting an e-business and its products.

Niche A small, specialized part of a market.

Online auction A Web site that allows users to buy or sell items, usually through a bidding process, and pay a small fee to the site operator, who does not handle the products, but simply facilitates the transaction.

Online storefront A Web site designed to display and provide information about products or services, and then accept orders from customers for those products or services.

Operating expenses The administrative and selling expenses incurred over a period to deliver a product or a service.

Outsourcing Paying another company to manage some aspect of a business's functions, for example, fulfillment.

Owner's equity The amount of claim the owner(s) can make against the assets of the company.

Page view A statistic recorded when a Web site visitor views a particular page.

Partnership An association of two or more persons for the purpose of running a business for profit.

Pass-through entities Legal forms (including partnerships, LLCs, and S corporations) in which income and losses are passed through to the owners, who pay the appropriate income taxes on their personal returns.

Patent A property right granted to an inventor excluding others from making, using, importing, or selling their invention in exchange for a public disclosure of the invention.

Payment gateway An e-commerce service provider that communicates to credit card companies, banks, and Web sites, allowing online transactions to take place.

PayPal A global service that allows consumers to make Internet purchases without giving their personal financial information to an e-commerce site. Instead they use a PayPal account funded credit card, check, or bank transfer.

Per-hour pricing Web site development time is billed at an hourly rate, often with no upper limit for billing.

Pharming A scam (often delivered as an email virus) that reroutes Internet users away from a site the user intended to visit to a bogus lookalike site that steals personal data.

Phishing An email scam that poses as a legitimate source asking for personal information; instead the data is stolen.

Podcast A recorded audio program available online for download in a file format that can easily be transferred to an MP3 player.

Points for improvement (PfIs) Specific points in a security plan where a weakness needing correction has been identified.

Pop-up ad An ad consisting of a window that pops up on a user's screen whenever the user visits the advertised Web site or one on which ad placement has been purchased.

Portable document format (PDF) An electronic publishing format that keeps images, typefaces, and other layout features intact and allows viewing with Adobe Reader software, no matter what program was used to create the document.

Portal A Web site that offers a variety of Internet services from a single convenient location.

Press release A short document that is designed to make a newsworthy announcement about a business to the media.

Pricing floor The lowest price that should be charged for a product.

Privacy policy A policy detailing how an online business collects, treats, and uses the information it receives from customers and others who visit its Web site.

Profit The money left over after all costs are paid.

Psychographics The classification of people based on their attitudes or lifestyle choices.

Quoting An email feature that allows a user to copy portions of the message to which they are replying.

Random Access Memory (RAM) Memory that a computer uses to temporarily store information needed to operate programs; expressed in billions of bytes, or gigabytes (GB), or in megabytes (MB).

Real time Occurring in the same time frame experienced by people.

Referrer file A specialized log file that displays the sources of all Web page requests, usually other Web sites.

Resolution The number of pixels that make up an image on the computer screen, usually expressed as a horizontal by vertical measurement.

Return policy A written policy that details the conditions under which customers are allowed to return a product or decline a service.

RSS feed A system for converting the contents of a Web page to an extensible markup language (XML) file so that the file can be read quickly using an RSS reader software program.

S corporation A type of corporation that limits the number and type of shareholders, but avoids double taxation by allowing profits and losses to pass through to those shareholders.

Seal of approval A certification provided by a third-party organization that has examined a Web site and confirmed that the site meets minimum security requirements in a given area.

Search engine A Web site that provides a list of links in response to the user typing a word or phrase into a "search" box.

Search-engine ad An advertisement tied to specific keywords in a search engine. When selected keywords are typed in a search box, an appropriate ad is displayed.

Search-engine optimization The process of obtaining a prominent listing placement on a search engine, Web directory, or information portal.

Secure socket layer (SSL) encryption A method of communication for scrambling information as it travels across the Internet; only an authorized sender or receiver can view it.

Self-employment tax A combined Social Security and Medicare tax for self-employed individuals that is computed on Schedule SE of Form 1040.

Shared server One server (computer) that is shared to store the pages of many different Web sites owned by different companies.

Shipping policy A written policy that explains how and when customer orders are to be managed and shipped.

Shopping cart A computer program built into a Web site that mimics the shopping experience in a bricks-and-mortar store, allowing customers to place items in a virtual "cart" and pay at a "checkout".

Signature file A text statement that software automatically places at the bottom of email messages.

Site map A diagram showing the pages needed by a Web page to accomplish its desired functions, as well as the relationship of those pages to one another.

Social responsibility The obligations a business has to society.

Sole proprietorship A business owned and controlled by one person.

Spam Unsolicited advertising emails, often sent in large batches to promote a product or service; the online equivalent of junk mail.

Spam filter Software programs that block unwanted spam.

Spyware A type of malicious software that plants itself deep into a computer system, posing as a legitimate program.

SWOT analysis A decision-making tool for business that evaluates the strengths, weaknesses, opportunities, and threats of an idea.

Target market A group of consumers who behave in a similar way and have been identified as potential customers for a firm's products or services.

Tax attorney An attorney who specializes in dealing with issues pertaining to tax law.

Tax year The defined accounting period used for evaluating a business's financial status and for filing taxes with the Internal Revenue Service.

Three-rings exercise A system for evaluating a business idea in which feedback is gathered first from family and friends, then from industry experts, and finally from potential customers.

Tickler A reminder, an offer, or an update directed to a customer that is automatically distributed by email.

Trademark A mark that legally protects the name, words, or symbols used by a firm to distinguish its products or services from those provided by another firm.

Trojan Horse Malware delivered in a seemingly harmless package (usually via email) that sneaks onto a computer, opens, and performs unwanted activity.

Umbrella policy An extra layer of liability coverage in addition to the basic business insurance policies.

Universal Resource Locator (URL) The unique address that identifies every World Wide Web page and other resources on the Internet.

Use tax A tax imposed on goods purchased in another state that replaces sales tax that would have been paid if the goods had been purchased in the home state.

User agreement A document published on a Web site that specifies the terms or conditions under which visitors are allowed to use the site.

Variable expenses Costs that may fluctuate periodically.

Venture capital Financing provided by a specialized investment firm that operates with the expectation of high risk and high return on its investment.

Virtual dedicated server A server used by multiple clients that provides increased control by partitioning the server into storage and access units dedicated to just one client.

Virus A program or piece of programming code that spreads from computer to computer, usually through email attachments.

Web browser Software that allows users to view and navigate the World Wide Web.

Web-hosting service A company that stores Web site files on a specialized computer (called a server) and makes the files available on the Internet.

Web page editor A program that allows creating and editing the HTML content that makes up a Web site.

Web portal A Web site that offers a broad array of information, services, and links related to a single topic.

Wholesale Products that are purchased at a discounted price and then resold at a marked-up price.

World Wide Web A worldwide collection of electronic documents.

Worm A type of virus that replicates itself and spreads to other computers through a shared network.

Zoning Ordinances that define how a particular piece of land or group of properties can be used.

INDEX

PERMISSIONS

Chapter 1 Tool Box — E-Bay homepage screenshot: Courtesy of E-Bay www.ebay.com

Chapter 2 Tool Box — Sample partnership agreement: Courtesy of Small Business Notes http://www.smallbusinessnotes.com/operating/legal/samplepartnership.html

PepsiCo Corporate code of conduct: Courtesy of PepsiCo http://www.pepsico.com/PEP_Investors/CorporateGovernance/CodeofConduct/english/images/Conduct07-v6.pdf

Chapter 3 Tool Box — A sample business plan for a children's Web site: "Written with Business Plan Pro, Palo alto Software, www.paloalto.com"; http://www.bplans.com/spv/3133/index.cfm?affiliate=sba

Chapter 4 Tool Box — Employee form required of small businesses (W-9): Courtesy of the IRS http://www.irs.gov/pub/irs-pdf/fw9.pdf

Chapter 5 Tool Box — Schedule SE (Form 1040): Courtesy of the IRS http://www.irs.gov/pub/irs-pdf/f1040sse.pdf

Chapter 6 Tool Box — Shopping cart screenshots from Ten Thousand Villages: Courtesy of Ten Thousand Villages www.tenthousandvillages.com

Shopping cart screenshot from Apple: Courtesy of Apple Inc. www.apple.com

Chapter 9 Tool Box — Yahoo!'s page for submitting a Web site for free: Reproduced with permission of Yahoo! Inc. ® 2007 by Yahoo! Inc. YAHOO! and the YAHOO! logo are trademarks of Yahoo!

Chapter 10 Tool Box — Excerpt from an e-businesses FAQ: Courtesy of Random Shirts http://www.randomshirts.com/store/pages.php?pageid=7

An online customer service form: Courtesy of Apple Inc. http://www.apple.com/support/itunes/store/lostmusic/

Chapter 13 Tool Box — A sample of a log-in feature used to collect customer information: Courtesy of BLUEFLY https://www.bluefly.com/pages/myaccount/signin.jsp

Chapter 14 Tool Box — An excerpt from the privacy policy of Craigslist: Courtesy of Craig's List http://www.craigslist.org/about/privacy.policy.html